GENESIS to REVELATION

A Comprehensive Verse-by-Verse Exploration of the Bible

HEBREWS, JAMES 1 AND 2 PETER 1, 2, AND 3 JOHN JUDE

KEITH SCHOVILLE

LEADER GUIDE

GENESIS to REVELATION

A Comprehensive Verse-by-Verse Exploration of the Bible

HEBREWS, JAMES
1 AND 2 PETER
1, 2, AND 3 JOHN
JUDE

KEITH SCHOVILLE

LEADER GUIDE

GENESIS TO REVELATION SERIES:
HEBREWS; JAMES; 1 AND 2 PETER; 1, 2, 3 JOHN; JUDE
LEADER GUIDE

ISBN 9781501855399

Manufactured in the United States of America
This book is printed on acid-free paper.
18 19 20 21 22 23 24 25 26 27—10 9 8 7 6 5 4 3 2 1

ABINGDON PRESS
Nashville

HOW TO TEACH GENESIS TO REVELATION

Unique Features of This Bible Study

In Genesis to Revelation, you and your class will study the Bible in three steps. Each step provides a different level of understanding of the Scripture. We call these steps Dimension One, Dimension Two, and Dimension Three.

Dimension One concerns what the Bible actually says. You do not interpret the Scripture at this point; you merely take account of what it says. Your main goal for this dimension is to get the content of the passage clear in your mind. What does the Bible say?

Dimension One is in workbook form. The members of the class will write the answers to questions about the passage in the space provided in the participant book. All the questions in Dimension One can be answered by reading the Bible itself. Be sure the class finishes Dimension One before going on to Dimensions Two and Three.

Dimension Two concerns information that will shed light on the Scripture under consideration. Dimension Two will answer such questions as

- What are the original meanings of some of the words used in the passage?

- What is the original background of the passage?

- Why was the passage most likely written?

- What are the relationships between the persons mentioned in the passage?

- What geographical and cultural factors affect the meaning of the passage?

The question for Dimension Two is, What information do we need in order to understand the meaning of the passage? In Dimension One the class members will discover what the Bible says. In Dimension Two they will discover what the Bible means.

Dimension Three focuses on interpreting the Scripture and applying it to life situations. The questions here are

- What is the meaning of the passage for my life?

- What response does the passage require of me as a Christian?

- What response does this passage require of us as a group?

Dimension Three questions have no easy answers. The task of applying the Scripture to life situations is up to you and the class.

Aside from the three-dimensional approach, another unique feature of this study is the organization of the series as a whole. Classes that choose to study the Genesis to Revelation Series will be able to study all the books of the Bible in their biblical order. This method will give the class continuity that is not present in most other Bible studies. The class will read and study virtually every verse of the Bible, from Genesis straight through to Revelation.

Weekly Preparation

Begin planning for each session early in the week. Read the passage that the lesson covers, and write the answers to Dimension One questions in the participant book. Then read Dimensions Two and Three in the participant book. Make a note of any questions or comments you have. Finally, study the material in the leader guide carefully. Decide how you want to organize your class session.

Organizing the Class Session

Since Genesis to Revelation involves three steps in studying the Scripture, you will want to organize your class sessions around these three dimensions. Each lesson in the participant book and this leader guide consists of three parts.

The first part of each lesson in the leader guide is the same as the Dimension One section in the participant book, except that the leader guide includes the answers to Dimension One questions. These questions and answers are taken from the New International Version of the Bible.

You might use Dimension One in several ways:

1. Ask the group members to read the Scripture and to write the answers to all the Dimension One questions before coming to class. This method will require that the class covenant to spend the necessary amount of study time outside of class. When the class session begins, read through the Dimension One questions, asking for responses from the group members. If anyone needs help with any of the answers, look at the biblical reference together.

2. Or, if you have enough class time, you might spend the first part of the session working through the Dimension One questions together as a group. Locate the Scripture references, ask the questions one at a time, and invite the class members to find the answers and to read them aloud. Then allow enough time for them to write the answers in the participant book.

3. Or, take some time at the beginning of the class session for group members to work individually. Have them read the Dimension One questions and the Scripture references and then write their answers to the questions in the spaces provided in the participant book. Discuss together any questions or answers in Dimension One that do not seem clear. This approach may take longer than the others, but it provides a good change of pace from time to time.

You do not have to organize your class sessions the same way every week. Ask the class members what they prefer. Experiment! You may find ways to study the Dimension One material other than the ones listed above.

The second part of each lesson in this leader guide corresponds to the second part of the participant book lessons. The Dimension Two section of the participant book provides background information to help the participants understand the Scripture. Become familiar with the information in the participant book.

Dimension Two of this leader guide contains additional information on the passage. The leader guide goes into more depth with some parts of the passage than the participant book does. You will want to share this information with the group in whatever way seems appropriate. For example, if someone raises a question about a particular verse, share any additional background information from the leader guide.

You might raise a simple question such as, What words or phrases gave you trouble in understanding the passage? or, Having grasped the content of the passage, what questions remain in your mind? Encourage the group members to share confusing points, troublesome words or phrases, or lingering questions. Write these problems on a posterboard or markerboard. This list of concerns will form the outline for the second portion of the session.

These concerns may also stimulate some research on the part of the group members. If your study group is large enough, divide the class into three groups. Then divide the passage for the following week into three parts. Assign a portion of the passage to each group. Using Bible commentaries and Bible dictionaries, direct each group to discover as much as it can about this portion of the passage before the class meets again. Each group will then report its findings during the class session.

The third part of each lesson in this leader guide relates to Dimension Three in the participant book. This section helps class members discover how to apply the Scripture to their own lives. Here you will find one or more interpretations of the passage—whether traditional, historical, or contemporary. Use these interpretations when appropriate to illumine the passage for the group members.

Dimension Three in the participant book points out some of the issues in the passage that are relevant to our lives. For each of these issues, the participant book raises questions to help the participants assess the meaning of the Scripture for their lives. The information in Dimension Three of the leader guide is designed to help you lead the class in discussing these issues. Usually, you will find a more in-depth discussion of portions of the Scripture.

The discussion in the leader guide will give you a better perspective on the Scripture and its interpretation before you begin to assess its meaning for today. You will probably want to share this Dimension Three information with the class to open the discussion. For each life situation, the leader guide contains suggestions on facilitating the class discussion. You, as the leader, are responsible for group discussions of Dimension Three issues.

Assembling Your Materials

You will need at least three items to prepare for and conduct each class session:

- A leader guide
- A participant book
- A Bible—you may use any translation or several; the answers in this leader guide are taken from the New International Version.

One advantage of the Genesis to Revelation Series is that the study is self-contained. That is, all you need to lead this Bible study is provided for you in the participant books and leader guides. Occasionally, or perhaps on a regular basis, you might want to consult other sources for additional information.

HOW TO LEAD A DISCUSSION

The Teacher as Discussion Leader

As the leader of this series or a part of this series, one of your main responsibilities during each class period will be to lead the class discussion. Some leaders are apprehensive about leading a discussion. In many ways, it is easier to lecture to the class. But remember that the class members will surely benefit more from the class sessions when they actively participate in a discussion of the material.

Leading a discussion is a skill that any teacher can master with practice. And keep in mind—especially if your class is not used to discussion—that the members of your group will also be learning through practice. The following are some pointers on how to lead interesting and thought-provoking discussions in the study group.

Preparing for a Discussion—Where Do I Start?

1. Focus on the subject that will be discussed and on the goal you want to achieve through that discussion.

2. Prepare by collecting information and data that you will need; jot down these ideas, facts, and questions so that you will have them when you need them.

3. Begin organizing your ideas; stop often to review your work. Keep in mind the climate within the group—attitudes, feelings, eagerness to participate and learn.

4. Consider possible alternative group procedures. Be prepared for the unexpected.

5. Having reached your goal, think through several ways to bring the discussion to a close.

As the leader, do not feel that your responsibility is to give a full account or report of the assigned material. This practice promotes dependency. Instead, through stimulating questions and discussion, the participants will read the material—not because you tell them to but because they want to read and prepare.

How Do I Establish a Climate for Learning?

The leader's readiness and preparation quickly establish a climate in which the group can proceed and its members learn and grow. The anxiety and fear of an unprepared leader are contagious but so are the positive vibrations coming from a leader who is prepared to move into a learning enterprise.

An attitude of shared ownership is also basic. Group members need to perceive themselves as part of the learning experience. Persons establish ownership by working on goals, sharing concerns, and accepting major responsibility for learning.

Here are several ways the leader can foster a positive climate for learning and growth.

1. Readiness. A leader who is always fully prepared can promote, in turn, the group's readiness to learn.

2. Exploration. When the leader encourages group members to freely explore new ideas, persons will know they are in a group whose primary function is learning.

3. Exposure. A leader who is open, honest, and willing to reveal himself or herself to the group will encourage participants to discuss their feelings and opinions.

4. Confidentiality. A leader can create a climate for learning when he or she respects the confidentiality of group members and encourages the group members to respect one another's confidentiality.

5. Acceptance. When a leader shows a high degree of acceptance, participants can likewise accept one another honestly.

How Can I Deal With Conflict?

What if conflict or strong disagreement arises in your group? What do you do? Think about the effective and ineffective ways you have dealt with conflict in the past.

Group conflict may come from one of several sources. One common source of conflict involves personality clashes. Any group is almost certain to contain at least two persons whose personalities clash. If you break your class into smaller groups for discussion, be sure these persons are in separate groups.

Another common source of group conflict is subject matter. The Bible can be a very controversial subject. Remember the difference between discussion or disagreement and conflict. As a leader you will have to decide when to encourage discussion and when to discourage conflict that is destructive to the group process.

Group conflict may also come from a general atmosphere conducive to expression of ideas and opinions. Try to discourage persons in the group from being judgmental toward others and their ideas. Keep reminding the class that each person is entitled to his or her own opinions and that no one opinion is more valid than another.

How Much Should I Contribute to the Discussion?

Many leaders are unsure about how much they should contribute to the class discussions. Below are several pitfalls to avoid.

1. The leader should remain neutral on a question until the group has had adequate time to discuss it. At the proper time in the discussion the leader can offer his or her opinion. The leader can direct the questions to the group at large, rechanneling those questions that come to him or her.

    At times when the members need to grapple with a question or issue, the most untimely response a leader can make is answering the question. Do not fall into the trap of doing the group members' work for them. Let them struggle with the question.

    However, if the leader has asked the group members to reveal thoughts and feelings, then group members have the right to expect the same of the leader. A leader has no right to ask others to reveal something he or she is unwilling to reveal. A leader can reveal thoughts and feelings, but at the appropriate time.

    The refusal to respond immediately to a question often takes self-discipline. The leader has spent time thinking, reading, and preparing. Thus the leader usually does have a point of view, and waiting for others to respond calls for restraint.

2. Another pitfall is the leader's making a speech or extended comments in expressing an opinion or summarizing what has been said. For example, in an attempt to persuade others, a leader may speak, repeat, or strongly emphasize what someone says concerning a question.

3. Finally, the pitfall of believing the leader must know "the answers" to the questions is always apparent. The leader need not know all the answers. Many questions that should be raised are ultimate and unanswerable; other questions are open-ended; and still others have several answers.

GENESIS TO REVELATION SERIES

HEBREWS; JAMES; 1 AND 2 PETER; 1, 2, AND 3 JOHN; JUDE

Leader Guide

Table of Contents

About the Writer

Dr. Keith Schoville, the writer of these teacher book lessons, served as professor emeritus in the Department of Hebrew and Semitic Studies at the University of Wisconsin-Madison. He is the author of *Biblical Archaeology in Focus*, an introduction to archaeology, and numerous articles in dictionaries and journals on archaeology and the biblical world. Dr. Schoville has excavated at Tel Dan in northern Israel, Tel Lachish in the south-central region of the country, and Tel Aroer in the southern region.

In these last days [God] has spoken to us by his Son. (1:2)

1

JESUS, GOD'S SUPERIOR MESSENGER

Hebrews 1:1–4:13

DIMENSION ONE: WHAT DOES THE BIBLE SAY?

Answer these questions by reading Hebrews 1

1. List the characteristics that set God's Son above the prophets. (1:2-3)

He is the heir of all things, the creator of the universe, the one who radiates Gods glory and "the exact representation of his being. " The Son also sustains all things by the power of his word. He made purification for sins, and he is seated at Gods right hand.

2. How is the Son superior to the angels? (1:6-7, 14)

The angels are to worship the Son. They are servants; the inferior worships the superior.

3. Why was the Son anointed above all his companions? (1:9)

The Son was anointed above his companions because he "loved righteousness and hated wickedness."

Answer these questions by reading Hebrews 2

4. In 2:1, the reader is warned of the danger of drifting away. What is the reader warned of in 2:3a?

> *The reader is warned not to "ignore so great a salvation."*

5. Identify the three sources that testify to the "great salvation" provided in Christ. (2:3b-4)

> *The great salvation was announced by the Lord (Jesus), "confirmed to us by those who heard him" (disciples and apostles), and testified to by God through signs, wonders and various miracles, and "gifts of the Holy Spirit."*

6. Why was the Son, who is superior to the angels, made lower than the angels for a time? (2:9)

> *The Son was made lower than the angels so that he could "taste death for everyone."*

7. The writer of Hebrews emphasizes the human experience of the Lord (2:14-18). What specific human experiences are mentioned in this section?

> *The specific human experiences of the Lord mentioned in the section are death (2:14), suffering, and temptation (2:18).*

Answer these questions by reading Hebrews 3

8. Jesus and Moses are both described as faithful to God in 3:1-6. What phrases indicate Moses' relationship to God and the superior relationship of Christ to God? (3:5-6)

> *Moses was faithful to God "as a servant"; Christ was faithful to God "as the Son."*

9. In 3:7-19, three dangers are listed: never entering God's rest, turning away from the living God, and the possibility of not sharing in Christ. What is the basic cause for these disasters? (3:12, 19)

> *The basic cause for these disasters is unbelief.*

10. What can be done to safeguard the believer from the danger of unbelief? (3:13)

> *By encouraging one another daily, believers safeguard themselves against the danger of unbelief.*

Answer these questions by reading Hebrews 4:1-13

11. In the previous section, failure to enter into God's rest was the result of unbelief. In 4:1-13, a different but equivalent word is used. What is that word? (4:11)

In 4:11, "disobedience" is the cause of failure to enter God's rest.

12. Why is it impossible to hide unbelief from God? (4:12-13)

The penetrating word of God discerns "the thoughts and attitudes of the heart. Nothing in all creation is hidden from God's sight."

DIMENSION TWO: WHAT DOES THE BIBLE MEAN?

Exploring Hebrews. Every teacher wants to communicate effectively. To enable group members to understand the message and the meaning of Hebrews, you must have a grasp of the basic information about the book. The following brief overview will provide direction toward your goal of helping group members benefit from their study of this fascinating book.

A Sermon, Not a Letter. The translators of the King James Version confidently entitled this book "The Epistle of Paul the Apostle to the Hebrews." Unlike the majority of the letters in the New Testament, however, Hebrews lacks the features we would expect in a letter. The text includes no introduction, indicating the sender and the recipient or recipients, and no greeting of grace, peace, and the like. The writer begins with a theological discussion that sets the stage for the major emphasis of the, book, that Jesus Christ is God's final and complete revelation.

The writer's main arguments are followed by exhortations to the readers. In the last chapter, the writer calls this communication "my word of exhortation" (13:22). Hebrews appears to be a written sermon to which has been added a brief closing such as we find in letters (13:22-25).

You will want to understand the major points in the sermon outline in order to follow the main thought of the writer.

Outline of Hebrews.

I. Jesus, the superior messenger (1:1–4:13)
    A. Superior to prophets (1:1-3a)
    B. Superior to angels (1:3b–2:18)
    C. Superior to Moses and Joshua (3:7–4:10)
    D. Exhortation (4:11-13)
II. Jesus, the superior high priest (4:14–10:18)
    A. A superior appointment (4:14–5:1 0)
    B. Exhortations (5:11–6:20)

C. Seven superior aspects of his priesthood (7:1–10:18)

    1. An earlier order of priesthood (7:1-19)

    2. A priest by oath (7:20-22)

    3. A permanent priesthood (7:23-25)

    4. A sinless priest (7:26-28)

    5. Priest of a new covenant (8:1-13)

    6. Priest of a more perfect tent (9:1-28)

    7. Priest of a "once for all" sacrifice (10:1-18)

III. Exhortation: faith and endurance (10:19–12:29)

    A. Faith and endurance defined and illustrated (10:19–11:40)

    B. Exhortation to persevere (12:1-29)

IV. Concluding exhortations (13:1-25)

You will notice that our lesson divisions do not exactly follow the outline above. The lessons were arranged with space considerations in mind as well as the time available to study each lesson. This first lesson, however, does conform to the first section of the outline of the book.

The Origin of Hebrews. No one knows who wrote Hebrews, the place in which it was written, the date of writing, or who the intended first readers were. Even the original title, if one existed, is not known. The title, "The Letter to the Hebrews," seems to be based on the content of the book rather than being a formal title.

The writer was probably not the apostle Paul. He looks back on "those who heard" the Lord (2:3), suggesting that he is a second-generation believer. Among other possible writers are Luke, Silas, Peter, Apollos, Barnabas, and Aquila and Priscilla. The Greek style of the book differs from that of Paul's letters. Hebrews approaches Luke and Acts in excellence of style. Detailed study of the ideas in Hebrews also confirms that Paul is unlikely to have written the book.

For whom was this document first intended? The content indicates that the first readers were Jewish Christians. The writer, however, makes no mention of circumcision, worship in the Jerusalem Temple, or ritual law, though he does refer to the Temple and ritual. Many converts from Judaism lived in the Diaspora, away from Palestine and in the Greek Roman world. Also, many God-fearing Gentiles who attended Jewish synagogues accepted Jesus as the messiah. They had a general acquaintance with the Old Testament traditions that the writer assumes the readers know.

The first recipients of the letter were probably members of a mixed congregation of converted Jews and Gentiles. The document was likely sent to Alexandria, Rome, or Jerusalem. Rome is the best possibility. The writer exhorts the readers to stand fast in the face of persecution and suffering. Christians in Rome had experienced such hardships. Also, with the writer were "those from Italy" (13:24); and their greetings may have been sent "back home" to Rome.

Possible dates for the writing of Hebrews range from AD 65 to AD 95. The first reference to the work is that of Clement of Rome, about AD 96. Since the concerns of the book are with conditions in the period after the apostles, the date was probably close to the end of the century.

The Significance of Hebrews. Hebrews provides a powerful case for the uniqueness of Jesus Christ as God's final revelation for the salvation of people. From the time it was first written to the present, the work has provided instruction that makes specific what Jesus expressed in general terms in Matthew 5:17: "Do not think that I have come to abolish the Law or the Prophets; I have not come to abolish them but to fulfill them." To become familiar with Hebrews is to receive essential instruction in the faith, once for all delivered to the saints. It is to receive the exhortations to constancy that every generation seems to need. The message of Hebrews is of timeless value.

Hebrews 1:1-3. This introduction reminds us of the creation account in Genesis, where God speaks and the material universe comes into existence. The passage also reminds us of the first eighteen verses of the Gospel of John, where the creative Word of God is identified with Jesus. In John also, the testimony is that the Son was the active agent in creation; and he has made God known.

The idea of the Son having the same nature as God and radiating God's glory echoes the words of Jesus, "Anyone who has seen me has seen the Father" (John 14:9b), and of Paul, "For God was pleased to have all his fullness dwell in him" (Colossians 1:19).

The writer introduces in the first three verses the two basic themes that will be expanded later: Jesus Christ is the superior revelation of God, and he has made purification of sins. This last idea will include both Jesus Christ's role as a fitting sacrifice for sin and as a supremely capable high priest.

Hebrews 1:4-14. The writer proves the superiority of the Son over angels by referring to Scripture. The writer assumes readers are familiar with the quoted passages. These quotations may pose a problem for modern readers, who frequently are not as familiar with the Old Testament as believers were in the early church.

The sources for the quotations are discussed in the participant book. The writer tends to quote from the Septuagint, the earliest Greek version of the Old Testament. The translation may not always agree exactly with the New International Version, which was translated from the Hebrew text. Textual variations existed in Hebrew manuscripts even before the Septuagint was translated in the third century BC. These variations were usually minor in extent and importance. They caused little concern to either Christians or Jews.

Sometimes the quotations in Hebrews are not exactly what we have in the Septuagint or the Hebrew. We can assume that the writer was quoting freely rather than exactly, or quoting from a manuscript that did not follow exactly the known Greek version.

"The name" (v. 4) is more excellent than that of the angels in several respects.

1. It signals a more intimate relationship with God. The Son is the firstborn of God. None of the angels is as intimate with God.

2. At his birth, the angels are called to worship him, recalling the angelic praise at the nativity of Jesus (Luke 2:13-14).

3. The Son is enthroned as a king forever. Angels are messengers for the heavenly king. They do not rule.

4. The Son is the source of salvation, as the writer will emphasize later in the letter. Angels, while servants of the king, are ministering spirits sent forth to do his will by serving the saved.

Hebrews 2:1-4. "Therefore" introduces the first of several exhortations in Hebrews. The writer fears that readers may drift away from the revelation in Jesus that they have heard. Or they may neglect—that is, pay no attention to—what has been revealed, such a great salvation. Much of what is presented later in the book provides details of just how great that salvation is.

The *previous* message is the law of Moses (see the participant book). Its promises were substantial and valid, as one would expect of a message delivered by angels. Anyone who drifted away from that message faced the consequences.

The *superior* message, the revelation in and by Jesus, was attested by more impressive evidence than was the law of Moses. Jesus delivered the message; the disciples who heard him speak confirmed it; and God bore witness to the validity of that message. God did this during the ministry of Jesus through signs, wonders, and miracles. These words echo those of Peter in his great sermon on Pentecost: "Jesus of Nazareth was a man accredited by God to you by miracles, wonders and signs, which God did among you through him, as you yourselves know" (Acts 2:22).

God also bore witness to the validity of the message after the ascension of Jesus through the gifts of the Holy Spirit. Spiritual gifts are referred to in several places in the New Testament (Romans 12:3-8; 1 Corinthians 12; Ephesians 4:8-16).

Hebrews 2:5-13. Read the comments for this section in the participant book. The idea of the superiority of the Son over angels is directly followed by the astounding evidence of the humanity of Jesus. While this happened historically, it has its ultimate effect in "the world to come" (v. 5), when everything will be under subjection to Jesus Christ. He will be clothed again in heavenly glory, and many will share his glory (vv. 10, 13b). Jesus referred to these ideas in his prayer in the upper room (John 17:5).

The quotations in 2:12-13 are from Psalm 22:22 and Isaiah 8:17-18, yet our writer has treated them as the words of Jesus. As the fulfillment of God's revelation, Jesus is seen as speaking through the psalmist and the prophet. To hear the prophetic word is to hear the voice of Christ.

Hebrews 2:14-18. It may be more a judgment of our time than of Scripture, but the major difficulty you confront in discussing this section with the group may be the reference to the devil. We do not need to sidestep the issue of evil, represented here by the devil. In a materialistic world, the reality of spiritual forces is often denied, but this is to deny an essential part of our being; for we are more than matter.

The devil does not have the power of death in the sense of determining who dies and when. That power is retained by the Creator. The power of death here is the power of sin, the power to divert us from the true source of happiness in life, the fulfillment of God's will for our lives. The diversion is to a substitute, which looks alluring but finally does not satisfy. Satisfying self is the substitute that draws people away from fulfilling God's will. Ultimately, such bondage to self ends in death "and after that . . . judgment" (9:27). Jesus suffered and died to save individuals from both bondage and judgment.

In 2:14, *destroy* can signify "to nullify; to render incompetent, inconsequential." The devil has been rendered impotent, but not to everyone. The devil is impotent to those who follow Jesus, the pioneer of their salvation.

Hebrews 3:1-6. Jesus is both an apostle (messenger) who brought God's superior revelation and the high priest who hears our confession. The confession here is connected with worship. An example of a confession that an Israelite was to make when bringing an offering to God before the priest is found in Deuteronomy 26:5-10. Essentially, the confession recounts God's deliverance and blessings.

The content of the Christian confession in mind here is also recognition of God's deliverance from sin and blessings given to us in Jesus. Essentially this confession is praise to God.

The word *house* in this passage has no connection with a physical building. Verse 6 clarifies the meaning: "we are his house." This meaning of *house* is in line with, for example, Ephesians 2:19-22; the church—the people of God—are God's house.

Hebrews 3:7-19. Moses was faithful over God's people as a servant. Yet the generation over which he was faithful provoked the wrath of God by rebelling, by refusing to follow God's ways. The result was God's solemn oath "that they would never enter his rest" (v. 18). As the participant book indicates, the rest is the Promised Land.

Unbelief and disobedience are essentially the same. They lead people to turn away from the living God. The protection against the danger of unbelief is daily encouragement of one another (v. 13).

Hebrews 4:1-13. *Therefore* introduces an exhortation. This exhortation is based on the example of the Israelites under Moses who failed to enter into the Promised Land. A greater-than-Moses has brought good news to us, the writer indicates in 3:5-6. The promise of entering God's rest remains.

The writer's point is that, long after the Hebrews rebelled and failed to enter the Promised Land, God spoke of a rest again through David (4:7). The exhortation is that the readers have entered into that rest through faith (4:3). But a further aspect of that rest remains to be attained (v. 11). The danger is that they will not reach that ultimate rest because of a lack of faith (vv. 1-2).

The sabbath rest of God began with the completion of Creation; however, according to Jesus, God was still at work (John 5:17). That work was completed in Jesus when, on the cross, he cried, "It is finished" (John 19:30). The rest of God in Christ is available for now and for eternity. Belief is the means of entrance now, and obedience is the manner by which we attain the future rest.

DIMENSION THREE:
WHAT DOES THE BIBLE MEAN TO ME?

Hebrews 1—Pluralism and the Church

The problem of how to live as a Christian in a pluralistic society is not limited to our time. The Christians who first read Hebrews lived in a world in which a variety of religions and superstitions abounded. Christians were a minority group in the last half of the first century. Some Christians apparently were tempted to turn their backs on what they had confessed. Our writer wrote to those so tempted, emphasizing the superior and exclusive claims of Christ.

This emphasis is exactly the antidote for timid believers today. The hope of the Christian must be in Jesus Christ as Lord. The testimony of the apostles is unswerving: "Salvation is found in no one else, for there is no other name under heaven given to mankind by which we must be saved" (Acts 4:12). The central teaching of the New Testament is the foundation on which churches stand.

At the same time, we must treat those who differ from us in a Christlike way. First and foremost, we must love others—ALL others—as Christ has loved us. We share Christ's love in the way we live and act often more than even the words we use. Our lives must be positive testimonies to Christ's love. That is the primary way in which we can share the gospel of Jesus Christ with those around us.

Hebrews 2:1-4; 3:7–4:13—Counteracting the Danger of Apostasy

Everyone ought to recognize that the danger of apostasy exists. The way is narrow, as Jesus taught. Those who find it have a climb to make. Perhaps the most helpful truth as we make our spiritual pilgrimage is to realize that we are not alone. Besides the help of Christ through the Holy Spirit, Hebrews tells us to "encourage one another daily" (3:13). The mutual support of Christians is essential to our lives. Be a friend, and draw on the strength of your Christian friends. Jesus did.

Hebrews 2:9–3:6; 4:13—Developing a Personal Relationship with Christ

Drawing on our lesson material, we learn that we are encouraged to develop a personal relationship with Jesus Christ by God. For example, in 2:9, we are told that Jesus tasted death for us "by the grace of God." The atoning death of Jesus is for each of us individually. Further, the human experiences of Jesus indicate his concern for each of us. He is able (and interested) to help us when we are tempted.

Prayer is one means of personal access to God. A further step in communicating to God your personal love and loyalty is being an obedient servant.

[W]e have a great high priest who has ascended into heaven, Jesus the Son of God. (4:14)

JESUS, GOD'S SUPERIOR HIGH PRIEST

Hebrews 4:14–7:28

DIMENSION ONE: WHAT DOES THE BIBLE SAY?

Answer these questions by reading Hebrews 4:14–5:14

1. Why should Christians expect to receive a sympathetic hearing at the throne of grace? (4:15)

   Our high priest, Jesus, sympathizes with us; for he "has been tempted in every way, just as we are."

2. What is the function of a high priest? (5:1)

   A high priest offers to God gifts and sacrifices on behalf of believers.

3. Of what benefit to other people was the obedient suffering of Jesus? (5:8-9)

   Through his suffering, Jesus became "the source of eternal salvation for all who obey him."

4. Why was the writer of Hebrews annoyed with those to whom the book was written? (5:11-14)

   The writer thought that readers had failed to mature in their understanding of God's revealed word.

Answer these questions by reading Hebrews 6

5. The "elementary teachings about Christ" are mentioned in 6:1. What are included in these teachings? (6:1-2)

   The elementary teachings include repentance, faith, instruction on baptisms, "the laying on of hands, the resurrection of the dead, and eternal judgment."

6. To what spiritual blight does the writer compare cultivated land that bears thorns and thistles? (6:4-8)

   The writer compares such land to the sin of apostasy.

7. In what way does the faithful person show love for God? (6:10)

   The faithful person shows love for God in helping God's people.

8. What has been the basis of hope for believers from Abraham to the time when Hebrews was written? (6:13-18)

   The basis of hope for believers has been faith in God's promises.

Answer these questions by reading Hebrews 7

9. Why was the priesthood of Melchizedek considered endless? (7:3)

   No record of his birth or death exists; nor is there any record of a beginning or ending to his priesthood.

10. In verse 7, the words *lesser* and *greater* are used. To whom do they refer? (7:4-7)

    The lesser is Abraham; the greater is Melchizedek.

11. Why was the Levitical priesthood replaced by "the order of Melchizedek"? (7:11)

    Perfection (spiritual maturity) was not attainable through the Levitical priesthood.

12. The priesthood of the tribe of Levi was established under the law of Moses. How is the priesthood of the Lord justified? (7:12-17)

    The priesthood of the Lord is justified by a change in God's law. The evidence for the change is Christ's indestructible life.

13. What makes Jesus "the guarantor of a better covenant"? (7:20-22)

    His priesthood was established on the oath of God.

4. List the ways in which Jesus, as permanent priest, is superior to the former priesthood. (7:26-27)

> *Jesus is "holy, blameless, pure, set apart from sinners, exalted above the heavens." None of these words were applicable to the other priests. They offered sacrifices often, for themselves and the people. Jesus offered himself as a sacrifice once for all people and for all time.*

DIMENSION TWO:
WHAT DOES THE BIBLE MEAN?

Having covered the superiority of Jesus as the revealer of God's will, beyond that of prophets, angels, and the major Israelite leaders, Moses and Joshua, the writer of Hebrews turns to this second emphasis: the function of Jesus as God's superior high priest. Jesus' priestly office is presented as superior to that of the line of Levitical high priests that began with Aaron, the brother of Moses.

The Levitical Priesthood. The basic information on the Levitical priesthood given below will help you and the group members understand more clearly the propositions of the writer of Hebrews. Comprehensive articles on the subject can be found in Bible dictionaries and encyclopedias.

The Israelite priesthood fell to the men of the tribe of Levi. Aaron and Moses were of that tribe. After the Exodus from Egypt and the subsequent establishment of the covenant between God and the Israelites at Mount Sinai, Aaron was appointed high priest (Exodus 28:1; Leviticus 8).

Aaron and his sons were to serve God in the tabernacle. Priests always function in connection with sanctuaries, special facilities that are restricted for specific religious rituals. The tent of meeting was a portable sanctuary. As long as the Israelites lived in tents, migrating in the Peninsula of Sinai and in the desert, it was appropriate that God's sanctuary among them should also be a tent. It was a grand tent, as befitting God, in contrast to the simple tents of the people.

The instructions for building the tent of meeting (tabernacle) and its furnishings are recorded in Exodus 25–27. The actual construction is detailed in Exodus 35–38, and the erection of the tabernacle follows in Exodus 40. Without the tabernacle, the people would not have needed a priesthood.

The priestly office was planned as an integral part of the tabernacle. The tent represented the presence of God: "Have them make a sanctuary for me, and I will dwell among them" (Exodus 25:8). It is dangerous to live in the vicinity of God, who is utterly holy and who hates sin. Even when God met Moses on the mountain, the people encamped at the base were warned, on penalty of death, to neither draw near nor touch the mountain (Exodus 19:10-13). Yet God desired "a kingdom of priests and a holy nation" (Exodus 19:6).

How could this problem be solved? The answer was the tabernacle and the priesthood. Aaron and his sons were set apart (consecrated) to serve as intermediaries between the holy God and the unholy people. In order to carry out this function, the priests attained a higher level of holiness than the common people. The priests wore special clothing. They were restricted in their non-priestly activities; they did not engage in anything that might make them ritually unclean. To do so would have made them unfit to serve in the tabernacle and liable to die (Exodus 28:42-43).

Some of the restrictions for a priest included: a priest with a physical defect could not serve, nor could a priest under the influence of alcohol. Priests were allowed to marry only a virgin of Israel, not a divorcee, prostitute, convert, nor, for the high priest, even a widow. A priest was not to touch the dead for fear of ritual defilement. The high priest could not have contact with the dead, even of his immediate family.

Despite all the restrictions on the lives of the priests, and especially of the high priest, their purity could not be completely established or maintained. On the Day of Atonement each year, the high priest had to make an offering for his sins as well as for the sins of the people. The people could bring their offerings to the door of the tabernacle, but it was the priests who actually performed the sacrifices. The holiness within the sanctuary was too great to allow individual Israelites to come nearer than the outer door.

The holiness of the sanctuary increased from the outer door and courts toward the Holy Place within the tent and into the Most Holy Place. The Most Holy Place was separated from the Holy Place by a veil (a heavy curtain). This inner sanctum contained the ark of the covenant and represented God's presence. Priests entered daily into the Holy Place, but the Most Holy Place was entered only once a year, on the Day of Atonement, and only by the high priest after he had offered sacrifices for his sins and the people's sins. Thus the presence of the holy God in the midst of the people was maintained through the priestly functions.

The Tabernacle and the Temple. The system of the tabernacle and the priesthood continued in Israel after the conquest of Canaan until the Temple in Jerusalem was built by King Solomon. The priests functioned in the permanent sanctuary as they had in the tent. That first Temple continued in use for over three hundred years, until it was destroyed by Nebuchadnezzar in his conquest of Jerusalem in 587 BC.

The Second Temple was built on the ruins of Solomon's Temple after the return of the Jews from the Babylonian Exile, about 520 BC. The plan of both temples was the same as that of the tabernacle. The Second Temple underwent a major reconstruction in the time of Herod the Great. It was this Temple Jesus taught at, cleansed of money changers, and wept over. The Temple was destroyed by the Romans in AD 70 as they crushed a revolt of the Jews. The priesthood of the Temple ceased to function after the destruction.

Hebrews 4:14-16. Just as the Levitical high priest passed through the outer sections of the tabernacle and through the veil to reach the Most Holy Place, Jesus "ascended into heaven" (v. 14) as he drew near to the true sanctuary—the actual abode of God—heaven itself. Christians can draw near with confidence to the "throne of grace" (v. 16). The equivalent in the earthly tabernacle was the ark of the covenant in the Most Holy Place, a symbol of God's throne and presence.

The emphasis of this section is to "hold firmly to the faith we profess" (v. 14). Jesus is the subject of the "faith we profess" (see Matthew 16:16).

Hebrews 5:1-10. Jesus and Aaron served similar priestly functions, acting on behalf of people in relation to God. The writer has pointed out that Jesus was tempted in every human way, yet without sin (4:15). Not so Aaron; he sinned when tempted. Jesus and Aaron do share one thing: they did not seek the priestly role. God called them both. In the case of Jesus, however, he was designated "high priest in the order of Melchizedek" (5:10).

Jesus not only experienced temptations like all individuals during the course of his life. He experienced excruciating suffering in those last hours of his life in Gethsemane (Luke 22:40-44), in his humiliating trials, and on Calvary. He "learned obedience" (Hebrews 5:8) through these experiences. But did God answer his prayers and supplications?

The answer is clearly yes, and the answer was the provision of strength to fulfill God's will and purpose for his life. Jesus' words throw light on this subject in the incident when one of his disciples cut off the ear of the high priest's servant with a sword. Jesus ordered him to put the sword away, adding, "Do you think I cannot call on my Father, and he will at once put at my disposal more than twelve legions of angels? But how then would the Scriptures be fulfilled that say it must happen in this way?" (Matthew 26:53-54).

Jesus fulfilled the will of God for his life. He was made perfect. He completed his life's purpose, and that purpose was that he would become "the source of eternal salvation for all who obey him" (Hebrews 5:9).

Hebrews 5:11–6:8. Consult the participant book for the comments on this section. Paul expressed similar thoughts in Philippians 3:13-15, pressing toward the goal of the heavenward call of God in Christ Jesus and calling on the mature to be like-minded. The mature are those who, by exercising mental discipline, have developed the ability to distinguish between the good and the less than good (5:14).

Being born into the kingdom of God does not assure maturity to the individual. Jesus provides the example for believers who want to develop into mature, well-rounded individuals. He increased in wisdom (Luke 2:52). Our spiritual sensitivities must be developed by exercising them. The inquisitive Jesus was discussing difficult questions with the religious leaders in the Temple when he was just twelve years old (Luke 2:46).

Constant discussions and bickering in churches and between Christian groups over the elemental doctrines of the faith indicate immaturity. The New Testament teaching, taken at face value, should be sufficient in respect to the first principles. All believers should seek to be united in matters of faith. Jesus prayed for the unity of believers. Friendly discussions of matters of opinion and nonessentials are acceptable. As Christians exercise their spiritual faculties, however, they should be able to go beyond the elementary teachings (6:1-2).

The reason for our writer's emphasis on this matter is simply that immaturity opens believers to the danger of falling away (6:4-6). If the roots of faith are shallow, reaching only into the topsoil, the strong winds of adversity will uproot the weak. Apparently others in the early church were like Demas, Paul's traveling companion: "because he loved this world," he forsook the apostle and the faith (2 Timothy 4:10).

One problem in the early history of the church was how to deal with the lapsed. The lapsed were those who, under persecution, complied with the Roman order to burn incense to the emperor. The church was faced with the problem of what to do with such people who had conformed to civil law rather than face martyrdom. The viewpoint that finally won the day was that no human sin is beyond God's forgiveness. That forgiveness should be seen in the visible church as well as in the eternal church.

The apostates the writer of Hebrews has in mind, it appears, had fallen away from the Lord because they chose to remain immature rather than to grow in faith. Such were gullible enough to "abandon the faith and follow deceiving spirits and things taught by demons. Such teachings come through hypocritical liars, whose consciences have been seared" (1 Timothy 4:1-2). Falling from grace, they seem to have had their consciences seared too, so that they could not be moved again by the gospel of love and grace in the way they once had been moved.

We have every reason, however, to pray for and encourage those who have abandoned their faith. God is not willing that any be lost but that all should come to salvation. The story of the prodigal son is sufficient encouragement for us to continue in prayer for the lapsed of our time.

Hebrews 6:9-20. We ought to assume that most of the people in the church are honest, sincere, committed Christians who are attempting to live their lives to the praise of Christ's glory. That is really what our writer is doing in terms of the readers (v. 9). We need not hunt for the negative, faithless person in the church. Jesus taught that the weeds should grow up with the wheat until the time of harvest (Matthew 13:24-30). And the harvest is God's.

The "better things" that belong to salvation for the sincere believer (Hebrews 6:9) are not specified. The writer was certainly not suggesting that persecutions would cease. Perhaps the idea here is the word of the Lord to his productive servant: "Well done, good and faithful servant" (Matthew 25:21).

The servant attitude fits well on the follower of Jesus. He said of himself, "The Son of Man did not come to be served, but to serve" (Matthew 20:28). The disciple, when mature, will be like the master. The people who first read The Letter to the Hebrews were not among the apostate; of this the writer was certain. They showed the marks of true discipleship. They loved one another (John 13:35). They looked after fellow Christians.

Believers who work for others in the name of the Lord can suffer burnout, the equivalent of being "lazy" (Hebrews 6:12). To guard against this possibility, the writer urges the readers to imitate the people of the past who attained the promises of God through faith and patience. Abraham is a prime example of one who patiently endured and who "received what was promised" (v. 15).

Abraham had been promised a son, and the promise was affirmed by the oath of God (vv. 13-14). The fulfillment of the promise was in Isaac. God also promised Abraham that through his seed all the nations of the earth would be blessed (Genesis 22:18). This blessing is accomplished through faith in Jesus Christ.

Those who believe the promises of God in Christ are children of Abraham by faith. He is the father of the faithful. Those who trust in the promises of God in Jesus, as Abraham trusted in God's promises, have strong encouragement. We are encouraged to hold on doggedly to our hope. Our hope is Jesus, who is stable and unswerving, as solid as an anchor. "Heaven and earth will pass away," he said, "but my words will never pass away" (Matthew 24:35). Jesus, our hope, is not something visible on earth. He has entered heaven on our behalf. His promise to his followers is "that you also may be where I am" (John 14:3).

Hebrews 7:1-28. The last verse of chapter 6 ends the long exhortation that began in 5:11, right after a reference to Melchizedek. The writer turns the readers' attention back to the main topic: Jesus as a high priest in the order of Melchizedek. Then the writer presents the seven proofs of Jesus' superiority as a high priest. The first four are contained in chapter 7.

The first of the proofs is a long argument presented in 7:1-19. The point is that the priesthood of Jesus in the order of Melchizedek is a higher order of priesthood than the Levitical priesthood.

Just before this (6:13-18), readers were reminded of God's sworn promise to Abraham. Everyone who read the letter was aware of the primary place the patriarch Abraham held as a model in the biblical faith. The biblical information about Melchizedek is directly related to Abraham, so the arguments presented in Hebrews are weighty.

What does the writer indicate about the mysterious figure of Melchizedek?

      I. Melchizedek is a historical shadow of Jesus as a high priest. He resembles the Son of God (7:3). Note these points of comparison:

          a. Both are priests of the Most High God;

          b. The name *Melchizedek* anticipates the character of Jesus, who is righteous and the Prince of Peace (Isaiah 9:6);

          c. Each is a priest forever, because there is no written record of the beginning and end of the priesthood.

      II. In relation to Abraham, Melchizedek was greater, because Abraham paid tithes to him and he blessed Abraham. (Symbolically, the forefather of the Levitical priests [Levi] also paid tithes to Melchizedek while Levi was yet unborn.)

The Levitical priesthood is shown to be imperfect (vv. 11-19), otherwise there would have been no necessity for the Son becoming a priest in the order of Melchizedek. The Levitical priesthood could not remove sin, so another priest was needed (v. 11).

A new priesthood could be established only by a change of law. The Levitical priesthood was based on the law of Moses. The new priesthood is based on the power of an indestructible life, not on a written, legal requirement (v. 16). The basis of the new priesthood is the statement of God in Psalm 110:4. This word of God was given in the psalm several centuries after the time of Moses. This change in the law allowed Jesus, who was from the tribe of Judah, to become a priest.

The second proof is that Jesus was not only called and appointed by God (5:4-5); his appointment was confirmed by the solemn oath of God (7:20-21). None of the Levitical priests were confirmed by an oath. So Jesus is our guarantor of a better covenant (v. 22).

The third proof is that Jesus is an unchangeable priest because he lives forever (vv. 23-25). He is always available to intercede and save. The Levitical priests were replaced at their deaths. They were temporary and changeable.

The fourth proof is that Jesus is a perfect priest (vv. 26-28). He offered himself once, a completely sufficient sacrifice for all people in all times. His perfection has brought him above the highest heavens. The Levitical priests were sinners, offering up animal sacrifices frequently for their own sins as well as for the sins of the people.

If you feel inadequate to deal with the ideas presented above, please do not let that keep you from the effort. Deal with the ideas as best you can, realizing that the more you read and think about Jesus as high priest, the more other passages in the Bible help enrich the concept.

God will bless you with sufficient understanding to lead the group members to a more biblical understanding of what God was doing on our behalf in Jesus Christ. Please note that the last verse of chapter 7 says it was God's initiative ("the oath") that provided such a superior high priest for us. Let us be thankful for God's love.

DIMENSION THREE: WHAT DOES THE BIBLE MEAN TO ME?

Hebrews 5:11–6:8—Spiritual Maturity and the Danger of Apostasy

The fact that you and the group members are studying the Genesis to Revelation Series of Bible studies indicates an interest in going on in your quest for spiritual maturity. Here are some points to ponder out of the advice the writer gives to those who read Hebrews.

The writer suggests that we can become slow of learning if all we do is hear. We also ought to teach. How can one become a teacher rather than simply a person constantly being taught? Continuing education is an essential part of being a Christian. We are called to be disciples of Christ, and *disciple* means "learner." Yet part of our learning should also be learning how to teach. What should be done on the individual level to develop teaching skills? What programs exist in your local church or in the connection of churches to assist the members in developing their teaching abilities?

But does the text really demand that we all be teachers in a formal sense, that is, with a classroom full of students, books, and other equipment? What types of informal teaching might individual Christians do who would never feel comfortable standing before a group? Home Bible study groups are growing in popularity in many places. Could these groups be a good substitute for the formal teaching setting?

Finally, how useful is teaching as a tool for strengthening the faith and commitment of the individual teacher?

Hebrews 5:7-10—Prayer

Prayer is appropriate. If Jesus, the Son of God, depended on prayer in the midst of a crisis in his life, we ought to learn from his example.

Prayer can be an emotional experience. Let us develop a tender heart ourselves, and let us tolerate the tears of others. We pray to the One who has the power to save. With God, nothing shall be called impossible.

God's plan for your life, or for the life of the church in which you are involved, may mean that you must pass through the valley of the shadow of death. God's will for our lives must override our desires. Be prepared for negative answers to prayer and what may seem to be unanswered prayers. All prayers are heard, and God's will is being worked out in the midst of it all.

We do have . . . a high priest, who sat down at the right hand of the throne of the Majesty in heaven. (8:1)

JESUS, PRIEST OF A BETTER COVENANT, TENT, AND SACRIFICE

Hebrews 8:1–10:18

DIMENSION ONE:
WHAT DOES THE BIBLE SAY?

Answer these questions by reading Hebrews 8

1. Where is the high priest of Christians now located? (8:1b)

The high priest of Christians is now seated "at the right hand of the throne of the Majesty in heaven."

2. Moses constructed the earthly tabernacle after what pattern? (8:5)

Moses constructed the earthly tabernacle after the pattern of the heavenly sanctuary.

3. Why is the new covenant, under which Christ has his ministry, better than the old covenant? (8:6)

The new covenant is better because it "is established on better promises."

4. How can we be certain that the first covenant was not faultless? (8:7)

If the first covenant had been faultless, God would not have found it necessary to establish a new covenant.

5. With what people did the Lord promise to establish the new covenant? (8:8)

The Lord promised to "make a new covenant / with the people of Israel / and with the people of Judah."

6. What did the Lord promise to do for the people under the new covenant? (8:10)

The Lord promised to put the divine laws in the minds and on the hearts of God's people.

Answer these questions by reading Hebrews 9

7. What did the ark of the covenant contain? (9:4)

The ark of the covenant "contained the gold jar of manna, Aaron's staff that had budded, and the stone tablets of the covenant."

8. What did the high priest always carry with him when he entered the second (inner) room? (9:6-7)

The high priest always carried the blood of sacrifice when he entered the inner room.

9. How often did Christ enter into the "perfect tabernacle," and what did he take with him? (9:11-12)

Christ entered only once into "the Most Holy Place" taking with him his own blood.

10. What is the blood of Christ able to do? (9:14)

The blood of Christ is able to cleanse the conscience "from acts that lead to death, so that we may serve the living God!"

11. How did the old covenant make possible the forgiveness of sins? (9:22)

The forgiveness of sins was made possible by the shedding of blood.

12. For whose benefit did Christ appear before God in heaven? (9:24)

Christ appeared before God in heaven "for us."

13. For what purpose will Christ appear a second time? (9:28)

Christ "will appear a second time . . . to bring salvation to those who are waiting for him."

Answer these questions by reading Hebrews 10:1-18

14. What did Christ desire to do when he came into the world? (10:7)

Christ desired to do the will of God.

15. Under the new covenant, what two things did the Lord promise to do? (10:16-17)

Under the new covenant God promised to "put my laws in their hearts, / and . . . write them on their minds" and to remember "their sins and lawless acts/ . . . no more."

DIMENSION TWO: WHAT DOES THE BIBLE MEAN?

The entire Book of Hebrews focuses on the superiority of Christ over all who preceded him. We noted his superiority as the means of God's revelation (lesson 1) and his superiority as a high priest (lesson 2).

In this lesson, we will focus on matters directly related to Christ's priesthood. These are: the covenant that is connected to his priesthood, the tent (tabernacle/temple) in which he ministers, and the sacrifice that Christ presented to almighty God.

Hebrews 8:1-6. In 8:1, the writer draws on Psalm 110 for the idea of one "who sat down at the right hand of the throne of the Majesty in heaven." Verse 1 of the psalm reads: "The LORD says to my Lord: / "Sit at my right hand / until I make your enemies / a footstool for your feet.""

"Majesty in heaven" is a substitute for God. This phrase is the same as "the Majesty in heaven" of Hebrews 1:3. Using a substitute expression, rather than pronouncing the name of God, was the usual way of referring to God in the period in which the New Testament was written. This practice grew out of the awe in which God was held and the fear of breaking the commandment not to take the Lord's name in vain. Our writer, apparently a devout Jewish Christian, found it natural to write in this fashion.

The idea of a throne or a temple in heaven was widespread in Jewish circles in New Testament times. The idea had its roots in the Old Testament. There, the tabernacle first appeared as a unique tent in the desert camp of Israel. The tabernacle represented God's presence with the people. Such was the case until the Temple was built in Jerusalem. The Temple served a similar function as God's house. Solomon said of it: "I have indeed built a magnificent temple for you, a place for you to dwell forever" (1 Kings 8:13). He also prayed these words at the dedication of the Temple: "But will God really dwell on earth? The heavens, even the highest heaven, cannot contain you. How much less this temple I have built!" (1 Kings 8:27).

Jesus is called a minister in the (heavenly) sanctuary (Hebrews 8:2); that is, the Most Holy Place. The true tent is the entire sacred installation. As high priest, Jesus could serve as priest throughout the heavenly complex. Not all Israelite priests could enter all areas of the earthly sanctuary. Only the high priest had the authority and obligation to enter the Most Holy Place.

The writer envisions the heavenly sanctuary as a tent rather than a temple, using the expression "set up," meaning "pitched," rather than the word *built*. This heavenly sanctuary existed before the earthly tabernacle, which was built on the plan of the heavenly one (v. 5). The verse is a quotation of God's instructions to Moses on the matter in Exodus 25:40.

The thought of the writer progresses logically in these verses. Jesus is a superior high priest who serves a superior (heavenly) sanctuary, so his ministry is better than that of the earthly copy. His ministry is as much better as the covenant he mediates. This better covenant is the main point of the section. The reference to the better covenant leads naturally into the discussion of it in the following verses.

Hebrews 8:7-13. Just as the heavenly tent surpasses in importance the earthly tent, so the new covenant surpasses the old. The new covenant has better promises than the old (8:6). But the main reason a new covenant (agreement) between God and humans is needed is that the old covenant is faulted.

As if someone among the readers had raised the question "How do you know the old covenant is not faultless?" the writer refers to Jeremiah 31:31 in Hebrews 8:8. Long after Moses, in the time of the prophet Jeremiah (about 600 BC), God revealed that the Mosaic covenant was not faultless. The fault was that God's people "did not remain faithful to my covenant" (8:9b). So the coming of a new covenant was revealed by God.

Jeremiah also prophesied an exile of God's people from Judah and Jerusalem to Babylonia, which lasted seventy years (Jeremiah 29:10). The fulfillment of this prophecy is noted in Ezra 1:1.

The fulfillment of Jeremiah's prophecy about the Exile helped the Jews look forward to the fulfillment of his prophecy about a new covenant. The Essenes, a community of devout Jews who lived at the northwest corner of the Dead Sea before and during the days of the early church, believed they had been chosen by God to be members of the new covenant. Jesus mentioned the establishment of the new covenant in his blood at the Last Supper, according to 1 Corinthians 11:25.

Notice that the covenant was at fault on the human side rather than on God's side. The people failed to keep their side of the bargain, even though they had promised to do so. They had said, "Everything the Lord has said we will do" (Exodus 24:3). When Paul discusses the law in Romans 3:3-4, he notes, "What if some were unfaithful? Will their unfaithfulness nullify God's faithfulness? Not at all! Let God be true, and every human being a liar." This fault on the human side of the old covenant was the reason God planned to institute a new covenant "when the set time had fully come" (Galatians 4:4). That occurred with the appearance of Jesus.

Hebrews 8:10 indicates one of the ways in which the new covenant would be better than the old. Rather than being written on stone or scrolls, it would be written on the hearts of God's people. God's will would not be taught by specialized teachers under the new covenant. Here we must understand that God's Spirit would be at work in the hearts and minds of believers, as Joel prophesied (2:28-29).

Another blessing of the new covenant is God's promise to be merciful toward the people's iniquities. God promises to remember their sins no more (Hebrews 8:12).

Hebrews 9:1-14. Christ is the mediator of this new covenant (8:6). Having established the superiority of the new covenant, the writer now considers the superiority of the sacrifice of Christ under the new covenant. The writer does this by comparing that sacrifice with the pattern of sacrifices under the old covenant, and in the earthly tabernacle related to that covenant. Christ's sacrifice is related to the heavenly sanctuary, of course.

The writer assumes that the readers know considerable detail about the earthly tabernacle and the rituals connected with it. A brief discussion of the tabernacle is provided in this section of the lesson in the participant book. The biblical description of the tabernacle's construction is found in Exodus 35–40. The tabernacle consisted of two main parts, a rectangular enclosure and the tent proper, which was positioned within the enclosure. The enclosure was about 150-feet long and 75-feet wide, with an entrance at the east end. The enclosure was made of poles and connecting brackets of bronze that were covered with curtains. The enclosure was about 7.5-feet high.

The tent proper was situated toward the west end of the enclosure. It was 45-feet long by 15-feet wide, and it was 15-feet high. A heavy curtain (veil) separated the tent into two rooms. The eastern end was a room 30 by 15 feet, the Holy Place. An opening in the east end provided entry from the courtyard for designated priests. Within this room were a golden lampstand and a golden table for twelve loaves of bread, representing the twelve tribes of Israel.

The inner room of the tent, the Most Holy Place, was entered only once a year by the high priest on the Day of Atonement. The room was a perfect cube of 15 feet. Within it stood a golden incense altar and a gold covered wooden chest called the *ark*. Within the ark were the tablets of stone engraved with the Ten Commandments, a golden jar of manna, and Aaron's staff. The lid of the ark, decorated with angelic symbols called *cherubim*, represented God's footstool. God's throne was in heaven. The Most Holy Place was in utter darkness except when the high priest entered on the Day of Atonement. (This assumption is based on the words of Solomon in 1 Kings 8:12.) The Day of Atonement falls near the autumnal equinox in late September. Sunrise on that day may have cast the sun's rays directly through the eastern door, through the opened veil, to illuminate the interior of the Most Holy Place for the high priestly ritual.

The tabernacle was made of goat's hair cloth. Over this was a covering of red leather made of rams' skins. And over this was another covering of (goat?) skin. All the cloth of the panels of the entire complex was beautifully dyed, and the hardware consisted of bronze in the enclosure and silver and gold in the tent proper. The value of the materials increased nearer to the Most Holy Place.

The outer court contained the altar of burnt offering and the large bronze water container called the *laver*. The water was used for ceremonial washings of the priests and for washing the sacrifices. Many more people were permitted to enter the outer court than the tent. A number of priests would be on duty, and Israelite men who were ritually clean could enter this area. Here various offerings were sacrificed.

The sacrifices offered at the tabernacle are discussed in Leviticus 1–7. *Burnt offerings* were entirely burned. They consisted of young bulls, rams, goats, doves, and pigeons. *Cereal offerings* were of grain, flour, or cakes baked without leaven. A portion was burned; the remainder was given to the priests. *Peace offerings* were of cattle, sheep, or goats. The fat was burned, and the remainder was eaten partly by the priests, partly by the worshipers. *Sin and trespass offerings* were similar to those mentioned above but for a specific sin or trespass. The fat was burned, while the remainder was in some cases burned outside the camp and in some cases eaten by the priests.

Animals (unblemished) were brought by the worshipers to the entrance of the enclosure. There, in the presence of the officiating priest, the worshipers laid their hands on them, signifying that the animals were substitutes for themselves. The animals were slain, and some of the blood was sprinkled or smeared on the altar and poured out at its base. Then the appropriate part or the whole was burned.

Two lambs were offered daily, one in the morning and one in the evening, as burnt offerings. This number was doubled on the sabbath. On the first day of each month, additional offerings were made. At the great pilgrimage festivals (Passover, Pentecost, and Tabernacles), great numbers of sacrifices were offered. Special offerings and procedures were followed on the Day of Atonement. Individuals might bring offerings for special occasions at other times.

Hebrews 9:6-7 speaks of the normal ritual pattern of the Israelite priests in the earthly tabernacle. Verse 8 explains that the annual entrance of the high priest into the Most Holy Place was a sign that the way into the true, heavenly sanctuary was not yet opened to the worshiper, as it would be when opened by Christ (10:19-20). The ritualistic situation in the earthly sanctuary was incapable of actually cleansing the conscience of the worshiper. The focus of the system was on "food and drink and various ceremonial washings—external regulations" (9:10). Apparently, with the sacrificial system associated with the tabernacle, the worshipers were so isolated from the presence of God, whose forgiveness the worshipers were seeking, that their conscience was never completely at peace. The worshipers had no direct access to God.

This sanctuary and sacrificial system was only a dim copy of the heavenly sanctuary, and thus was not nearly as effectual as the true sanctuary and sacrifice to be established at the "time of the new order" (9:10). This expression must refer to the high priestly work of Christ and thus to the time in which the writer of Hebrews was living (see 9:11-14). The time of the new order, or correction, occurred "when Christ came as high priest of the good things that are already here" (v. 11). The "good things" would refer to the blessings that have come as the result of Christ's atoning death, burial, and resurrection. If the original text referred to "the good things that are to come" (see the NIV footnote to v. 11), the reference would be to the time when the promises of God in Christ would be fulfilled. That is the future hope of Christians.

Whichever version is accurate, the emphasis in 9:11-14 is on the superiority of Christ's ministry as high priest, on the better sacrifice he made, and on the superlative results. Christ's ministry actually accomplished what the inferior ministry and rituals only hinted at. The blood of Christ is the effective means for purifying the conscience. In every respect—in terms of the priestly ministry, in terms of the sanctuary and sacrifices, and in terms of the covenant—the heavenly realities are superior to the earthly copies.

Hebrews 9:15-28. Earlier in the lesson, we noted the reference to the new, better covenant (8:6-13). The writer now returns to that subject. The blood of Christ not only makes possible the purifying of the conscience from "acts that lead to death, so that we may serve the living God" (9:14); it also establishes the new, better covenant.

We have seen that the earthly tabernacle and priestly function offered an imperfect picture of the better, heavenly arrangement. The heavenly is the original and superior sanctuary, priesthood, and sacrifice. The new covenant on which the heavenly arrangement is based has better promises. Now, we are shown that the new covenant is mediated and ratified by a superior mediator.

The background of these ideas is the historical establishment of the old covenant at Sinai. There Moses was the mediator between God (on the mountain) and the people (at the foot of the mountain). The old covenant was ratified by animal sacrifices and by the sprinkling of blood on the people, on the book of the covenant, on the tabernacle (after it was built), and on all the ritual implements (vv. 18-21). The shedding of blood under the old covenant was for purifying the exterior of humans and of ritual things.

The new covenant was mediated by Christ and established by his blood. It redeems people from their transgressions under the old covenant. They are cleansed inwardly, in the conscience. The death of Christ put this new will, this new covenant, into effect. That his shed blood is more effective than that of sheep and goats is the focus of 9:23-28.

The pattern of the superiority of the heavenly reality to the inferior earthly copy continues. Christ has entered heaven, not just the Most Holy Place of an earthly sanctuary. He is in God's presence on our behalf, not on behalf of himself as well as others, as with the Levitical high priest.

Christ's sacrifice was so effective that it was offered only once and for all time. That sacrifice is in contrast to the annual sacrifice offered by the earthly high priest on the Day of Atonement. The purpose of Christ's sacrifice was to put away sin permanently for those who accept him. Christ dealt with sin while he was here the first time, suffering in the flesh. The next time Christ appears he will have no need to deal with sin (v. 28). Christ bore the sins of many, of any who will respond to his invitation. When Christ returns, it will be to save those who are eagerly awaiting his arrival.

Christ came to establish the new covenant at the "culmination of the ages" (v. 26), which does not mean at the end of the world. Rather the expression refers to the end of the era of the old covenant. There are still those on earth whose consciences have been purified by Christ's blood, and who eagerly wait for him. The "culmination of the ages" includes the span of the church's earthly existence until the Savior returns.

Hebrews 10:1-10. Earlier, our writer introduced the once-for-all nature of Christ's sacrifice. This section expands on that idea. Notice that the contrast here is between the ability of the sacrificial blood under the old system and that of Christ's blood under the new system to cleanse from sin.

Under the old system, there were "those who draw near" (v. 1). These are called worshipers in verse 2. Their consciences would have been free of a sense of sin had the sacrifices been effective. But they were not.

Then what of the sense of sin in Christians? Once we come to Christ in repentance, confessing our sins, dying to sin, and in baptism burying the old person dominated by sin, we rise to live a new life (Romans 6:4). Christians may sin and be aware of this after being initially cleansed by the blood of Christ, but they ought not to "live in it" (Romans 6:2). Prayer, confession, and Communion at the Lord's Table are means by which penitent Christians are cleansed. Any committed Christian who walks around bearing a burden of guilt for sin already forgiven is falling into a devilish trap. We are to accept God's assurances that in Christ we are free from that kind of perpetual burden. Christ's better sacrifice is final and effectual. We have been sanctified by Christ's sacrifice (Hebrews 10:10).

Hebrews 10:11-18. Whereas, in the earthly sanctuary, the high priest fearfully entered the Most Holy Place standing, and remained standing as he carried out the prescribed ritual; Christ sat down at God's right hand. His sacrifice was once and for all. There was no need for him to exit from the presence of God in order to return again in the future with another sacrifice for sin (v. 12).

Notice again how effective that sacrifice is for "those who are being made holy" (v. 14). In fact, the final emphasis in this section is on the meaning of Christ's sacrifice for us (v. 15). The Holy Spirit testifies to us here, through Scripture. The Scripture is Jeremiah 31:34. The testimony is that we are forgiven. When God forgives our sins, we have no more need of the Day of Atonement or any other kind of sacrifice to remove sin. No wonder the last words of Christ from the cross were, "It is finished" (John 19:30).

DIMENSION THREE: WHAT DOES THE BIBLE MEAN TO ME?

Hebrews 9:22-26—The Doctrine of the Blood Atonement of Jesus

The shed blood of Jesus is essential for the cleansing of our conscience before our Maker. Jesus died for me, and he died for you. His blood was a substitute for yours and mine, and we have life because he gave up his. God accepted this selfless act as sufficient, and God raised Jesus from the dead. So we have a living Savior, a living Lord. This is possible only because Jesus is the Lamb of God who takes away the sins of the world.

The shed blood is an essential part of the Christian faith. It is, in fact, the ultimate evidence of the love of Jesus Christ. This evidence is essential for the faith of the individual and essential to the existence of any church of the living Lord.

Hebrews 9:14, 15, 28; 10:10, 14—Those Who Read Hebrews

To answer the question in the participant book, see the section in this chapter on Hebrews 9:15-28, and draw on those ideas. We should recall that the word *gospel* means "good news." As Christians, we find very little good news if we are almost constantly reminded from the pulpit and from Christian publications that we are gross sinners under condemnation. We find the writer of Hebrews encouraging the readers in this way: "Do not throw away your confidence; it will be richly rewarded" (10:35).

Many New Testament passages teach the confidence Christians ought to have. For example, in 1 John 1:7 we read: "If we walk in the light, as he is in the light, we have fellowship with one another, and the blood of Jesus, his Son, purifies us from all sin." The "peace of God, which transcends all understanding" (Philippians 4:7), should keep the heart and mind of those in Christ; for he is our peace.

Faith is confidence in what we hope for and assurance about what we do not see. (11:1)

FAITH, THE SUPERIOR WAY TO DO GOD'S WILL

Hebrews 10:19–11:40

DIMENSION ONE: WHAT DOES THE BIBLE SAY?

Answer these questions by reading Hebrews 10:19-39

1. In 10:19-25, several exhortations begin with the words *let us*. What five actions does the writer call for?

> *The readers are urged to "draw near to God with . . . faith" (10:22); to "hold unswervingly to the hope we profess" (10: 23); to "spur one another on toward love and good deeds" (10:24); to "not give up meeting together" (10:25); and "encouraging one another— all the more as . . . the Day [approaches}" (10:25).*

2. Who should fear falling "into the hands of the living God"? (10:29-31)

> *The person who should fear falling into the hands of the living God is the one who has been sanctified by the blood of the covenant and has then treated it as an unholy thing and trampled the Son of God under foot, thus insulting the Spirit of grace.*

3. List the sufferings that early believers in Christ endured. (10:32-34)

> *Early believers in Christ (Christians) (1) suffered public insult and persecution, (2) shared the similar persecutions of fellow believers, and (3) willingly gave up earthly property.*

4. Who are the opposite of "those who have faith and are saved"? (10:39)

> *The opposite are "those who shrink back and are destroyed."*

Answer these questions by reading Hebrews 11

5. According to the writer of Hebrews, how can we understand the creation of the visible world out of things that cannot be seen? (11:3)

    We understand that the "universe was formed at Gods command" by faith.

6. List the patriarchs given as examples of faith in 11:4-7.

    The examples of faithful patriarchs are Abel, Enoch, and Noah.

7. What did Abraham and Sarah have faith in? (11:8-13)

    Abraham and Sarah believed the promises of God.

8. What is the common feature of the faith of Abraham, Isaac, Jacob, and Joseph? (11:17-22)

    Each of these patriarchs trusted God for future blessings.

9. List the three things that Moses did by faith. (11:23-28)

    "By faith Moses . . . refused to be known as the son of Pharaoh's daughter," "by faith he left Egypt," and "by faith he kept the Passover."

10. Identify the two historical events that illustrate the faith of the Israelites. (11:29-30)

    The faith of the Israelites is illustrated by the crossing of the Red Sea and by the conquest of Jericho.

11. The accomplishments of God's judges and prophets are listed in 11:32-38. How were these great deeds done?

    The deeds of the judges and prophets were accomplished through faith.

12. The heroic figures of faith mentioned in Hebrews 11 did not receive in their time what was promised. Why not? (11:39-40)

    God intended that they would share in "something better" with us, that they should be made perfect with us.

DIMENSION TWO:
WHAT DOES THE BIBLE MEAN?

In our study of Hebrews we have reached the end of the writer's arguments that Jesus is superior to every aspect of the Israelite religion established under the law mediated through Moses. The previous presentation was intended to help readers see that to fall back to the older way from which they had been freed would be to turn their backs on the better way, approved by God through Jesus Christ. Nothing remains for the writer but to exhort readers to hold fast to what they have received through Christ and add some final comments.

Hebrews 10:19-25. We have seen the word *therefore* introduce exhortations before in this book. Chapters 2, 3, 4, and 6 open with this word. *Therefore* is a conjunction, a word that joins what follows with what has gone before. The writer intends to say, "Therefore, brothers and sisters . . . let us draw near" (vv. 19, 22). But the writer summarizes in two clauses what has been presented before, beginning each clause with *since*. We need to keep them in mind when we read, "let us draw near."

The first *since* clause reminds the readers of what they most need to hear: "we have confidence to enter" the presence of God. The first readers were tempted to give up Christ to return to the old covenant ways. They needed the confidence that, the writer assures them, they have. That confidence was based on the sacrificial blood of Jesus. Our writer already had pointed out that this sacrifice meant that God would remember their sins and misdeeds no more (v. 17). Thanks to the sacrifice of Christ, Christians are cleansed and can confidently enter the presence of God.

The other *since* clause (v. 21) draws attention to the high priestly presence of Jesus in heaven. He is at God's right hand. Christians have a friend in the house of God who has so loved them that he gave his life for them. He is seated on the right hand of the One who loved the world so much that he gave his only begotten Son in order that no one need perish. All can now have everlasting life. No wonder the writer encourages readers to approach God confidently.

The condition of those who draw near is described next in verse 22. One condition is that they have a "sincere heart." A sincere heart is a loyal heart. Such a heart does not question the truth that it is the shed blood of Christ—not works—that provides salvation. A sincere heart is a heart "sprinkled to cleanse [it] from a guilty conscience." Recall that the blood of Christ cleanses the conscience (10:1-4). The other condition is that they have their "bodies washed with pure water." Sacrifices were washed in the tabernacle, but this is more likely a reference to Christian baptism, a symbol of cleansing from sin (Acts 22:16).

Besides the encouragement to draw near, the writer urges readers to "hold unswervingly to the hope we profess" (Hebrews 10:23). What is this hope? It is that God will soon bring to complete fulfillment the promises he made to Abraham. We will see at the close of chapter 11 that none of those who lived by faith "received what had been promised, since God had planned something better for us so that only together with us would they be made perfect" (11:39-40). The promises of God to Abraham are fulfilled in Christ. Paul expressed the idea this way to the church in Galatia: "If you belong to Christ, then you are Abraham's seed, and heirs according to the promise" (Galatians 3:29). The final consummation of the ages and the realization of those promises await the return of Christ; that is why it is yet a hope. Christians have great confidence in this hope, however, because they have a guarantee—the Holy Spirit (Ephesians 1:13-14).

Besides drawing near and holding fast, the writer urges readers to "consider" (Hebrews 10:24). Instead of wondering about when the hope will finally be realized, the readers are pointed to constructive activities. To consider is to seriously think about something. The idea is to spend time encouraging one another, to care for one another. This kind of encouragement comes from providing an example. When Christians are showing loving concern for one another, they have no time to become discouraged and to grumble.

One of the best settings for stirring up support within the community of Christians is the assembly of believers. Not only are the problems and needs of individuals brought to the attention of the group in that setting; that setting also provides the mutual encouragement that comes from sharing what God is doing in the lives of believers. The day of the final fulfillment of the promises draws ever nearer. That, too, is encouraging. The promised victory in Christ draws nearer.

Hebrews 10:26-31. The opening lines of the exhortation (10:19-25) provide a powerful encouragement to faith. The other side of the coin is presented in these verses. If the readers fail to act confidently on their faith in the blood of Christ and his high priestly efforts on their behalf, grave danger lies near. The writer is concerned about the danger of deliberate sin, in contrast to unwitting sin.

The particular sin that the writer has in mind is specifically mentioned in 10:29. He draws a picture of a person who had at one time received the knowledge of the truth. Then that person spurned (trampled underfoot) the Son of God. That individual also profaned the very means by which salvation comes—the blood of Christ. To profane is to make common, to treat that which is sacred as unclean. The result of not only turning away from the Savior but also treating the Savior with contempt is to insult the Spirit of grace, the Holy Spirit.

God is patient, but God's patience can wear thin. Vengeance is the punishment inflicted on an enemy to retaliate for indignities done by the enemy. Here, to judge is to condemn as guilty and to punish. Anyone who would accept God's gracious gift of salvation only to later treat it with contempt faces a terrible consequence at the hand of God. When we deal with the God of the Bible, we are dealing with the living God. God is not a lifeless idol manufactured by human hands.

Hebrews 10:32-39. The writer has not charged readers with the sin of apostasy, but has only reminded them of the danger in order to spur them on to greater endurance. In 10:19-25, the writer has used encouragement; in 10:26-31, warning is used. Verses 32-39 call them to greater efforts in the faith by reminding them of their heroic lives in the past.

To receive the light is to come to a saving knowledge of the Lord Jesus Christ (2 Peter 1:3-4). Light expels darkness, permitting hidden truths to be seen. With the light of truth, one can distinguish God's will for one's life. The commitment of life to Christ brings peace with God but enmity with the world. The writer knew that the readers have suffered for their faith. The early days of Christianity were filled with open and sometimes violent persecution.

The sufferings experienced by the first readers of Hebrews fell into two categories. They personally suffered public abuse and affliction. This abuse could be physical abuse or the cutting remarks and disdain of their former friends or both.

The other category was the equally difficult struggle of seeing Christian brothers and sisters suffering and being unable to do anything about it but to endure. Paul, in Galatians 6:2, commanded: "Carry each other's burdens, and in this way you will fulfill the law of Christ." In Romans 12:15, he urged Christians to "mourn with those who mourn."

The first readers of Hebrews have endured such afflictions. The writer commends them in 10:34. Confidence in their future under the promises of God is what sustains them. Their possessions in this world, used to support prisoners or taken from them by the pagan society that afflicts them, count for nothing. They joyfully accept such events in their lives. All this is temporary; but the treasures in heaven are abiding treasures.

The mention of prisoners reminds me of the difference between prison life then and now. Today, prisoners are given the necessities of life by the state. The survival of prisoners in the Roman world depended on food, blankets, and clothing provided by friends and families. That is why visiting those in prison was so vital and was commended by Jesus (Matthew 25:36).

Through all these activities—struggling with suffering, accepting insult and persecution, sharing the pain of others so treated, and suffering material loss for the sake of the Christian faith—the readers have persevered. They suffered while living in the will of God (Hebrews 10:36). The call is to continue to persevere. What is promised will come only to those who persevere.

To prove the point, the writer of Hebrews uses a quotation from Habakkuk 2:3-4. The need is to persevere to the end. The end will come "in just a little while." "He who is coming" is the Christ. The "righteous one" is the faithful believer, the person who has suffered ridicule and persecution for the faith and has persevered. Recently, that person has been tempted to give up. The point of the quotation in 10:38 is that such a person needs faith in order to live and to persevere until "he who is coming" comes. God will have no pleasure in the one who *almost* remains faithful to the end.

The writer hastens to reassure readers that, while mentioning these things to urge them on, no charge of unfaithfulness is being made. They have what it takes to persevere—faith—and the writer recognizes their faith. But that faith can be deepened and strengthened, to which end the text now turns.

Hebrews 11:1-3. Encourage group members to memorize this powerful definition of faith (11:1).

The word translated *confidence* has the basic meaning of "that which stands under anything." So it can also be translated as "groundwork, title-deed, or substance." Faith is the foundation or basis for hope. One who has faith has a base on which to stand in the difficulties of life.

The other side of the coin of faith is *assurance*. Having a foundation of things hoped for is not enough. Hope can be an empty exercise, based on what is imagined rather than on reality. When confident hope is joined to assurance of the truth of God and God's promises—what we do not see—sustaining faith exists. This combination of having a confident hope based on the assurance of what we cannot see is faith.

Biblical faith is trust in the reality of God and the truth of God's revealed word. Both "the ancients" (v. 2) and people today receive divine approval through faith. As the readers are told in 11:6, "Anyone who comes to [God] must believe that he exists and that he rewards those who earnestly seek him." God, of course, is the great Unseen. "No one has ever seen God, but the one and only son, who is himself God and is in closest relationship with the Father's side, has made him known" (John 1:18).

The last idea in this section is that God created the universe by command, out of things not seen. The writer's exact meaning is not clear to us, although it certainly does not include our modern understanding of the nature of things: unseen atoms, atomic particles, and energy. But it is amazing how well this expression of how the world came to be fits the scientific evidence that the material universe is made of unseen particles.

Hebrews 11:4-40. After defining faith, the writer of Hebrews presents illustrations of that definition based on the flow of biblical history. After mentioning the creation of the universe, which we understand by faith, the text moves on to note faith before the Flood (vv. 4-7), the faith of the patriarchs (vv. 8-22), faith in the period of the Exodus and the conquest of Canaan (vv. 23-31), and the faith of later generations of biblical people (vv. 32-38). The writer then brings the saga of the faithful down to the rewarding of the faith of the past in the present. That present was the end of the first-century AD (vv. 39-40).

Hebrews 11:4-7. The biblical people mentioned in this section who exhibited faith include Abel, the first victim of murder; Enoch, who walked with God; and Noah, who was considered righteous in his generation. The stories of these three are found in the first few chapters of Genesis.

The participant book mentions that the Bible gives no direct statement to indicate why Abel's offering was accepted by God while Cain's was not. However, an expanded Jewish translation and paraphrase of Genesis does discuss the faith of Cain and Abel. The explanation given for Cain rising up and killing Abel is that they were arguing about why Abel's sacrifice was accepted and Cain's was not. Essentially, Abel argued that the world is created by the mercy of God and is governed according to the fruit of good works. Cain insisted that the world is not governed by good works. Then he went on to deny a judgment, a judge, and another (heavenly) world. Abel insisted otherwise, and Cain rose up in anger and killed him.

To the writer of Hebrews, the fact that God accepted Abel's gifts is evidence that Abel was righteous. First John 3:12 explains the first murder thus: "Why did he murder him? Because his [Cain's] own actions were evil and his brother's were righteous."

Enoch was the father of Methuselah. We are told in Genesis 5:24 that "Enoch walked with God; then he was no more, because God took him away." In a sense, Enoch is mysterious like Melchizedek. The writer of the intertestamental Book of Jubilees (10:17) considered Enoch as more righteous than Noah. In Genesis, "God took him away" means Enoch did not see death. The Septuagint (Greek) translation of the Old Testament says that Enoch was "pleasing to God."

Abel and Enoch are examples that establish the principle that "without faith it is impossible to please God" (11:6). God will reward those who believe that God exists and who seek God.

Noah's faith was established on the truth of God's testimony to him. He believed the Flood would come, even though it was unseen for a long time before it actually occurred. Noah's faith was expressed in a tangible form. He built an ark.

Hebrews 11:8-22. The faith of Abraham, his wife Sarah, his son Isaac, his grandson Jacob, and his great-grandson Joseph, is related to incidents in Genesis 12–50. The common thread that runs through all these incidents is the idea of a promise. A promise is a thing hoped for, something not seen. The faith of the patriarchs and matriarchs was a sense of assurance, a conviction of the reality of the promise.

Abraham and Sarah obeyed the call of God to go to a land they had never seen but a land they trusted existed. They saw that land and lived in it. Yet they did not see the fulfillment of God's promise that their descendants would possess the land of Canaan (Genesis 17:8). Isaac and Jacob, as Abraham, lived as wandering strangers in the land of promise. The contrast is between living in a tent as a sojourner and living in a city as a permanent inhabitant of the land. But in Hebrews 11:10, the writer spiritualizes the city. God builds this city.

Sarah's faith is not evident in Genesis 18:9-15. When she is informed that she (a woman past childbearing age) will have a son, she laughs. The writer of Hebrews says that she "considered him faithful who had made the promise (Hebrews 11:11), and so Isaac was conceived and born (Genesis 21:1-2).

Again, in Hebrews 11:13-16, the writer of Hebrews spiritualizes the promises to the patriarchs. The patriarchs are represented as desiring a heavenly city and country. This desire suggests prophetic insight on their part.

The theme of future unrealized promises is continued with examples of Abraham and the offering of Isaac, the blessing of Jacob by Isaac, the blessing of Joseph's sons by Jacob, and the directions for his burial that Joseph gave to the Israelites. In each case, something to be realized in the future required faith on the part of a patriarchal family member.

Hebrews 11:23-32. Moses provides another example of one who trusted in the promises of God. The example begins with his parents. The writer implies that they saw the potential of the child. Moses was "looking ahead to his reward" (v. 26). He endured because, in his mind's eye, he saw "him who is invisible" (v. 27), that is, God. Moses believed the promise that the death angel would pass over the houses with blood on the doorway.

The faith of the Israelites crossing the sea and marching around Jericho also contains the element of a promise believed before they saw it realized. Rahab envisioned the future when the Israelites would conquer Jericho by God's help, and acted on her belief. The confident hope and assurance that these things would come to pass was the expression of their faith.

Hebrews 11:32-38. The allusions to biblical characters and events in this section are so general that specific incidents are difficult to identify. The participant's guide suggests some possibilities. For the writer of Hebrews, the point is that these kings, judges, prophets, and common people struggled against tremendous odds and suffered exceedingly. They were willing and able to do what they did because they had faith in things envisioned but unfulfilled. In other words, they trusted the promises of God.

Hebrews 11:39-40. To this point the writer has listed the faithful of the past as examples. Everyone on this list hoped for something that God promised. To some degree or other, each of them shared in the promises to Abraham. Those promises were yet unfulfilled when they died.

Now, the writer insists, the promises are being fulfilled in the very time in which the readers are living. All the saints of the past are depending on the writer's generation to be faithful. If the readers become apostates, then the saints of God of the past will not be perfected. They will not see the promises fulfilled. God's intent is to bring to fruition God's promises of the ages in the time of the writer and the first readers of Hebrews. We are to understand that this fulfillment is in Jesus Christ as revealer of God's will and as high priest and sacrifice.

DIMENSION THREE: WHAT DOES THE BIBLE MEAN TO ME?

Hebrews 10:19-39—Christian Perseverance

For the church—the corporate body—and for the individual Christian, the sources of strength to live by faith are still the same as for the writer and first readers of Hebrews. These include looking to Jesus as an example and to the examples of the faithful in times past. The history of the church is filled with heroes and heroines of the faith. We should keep constantly before us stories of Christians who suffered and triumphed by faith.

But more than this, an effort should be made to arouse the awareness in the church and in the individual Christian of living examples of persevering faithful. In practically every church there are persons who trust in the promises of God in the midst of adversity and suffering. These persons should be recognized and celebrated.

Hebrews 11:4-38—Biblical Heroes and Heroines of the Faith

This section links closely with the one above. Think first of the pioneers in the faith who helped establish your local congregation. Try to discover some of the problems they confronted and overcame by faith. Often, the present realities of the congregation are the result of envisioning things not seen but hoped for on the part of older brothers and sisters in the faith. Some of them are now gone from the scene, but their works follow after them.

One way of stimulating group members to think about significant people of faith is to ask, What Christians have been influential in your life?

[L]et us run with perseverance the race marked out for us. (12:1)

THE DEMANDS OF ENDURING FAITH

Hebrews 12–13

DIMENSION ONE: WHAT DOES THE BIBLE SAY?

Answer these questions by reading Hebrews 12

1. The readers of Hebrews are called to take three positive steps in 12:1-2. List them below.

    They are called to (1) "throw off everything that hinders and the sin that so easily entangles," (2) "run with perseverance the race" before them, and (3) look to Jesus, "the pioneer and perfecter" of their faith.

2. The writer of Hebrews viewed the struggles of the Christian as the discipline of God. How should the discipline of God be understood by the Christian? (12:5-7)

    The discipline of God is evidence of God's love, proof that God is dealing with the believer as God's child.

3. For what two things ought we to strive as we run our race of life? (12:14)

    We are to "live in peace with everyone and to be holy."

4. Trouble that defiles many is the opposite of peace with all (12:14-15). What is the best guard against this cause of trouble? (12:15)

    The best guard against this cause of trouble (a "bitter root") is to obtain the grace of God.

5. Why were the Israelites and even Moses fearful at the place where they met God? (12:18-21)

    They were fearful because the sight was so terrifying.

6. Thanks to the new covenant that Jesus mediated, what will be the nature of the heavenly assembly of God's people? (12:22-24)

They will join in joyful gathering with the angels.

7. Why will the earth and the heaven be shaken once more? (12:25-27)

They will be shaken once more so that "what cannot be shaken may remain."

8. As a part of an unshakable kingdom, what two things are Christians urged to do? (12:28)

They are urged to be thankful and to offer acceptable worship to God.

Answer these questions by reading Hebrews 13

9. How many admonitions are given to the readers of Hebrews in 13:1-5? What are they?

Eight admonitions are given to the readers: (1) on loving one another, (2) on hospitality, (3) on those in prison, (4) on the mistreated, (5) on marriage, (6) on the marriage bed, (7) on the love of money, and (8) on being content.

10. List the three things Christians should do in respect to their leaders. (13:7)

Christians should remember their leaders, consider their lives, and imitate their faith.

11. Where did the sacrificial suffering of Jesus take place? (13:12)

Jesus suffered outside the city gate.

12. Identify three sacrifices Christians are to offer to God. (13:15-16)

Christians are to offer God praise ("the fruit of lips"), to perform good deeds, and to share what they have with others.

13. The writer asked readers specifically to pray for what? (13:18-19)

The writer asked them to pray that "I may be restored to you soon."

14. The writer included a prayer for readers. What request is made of God for them? (13:20-21)
The writer prayed that they would be equipped to do God's will and that God would work God's will in them through Jesus Christ.

DIMENSION TWO:
WHAT DOES THE BIBLE MEAN?

In lesson 4, we saw faith defined and then illustrated with a roll call of heroes and heroines of the faith. The intent of the writer was to set the stage to exhort readers to endure. That exhortation makes up the first half of this lesson, chapter 12.

Hebrews 12:1-2. As we noted in the preceding lesson, the saints of the Old Testament died without having seen the promises of God fulfilled. They were not made perfect apart from the writer of Hebrews and the first readers (11:40).

Those prophetic foreseers are now pictured by the writer of Hebrews as looking down on the arena of life in which Christians struggle. One can almost hear them cheering the struggling Christians on toward the goal.

The figures of speech used in 12:1-2 are taken from the athletic arena. A runner in the games of the classical world removed the clothing that would hamper full exertion; the writer urged the readers to lay aside anything that might hinder their speed and progress in the faith.

The Christian is also to lay aside "the sin that so easily entangles." This phrase is translated as "the sin which doth so easily beset us" in the King James Version. The Latin Vulgate translation has "the sin standing around us." The picture painted here is of sin, like a surrounding pack of dogs, hindering the forward motion of the runner.

Jesus is pictured as an example of faith as well as the One who brings the believer's faith to completion, if the believer's gaze is kept on Jesus. In keeping with the definition of faith in 11:1, Jesus was assured of what he hoped for and was convinced of the joy in the future after he endured the cross. He died as a common criminal, but he took no thought of it for the sake of doing God's will. The main point of the example is that Jesus endured.

Hebrews 12:3-11. For Jesus, a part of the despicable situation at the cross was the hostility of the crowd. Even one of the criminals who was crucified at the same time railed against Jesus (Luke 23:39). Yet Jesus endured the cross, scorning the shame. The readers are asked to consider this example. Recalling what Jesus suffered becomes the antidote for curing fainthearted feelings or being tired in the faith.

Jesus struggled under the burden of the sin of others rather than under his own sin; for, as we have seen, he was sinless. Jesus shed his blood in his sacrificial death. While the readers of Hebrews had "endured in a great conflict full of suffering" (10:32), they had not resisted to the point of death, as Jesus did.

The suffering of Jesus was within the will of God for his life. God's children can expect suffering too. The writer notes that God addresses them as God's children. The basis for the writer's understanding of Christians' relationship to God is the Scripture. To emphasize this point, the writer quotes Proverbs 3:11-12.

The emphasis, as with the example of Jesus, is on enduring a painful period. The suffering the readers experience is the discipline of God. The fact that they suffer for their faith is evidence that they are indeed the children of God. For God disciplines only God's actual children.

"Father of spirits" in 12:9b is the equivalent of "God." God certainly is that, for "in him we live and move and have our being" (Acts 17:28).

We endure the discipline of earthly fathers and respect them. How much more should we endure and respect the discipline of the "Father of spirits." By doing so, we live. God's discipline is for our good, producing holiness, while our earthly fathers discipline us for our good, but at their pleasure. The motivation for discipline differs.

The word *discipline* has a connection with the idea of being trained. A disciple is a learner. One undergoes the rigors of discipline in order to attain the benefits. The benefit of enduring God's discipline is "a harvest of righteousness and peace" (Hebrews 12:11). Nothing gives greater satisfaction than being right with God and our fellow humans.

Hebrews 12:12-17. This *therefore* in Hebrews (one of the last in the book) introduces the urging of the writer based on the first part of the chapter. The cloud of witnesses, the example of Jesus, and the assurance that the readers are God's legitimate children are the basis for encouragement. A part of the exhortation consists of specific steps to be taken by the readers.

Verses 12-13 picture the readers as tired and lame. They are urged to shake off these feelings. The "level paths" refer to religious paths. Walking in the narrow way will bring healing rather than injury.

Striving for "peace with everyone" and for holiness (v. 14) are ways of making level paths for the feet. How could a believer miss "the grace of God" (v. 15)? John Chrysostom, a powerful preacher and patriarch of Constantinople (AD 398–404), explained this expression as similar to a group of travelers in which one lags behind and never makes it to the end of the long, difficult journey. The person who endures to the end shall be saved.

"Bitter root" in verse 15 is taken from Deuteronomy 29:18. There it reads "root . . . produces such bitter poison." The context indicates that idolatry and apostasy comprise the root. Potential apostasy was a major concern, too, of the writer of Hebrews. The point is that apostasy can cause a person to fail to attain the grace of God. It can also bear poisonous and bitter fruit by influencing many others, causing them to be defiled, that is, to fall away from the promise of God.

Not only must one guard against apostasy, one must guard against being immoral or godless. Esau is charged with acting without due reverence for the things of God. The birthright belonged to the eldest son by custom. Jacob purchased the birthright when Esau was very hungry. Later, when Esau wanted to inherit the blessing, he could not reverse the foolishness of his earlier actions (Genesis 27). This is the intended meaning of "he was rejected" (v. 17).

The reader is warned by the example of Esau. Do not do something foolish that will forfeit your obtaining the grace of God. Walk carefully on the road of life.

Hebrews 12:18-24. The writer of Hebrews urged endurance in the race of life, and warned against the folly of apostasy and unthinking, godless actions. Now the writer compares appearing before God under the old covenant and under the new covenant.

Notice the similarity of the beginnings of verses 18 and 22. All the Israelites, even Moses, were absolutely terrified at Mount Sinai. "A mountain that can be touched" was a physical mountain. In contrast, the Mount Zion of 12:22 is a heavenly mountain. The earthly Mount Zion was a part of the earthly city of Jerusalem. It could be touched. But the earthly Jerusalem was a poor imitation of the heavenly Jerusalem, which could not be touched.

Earthly Mount Sinai was awesome when God's presence was there. The blazing fire, darkness, gloom, storm, trumpet sound, and sound of God's voice were elements of that experience. References to them are found in Deuteronomy 4:11 and Exodus 19:16-19; 20:18-20.

In contrast to earthly Sinai, the readers are reminded that they have come to a heavenly Mount Zion. Instead of hovering in fear at the foot of the mountain, they have entered a joyful gathering of angels. With the angels is the "church of the firstborn, whose names are written in heaven" (v. 23). *Firstborn* may refer to Jesus. In Colossians 1:15, he is referred to as "the firstborn over all creation." More likely, though, the writer of Hebrews has Christians in mind. James 1:18 refers to believers in this way: "He chose to give us birth through the word of truth, that we might be a kind of firstfruits of all he created."

Those "whose names are written in heaven" (v. 23) are those "whose names are in the book of life" (Philippians 4:3). Jesus told his disciples to "rejoice that your names are written in heaven" (Luke 10:20). Several references to the book of life appear in the Book of Revelation (3:5; 13:8; 17:8; 20:15; 21:27).

The readers need not fear in the presence of God because there is no sin there, only "the spirits of the righteous made perfect" (Hebrews 12:23). These include all the saints of old who looked forward to the time when the promises of God would be fulfilled in Christ. The reason they are made perfect is that Jesus is the mediator of the new covenant. The sprinkled blood of Jesus speaks graciously of forgiveness. Abel's blood cries out for vengeance. Both died unjustly.

Hebrews 12:25-29. The readers are warned not to refuse "him who speaks" (v. 25). The writer refers to the Israelites at Mount Sinai again. There the people wanted to be excused from speaking directly to God (Exodus 20:18-20). They asked Moses to talk with God on their behalf. "Him who speaks" must be God, as at Sinai. This time God speaks from heaven.

God's voice shook the earth at Sinai. Through the prophet Haggai, God promised to shake the earth again and with it, heaven (Haggai 2:6). Heaven and earth represent the entire universe. This second shaking is interpreted as a time when everything changeable will be removed. This probably refers to the faulted old covenant mentioned in 8:7-13. The old covenant is described there as aging and ready to disappear.

What cannot be shaken then remains. This is the kingdom of God (12:28). The writer urges the readers to be grateful, for they have received this unshakable kingdom.

Showing gratitude to God for receiving an unshakable kingdom is done by offering God acceptable worship. Recognizing God's real nature is what the writer is emphasizing. Acceptable worship is offered by those who respect and honor God as the Creator of the universe and the Source of salvation.

Perhaps nothing in human experience is as awesome as a consuming fire, such as a rampaging wildfire. Until the development of the atomic bomb, itself a consuming fire, a mighty fire was one of the most terrifying and destructive natural forces observed by humans. God's awesome power is likened to that.

Hebrews 13:1-6. Having completed the persuasive argument that the salvation offered through Jesus Christ is completely superior to all else, the writer of Hebrews closes with several exhortations. The first concerns general Christian responsibilities.

The admonitions in these verses relate to a Christian community or congregation, rather than to Christians dealing with unbelievers. Loving one another is to be a hallmark of the Christian. Jesus said, "Everyone will know that you are my disciples, if you love one another" (John 13:35). Paul called on the Roman Christians to "be devoted to one another in love" (Romans 12:10).

Love for other members of the family of God includes a genuine concern for fellow-believers whom we may not know personally. In an era before motels and hotels, showing hospitality to Christians who were passing through was widely practiced. The reference to "angels without knowing it" in verse 2, is likely a reference to the hospitality that Abraham showed to some visitors who later were discovered to be angels (Genesis 18).

As strangers needed travel mercies, so those in prison needed the ministrations of the faithful. These prisoners were not common criminals justly imprisoned. These were brothers and sisters in the faith who were suffering for the faith (10:32-34). Such prisoners required food and clothing from outside the prison, since the necessities of life were not provided by the authorities.

Visiting those imprisoned for the faith was a form of identification with them. Christian support of the members who were suffering was the same as taking part in their suffering. "If one part suffers, every part suffers with it; if one part is honored, every part rejoices with it" (1 Corinthians 12:26).

Along with the loving deeds one ought to do, Christians must refrain from immoral and adulterous actions. Marriage is a sacred bond. Adulterous relationships are exactly the opposite of genuine concern for one another, which is Christian love. And any adulterous thought or temptation can be squelched if the thinker will be genuinely concerned about the other person.

Sex and money have been the downfall of many. Sex alone can be a stumbling block. Money alone can cause an unwary person to fall away. Together the threat is doubled. The antidote for such sins is contentment. Contentment is the result of confidence in God's ability and willingness to provide for the needs of God's children.

To instill confidence in God's provision for the people, the writer quotes Deuteronomy 31:6. There Moses assures his people that God will not forsake them as they fight the Canaanites in the conquest of the Promised Land. Here the text is used to assure Christians that God will provide the necessities of life to them.

Hebrews 13:7-17. Verse 7 suggests that the leaders to be remembered had died for their faith or in the faith. Notice that the writer is not simply suggesting a line of action to the readers, but commanding them to "remember . . . consider . . . imitate."

Verse 8 sounds like a confession of faith. This saying has a double function. First, Jesus Christ is included in the group of leaders to be remembered, considered, and imitated. Second, Jesus Christ is the object of the faith of the leaders.

The Christian confesses an unchanging Christ who is able to save completely those who come to God by him (Hebrews 7:25). So the command in verse 9 is "do not be carried away." What might carry a believer away into apostasy are "all kinds of strange teachings." What these teachings are is not clearly indicated, but the reference to foods suggests the dietary restrictions practiced in the Judaism of the time. These restrictions might have held some attraction for Jewish Christians who were suffering for their faith in Christ. We should keep in mind that it was to such believers, who were being tempted to return to the rules and rituals of the law of Moses, that this letter was written.

The heart and mind should be strengthened by grace rather than by rules concerning foods. Jesus taught that it is not what goes into the mouth that defiles a person but what comes out of the mouth (Mark 7:14-23). So the writer warns against teachings that do not focus on the grace of God in Christ Jesus.

Loyalty to Christ means adhering to the faith "that was once for all entrusted to God's holy people" (Jude 1:3). That loyalty also means identifying with Christ's sacrifice. Christians find no value in adhering to the rituals of sacrifice in the tabernacle or temple. Christ's sacrifice was not in the sanctuary; it was outside the gate of the Temple and of the city. The blood of Christ's sacrifice can sanctify the people outside the city, that is, outside the old system of rituals connected with the Temple.

To go to Christ outside the old sacrificial system is to share in the abuse that he endured (Hebrews 13:13). Jesus was misunderstood, falsely arrested, imprisoned, jeered at, spit on, beaten, whipped, and killed. An earthly city (Jerusalem) with its sanctuary and rituals is no permanent place for the followers of Christ. Our place is in heaven.

Jesus has gone to prepare for our arrival (John 14:2-3). In the meantime, Christians have a holy ministry to carry out. It involves praising God and doing good to others (Hebrews 13:15-16). Do not forget, the writer repeats, to pay heed to your present leaders (v. 17).

Hebrews 13:18-19. This chapter begins by urging that love for one another continue. The writer has shown a genuine concern for the readers, writing frankly and fully, intending to help them endure in the faith. Now readers are asked to show love toward the writer. Intercessory prayer is clear evidence of Christian love. The prayer requested is that the writer may return to them.

Hebrews 13:20-21. This prayer is like the songs in our hymnal. Many were written by brothers and sisters in the faith who are long since dead. Yet each new generation of Christians sings their thoughts and words afresh. They speak to us and for us. The writer of Hebrews prays for us as well as the first readers.

Hebrews 13:22-25. Apart from speculating about some items in the content (see the participant book), this postscript is of great value to us because it reflects the concern the writer had for the readers. Not content to write to them only about religious and theological ideas, the writer included items about persons they knew. This sense of Christian belonging and fellowship is vital to the life of the church in all times and places.

DIMENSION THREE:
WHAT DOES THE BIBLE MEAN TO ME?

Hebrews 12:1-2—Running the Race of Life

Perseverance in running the race of life requires that we have hope in someone or something that makes living worthwhile. For the Christian, one motivation of living is to attain the joy that is set before us in the Christian life, heaven itself. But most Christians find joy in this life in serving others. We are most motivated when we look beyond ourselves to find purpose and fulfillment in living. The church at its best is a community of like-minded persons who share the servant mentality and encourage one another to love and good works.

Hebrews 13:1-6—Love and Caring

More and more, the church and individual Christians are being challenged to respond to the needs of individuals and groups in our society and in the world. Perhaps you have contributed to feed others in need of food in a particular part of the world or to assist desperate farmers in a time of economic crisis or to work with the homeless in your city; the list can go on and on. Giving money is often the easiest way to respond to such needs, but personal involvement as a volunteer is more rewarding.

The needs in every place outstrip the responses. What programs does your church support locally? Nationally? Internationally?

Hebrews 13:18-22—Intercessory Prayer

We should think of prayer in three terms: prayer in our personal/individual practice; prayer in small groups (family, Bible study, and the like); and prayer when the congregation is assembled.

A personal prayer list can be useful. Update it regularly and pray at a particular time each day. I have found that meeting once a week, other than Sunday, with a small group of believers for Bible study and prayer is a blessing to me personally as well as to those for whom we pray.

The small congregation that I am a part of has enriched the prayer period of the Sunday morning worship with brief prayers from the congregation and with prayer requests provided by individuals to the worship leader. In any size congregation, the worship leader can mention specific needs and individuals for whom the congregation can pray. A slightly lengthened prayer period will benefit both the worshipers and those for whom intercessory prayers are raised. God will surely bless such Christian concern.

If any of you lacks wisdom, you should ask God, who gives generously to all without finding fault, and it will be given to you. (1:5)

A MANUAL OF WISE INSTRUCTION, PART 1

James 1–2

DIMENSION ONE: WHAT DOES THE BIBLE SAY?

Answer these questions by reading James 1

1. What should happen when a Christian meets various trials? (1:2-3)

    The testing of a Christian's faith should produce perseverance.

2. Under what conditions will God answer a request for wisdom? (1:5-8)

    The request for wisdom must be made with belief and not doubt; for a "double-minded" person will not receive anything from God.

3. How does temptation develop into death? (1:14-15)

    Each person is tempted by personal desire. Then desire gives birth to sin, "and sin, when it is full-grown, gives birth to death."

4. What happens to the person who looks into the perfect law that gives freedom and perseveres? (1:25)

    The person who looks into the perfect law that gives freedom and perseveres does not forget the law but acts. That person will be blessed in doing.

5. James provides a concise definition of pure religion. What is it? (1:27)

    Religion that is pure and faultless is this: "to look after orphans and widows in their distress and to keep oneself from being polluted by the world."

Answer these questions by reading James 2

6. Why should a Christian show as much respect to a poor person as to a rich person? (2:5)

A Christian should show as much respect to a poor person as to a rich person because God has "chosen those who are poor in the eyes of the world to be rich in faith and to inherit the kingdom he promised to those who love him."

7. What is the royal law believers are expected to fulfill? (2:8)

The royal law is, "Love your neighbor as yourself."

8. What example of dead faith does James give? (2:14-17)

The example of dead faith is a person who fails to clothe and feed another who is hungry and cold, yet who says, "Go in peace; keep warm and well fed."

9. What two Old Testament examples does James use to prove that faith is completed by deeds? (2:21-25)

The two examples that prove that faith is completed by deeds are Abraham, when he was willing to offer his son Isaac on the altar, and Rahab, when she received the explorers and sent them out another way.

DIMENSION TWO: WHAT DOES THE BIBLE MEAN?

Among the books of the New Testament, James is in a class by itself. It is not like one of the Gospels, nor like Acts or Revelation. Nor does James have the characteristics of an epistle, except for the salutation (1:1). As a not-quite epistle, it fits better among the general letters than it would among the letters of Paul. Hebrews does not read like a letter, either, except for the very end of that book. First and Second Peter do sound like letters, as do Second and Third John and Jude. James is a bit more like First John, which also lacks some of the characteristics we expect in a letter. Yet James is not exactly like any of these books.

What kind of work is James, then? We classify James as wisdom literature, something like the Book of Proverbs in the Old Testament. James is a collection of teachings to give specific instructions to Christians on practical matters. The Letter of James is like a manual of discipline for the individual Christian and for Christian groups. As a book of practical wisdom for living the Christian life in the midst of trials and temptations, James holds a unique position in the New Testament.

The Writer. The first word in the book is the name *James*. He calls himself "a servant of God and of the Lord Jesus Christ" (1:1). The only other information he gives about himself is that he is a teacher (3:1). Who could this James have been? Two apostles were named James: James the son of Zebedee and James the son of Alphaeus. But the first was executed around AD 44 (Acts 12:2), before the probable date when this letter was written. James the son of Alphaeus did not hold the important role in the early church that the writer of this book seems to have held.

The writer of the letter, then, must be James, the brother of Jesus (Galatians 1:19). The immediate family of Jesus seems not to have accepted him as the Messiah/Christ until near the end of his ministry. Mary, his mother, of course, appears never to have doubted his destiny. Following the Ascension, the brothers of Jesus, along with their mother, were in the upper room prior to the events on the day of Pentecost (Acts 1:12-14). Their presence indicates that they had accepted Jesus as the Christ.

James came to be known as the Righteous One or the Just. He became the most important leader in the Jerusalem church from about AD 40 until his death in AD 62 (Acts 12:17; 15:13; 21:18; Galatians 2:9). James was admired even by non-Christian Jews for his pious life, according to Josephus. (The works of Josephus, a Jewish historian, were all written after AD 70 and before AD 125.) According to Eusebius (AD 260–340), the first historian of the church, James was beaten to death with a club. But Josephus indicates that James, along with several others, was stoned to death at the instigation of the high priest. Another tradition has it that James was cast down from the pinnacle of the Temple. In whatever manner, James was probably martyred in an outbreak of the Jews following the death of the procurator Festus in AD 62.

The authorship of the letter was in dispute in the period after the apostles and before its acceptance as an authoritative work in the New Testament. Official approval came at the Council of Carthage in AD 397. Previously, Origen (AD 185–254) had viewed the book as scripture and James the Just as the writer. Eusebius cited it as scripture, but he also noted that it was among the disputed books. Jerome (AD 340–420) included James in his translation of the Old and New Testaments into Latin (the Vulgate).

Modern scholars are divided on the identity of the writer. The primary views on the problem, but without the supporting arguments, are listed here:

1. The letter was written by James, the brother of Jesus, before the Jerusalem Conference of Acts 15 (about AD 50);

2. Much of the material was given orally or written by James before AD 50, then revised by another person between AD 55 and AD 65, or possibly AD 75 and AD 85;

3. The book was written by another person under the name of James, the brother of the Lord, between AD 75 and AD 125. This unnamed person might well have been a disciple of James the Righteous One and in a position to write in his name.

For the purposes of our study, it is not necessary to answer this question of authorship. We will assume that the letter is connected to James, the brother of Jesus. The problem of authorship has no direct bearing on the validity of the Book of James as authoritative scripture. Generations of Christians from early in the history of the church have turned to James for instruction in Christian living. We, too, can find instruction and inspiration in James for individuals and for the church in the midst of the trials and temptations of our day.

Place of Writing. Just as the question of authorship is unclear, so the place of writing remains an open question. If James the Just wrote it, then the Letter of James came from Jerusalem. If an unknown person wrote the book, suggested points of origin are Antioch in Syria, Caesarea in Palestine, Egypt, and Rome.

The Readers. In the salutation (1:1), the writer addresses "the twelve tribes scattered among the nations." Taken literally, this would refer to the tribes of Israel. But the tribal distinctions were essentially lost among the Jews at the time of the Babylonian exile. In the Dispersion, the tribes were blended. The letter could have been addressed to Jewish Christians only, or, more likely, to Christian congregations scattered across the Roman world. The congregations could include both Gentile Christians and Jewish Christians.

The reference to the twelve tribes is rooted in the understanding that the church is the spiritual Israel. Peter, at the home of Cornelius, perceived that "[God] accepts from every nation the one who fears him and does what is right" (Acts 10:35). Paul taught that "it is not the children by physical descent who are God's children, but it is the children of the promise who are regarded as Abraham's offspring" (Romans 9:8).

First Peter opens with a similar expression. The letter is addressed "to God's elect, exiles scattered throughout the provinces." All believers in Christ are included in this expression.

Purpose of the Letter. The instruction in the letter is intended to strengthen the faith of the readers in the midst of the difficulties of life. We touched on this matter above, but a further word is in order.

Martin Luther's opinion of the Book of James is well-known. Compared to the Gospel of John, Romans, Galatians, and First Peter, Luther stated that James is a "right strawy [sic] epistle"; he saw in it no real gospel character. Luther thought that James teaches against justification by faith because it emphasizes works. Luther was reacting to the medieval Roman Catholic emphasis on salvation by works. Luther knew from his experience that pious works and penance do not bring salvation, since salvation is by grace to everyone who believes. But, as we will see, James does not set faith against works; he joins them together.

Outline of James.

I. Salutation (1:1)

II. How to confront various trials (1:2-18)

    A. Be steadfast in trials (1:2-4)

    B. Pray for wisdom (1:5-8)

    C. Hold a balanced view of poverty and wealth (1:9-11)

    D. Recognize the real basis of temptation and the antidote (1:12-18)

III. Listen carefully; act rightly (1:19-27)

IV. Avoid the sin of snobbery (2:1-13)

V. Show your faith by your deeds (2:14-26)

VI. The tongue is dangerous; bridle it (3:1-12)

VII. Instruction on the wise way to live (3:13–4:12)

    A. Show true wisdom; lead a humble life (3:13-18)

    B. Control your passions; submit to God and resist the devil (4:1-10)

    C. Do not judge your neighbor; leave that to God (4:11-12)

VIII. Observations on the arrogant and the dishonest wealthy (4:13–5:6)

    A. Against arrogant boasting (4:13-17)

    B. Against ill-gotten gain (5:1-6)

IX. Wise comments on various subjects (5:7-20)

    A. On waiting patiently for "the Lord's coming" (5:7-11)

    B. On avoiding oaths (5:12)

    C. On mutual prayer and confession (5:13-18)

    D. On bringing wanderers back (5:19-20)

James 1:1. The name *James* is the Greek form of the Hebrew *Jacob*. It has been a popular name through the centuries, taken from the patriarch Jacob, the grandson of Abraham.

James is "a servant [a slave] of God and of the Lord Jesus Christ." Paul used the same word of himself (Romans 1:1; Philippians 1:1; Titus 1:1). This designation is based on the concept that Christians are "bought at a price" and are not their own (1 Corinthians 6:20).

James is not a theological work. Jesus is mentioned only here and in 2:1, but clearly Jesus is the Messiah. He is to be served as God.

We have already noted the expression "the twelve tribes scattered among the nations" (the Dispersion). Jews still speak of the Diaspora, that is, those Jews living outside Israel. The expression "the twelve tribes" indicates the unity of God's people. James was saying that wherever Christians may be scattered in the world, they are a part of the one church.

James 1:2–27. In this section, we can identify four main teachings about confronting trials. They are tied together only loosely, with phrases and words, such as *lacking* in 1:4-5 and *ask* in 1:5-6. These teachings may have existed independently as oral sayings that were collected and arranged on the basis of these repeated words. This method of grouping sayings with similar words can assist memorization. The writer, a teacher, might have had the student in mind when arranging the material in his book.

James 1:2-4. This teaching is for congregations, primarily, and for individuals otherwise. James identifies with those to whom he writes and writes from his own experience.

Not every member of a congregation might undergo trials at the same time, but the church is the body of Christ. "If one part suffers, every part suffers with it" (1 Corinthians 12:26). In a world essentially hostile to people of the faith, various trials are certain to come. James tells us the way to meet these trials.

"Consider it pure joy" (v. 2). Do not consider confronting various trials as part joy and part misery. Regard it as complete joy. Persecution is no fun, and the early Christians were being oppressed (2:6). Apparently, some of them had known sickness (5:13-16) and some poverty (5:1-6), neither of which brings pleasure. How then could James's first readers do what he suggests?

Jesus taught in the Sermon on the Mount:

> Blessed [Happy] are those who are persecuted because of righteousness,
> for theirs is the kingdom of heaven.

> Blessed are you when people insult you, persecute you and falsely say all kinds of evil against you because of me. Rejoice and be glad, because great is your reward in heaven, for in the same way they persecuted the prophets who were before you. (Matthew 5:10-12)

First Peter 3:14 points out that "even if you should suffer for what is right, you are blessed." When James calls on Christians to consider difficulties a positive good, it is in line with biblical truth.

But the main reason for demanding that Christians count trials they meet as pure joy is that such trials are tests of one's faith. Meeting trials equals finding opportunities to develop steadfastness. Various trials have a bright side to them. They can be turned to our highest good. When our endurance is completely developed, we reach maturity in the faith and lack nothing that will separate us from eternal blessings with God.

James 1:5-8. A help in meeting temptations is to face them wisely. When James writes, "If any of you lacks wisdom," he assumes that some do lack wisdom. "The fear of the LORD is the beginning of knowledge, / but fools despise wisdom and instruction" (Proverbs 1:7). Knowledge consists of facts learned; wisdom guides the use of knowledge. Jesus was realistic in instructing the Twelve when he sent them forth on a missionary journey: "I am sending you out like sheep among wolves. Therefore be as shrewd as snakes and as innocent as doves" (Matthew 10:16).

The main point of this section, however, is not wisdom but how to obtain wisdom. God is the source of wisdom. To obtain it, ask. Pray for it. Recall what Jesus said, "Ask and it will be given to you" (Matthew 7:7). God gives outright, with a single mind. It is God's good pleasure to give (Luke 12:32). But let the request be a prayer of faith. Doubting that God will grant the request destroys the purpose of prayer. Doubting while asking is the mark of a person unstable in the faith.

James 1:9-11. One of the constant temptations through the ages has been to count the rich as favored by God and the poor as sinners, suffering God's disfavor. Such a conclusion is not biblically valid.

"Believers in humble circumstances" are poor, yet they are to "take pride in their high position" (1:9). To take pride here is to glory in the high position God has accorded them (2:5). Many poor persons were part of the early church. Paul wrote, "Brothers and sisters, think of what you were when you were called. Not many of you were wise by human standards; not many were influential; not many were of noble birth" (1 Corinthians 1:26).

Rich Christians, however, have nothing to take pride in except being humbled. Wealth can puff a person up with pride, yet Christians are called to be humble (4:6). Further, wealth must be left behind. Rich Christians will exult in the fact that any pride held before coming to Christ has now been shattered. Selfishness is replaced by stewardship under God. Christians must hold a balanced view of poverty and wealth.

James 1:12-18. The wise instruction in this section begins with what sounds like a beatitude, as in Matthew 5:10. *Blessed* means "happy." The crown of life should make any Christian happy.

The crown is the victory wreath, similar to those bestowed by the Greeks on winners of Olympic races. The thought echoes Revelation 2:10.

God is not the source of temptation. God is the source of "every good and perfect gift" (1:17). God is untouched by evil but knows its nature. God also knows people; God is well aware of our tendency toward evil. The source of temptation is a person's own desire. Desire is neither good nor evil; it is neutral. But desire lures and entices. Unchecked, the effect can be deadly. Desire can conceive and give birth to sin. Sin can fully develop into complete separation from God. That separation is death in the most profound sense.

Desire can be controlled. "No temptation has overtaken you except what is common to mankind. And God is faithful; he will not let you be tempted beyond what you can bear. But when you are tempted, he will also provide a way out so that you can endure it" (1 Corinthians 10:13). God has provided the antidote to temptation. We have been born again by God's word (1 Peter 1:23). As firstfruits, we are to offer ourselves to God as a living sacrifice (Romans 12:1). The first fruits are always God's.

James 1:19-27. "Take note of this," introduces a new wise instruction. What the dear believers are to know is what follows. Christians should be quick to listen to the word of God and to what is said by others. Everyone should also be slow to speak; that is, everyone should think before speaking. The quick reply often comes off the top of one's head and out of anger. So James warns everyone to be "slow to become angry" (v. 19).

James is writing to believers. Uncontrolled anger is unacceptable behavior for Christians. It does not accomplish good for God. To the contrary, uncontrolled anger will prove a stumbling block to those outside of Christ who see it in Christians. God will provide a way to overcome the temptation to get angry. James ranks anger as a part of "moral filth and the evil that is so prevalent"; anger will threaten the soul; "the word planted in you" has the power to save (v. 21).

Just hearing the word is not enough; to hear and not to do is to fool ourselves. The illustration James uses to make his point is quite clear. The face one sees in the mirror may soon be forgotten, but one who has looked into the mirror of God's Word cannot forget that believers are sinners saved by grace. In Christ there is freedom from sin and liberty to love (Galatians 5:13). To look intently into the perfect law is to be moved to do and to be blessed in the process.

The coin of hearing and doing has two sides (1:26-27). One side is hearing. But that side is not enough. It brings forth only empty words from an unbridled tongue without appropriate deeds. The result is a worthless religion. Pure and faultless religion, according to James, also requires doing. The doing side of the coin involves visiting the weak and vulnerable in society and supplying their needs.

"To keep oneself from being polluted by the world" (v. 27) is a necessary part of pure religion as well. The world always exhibits a selfish or self-seeking attitude toward worldly goods. A Christian must constantly guard against adopting that view, else giving to the needy will cease.

James 2:1-13. This teaching would not have been included if showing favoritism were not a problem in the church. James is dead set against favoritism. An example of what was going on is given in 2:2-3.

Favoritism is not acceptable to those who trust in the saving grace of Jesus (2:9). He is "our glorious Lord Jesus Christ" (2:1); and all human glory, even that of a rich person, is as filthy rags in comparison. The ground is level at the foot of the cross. All are saved by grace through faith, as a gift of God, and none is worthy. There is neither Jew nor Gentile, bond nor free, male nor female in Christ; snobbish distinctions among believers are unwarranted.

Further, favoritism dishonors those chosen of God "to be rich in faith and to inherit the kingdom he promised those who love him" (2:5). The rich tend to love riches. Jesus taught that we cannot love God and money (Matthew 6:24). The rich trust in wealth; the poor cannot do that. They trust in God.

Further, the love of money is the root of all kinds of evil (1 Timothy 6:10). That includes the evil of oppressing the poor (James 2:6). The rich slander "the noble name of him to whom you belong" (v. 7). This is the name of Jesus and is likely a reference to the baptismal formula (Acts 2:38; 8:16; 10:48).

Apparently the rich persons James has in mind in this passage are not rich Christians, as perhaps in 1:10-11. Rather, these are wealthy non-Christians from the community who have come to visit the meeting, either on someone's invitation or out of curiosity.

The correct Christian practice is to love others without showing favoritism. That is the royal law of love that Jesus taught (Matthew 22:39). Just as breaking the Mosaic law made one guilty, so breaking the law of love by showing favoritism makes one guilty.

In 2:12-13, James concludes his teaching on the important matter of snobbery. His point is that Christians should speak and act with the Last Judgment in mind. God has graciously covered our sins by the blood of Jesus Christ, but we can hardly expect to be shown mercy for the sin of favoritism, if we practice it. Christians are still required to do unto others as we would have them do unto us (Matthew 7:12). We are to be hearers *and* doers of the word.

James 2:14-26. The question in 2:4 introduces the core of this section's important instruction. The instruction in these verses deals with faith and deeds and the relationship between the two.

Faith, here, consists of the gospel facts and all that belief in them implies: repentance from sin, confession of Jesus as Lord and Savior, dying to self and rising to live a new life through Christian baptism, and living to the praise of God's glory. Faith alone cannot save. (The assumption is that the person with faith has the opportunity to live a life of faith.)

The person who has a warm feeling toward someone in need and has the resources to meet that need but fails to do so accomplishes nothing (2:15-16). So faith without deeds is without accomplishment. It is valueless. A living faith is always shown by deeds.

To the person who might raise the question in 2:18, James provides three examples in response. The first example is of belief without deeds ("even demons believe," v. 19). Two biblical examples follow. In the first biblical example, James states that Abraham was justified by deeds when he showed his willingness to offer Isaac on the altar (Genesis 22). Read carefully 2:22 and the conclusion of the example of Abraham in 2:24.

In 2:23, James quotes Genesis 15:6. Paul also used Abraham and this verse to establish that Abraham was justified by faith apart from deeds (Romans 4:1-12). Much has been made of the seeming contradiction between Paul and James on the matter of faith and deeds. But I can see no direct or indirect contradiction. Paul had in mind justification in connection with conversion and baptism; that is by faith. He also encouraged acts of Christian love, however, as does James. James sees justification in terms of the Last Judgment. The deeds a believer does, or fails to do, determine the result of that judgment. Paul also held that the final judgment will be determined on the basis of the deeds of a believer (1 Corinthians 3:13-15; 2 Corinthians 5:10). This is in line with what Jesus taught on the Last Judgment (Matthew 25:31-46).

So a believer is also justified by deeds and not by faith alone. Rahab (Joshua 2:1-21) is the second biblical example of this basic principle. She saved the lives of the spies Joshua sent to Jericho. She acted on her faith that God had given the land into the hands of the Israelites (Joshua 2:9). So Rahab is listed in the great roll call of the faithful in Hebrews (11:31).

James concludes his teaching on the relationship between faith and deeds with an observation. The body without the spirit is dead; it cannot fulfill a purpose or function. Just so, faith without deeds is without value; it is profitless.

DIMENSION THREE: WHAT DOES THE BIBLE MEAN TO ME?

James 1:13-15—Placing Desires Under the Lordship of Jesus

Essentially, the answer to the question in the participant book for this section lies in the effort to bring every desire under the lordship of Jesus. Paul urged the Roman Christians to "put to death the misdeeds of the body" (Romans 8:13). We can assume that the deeds were stimulated by desires. Again, he told the Christians in Colossae: "Put to death, therefore, whatever belongs to your earthly nature: sexual immorality, impurity, lust, evil desires and greed, which is idolatry" (Colossians 3:5). Of himself, Paul also said, "I strike a blow to my body and make it my slave so that after I have preached to others, I myself will not be disqualified for the prize" (1 Corinthians 9:27).

If we consider any particular desire that may arise within us, we can always find a way to control it, often by turning our minds to other, more constructive thoughts. As Paul indicated in Philippians 4:8: whatever is true, noble, right, pure, lovely, admirable, excellent, praiseworthy—think about these things.

The church can assist its members to overcome desires by being aware of them. Support groups for particular problems can help. Frankly facing the problems that individual Christians confront in overcoming potentially harmful desires is important.

James 1:27—Pure and Faultless Religion

The question in the participant book is not to be isolated from the matter of faith and deeds. The problem in our society is to identify the equivalent of the widows and orphans of whom James speaks. The widows were vulnerable to those who coveted and stole their houses. This thievery was particularly bad in a culture in which almost every woman was under the protection of a father, husband, or male kin. The orphan, too, was vulnerable to exploitation and to suffering due to the lack of family support. Together, widows and orphans made up the most vulnerable elements of society.

Who are the most vulnerable, the most disadvantaged in our society? Who are the vulnerable in your neighborhood? These are known of God. Do you know them? Does your church know them? Identifying and meeting the basic needs of such people will be the equivalent of caring for the widow and the orphan. These vulnerable people will include the homeless, the helpless, and the economically oppressed.

Helping individuals and groups that fall into these categories may require the cooperative efforts of many Christians. Most of us, however, can find those to whom we can minister personally. Let us act creatively to practice pure and faultless religion before God.

James 1:27—Faith and Deeds

As discussed in the introduction to James, the writer's focus on works is not in order to receive salvation. To James, deeds are an outpouring of received faith and salvation: I have received God's salvation, and that reception of salvation compels me to act to improve the world for others.

This is the response of faith supported by John Wesley, the founder of Methodism. Wesley's idea of social justice and the social gospel was that one's faith was lived out in serving others. Our response in faith doesn't have to be grand scale and world altering in nature. We don't have to serve thousands; we can serve one. And we will have served. Encourage group members to begin responding to the grace they have received from God by exploring ways they can make a difference in one person's life.

[T]he wisdom that comes from heaven is first of all pure; then peace-loving, considerate, submissive, full of mercy and good fruit, impartial and sincere. (3:17)

7

A MANUAL OF WISE INSTRUCTION, PART 2

James 3–5

DIMENSION ONE: WHAT DOES THE BIBLE SAY?

Answer these questions by reading James 3

1. Why does James discourage many of his readers from becoming teachers? (3:1)
    Teachers "will be judged more strictly."

2. What evidence does James provide to show that the tongue is "a restless evil, full of deadly poison"? (3:7-10)
    "All kinds of animals" can be tamed by humans but not the tongue. The tongue gives both blessings and curses.

3. How does James describe the wisdom that does not come from heaven? (3:15-16)
    The wisdom that is not from heaven "is earthly, unspiritual, demonic." It is found "where you have envy and selfish ambition . . . disorder and every evil practice."

4. What are the characteristics of the wisdom that comes from heaven? (3:17)
    The wisdom from heaven is "Pure; then peace-loving, considerate, submissive, full of mercy and good fruit, impartial and sincere."

Answer these questions by reading James 4

5. Why do people fight, quarrel, and kill? (4:1-2)
    People fight, quarrel, and kill because of their desires. They want and do not have, so they kill. They covet and cannot obtain, so they fight and quarrel.

6. What positive actions can believers take to show humility and receive God's grace? (4:6-8)

To show humility and to receive God's grace, believers should submit themselves to God, resist the devil and come near to God.

7. Who is capable of judging another Christian? (4:12)

"There is only one Lawgiver and Judge, the one who is able to save and destroy."

8. To what statement does James refer when he says, "you boast in your arrogant schemes"? (4:13-16a)

James refers to this statement as boasting: "Today or tomorrow we will go to this or that city, spend a year there, carry on business and make money."

Answer these questions by reading James 5

9. James foretold that the rich would suffer miseries (5:1-6). Why would this come upon them in the last days?

James foretold that the rich would suffer miseries in the last days because they kept back by fraud the wages of the laborers and harvesters who mowed their fields.

10. James gives three examples of patient people in 5:7-11. Identify them.

The three examples of patient people that James gives are the farmer waiting for the harvest, the prophets "who spoke in the name of the Lord," and Job.

11. Why is James against swearing by an oath? (5:12)

James is against taking oaths because those who do might "be condemned."

12. What are James's recommendations for people who are in trouble, happy, or sick? (5:13-14)

James recommends that people who are in trouble should pray, that those who are happy should sing, and that the sick person should call for the elders of the church and let them pray over the sick person, anointing the sick person with oil "in the name of the Lord."

13. Who is a good example of a righteous man whose prayers were effective? (5:16b-18)

The prophet Elijah is a good example of a righteous man whose prayers were effective.

14. What is the proper thing to do when a Christian brother or sister wanders from the truth? (5:19-20)

The proper thing to do when a Christian brother or sister wanders from the truth is to bring that sinner back from the error of his or her way.

DIMENSION TWO: WHAT DOES THE BIBLE MEAN?

In lesson 6, we studied the first four of James's wise instructions for Christians. The topics covered were confronting various trials, listening carefully and acting rightly, avoiding the sin of snobbery, and showing your faith by your deeds.

In this lesson, James is teaching about bridling the dangerous tongue, giving instruction on the wise way to live, observing the arrogant and the dishonest wealthy, and commenting wisely on various subjects, including waiting patiently for the coming of the Lord, avoiding oaths, praying mutual prayers and confession, and bringing wanderers back.

James 3:1-12. In a sense, the subject in these verses was introduced when James admonished his readers to be quick to hear, slow to speak, and slow to anger. But the main focus of that section (1:19-27) was on being doers of the word and not just hearers. Here, the focus is on the importance of controlling the tongue.

Three segments make up this section. Verses 1-2a introduce the problem of proper speech. Then 3:2b-5a is a segment on the difficulty of controlling the tongue, and 3:5b-12 is a second supporting segment on the danger of a poisonous tongue.

James is writing to a congregation ("meeting" in 2:2) or a group of congregations. One of the spiritual gifts God gives is teaching (1 Corinthians 12:28; Ephesians 4:11). The calling to teach is a high calling. Jesus is the example to follow, for he was recognized as a teacher by the Jewish Sanhedrin (ruling council) (John 3:1-2). He was also called *rabbi* by his followers and by those who entered into discussions with him. As John 1:38 explains, *rabbi* means "Teacher."

Apparently, many of the believers in the congregation James wrote to thought themselves called to be teachers. James warns against taking on the responsibility of testifying to the faith publicly and instructing others in the faith. Teaching is a calling that is privileged, but the teacher is liable to more severe condemnation for errors than the layperson is.

James considers himself a teacher and is aware of the weight of responsibility. The wise instructions and advice that make up this letter prove that he was conscientious in carrying out his responsibilities.

A teacher, like everyone else, makes mistakes. The teacher has to be more accountable for errors than others, however, because what the teacher says directly affects the hearers (students). We all must answer to God for how careful and conscientious we are in our work. We all will "give account" for our words and either be justified by them or condemned (Matthew 12:36-37).

James may have the teacher in mind as he continues with the first supporting paragraph; but what he says fits every Christian. The perfect (spiritually mature) person makes no mistakes in the content of what he or she says or the manner in which it is said.

None of us would claim that perfection. In striving for excellence, however, we attempt to make no mistakes. James indicates that the control (taming) of the tongue is an essential part of becoming mature. In fact, control of the tongue is a major factor in controlling the whole body.

Why can James say this? Because, as a person thinks in his or her heart (mind), so is that person. Out of the heart "evil thoughts come—sexual immorality, theft, murder, adultery, greed, malice, deceit, lewdness, envy, slander, arrogance and folly" (Mark 7:21-22). Out of the abundance of the heart the mouth speaks (Luke 6:45). The Christian is to be transformed by the renewing of the mind (Romans 12:2), an ongoing process. The change will include controlling the tongue so that evil speech, slander, and foolishness do not gush forth.

We no longer live in the days when the horse was used for work more than pleasure. Yet most of the group members should be able to relate to the word *bit* and how a bit functions to control a horse. The point is, as a small thing like a bit can control the entire body of a horse, so by a tamed tongue, a person attains self-control.

Small things do control large things. The pilot of a ship guides it with a small rudder. The pilot can even control the ship with the rudder when strong winds are blowing against the ship. Like a rudder or a bit, the tongue is a small part of the body. The tongue boasts of great things because it controls the whole body.

Forest and brush fires occurred in ancient times as well as modern times. James uses a timeless saying: "Consider what a great forest is set on fire by a small spark" (v. 5). A forest fire is awesome in its devastating power. It can destroy the one who set it, whether accidentally or on purpose, and it can destroy others. Just so, the tongue, when used maliciously, can destroy both the speaker and the object of the words spoken.

Evil speech is what James has in mind; verses 6b-12 make that clear. The tongue is a fire kindled from hellfire. That is, Satan is the source of acid, burning speech. It is "a world of evil."

The background of 3:7 is Genesis 1:28; 2:19; and 9:2. Humans are given the power to rule over animals. But who can tame the tongue? No one alone, but by God's grace the tongue can be controlled.

The tongue is a "restless evil" always moving like a snake on the go and venomous as a rattler. Psalm 140:3 may lie behind the words of James: "They make their tongues as sharp as a serpent's; / the poison of vipers is on their lips."

The tongue is an instrument of deception. We expect consistency in nature, as with a spring producing either fresh or salt water, or as in the other examples James provides. But the evil, uncontrolled tongue spews forth from the same source both blessings and curses.

We should be able to expect consistency in the speech that comes forth from the mouths of Christians. They should be slow to speak. They should refrain from speaking in anger. "Do not let any unwholesome talk come out of your mouths, but only what is helpful for building others up according to their needs, that it may benefit those who listen" (Ephesians 4:29).

James 3:13–4:12. This section of the letter does not appear to be directly connected with the teaching on the dangers of the tongue. Some persons, however, think that these verses appear here to make the point that pure speech comes from wisdom. I believe the main concern is on how to live a good life.

James 3:13-18. In 1:5, the person who lacked wisdom was encouraged to ask God for it in faith. Here, the attention is on those who think themselves wise and understanding (among the Christians in the congregation to whom James writes).

James will draw a sharp line between the wisdom from heaven and earthly wisdom. Here, as soon as he raises the question, he provides the test of the wisdom that is from heaven. The wise person lives a good life. That person shows evidence of wisdom and understanding.

The works the wise person performs are done "in the humility that comes from wisdom" (v. 13). Humble wisdom is the opposite of bitter jealousy and selfish ambition. Humble wisdom is not weakness; it is gentleness. A Christian should be tough but gentle.

One of Jesus' Beatitudes speaks of the meek (Matthew 5:5). Paul exhorted Christian teachers not to be quarrelsome but to be kindly toward everyone, forbearing and correcting those in need of correction with gentleness (2 Timothy 2:24-25a). Peter urged defenders of the faith to speak gently and reverently (1 Peter 3:15b). These verses help us put the problem James is dealing with in perspective.

Earthly wisdom is looking at circumstances in an unspiritual way, even a demonic way (3:15). Paul stated flatly that "God made foolish the wisdom of the world" (1 Corinthians 1:20d). Bitter envy, selfish ambition, boasting, and lying are evidences of earthly wisdom. They do not bring the good life. They do not bring peace with God or other people. They result in "disorder and every evil practice" (James 3:16).

Contrast the wisdom from heaven with earthly wisdom. The wisdom from heaven is pure. A Christian is cleansed by the blood of Jesus Christ, and that person's mind is set on things that are above (Colossians 3:2). The peace of God that passes all understanding is available to the believer (Philippians 4:7) because of the reconciliation with God and people. Christians are to be open to reason and full of mercy and good fruits because they know what it means to have received mercy from God. We are to follow in the footsteps of Jesus, who went about doing good (Acts 10:38).

All these elements of the wisdom that is from heaven should be clearly evident in the life of the spiritual person. This wisdom, if any lack it, can be received by asking God for it (1:5). Instead of disorder, the result is peace.

James 4:1-10. Perhaps this section is logically connected with 3:13-18 because the wisdom from heaven results in peace, while the wisdom of the world results in conflict. James may have had in mind the conflicts within a community of believers. He may have had in mind war in the world. Or, he may have been thinking of both. At any rate, his explanation of the cause of conflict

Just as desire can lead to sin and death (1:14-15), so a person's desires can cause fights and quarrels. Paul wrote of the conflict between the law of sin and the law of the mind (Romans 7:23). Christ gives the victory, but there is a struggle.

In 4:2-3, James weaves the picture together so that we have no doubt about the cause of conflicts. Desire can even lead to murder. Coveting not only breaks the tenth commandment (Exodus 20:17); it also leads to savage efforts to obtain what is coveted.

The Christian has but to ask in order to receive all that is *needed* (Matthew 7:7-8). But God does not promise all that is *desired*. A parent does not give that which will harm his or her children just because they ask. Needs are not measured by desires.

James 4:4 opens with a strong statement. The original Greek actually says, "adulterers and adulteresses." This strange expression becomes clear in the light of the scriptural pattern of thinking. Spiritual infidelity is spoken of as adultery in Hosea 3:1, for example, and elsewhere among the Old Testament prophets. Jesus, too, spoke of "this adulterous and sinful generation" (Mark 8:38). Underlying these expressions are the metaphors of God as the spouse of Israel and Christ as the spouse of the church.

Those who can receive the wisdom from heaven by asking for it are committing spiritual adultery when they live by the wisdom of this world, when they are driven by their desires (James 4:4). Jesus taught essentially the same thing: "You cannot serve both God and money" (Matthew 6:24c).

The exact quotation in James 4:5 cannot be found in the Bible, nor has it been found in other known writings. The general thought occurs in Genesis 6:5-6 and Isaiah 63:8-16. The spirit God caused to live in us may be the human spirit, created in God's image. Or "the spirit" may refer to the indwelling Holy Spirit, given as a gift to those who come to God through Christ. We do not have to make a final decision on which of these views is correct, since both are. James may also be speaking of Scripture generally, summarizing the biblical view of God's concern for people.

The quotation in 4:6 is from Proverbs 3:34. The point of the quotation is to support the fact that God gives abundant grace to the humble. John wrote in his gospel, "Out of his fullness we have all received grace in place of grace already given" (1:16). The gift of grace is a reflection of God's active yearning for believers to triumph over their desires. God wants every Christian to be God's friend, rather than to be a friend of the world. God desires peace for God's children, not wars and fighting.

Humility is an essential ingredient in the make-up of a sincere follower of Jesus. Jesus provides the example to follow: "Being found in appearance as a man, / he humbled himself / by becoming obedient to death— / even death on a cross!" (Philippians 2:8). Humility is the opposite of the pride and vanity that characterize the wisdom of the world.

James 4:7-10 clarifies the wise way to live. Two actions are required: submission to God, which is evidence of humility; and resistance to the devil, which provides the way of escape from the temptations that desire and passion arouse.

The world seeks self-exaltation. James calls on people to do things God's way. God is ready to meet the sincere seeker of grace more than halfway. God is like the father in the story of the prodigal son, gazing longingly down the road, awaiting some sign of his son's return, ready to run forth to meet him in glad embrace (Luke 15:20b).

God has also, by grace, made it possible for the erring person to be cleansed, the contaminated heart (mind) to be purified, and the double-minded person to find direction and stability. These blessings are possible thanks to the completed work of Jesus Christ.

Repentance, shown by sincere sorrow (4:9), is essential to receiving the gift of the Holy Spirit (salvation) through God's grace (Acts 2:38). Repentance, a complete reversal of the way one thinks and acts, is evidence of true humility before God. What the world seeks and grasps hungrily through self-exaltation, God accomplishes for those who are humble before God. God exalts them.

James 4:11-12. The believer who lives wisely will refrain from condemning another Christian, for all are sinners saved by grace. Judgmental thinking about other believers followed by slander (harsh, critical words) judges rather than obeys the law. That is, that judgmental person has, in practice, rejected the royal law to love neighbor as self (2:8). Further, to judge a brother or sister in Christ is to place oneself in opposition to the one valid judge. God alone is able to save and to destroy (Matthew 10:28). Since God will be my judge (and yours), who am I to condemn my brother or sister in Christ?

James 4:13–5:6. Two segments make up the wise instruction of this section. The first is against arrogant boasting (4:13-17) and the second against ill-gotten gain (5:1-6).

James does not object to good business planning. Jesus taught that planning is necessary, as in the parable of the shortsighted virgins who ran out of oil at the crucial moment (Matthew 25:1-13). The need for planning is understood, too, in the case of the man in tending to build a tower and the king plotting a conquest (Luke 14:28-32). What James objects to is the arrogance of a Christian planning a venture without any thought of the One who controls history. Believers, above all others, should realize that "my times are in your hands" (Psalm 31:15).

To plan, as in James 4:13, is to be arrogant. Such planners lack humility and a sense of living under the lordship of Christ. Their thinking and actions reflect a bad (inappropriate) way for Christians to think. Such people need to hear the Word, to be taught, so that they know what is right to do. Ignorance does not justify arrogant attitudes. Even worse is the person who knows what to do and fails to do it. Knowing what to do and not doing it is a grievous error that misses the mark of God's will, and that is sin.

Does James address his remarks in 5:1-6 to rich Christians or to the rich outside the church? He seems to have in mind those outside the church, but echoes of what he says may apply to wealthy Christians.

The rich are often considered happy and carefree, in contrast to the poor, who are burdened with labor in order to obtain the necessities of life. But the poor are a special concern of God's.

James calls on the rich to weep and wail. The reason is anticipation of the coming "last days" and the judgment of God (5:1-3). All the treasure the rich have laid up will prove to be worthless. In fact, what they have laid up will be evidence against them, evidence of their greed and coveting. What they trusted in will destroy them, consuming them like fire. This instruction reminds us of the story Jesus told of the rich man and Lazarus, the beggar (Luke 16:19-31).

The things treasured by the rich will condemn them because they were acquired through fraud and injustice (5:4). The poor, in particular, suffered because of the rich's fraud and injustices.

fraud and injustice (5:4). The poor, in particular, suffered because of the rich's fraud and injustices. The Bible has many teachings against paying wages late or bilking workers out of their just wages (Leviticus 19:13b; Deuteronomy 24:14-15; Job 7:1-32; Malachi 3:5; Matthew 20:8).

James 5:7-11. This teaching may be directly connected with the preceding warning to the rich. It could also stand as an independent instruction. Encouragement to patience is needed in the face of economic oppression, but it is also useful in other circumstances of life.

The first example of patience is that of the farmer. He plants and then must await both the early rains, which help the plants get off to a good start, and the late rains, which help the grain come to full development. The agricultural picture is that of the Middle East. Weather patterns there produce the early rains of the growing season after a long dry summer. The late rains fall before harvest the following spring.

James urges the readers to be patient for the harvest of souls with the coming of Christ. In anticipation they are to "stand firm" (v. 8). The coming of Christ will be soon and as certain as harvest time follows the rain. The coming of Christ was anticipated in the first generation of Christians, and it continues to be a living hope.

In 5:9, James admonishes his readers not to grumble. Grumbling is the result of impatience. Grumbling may be aimed at one another, blaming the stress of the times on a Christian brother or sister and generating disunity in the process.

Rather than grumbling and impatience, believers are called to patience in suffering (5:10). Suffering may result from the words and deeds of others, as in the case of oppression by the rich. Suffering may also come from one's own mistakes or foolish actions.

James also gives two other examples of patience in suffering. The prophets suffered for speaking "in the name of the Lord" (v. 10). Job remained steadfast despite the afflictions imposed on him at the hand of Satan.

James 5:12. Taking oaths seems to have been overdone in both Jewish and pagan society in the time of Jesus and the early church. What James says here echoes the words of Jesus in Matthew 5:34-37. An oath was taken by swearing by something or someone of higher position or authority than the oath taker. What James condemns is confirming the most mundane matters by an oath. Christians should always speak the truth; for the Christian, *yes* should mean "yes" and *no* should mean "no," without further emphasis.

That this is not an absolute prohibition against calling God to witness is shown by Paul (2 Corinthians 1:23; 11:31; Galatians 1:20; Philippians 1:8). Some serious occasions may call for an oath, but never trivial matters.

James 5:13-18. James presents his most positive teaching at the end of his letter. These verses and the last comment (5:19-20) are exemplary of the idea that the fellowship in the faith is the priesthood of all believers, "a royal priesthood" (1 Peter 2:9).

Christians can do some things for themselves. If they are suffering, they can bring the matter before the throne of grace. Jesus taught the importance of persistence in prayer (Luke 11:5-10). If they are joyful, they can respond to that joy through singing. The redeemed of God have much to be grateful for, even in the midst of suffering and trouble. Let the cheerful sing praise, "speaking to one another with psalms, hymns and songs from the Spirit. Sing and make music from your heart to the Lord, always giving thanks to God the Father for everything, in the name of our Lord

But Christians must also function in community. Is anyone sick? James gives a prescription that many churches do not follow. True, prayer for the sick is raised by members of the congregation corporately and individually. Here, the sick person is told to take the initiative. Call for the elders of the church. They should pray over that sick person and anoint that person with oil "in the name of the Lord" (v. 14). They are acting on behalf of the Great Physician. Some persons will question anointing with oil. They may wonder of what value that can be. We certainly don't anoint in place of seeking medical treatment. But healing is more than diagnosis, prescriptions, and prognosis. The prayer of faith combined with the act of faith (anointing) will have the effect of spiritual healing, which goes much further than physical curing.

Sometimes sin is the cause of sickness. Physical difficulties are often related to mental and spiritual causes. In these cases, confession is therapeutic. Confession is to one another, to brothers and sisters within the household of faith. No one is without sin; "We all stumble in many ways" (3:2), so we all need to confess our sins to one another and to pray for one another. The healing we need may be physical, mental, emotional, or spiritual.

Prayer is the key to healing, following confession. Elijah is a good example of the truth expressed in 5:16b (see his story in 1 Kings 17–18.)

James 5:19-20. James's final word of encouragement is indirectly related to the preceding instruction. A wanderer (backslider) has gone away from the caring, sharing fellowship of the church that is depicted in 5:13-18. This person has wandered from the truth of the gospel, which is the basis of the church.

Such wanderers are worthy of an effort to be brought back. Those who make that effort will experience the profound pleasure of knowing that the effort has saved a sinner (the wanderer) from eternal death (Revelation 21:8). A multitude of sins will be covered in the process (1 Peter 4:8). That is because the blood of Jesus Christ is able to cover all sin and to cleanse all from unrighteousness.

DIMENSION THREE: WHAT DOES THE BIBLE MEAN TO ME?

James 3:1–4:17—Your Christian Experience

This discussion topic is not intended to damage persons but to stimulate self-evaluation. Group members may have experience dealing with one or more of the concerns listed in the participant book. They may have come to grips with one or more of the concerns in their own life, or they may have suffered the effects of these concerns at the hands of others. They may still be struggling with a concern. Be sure participants can share their experiences in an open, supportive environment, and not be afraid of ostrization or judgement because of their struggles. We all have areas of our Christian experience with which we struggle.

Seek to find, in the context of each concern, the positive instruction that will help with the problem. The scriptural solutions to the problems raised by these concerns should apply to the person or to a dominant problem in the life of a congregation. Solutions to such problems come as the result of an awareness that a problem exists, understanding the nature of the problem, determining through prayer and consultation the action to be taken, and by the grace of God acting positively to remedy the concern.

James 5:13-18—Your Influence in the Life of Your Church

One hindrance to fellowship is the stress on individualism in our culture. The church is a community. Membership in it provides privileges and requires responsibilities. Christians are to share life. They are to "rejoice with those who rejoice; mourn with those who mourn" (Romans 12:15). In James, we see that we are also to sing praises to God for the benefit of one another, to confess our sins to one another, and to pray for one another.

Explore the problem of retaining our individualism while we practice being members of a community of the faithful. In what practical ways can we be more actively involved in the lives of fellow believers? What are some practical means by which we can allow Christian brothers and sisters to share more intimately in our lives?

Live such good lives among the pagans that . . . they may see your good deeds and glorify God. (2:12)

HOW TO LIVE IN A HOSTILE WORLD

1 Peter

DIMENSION ONE: WHAT DOES THE BIBLE SAY?

Answer these questions by reading 1 Peter

1. To whom is this letter addressed? (1:1)

The letter is addressed to "God's elect, exiles scattered throughout the provinces of Pontus, Galatia, Cappadocia, Asia and Bithynia."

2. What was the basis of the living hope in which the readers rejoiced? (1:3b)

The basis of the living hope was "the resurrection of Jesus Christ from the dead."

3. What did the prophets predict about Christ? (1:10-11)

The prophets predicted "the sufferings of the Messiah and the glories that would follow."

4. If someone claims God as Father, what effect should the claim have on that person's manner of life? (1:14-16)

The person who claims God as Father should be holy in conduct, for God is holy.

5. What four expressions are used to describe all those who have received mercy? (2:9-10)

Those who have received mercy are described as "a chosen people, a royal priesthood, a holy nation, God's special possession."

6. If we follow in the steps of Jesus, what specific things will we try to do? (2:21-23)

If we follow the example of Jesus, we will try: to commit no sin, to have no deceit in our mouths, to not retaliate when we are insulted, to not threaten when we suffer, and to trust ourselves to "him who judges justly."

7. In relation to one another, how should wives and husbands act? (3:1, 7)

Wives are to be submissive to their husbands, and husbands are to live considerately with their wives.

8. What characteristics should Christians show toward one another? (3:8)

Christians should be like-minded, sympathetic, love one another, be compassionate, and humble.

9. First Peter 4:7-11 lists a number of practices Christians should follow. Why should Christians practice these things? (4:11 b)

Christians should practice these things "so that in all things God may be praised through Jesus Christ."

10. Suffering as a Christian is acceptable, but Christians are warned not to suffer for certain things. What are they? (4:15)

Christians should not suffer "as a murderer or thief or any other kind of criminal, or even as a meddler."

11. Identify the main theme in 1 Peter 5:1-6.

The main theme of these verses is Christian humility.

12. First Peter 5:7-11 has two comforting promises for Christians. What are they?

God "cares for you" (5:7). After you have suffered as a Christian, God will "restore you and make you strong, firm and steadfast" (5:10).

DIMENSION TWO:
WHAT DOES THE BIBLE MEAN?

The First Letter of Peter is a message of instruction and encouragement for believers who are under the stress of trials and persecution. Its content and tone of expression have strengthened Christians from the first century and into the twenty-first century.

Writer, Date, and Place of Writing. The authorship of this letter is a matter of controversy. The opening verse of the letter indicates the apostle Peter is the writer. But several arguments against his authorship have been raised:

1. The excellence of the Greek could not be expected from the hand of a simple Galilean fisherman;

2. The intense persecutions mentioned in the letter did not take place until after the end of the first century AD, long after Peter's death;

3. The expressions and ideas are too much like Paul's to come from Peter;

4. The letter does not reflect the personal acquaintance of Peter with Jesus that the Gospels indicate.

On the basis of these objections, the assumption is that the letter was written by a disciple of Peter in the apostle's name about AD 112.

Against this view and for Peter as the writer are the following points:

1. The Greek was from the hand of Silas, who wrote under Peter's direction (5:12);

2. The persecutions need not be considered late but in the time of Peter;

3. The influence of Paul is apparent only because the expressions were a common core used by both Peter and Paul;

4. That the letter lacks evidence of a close bond between Jesus and the writer is not valid and is overstated.

Our assumption is that Peter wrote this letter before his death as a martyr in Rome around AD 64. This view is based on early traditions in the church and the lack of compelling arguments to the contrary. Irenaeus (about AD 185) was the first to quote First Peter by name. Eusebius (before AD 340) placed the letter among the acknowledged books of the New Testament.

The belief that Rome was the place of origin for the letter is based on the view that "Babylon" (5:13) is really a reference to Rome. Similar usage is found in the Book of Revelation (14:8; 17:5; 18:2).

The Readers. Peter wrote to Christians living in five provinces of Asia Minor (part of modern Turkey): Pontus, Galatia, Cappadocia, Asia, and Bithynia. These Christians lived in the region originally evangelized by Paul. The congregations likely consisted of Jewish and Gentile Christians.

The readers seem already to have faced some persecution. Peter writes to encourage them to stand fast in "the true grace of God" (5:12). They needed that because of a "fiery ordeal" that they were now facing (4:12). It was a time that tried their faith and their souls.

Outline of First Peter.

1 Peter 1:1-2. The letter opens with Peter's name. Peter was an interesting member of the small group of disciples that followed Jesus throughout his ministry. An enthusiastic and forceful man, some of Peter's character seems to be reflected in the forcefulness of this letter.

Peter's Hebrew name was *Simon Bar* (son of) *Jonah* (Matthew 16:17). Jesus gave him the nickname *Cephas*, an Aramaic word meaning "rock." The Greek form of *Cephas* is *Petros* with the same meaning; and *Petros* is the basis of the English name *Peter*.

Peter was married, and his wife apparently accompanied him on his missionary journeys. He was originally in business as a fisherman, but left that at the call of Jesus. He had a mountaintop experience at the transfiguration of Jesus (Matthew 17:1-18). It was an unforgettable experience that he mentions in Second Peter (1:17-18).

Peter walked on water (Matthew 14:28-29), rebuked Jesus for suggesting Jesus' coming death (Matthew 16:21-23), and emphasized his allegiance to Jesus shortly before denying him (Mark 14:29, 66-72). Restored by Jesus (see John 21:15-19), Peter went on to preach the first gospel sermon after the Ascension, on the Day of Pentecost (Acts 2). Peter was instrumental in the conversion of the first Samaritans and Gentiles won to Christ. He traveled with the gospel among the Jews of the Dispersion (Galatians 2:9), while Paul went to the Gentiles. According to apparently authentic tradition, both Peter and Paul were martyred in Rome during the persecutions of Christians by Nero.

We discussed the Dispersion (or Diaspora) in lesson 6. While the expression originated with the Jews, it was later applied to Christians. Later in this letter Peter addresses the readers as "foreigners and exiles" (2:11).

Notice 1:2, which specifies the privileged position the readers hold. They are the elect, the chosen ones. (Peter anticipates his teaching on the chosen ones that follows in 2:4-10.) God chose them "according to the foreknowledge of God the Father." The Good News Bible (GNT) translates this as "according to the purpose of God the Father."

God chose them, destined them to be sanctified (to be made holy) by the Holy Spirit. A similar expression is found in 2 Thessalonians 2:13. They are destined as sanctified people to obey Jesus Christ and to be "sprinkled by his blood" 1 Peter 1:2). At baptism, believers receive the sanctification of the Spirit (Titus 3:5); and in baptism they come into contact, symbolically, with the shed blood of Jesus, in that they are baptized into his death (Romans 6:3).

In other words, 1:2 acknowledges that the readers have been brought by God's providence into God's nation. Such believers receive grace and peace. Peter prays that these two benefits will be multiplied to them.

1 Peter 1:3-12. Peter proceeds from the theological to the practical in this letter. In this section, he establishes the basis for the instruction that will follow. He will later challenge the believers to face courageously the difficulties ahead. They can triumph over every trial if they can catch a vision of what God has done for them in Christ Jesus. Peter, perhaps in his early sixties, has never lost the sense of wonder at what he has witnessed and experienced. He must bless God.

Peter wants the Christians to appreciate their new life in Christ. They have this new life by God's great mercy (v. 3b). God was motivated by love and pity toward undeserving people (Titus 3:5).

Peter and his readers—all who have accepted God's grace and mercy—are born again. Jesus told Nicodemus that unless one is born again that person cannot see the kingdom of God (John 3:3). Obedient believers are born again to a living hope. The resurrection of Jesus from the dead holds promise of the believer's resurrection (1 Corinthians 15:16-23). The living hope goes on beyond resurrection to include a heavenly inheritance, described in the timeless adjectives of 1 Peter 1:4. That inheritance is eternal life. The earthly shadow of this heavenly reality was the land of Canaan, ancient Israel's Promised Land.

The inheritance is kept in heaven; there those who will inherit are guarded by God's power. That guarding power is activated by the faith of the believer. The inheritance is salvation, anticipated now by faith, realized in "the last time" (1 Peter 1:5).

Christians have a foretaste of salvation now, a guarantee. They are sealed with the Holy Spirit (Ephesians 1:13-14). They can rejoice in this guarantee while they face various trials. The trials will prove the genuineness of their faith. Their faith is more precious than gold because the end result is the "inheritance that can never perish, spoil or fade" (1 Peter 1:4). Even gold is perishable here on earth. The testing of faith will show the faith to be genuine. When the faithful are tested by fire and stand the test, they bring praise, glory, and honor to Christ now and at his appearing (Revelation 7:9-17).

Peter, who had seen Jesus, commends the faith of the readers who have not seen him. Even so, they love him. They find exquisite joy in Christ, and by faith they are in the process of obtaining salvation. Salvation in Christ has a past, present, and future aspect. In the present, "we live by faith, not by sight," as Paul said in 2 Corinthians 5:7. The full inheritance is received only at the appearing of Christ.

First Peter 1:10-12 indicates that Christians have an advantage over the pious of ages past. Christians walk by faith, and they have a much clearer picture of grace in Christ than even the prophets.

The prophets predicted the sufferings of Christ and "the glories that would follow" (v. 11). That is the same pattern the readers must repeat—to suffer, then to attain glory.

The fact that the prophets were really serving the purposes of God for the time of the readers is stressed in 1:12. What the prophets foresaw has been preached to the readers. The good news (gospel) came through speakers under the inspiration of the Holy Spirit. The mysteries of God in Christ were so great that even the angels did not know them. (No wonder the angels sang with joy at the birth of the Messiah; the mystery was unfolding before them!)

The reason Peter wrote this section is clear. These Christians have received what prophets and angels could not comprehend. This information would help the readers even more to appreciate their new life in Christ.

1 Peter 1:13–2:10. Peter has pointed out the incredibly great blessings of being chosen, destined, and sanctified by God's grace. Believers have every reason to be thankful for a living hope, a hope that in reality exceeds all that the human mind can imagine. Now Peter turns to call the readers to live a holy life before God.

1 Peter 1:13. The call to have "minds that are alert and fully sober" (RSV has "gird up your minds") is related to girding up the loins. The common dress for men at this time was in robes. When in a hurry or preparing for activities that the robes would hamper, they would bind their clothing up around the waist with a rope (girdle). This girding up their clothes would free them for energetic activity.

Peter calls for preparing the mind for intense activity. (Paul called for similar actions in Romans 12:1-2.) A determined effort is required by a person to live a holy life and to obtain the grace that is coming.

Being prepared includes being self-controlled. Being self-controlled is facing realistically what the situation requires. It is counting the cost. The other activity that preparing the mind requires is setting one's hope on the promised future inheritance.

1 Peter 1:14–2:3. While Peter uses the plural ("children," 1:14), what he calls for in Christian conduct must be done individually.

Peter calls Christians to be obedient. What are the specifics of obedience Peter has in mind? (1) Do not allow the "evil desires" of your former way of life to control you. (2) To the contrary, conduct yourself in a holy way. Be holy like the Holy One (vv. 15-16). (3) Live out your time here on earth with reverent respect for the Father to whom you pray. God is an impartial judge of the actions of each one of us (v. 17).

At the same time, you can have confidence in God (v. 21). You were ransomed from a hopeless life, like that of your ancestors, at an incredible price—the precious blood of Christ. This ransom was all God's work. Christ shed his blood in death, was raised from the dead, and is given glory, all for your sake. So you can have confidence in God. You can put your faith and hope in God (v. 21).

To live as a child of God, love others deeply with all your heart (v. 22). You are able to do this because you have purified your souls by obedience to the truth. The first readers of Peter's letter would understand the *truth* as the gospel. A positive response to the gospel involves repentance of past sins, confession that Jesus is the Christ (therefore both Savior and Lord), and baptism into Christ. This response justifies a person before God and brings a person into the community of the redeemed, the church.

Purification of the soul is connected with baptism. At Paul's conversion, Ananias instructed him, "Get up, be baptized and wash your sins away, calling on his name" (Acts 22:16b). The cleansing is symbolized by the water but is actualized by sharing in the death, burial, and resurrection of Jesus (Romans 6:1-11). In relationship to Jesus' death, we come into contact with the cleansing blood of his sacrifice. Purified, the baptized believer rises to walk in newness of life, no longer under the domination of sin or the condemnation of God.

Peter describes the believer's new relationship in Christ with family metaphors ("sincere love for each other," 1:22). We are conceived by imperishable seed, the word of God. This picture is similar to Jesus' parable of the sower (Matthew 13:18-23). In that parable, the seed is the word of the kingdom. When the living and abiding word of God has developed within us, we are born again. The good news that was preached has borne fruit (1 Peter 1:25b).

The new life that comes with the new birth is different from the futile ways of the old life. Living the new life in Christ requires action. "Rid yourselves of" malice (wickedness), deceit, hypocrisy, envy (jealousy), and all slander (insulting language) (2:1). All these are the opposite of loving one another sincerely.

Besides the action of putting away the negative things mentioned in 2:1, Peter exhorts the readers to positive action in 2:2. "Crave pure spiritual milk" like newborn babies long for their mother's milk. The spiritual milk must be something taken into the mind of the believer that is the opposite of malice, deceit, and so on. This new thing must be the word of God. The King James Version (KJV) uses the phrase "desire the sincere milk of the word." Rather than feeding on the deceit of the world, as they had in the past, the newborn children of God take into their mind God's word, so as to grow up to salvation. Salvation here is final salvation. No one will ever attain final salvation who does not first begin as a babe in Christ, then move on toward spiritual maturity. The first readers have already "tasted that the Lord is good" (2:3; see Psalm 34:8).

1 Peter 2:4-10. To live as a Christian in a hostile world requires girding up the mind, purifying the soul, being born again, putting away malice and the like, and craving spiritual food. But God's children do not exist in isolation. The "family" metaphor used earlier now becomes a "spiritual house" metaphor. The spiritual house image is probably based on the Temple in Jerusalem. Believers are to "come to him, the living Stone" (v. 4). That stone is Jesus Christ. Peter establishes that fact by the quotations that follow in verses 6-8 (Isaiah 28:16; Psalm 118:22; Isaiah 8:14-15).

Jesus also quoted Psalm 118:22 in Matthew 21:42. He saw himself as the stone rejected by the builders. But God has made Jesus the head of the corner. Peter referred to Jesus as the rejected stone, now head of the corner, before the Jewish leaders in Jerusalem years earlier (Acts 4:10-11).

Now the believers, who are also living stones, are instructed to be built into a spiritual house on the living foundation stone (1 Peter 2:5). They are also to be a holy priesthood in that living temple, presenting their bodies as living sacrifices to God (Romans 12:1).

Committed Christians belong to the family of God by the new birth. They have become a chosen people (Isaiah 43:20b), a royal priesthood, a holy nation (both from Exodus 19:6), a people belonging to God (Exodus 19:5), like Israel of old. The purpose of God's people is given in 2:9. Verse 10 is based on Hosea 1:9-10.

1 Peter 2:11-12. The readers are God's people in exile, aliens in a Gentile world. They are to refrain from indulging sinful desires. Peter agrees with James 3:13–4:10. These sinful desires war against the soul. God's people are to live a life that declares the wonderful deeds of God (1 Peter 2:9) through their own good deeds. The church is a letter from Christ, to be known and read by all persons (2 Corinthians 3:2-3).

1 Peter 2:13-17. To live a holy life before the world, submit to civil authorities. Do this for God's sake, for the sake of God's concern to redeem the lost and God's concern for the people. Show appropriate respect (honor) to all. But have a deep and abiding concern for the people of God—you and they are God's people—and show God profound respect.

1 Peter 2:18-20. Slavery was a fact of life for many of the early Christians. A slave, in order to live a life holy before the world, must be submissive to the master. This submission may require unjust suffering, but this suffering can be endured if one is "conscious of God" (v. 19).

1 Peter 2:21-25. Patience in suffering will win God's approval. To be patient is to follow in the footsteps of Jesus. God allowed Jesus to suffer on behalf of the believers, and they have benefited. Christian suffering for doing right will benefit others also.

1 Peter 3:1-12. Submission and consideration for others is a way of life for Christians. Christ submitted to those who had authority to crucify him. The principle works in more intimate relationships as well.

1 Peter 3:1-7. Wives are to be submissive to their husbands, some of whom are not Christians. The lifestyle of a Christian wife can affect the faith of her husband. Submission involves doing right and can be done without fear of intimidation. Read this in the cultural context of the first-century AD.

Husbands are to be considerate and understanding toward their wives. Do not use greater physical strength to intimidate your wife, Peter writes. Honor her as one who is a joint heir of eternal life with you. Clearly, to fail to maintain this considerate treatment of your spouse will affect your spiritual life and your communication with God.

1 Peter 3:8-12. To live a holy life requires Christian unity. The unity of believers results from right attitudes, indicated in 3:8. Peter then quotes from Psalm 34:12-16, to remind the readers that God favors right conduct.

1 Peter 3:13-22. Ordinarily, no harm will come from doing good. But if suffering does come, set Christ in your heart. Through good behavior in Christ, opportunities may arise to share your reason for Christian hope. Within God's purpose and will, suffering for doing right may come. Jesus so suffered on our behalf (vv. 17-18).

Verses 19-20 present a difficult passage to understand: After being "made alive in the Spirit" (v. 18), Christ went to proclaim to "imprisoned spirits" (v. 19). Christ, who existed with God before the world began (John 1:1-5), moved Noah to warn his generation of the coming flood. Noah's warning was a call to repentance (see Genesis 6–9).

Although Noah's generation was destroyed, a few (eight persons) were saved through water; that is, they were saved by being in the ark, the water bore it up. In a similar way, water, the water of baptism, now saves the few from "this corrupt generation" (Acts 2:40). Water might cleanse the skin; but in baptism, water is not what saves you. Water is a symbolic appeal to God: "Give me, I pray, a clear conscience. I know you have made it possible through the resurrection of Jesus Christ." Baptism apart from repentance and commitment to God in Christ is not Christian baptism.

1 Peter 4:1-11. Like Christ, live by the will of God rather than by human desires. It is enough, Peter wrote, that you formerly lived as pagans (v. 3). But all will be judged, both those alive and those dead. The good news was preached to the dead while they were yet alive (v. 6). God has had a witness in every generation (Romans 1:19-23).

Every generation of Christians has lived on the edge of the end of all things. In fact, the end of all things in this world for us comes the moment we die. Live to the glory of God now. Keep clear minded and self-controlled now. Pray now. Love now. Be hospitable now. Use your spiritual gifts now. Do all these things now so that God will be glorified both now and "for ever and ever" (4:11).

1 Peter 4:12-19. Peter had experienced suffering. He advises his beloved readers not to be surprised when painful trials (persecutions) erupt. They are sojourners in an alien and hostile world.

Rather, be of good cheer when persecutions come, sharing in Christ's sufferings (the church is the body of Christ); you will also share in Christ's glory. Do not suffer as an evildoer. Suffer as a Christian, and praise God. Judgment is coming, beginning with the family of God, so do right. Do not worry about the Judgment. Trust your soul to God.

1 Peter 5:1-11. Verses 1-4 are addressed to the leaders of the Christian community, "the elders." Peter, though an apostle, sees himself also in the role of an elder, a shepherd of the flock of God, the people of the faith. Peter's emphasis here is on the proper attitude and actions. The appropriate attitude is one of humility.

Those subject to the elders should also be clothed with humility. Verse 6 seems to echo James 4:10. Humility now assures exaltation in God's tomorrow and by God's hand. Relax; God cares for you now. Let God bear your anxiety. "Do not be anxious about anything, but in every situation, by prayer and petition, with thanksgiving, present your requests to God. And the peace of God, which transcends all understanding, will guard your hearts and your minds in Christ Jesus" (Philippians 4:6-7).

First Peter 5:8-9 is just as valid as the preceding verses. The devil is the personification of evil, waiting to swallow up the unwary, enticing Christians to forgo suffering and cave in to desire. This advice is similar to that of James 4:7b: "Resist the devil, and he will flee from you." You are not alone in resisting. You are not alone in suffering. Both will end, and you will receive the reward for faithfulness—to share in the eternal glory of Christ.

1 Peter 5:12-14. Silas was responsible for drafting the letter. He is probably the Silas of Acts 15:22-40. He, along with Timothy, was also involved in writing First and Second Thessalonians.

The last part of 5:12 gives the specific reason Peter wrote. "The true grace of God" is the Christians' current situation of suffering. Stand fast in it. Rejoice in it (4:13).

Greetings from the church in Rome (Babylon) come with the letter. The Roman Christians, too, are chosen. Greetings also come from (John) Mark. We know Mark as the companion of Paul and Barnabas (Acts 15:37-40).

The warmth of the writer toward his readers is felt in the closing remarks. *Peace* refers to unity and harmony in the church. It is a fruit of the Holy Spirit (Galatians 5:22).

DIMENSION THREE:
WHAT DOES THE BIBLE MEAN TO ME?

1 Peter 2:5, 9—A Royal Priesthood

In Israel, priests represented the people in the ritual of the sanctuary. They mediated between God and the people. The high priest had a special role, as we have seen in the study of Hebrews. He entered into the Most Holy Place of the Tabernacle (Temple) to make atonement for the sins of the people. Christ has now become the believer's high priest. Immediate access to God is possible now through him.

All Christians are now able to offer spiritual sacrifices acceptable to God. All believers are now priests. In Romans 12:1, Paul explains that we are to present our bodies as a living sacrifice, and that is our reasonable or spiritual service. What he has in mind is a dedicated Christian life. The specific implications of that living sacrifice are given through the remainder of Romans 12.

Peter says that we (the royal priesthood) are also to declare the wonderful deeds of God, who called us "out of darkness into his wonderful light" (2:9). We are to be ready at any time to explain the hope that is within us (that you may declare the praises of him who called you," v. 9).

Another aspect of our priesthood is to offer sacrifices of praise. This praise is also called "the fruit of lips that openly profess [God's] name" (Hebrews 13:15). Beyond that, Hebrews 13:16 encourages doing good to others and sharing what you have, "for with such sacrifices God is pleased."

Make every effort to confirm your calling and election. For if you do these things, you will never stumble. (1:10)

HOW TO HANDLE THE CRISIS IN THE CHURCH

2 Peter

DIMENSION ONE:
WHAT DOES THE BIBLE SAY?

Answer these questions by reading 2 Peter

1. How does Peter describe his relationship to Jesus Christ? (1:1)

   Peter calls himself "a servant and apostle of Jesus Christ."

2. What can the believers in the great and precious promises of God expect to receive? (1:4)

   The believers can expect to "participate in the divine nature, having escaped the corruption in the world."

3. What one thing does Peter want to do for his readers? (1:12)

   The one thing Peter wants to do for his readers is to remind them of truths they already know.

4. What were the sources of the apostolic witness and the prophetic word? (1:16-21)

   The apostles were eyewitnesses of the majesty of Jesus (1:16); the prophetic word came through the Holy Spirit (1:21).

5. What does Peter say that the false teachers will do? (2:1-3)

   The false teachers will bring in destructive heresies, deny the Lord, act in shameful ways, and exploit the readers with false stories.

6. In 2:4-10a, Peter uses three examples to show that God knows how to keep the unrighteous under punishment. List the three examples.

   The three examples are the angels that sinned, the people of the ancient world who died in the flood, and the people of Sodom and Gomorrah.

7. The false teachers are seen as following in the footsteps of what biblical character? (2:12-16)

   The false teachers followed in the way of Balaam, the son of Bezer.

8. Why do the false teachers fail to deliver on their promise of freedom for their followers? (2:19)

   The false teachers cannot give freedom to those who follow them because "they themselves are slaves of depravity."

9. Why do scoffers say, "Where is this 'coming' he promised?" (3:3-4)

   Scoffers say this because "everything goes on as it has since the beginning of creation."

10. Why does the Lord delay the Day of Judgment and destruction of ungodly people? (3:9)

    The Lord delays the Day of Judgment because God does not wish any to perish, "but everyone to come to repentance."

11. According to the promise of God, for what do Christians wait? (3:13)

    Christians are waiting for "a new heaven and a new earth, where righteousness dwells."

12. Peter warns the readers to beware of two related things. What are they? (3:15-17)

    Peter warns them to beware of being "carried away by the error of lawless men and fall[ing] from [their] secure position."

DIMENSION TWO:
WHAT DOES THE BIBLE MEAN?

Writer and Date. After investigating the varying views on the authorship of this book, one remains perplexed. Every book in the New Testament is challenged by someone, but more scholars deny the genuineness of Second Peter than any other book in the canon.

There are two major scholarly views on the authorship of 1 Peter:

1. The letter is written as from the apostle Peter (1:1). The writer refers to the transfiguration of Jesus (1:17-18; Matthew 17:1-8; Mark 9:2-8; Luke 9:28-36). Peter was an eyewitness. The writer refers also to the words of Jesus about the coming death of Peter (John 21:18-19). A previous letter is referred to (2 Peter 3:1), doubtless to be understood as First Peter. The writer indicates a personal familiarity with the apostle Paul and accepts him as an inspired writer (3:15b-16). Based on this internal evidence, the traditional position is that Peter was the writer.

2. Second Peter was written by an unnamed follower of Peter sometime after the apostle's death. The writer's intent was to preserve the apostolic tradition. The language and imagery of the book is quite Greek in flavor. Peter, a Galilean fisherman, would be expected to write with a more Semitic flavor. Further, there is no new information about Jesus and the apostles in the letter that would not have been available to a follower of Peter.

The letter was written by this unnamed disciple about AD 90. Or, the letter was written between AD 125 and AD 150 by a member of the third generation from Peter. Reasons for dating the letter later are the following:

a. It draws heavily on the Letter of Jude, which was probably written about AD 90; and Second Peter is believed to be the borrower;

b. It mentions the death of the "ancestors," the early church leaders (3:4b);

c. It refers to the letters of Paul as "Scriptures" (3:16), an expression used during the time of the apostles to refer only to the Old Testament books.

Origen, Eusebius, and Jerome refer to Second Peter; but they indicate that some people doubt that the letter was written by the apostle. Eusebius put it in the category of "disputed books." Second Peter was accepted into the canon by the Council at Carthage (AD 397).

For our purposes, we will view the letter as written by the apostle Peter, shortly before his death, near AD 64. Despite differences between First and Second Peter that scholars have observed, the two books have significant similarities. Both letters emphasize Christ and his second coming as central doctrines; the importance of the story of the flood and Noah; the importance of the prophetic word, the Old Testament, similar to Peter's use of prophecy in his Pentecost sermon (Acts 2:14-36); and the necessity of Christian growth.

Place of Writing. Peter speaks of his approaching death (1:14). According to early Christian tradition, this took place in Rome about the same time Paul was killed, sometime between AD 64 and AD 67.

The Readers. Our writer mentions that this epistle is the second letter he has written to the readers (3:1). We can assume that it was written to the Christians in the five provinces of Asia Minor listed in 1 Peter 1:1.

The Form of the Letter. Second Peter is similar in form to a "testament." Testaments were a literary type begun by Jews in the intertestamental period. Christians also took up this literary form. Testaments in the New Testament include Jesus' farewell speech (John 13–17), Paul's farewell to the elders of Ephesus (Acts 20:17-35), and Second Timothy.

A testament is like a last will and testament to the church. It is written on the occasion of the approaching death of the writer. The content includes admonitions and edifying words that point out the difficulties that will come. Peter leaves this work as a legacy to help remind his readers of important truths.

Outline of Second Peter

I. Salutation (1:1-2)

II. Make your calling and election sure (1:3-11)

III. Keep the apostolic and prophetic word (1:12-21)

      A. The apostolic witness (1:12-18)

      B. The prophetic word (1:19-21)

IV. Beware of false teachers (2:1-22)

      A. False teachers will arise (2:1-3)

      B. They will be punished, but the righteous will be rescued (2:4-10a)

      C. The character and conduct of false teachers (2:10b-16)

      D. The folly of following them (2:17-22)

V. On the second coming of the Lord (3:1-18)

      A. Some will scoff at it (3:1-7)

      B. The answer for scoffers (3:8-10)

      C. How to await that day (3:11-18)

2 Peter 1:1-2. *Simon* is the Hebrew form of Peter's first name as it appears also in Acts 15:14. Compared to the opening of First Peter, here the words "a servant" are added.

Rather than identifying the place to which the letter was sent, Peter addresses the recipients as "those who through the righteousness of our God and Savior Jesus Christ have received a faith as precious as ours" (v. 1). This phrase likely refers to Gentile Christians. The expression shows that the ground is level at the foot of the cross. "There is neither Jew nor Gentile, neither slave nor free, nor is there male and female" in Christ Jesus (Galatians 3:28).

The desire for grace and peace for the readers, found in First Peter, is repeated here (1:2), with the addition: "through the knowledge of God and of Jesus our Lord." A deepening "knowledge of God and of Jesus our Lord" will result in multiplied grace and peace.

2 Peter 1:3-11. Verses 3-4 provide an introduction to the main statement that begins with verse 5. The main thought in this introduction is the gift God has given to people of faith (us). The gift mentioned here has several meanings. It is a complete package, providing all that is needed to live a godly life; it comes through knowledge of God, the One who called us through Jesus to share "his . . . glory and goodness" (v. 3); it provides a protective shield, a means of escaping the life-destroying effects of evil desires (v. 4; compare 1 Peter 4:1-6); and it provides the means for sharing God's essential nature (v. 4).

God has made spiritual gifts and knowledge available to people of faith. Through what God has granted, they may escape worldly corruption. However, supplementary effort is required (v. 5). They should do their utmost to add to what God has done for them. They need to confirm eagerly their calling and election (v. 10).

Verses 5-7 list eight qualities Christians should have in their lives. Each quality promotes acquiring the next.

Faith is the foundation of the Christian life. Faith is assurance (Hebrews 11:1). Without faith it is impossible to please God (Hebrews 11:6). Faith includes believing in God and believing God. The basis of faith is accepting the testimony (knowledge) God has revealed about Christ (Romans 10:14-17).

Goodness is moral power, goodness of life, and strength of Christian character.

Knowledge is the knowledge "of God and of Jesus our Lord" mentioned in 1:2-3. "This is eternal life: that they know you, the only true God, and Jesus Christ, whom you have sent" (John 17:3). The Bible is the disciple's textbook. Contained within it is everything "useful for teaching, rebuking, correcting and training in righteousness, so that the servant of God may be thoroughly equipped for every good work" (2 Timothy 3:16-17).

Self-control is promoted by knowledge of one's self. It involves the mind; thoughts can be controlled. People can choose what they think about. Paul urged Christians to think about things true, noble, right, pure, lovely, admirable, excellent, and praiseworthy (Philippians 4:8). Self-control also involves the body; Christians can subdue passions and desires. "When you are tempted, [God] will also provide a way out" (1 Corinthians 10:13c). The body can be controlled and directed to alternative activities.

Perseverance is sometimes rendered "patience," sometimes "steadfastness." Perseverance is the ability to stand firm. Jesus, in foretelling persecution against his apostles, said, "Stand firm, and you will win life" (Luke 21:19). The one "who stands firm to the end will be saved" (Matthew 24:13).

Godliness is a reverent attitude toward God. It includes devotion to God and imitating God's character. Practically, it means following in the footsteps of Jesus.

Mutual affection is love for the other members of the family of God. This quality of caring is also discussed in 1 Peter 1:22.

Love is a genuine concern for the good and welfare of another person. Christian love, like that exemplified in Christ, is not an emotional feeling. Such love is a deliberate attitude with related actions (Matthew 5:44).

The person who possesses an abundance of these qualities will actively apply the knowledge of the Lord to life situations. That person will be productive in the Christian life, full of love and good works. God saves people for a purpose, to be fruitful servants in the cause of righteousness.

However, the person who has saving faith, but who does not add these characteristics to that faith, is terribly handicapped (1:9). Shortsighted to the point of blindness and forgetful of the cleansing power of Jesus' blood, that person is destined for disaster. Faith without living a productive life is dead (James 2:26).

God in Christ chooses and calls us (1:3, 10). Whoever will, may come (Revelation 22:17). But the called must be zealous to confirm the call. This confirmation is done by adding to faith the qualities indicated in 1:5-7. Believers who diligently endeavor to confirm that call will be so engrossed in the effort and so engaged in the task that they will have no occasion to stumble. The end result will be a rich welcome into the eternal kingdom of God, into heaven itself. These are ample reasons to make one's calling and election sure.

2 Peter 1:12-15. Because of the importance of developing the Christian graces and thereby confirming their calling, Peter is determined to leave his readers a permanent reminder (v. 12). This letter is that reminder.

The permanent reminder is not some new information that they have not previously received. Peter is confident that the readers know and are established in the truth. But Christians forget and need to be reminded ("refresh your memory," v. 13).

The time had come to leave this permanent reminder. Peter was still alive ("in the tent of this body," v. 13), but he knew that he was soon to die. Jesus had predicted Peter's death: "'When you are old you will stretch out your hands, and someone else will dress you and lead you where you do not want to go.' Jesus said this to indicate the kind of death by which Peter would glorify God" (John 21:18b-19). The passage may also suggest a further revelation from Christ to Peter shortly before he wrote this letter (2 Peter 1:14).

In the remainder of this section, the apostle emphasizes the apostolic witness and the prophetic word.

2 Peter 1:16-18. Peter, writing to former pagans who were steeped in the myths of Greek and Oriental culture, is emphatic that Christ is no myth. He reminds the readers that he and the other apostles had made known to them the details about the first coming of Jesus Christ. (Peter will discuss the second coming of Christ later in the letter.)

Jesus came in power. Peter was an eyewitness to his powerful works. Peter's mother-in-law was healed by Jesus' power (Matthew 8:14-15). Peter shared that marvelous power of Jesus over the natural elements; he walked on water (Matthew 14:28-29). In Second Peter 1:16, the power Peter had in mind was what he witnessed on the Mount of Transfiguration (Matthew 17:1-8).

Peter witnessed more than power on that mountain. He, James, and John also witnessed the majesty of Jesus Christ. "His face shone like the sun, and his clothes became as white as the light. Just then there appeared . . . Moses and Elijah, talking with Jesus" (Matthew 17:2b-3).

Moses and Elijah were great channels of revelation for God's will, and Peter was ready to classify the majestic Jesus into a similar category. Then he heard a voice from heaven that he would never forget: "This is my Son, whom I love; with him I am well pleased. Listen to him!" (Matthew 17:5). All this was in Peter's mind as he wrote, and his readers knew the story well.

The Transfiguration was a personal experience of Peter's and a historical occurrence on a rock-solid mountain. Jesus, in all his power, glory, and majesty was no myth. That is the apostolic witness to be remembered, to be kept.

2 Peter 1:19-21. Jesus verified the testimony of the prophets. When God bore witness to him on the mountain, what the prophets had said of the Messiah was made even more certain. Everything foretold about Jesus was true. That includes what was fulfilled during his life and ministry. It also includes that yet to be fulfilled, his second coming.

Christians, the readers of Peter's testimony, will do well to pay attention to the prophetic witness. The prophetic word is like a lamp in a distant window, guiding travelers through the dark toward their destination. You are not in danger of going astray when you follow the prophetic light. The day when Christ comes again will dawn. The morning star, the dayspring from on high, will completely illuminate Christians' hearts. That is, they will understand completely what now is partly hidden.

To keep the prophetic word requires understanding its source. The prophets spoke under the inspiration of the Holy Spirit (v. 21). Likewise, the interpretation of Scripture must be by those inspired by the Holy Spirit (v. 20). Peter is one of these. But false prophets are everywhere, and he warns the readers against them.

2 Peter 2:1-3. "There were also false prophets among the people, just as there will be false teachers among you," Peter writes in 2:1. False prophets arose among God's people in Old Testament times (Deuteronomy 13:1-5; Jeremiah 6:13; 28:9; Ezekiel 13:9). Jesus warned against such false prophets (Matthew 7:15). Paul wrote to the Christians in Corinth, mentioning problems with false apostles and false believers (2 Corinthians 11:13, 26).

Peter describes the false teachers:

1. They subtly bring in ideas of their own, private interpretations that are not of the Holy Spirit, that pose a threat to the unity and spiritual health of the church (v. 1b);

2. They deny the Master who redeemed them, not by outright rejection but by cleverly twisting the truth about who he is, what he taught, and what he did (v. 1b);

3. They entice others into sexual immorality, discrediting thereby the way of truth (v. 2);

4. They are subtly covetous, using lies to exploit the gullible (v. 3a).

The downfall of false teachers is certain. Their judgment is not far off. To underline this, Peter gives examples of deserved destruction on the ungodly in the next section. Similarities to passages in Jude are striking; you may want to compare Peter's examples with the comments in lesson 13.

2 Peter 2:4-10a. Verses 4-8 contain a series of four *if* clauses. The *ifs* are the equivalent of "as surely as." The result clause, introduced by *then*, begins in 2:9. Each *if* clause contains an example of deserved judgment:

1. When certain angels sinned, they were cast out of heaven into hell. The Greeks believed hell was a dark and dismal place where the wicked dead were cast. The angels went from realms of light to darkest night, there to await the final judgment (v. 4; compare Jude 6).

2. The violence of the ancient world resulted in its destruction in the Flood. Only Noah, who was righteous in his generation, survived with his immediate family. They survived because God rescued them by means of the ark (v. 5; compare 1 Peter 3:20).

3. Sodom and Gomorrah were the epitome of cities where people lived by sexual passions. Fire from heaven consumed them. Since the time of Abraham, Sodom and Gomorrah have been examples of judgment on godlessness (v. 6).

4. However, God rescued "Lot, a righteous man" (v. 7). Here we have a view of Lot that is not included in the Old Testament account (Genesis 19). Peter pictures Lot as deeply troubled by the lawless deeds of his neighbors, even though he had chosen to live among them (2 Peter 2:7-8).

If God did all this in the past, and God did, then God knows how to save the faithful ones while punishing the godless. God is particularly set against those who indulge their polluting passions and despise divine authority (vv. 9-10).

2 Peter 2:10b-16. Peter is devastating in his description of the false teachers, so-called Christians. He has mentioned that their condemnation is coming, their destruction draws near. Just as the ungodly mentioned in the previous verses were punished for their godlessness, so the false teachers will be punished. Here is the catalog of their godlessness:

1. The false teachers "heap abuse on celestial beings" (or things, vv. 10-11). Some translate *celestial beings* as "dignitaries," others as "glorious ones," others as "glories of the unseen world." The act of abuse is the focus here. Instead of showing Christian humility, the false teachers exhibit arrogance and willfulness.

2. The false teachers act like brute animals and will be destroyed like beasts of prey (vv. 12b-13a).

3. The false teachers revel and entice others to join them in reveling (vv. 13b-14). They love to party, even in the daytime, looking for an opportunity to indulge in sinful lewdness. The false teachers entice others to share their pleasure, intending to take advantage of them to the profit of the false teachers.

4. These people are under God's curse. They started on the right way, and then forsook it. Now they follow the pattern of Balaam (Numbers 22–24). He corrupted his prophetic calling for gain and turned God's people, Israel, to sinful ways. Ironically, a donkey, by God's power, spoke a prophetic word to Balaam to stop his irrational actions.

2 Peter 2:17-22. False teachers give a false impression to the naive (those "who are just escaping from those who live in error," v. 18). They are like dry wells to the thirsty and empty rain clouds to the dry land. They promise a freedom they cannot deliver, because they are slaves to corruption.

The false teachers and those foolish enough to follow them will end up worse off than they were before they accepted Jesus Christ as Lord and Savior. To turn their backs on the sacred commandment (to love God and neighbor) in order to return to the defilements of the world is as sickening as to see the dog eat its vomit or the washed sow return to the mire (v. 22).

2 Peter 3:1-18. Peter wants to remind his readers to make their calling and election sure, to adhere to the apostolic and prophetic word, and to beware of false teachers. His last and major concern is the certainty of the second coming of Christ. Apparently, this concern was heightened by its rejection by the false teachers.

2 Peter 3:1-7. Scoffers will appear "in the last days" (v. 3). Many mock the idea of the Second Coming in every generation (compare 1 Peter 1:3-7; 4:7, 13; 5:4).

Scoffers are motivated by their own evil desires, not by the Spirit of God. Remove God, the heavenly hope, and the return of Christ, and all that remains is to live for fulfilling desires.

Scoffers deliberately ignore (forget) the power and certainty of the word of God. God created the earth and the heavens by God's word ("Let there be . . .," Genesis 1). From the heavens, God poured forth water in the Flood to destroy the earth (Genesis 6–9). The present heavens and earth will be destroyed by fire, according to God's word. No direct statement in the Old Testament says that the earth will be destroyed by fire. In New Testament times, though, the idea that the world would end in a great blaze of fire was widespread.

The destruction of the heavens and earth by fire will take place in conjunction with the end of time. The end will mark the Day of Judgment and the destruction of the ungodly as well.

2 Peter 3:8-10. Peter makes it clear that the delay in the Second Coming and the attendant end of the world is due to two factors: first, God does not mark time the way people do; and second, God is a gracious God. God is not willing that any shall perish but that all shall come to repentance. That day will come like a thief in the night, a quotation from Jesus (Matthew 24:36-44; Luke 12:35-40; and see Paul's expression in 1 Thessalonians 5:2). The day will come, unexpected and catastrophic.

2 Peter 3:11-18. In light of the catastrophic nature of the day of God, Christians should be waiting for that day (as Jesus taught, Matthew 24:36-44). They should be hastening its coming by living holy and godly lives. That day will hold no terror for the faithful of God's people, for they look for a new creation, a new world in which righteousness will be at home (Isaiah 65:17; Revelation 21:1).

In 1:10, Peter urges his readers to be eager to confirm their calling and election. Here, with a related meaning, he urges them to be eager to be holy and at peace, so they can be found that way when Christ comes. As they wait, they should "bear in mind that our Lord's patience means salvation," Peter advises (3:15). Judgment is delayed in order to allow others an opportunity to respond to the gospel.

Paul also urged godly living and preparation for Christ's return in his letters. Some ignorant and unstable people twisted his words, giving them false explanations. This false teaching will bring disaster on their heads (and on the heads of those who are gullible). They can twist his words because, like other Scriptures, some passages in his letters are hard to understand.

Peter closes the letter without the expected conclusion (as in 1 Peter 5:12-14). But he practically echoes his opening thoughts on "the grace and knowledge of our Lord and Savior Jesus Christ" (3:18). Peter saw Christ's glory on the mountaintop. Jesus Christ deserves that glory now and forever.

DIMENSION THREE: WHAT DOES THE BIBLE MEAN TO ME?

2 Peter 1:16-18—Jesus as a Historical Person

The contrast in 2 Peter 1:16-18 is between "cleverly devised stories" and an eyewitness account. The New Testament is written as a truthful record of historical people and events. The books are based on the testimony of eyewitnesses, as indicated, for example, in Luke 1:1-4. Indications of historical points are scattered throughout the accounts. We have no indication that anyone involved in the process of writing and transmitting the testimony was being devious. Every indication, in both the texts and the traditions of the early church, is that the apostles and the early disciples were willing to suffer and die attesting to what they had seen and experienced.

The writers of the New Testament books were well aware of the nature of cultural myths. Their world was engulfed in stories about pagan gods. Those stories were based on the imaginations of people rather than on historical events. The stories were connected to the rituals of pagan temples, in which sexual activities were carried out in the name of the gods. Rather than elevating the human spirit, mythological religion pandered to human passions in the guise of the sacred.

Despite the views of some scholars who think that they see similar myths in the New Testament, there is nothing false in it. The New Testament writers knew story and wrote history.

The validity of salvation in Jesus Christ rises or falls on the historical truth of the gospel. Paul stated it clearly in 1 Corinthians 15. If the gospel is not true history, then our faith is vain. Cultural myths cannot save. Only the shed blood of Jesus Christ is able to take away the sins of the world, including yours and mine.

For the church, since it is made up of sinners saved by the blood of Jesus Christ through the grace of God, the historical validity of the faith is as important as it is to the individual Christian. Either the church is in truth Christ's body on earth, because Jesus was what the Gospels state, or it is nothing.

2 Peter 3—The Second Coming of Christ

A brief summary of the main points presented by Peter will help you and the group members think about the question in the participant book.

1. There is no question about the fact of the Second Coming from the point of view of the person of faith. Let scoffers come and go; the fact of the second coming of Christ remains a basic Christian doctrine.

2. The question of when Christ will come remains unanswered. God is long suffering; we are to be patient.

3. The events connected with Christ's second coming are given only sketchily. It is fruitless to speculate about further details.

4. Those who patiently look for Christ's coming need have no fear at his appearing. They are new creations in Christ and await the creation of "a new heaven and a new earth" in which righteousness reigns.

5. Anticipation includes preparation through quality daily living. Holiness, godliness, and peace are three qualities of life Peter mentions.

If we walk in the light, as he is in the light, we have fellowship with one another. (1:7)

10

THE BASIS OF CHRISTIAN FELLOWSHIP

1 John 1–2

DIMENSION ONE: WHAT DOES THE BIBLE SAY?

Answer these questions by reading 1 John 1

1. With what physical senses had John experienced contact with the Word of life? (1:1)

   John had heard with his ears, seen with his eyes, and touched with his hands the Word of life.

2. What did John want the readers to share? (1:3)

   John wanted the readers to have fellowship with him and "with the Father and with his Son, Jesus Christ."

3. What benefits does walking in the light bring to the Christian? (1:7)

   The Christian who walks in the light will have fellowship with other Christians and will be purified from all sin through the blood of Jesus Christ.

Answer these questions by reading 1 John 2

4. How can Christians be sure that they know Christ? (2:3)

   If we obey his commands, then we can be sure that we know him.

5. How can a person know that he or she is in the light? (2:9-10)

   The one who loves a brother or sister in Christ lives in the light, "and there is nothing in them to make them stumble"; but the one who hates a brother or sister is in the darkness.

6. For what three things did John commend the young men to whom he wrote? (2:14b)

John commended the young men "because you are strong, / and the word of God lives in you, / and you have overcome the evil one."

7. What is the evidence that the last hour has come? (2:18)

The evidence that the last hour has come is that many antichrists have come.

8. How can an antichrist be identified? (2:22c)

An antichrist is anyone who denies the Father and the Son.

9. What is promised to those who remain in the Son and in the Father? (2:24b-25)

Those who remain in the Son and in the Father have the promise of eternal life.

10. How should those who remain in Christ act when he comes? (2:28)

Those who remain in Jesus Christ should "be confident and unashamed before him at his coming."

DIMENSION TWO:
WHAT DOES THE BIBLE MEAN?

The Writer. The three letters attributed to John in the New Testament do not have the writer's name stated in them. Neither does the Gospel of John give the name of its writer.

The belief that John, the son of Zebedee and companion of Jesus, is the writer appeared quite early in church history. Christian writers and works whose words seem to reflect expressions from First John, for instance, include Clement of Rome, who wrote about AD 96; Ignatius of Antioch, whose episodes are dated to about AD 110; and the Didache, an early Christian manual written sometime between AD 90 and AD 120.

Irenaeus of Lyons (about AD 185) testified that both Polycarp and Papias, bishops of Smyrna and Hierapolis in Asia Minor, respectively, in the early part of the second century, had known and heard the apostle John. Irenaeus quoted from First John and ascribed the quotation to John.

That First John and the Gospel are closely related is shown by phrases that are common to both, for example, "to make [y]our joy complete" (1 John 1:4; John 16:24); "walks around in the dark[ness]. They do not know where they are going" (1 John 2:11; John 12:35c); and Christ's title, "one and only Son" (1 John 4:9; John 1:14b, 18; 3:16). Many other words and phrases are common to First John and the Gospel: *remain, children of God, light, love, darkness, new command.*

Second John reflects the same concerns with love and truth that are expressed in First John. Second John appears to be addressed to a particular person (or church), but that person is not named. The writer identifies himself as "the elder." The writer of the third letter also identifies himself as "the elder." Third John is addressed to a particular person: Gaius. He is greeted with almost exactly the same expression as is used in the opening greeting in Second John. Concluding remarks in both Second and Third John are also strikingly similar.

Counter arguments to the early tradition of John as writer of these books have been offered. Some scholars have also argued against the internal support for the tradition. The majority of biblical scholars, however, accept that the writer of the Gospel and the letters is John, the beloved companion of Jesus, the son of Zebedee, and the brother of James.

Time and Place. The Gospel of John and the three letters probably were all written from the same place and in the same general period of time. According to early Christian tradition, John was the last of the original twelve disciples of Jesus to die. He lived in Ephesus in Asia Minor (western part of modern Turkey) during the later years of his life, carrying on a ministry to the church there and to the churches in the region. No one knows the date of John's death. The general assumption is that he died by AD 100. The letters and the Gospel would have been written, then, sometime between AD 90 and AD 100. The expression *dear children*, that appears scattered through the letters, suggests the writer was an elderly person, because it is used of young and old alike.

Persons Addressed. No particular person or group of persons is mentioned as the original recipients of First John. The letter is a general communication to all Christians. Perhaps it was originally intended for loyal believers in the region of Asia, the region in which the seven churches of the Book of Revelation were located. Because First John is a general communication to Christians wherever they might be found, the letter is of special significance to Christians today.

Purpose. The first four verses of First John provide an introduction to the remainder of the letter, and they contain the reason why John wrote. He wanted those who read to "have fellowship" with the Father and his Son Jesus Christ and with "us." The *us* must refer to the apostle and his supporters, the loyal Christians who received his testimony.

To have fellowship is to share. *Fellowship* implies certain things held in common; connected with this are the ideas of oneness, unity, and community. John expected that the testimony he proclaimed would bring fellowship, which would result in complete and lasting joy to himself, his associates, and the readers. This desire echoes that of Jesus for his disciples expressed in John's Gospel (15:11; 16:24; 17:13).

First John was also written to counter dangerous teachings that undercut the truth of the gospel and the basis of the fellowship John desired for Christians. The content of the letter indicates that these errors were threatening to lead unstable souls astray. The general label for the false teachings John opposed is Gnosticism.

Gnostics taught that the world was made by an inferior power rather than by almighty God. The idea is rooted in views of the world developed by Greek philosophers. They held that the material world is, by its nature, evil; and the unseen, spiritual world is, by nature, good.

Almighty God, who is spiritual and utterly holy, could not have created the sinful world. So some intermediate being must have created it.

Humans were viewed as both physical and spiritual. The spiritual (good) was trapped in the physical (evil). Salvation was spiritual and was made possible through special, secret knowledge. This secret knowledge was possessed by only special, gifted teachers and those who became their disciples.

Among the gnostic teachings was the denial of the humanity of Christ. They taught that he only appeared to be human, because to be human meant he was partly evil. In this view, Jesus was a man born as other men. Because he was very righteous and wise, the Christ-spirit descended on Jesus at his baptism and left him before the crucifixion. The human Jesus experienced death, burial, and resurrection; the Christ did not.

One aspect of gnostic thought was a focus on mental enlightenment while permitting the body to be involved in immoral activities. John, by contrast, emphasized the demands of holiness that true faith and love place on the believer.

The gnostic element was active within the church. Their teachings and practices threatened the survival of historic Christianity and the unity of believers. The problem became a crisis in the second century, which resulted in the consolidation of the orthodox teaching of the church. The books accepted as orthodox and authoritative are our New Testament. The writings of John played an important role in overcoming this threat to the unity and survival of the church.

Form of the Letter. First John does not have the formal features of a New Testament letter, such as we find in Paul's letters. No salutation indicates who the writer is and who the letter is intended for. No greeting of grace, peace, and the like is included. No conclusion appears, as in Second and Third John. Some people consider the book a sermon or a collection of notes on several sermons. Even though First John is technically not a letter, clearly it is a communication from an authoritative Christian leader to people he feels would heed his teaching, warnings, and encouragement.

Outline of First John

First John does not easily divide into a logical development of thought. Certain key words and ideas, however, surface again and again. The overall result is an emphatic statement of great truths of the faith. We will use the following outline as we consider the content of the letter:

I. Introduction. The testimony—foundation of fellowship (1:1-4)

II. The conditions of fellowship (1:5–2:29)

    A. Walk in the light (1:5-10)

    B. Walk in the footsteps of Jesus (2:1-6)

    C. Pass the test of Christian love (2:7-11)

    D. Know God and keep God's commandments (2:12-17)

    E. Shun the antichrists; remain in Christ (2:18-29)

III. Fellowship—a family relationship (3:1–4:6)

    A. Children of God (3:1-3)

    B. Children of the devil (3:4-10)

C. God's children love one another (3:11-18)

D. God's children keep God's commandments and have confidence (3:19-24)

E. God's children share God's Spirit (4:1-6)

IV. Facets of the fellowship (4:7–5:21)

A. The love of God (4:7-21)

B. Faith in Jesus, the Son of God (5:1-5)

C. Trust in the testimony of God (5:6-12)

D. The certainties of faith (5:13-21)

1 John 1:14. Verses 1-3 are complicated in construction. Note that verse 2 is an inserted remark. Having mentioned the "Word of life," John inserts this explanation before completing his main sentence. Verse 2 emphasizes that the testimony of John was based on his personal eyewitness of Jesus Christ.

We can summarize John's opening sentence this way: What we experienced with our senses concerning the Word of life, we proclaim also to you. We do this so that you may have fellowship with us and with the Father and with his Son Jesus Christ.

Expressions in 1:1 echo the opening verse of the Gospel of John (1:1). The subject in both instances is Christ. By using the word *we*, John associates himself with the disciples of Jesus, the "eyewitnesses and servants of the word" (Luke 1:2).

These people experienced the humanity of Jesus over a considerable period of time. They heard him speak and teach with their ears. They saw him with their eyes. They did more than just glance at the Christ; they observed him carefully. They personally touched him with their hands, even after the Resurrection (Luke 24:39). Jesus Christ was not a phantom. He was a living human being.

The Word of life can refer to Jesus or to the message of the gospel. Here it probably carries both meanings. The Christ was the Word. He was with God and was God. Both the Gospel of John and First John testify to the same truth about Christ.

John proclaimed the good news that through Christ individuals can be reconciled to God. Fellowship between people and God, both "the Father and . . . his Son, Jesus Christ" (v. 3) is possible. Fellowship among those who accept reconciliation is also possible.

When individuals are in Christ and Christ in them, they have reason for great happiness. The theme of joy fills the New Testament. Nothing made John happier than to hear that believers were following the truth (2 John 4; 3 John 3).

1 John 1:5–2:29. The testimony about Jesus Christ is the basis for the fellowship among believers and with God and Christ. But the fellowship is not without conditions. No one who is indifferent to sin can maintain the fellowship. In our outline above, we identified five conditions of fellowship covered in this section of the letter.

1 John 1:5-10. John indicates that he heard the truth about God "from him" (v. 5). *Him* obviously refers to Jesus. The truth is that God is light. The opposite of light is darkness. Light and darkness cannot exist in the same place, so there is no darkness whatsoever in God.

Light and darkness have long been used as images of truth and error, good and evil, righteousness and sin. John used these expressions frequently in the Gospel and in the letters

(John 1:5; 8:12; 12:35, 46; 1 John 2:8-9, 11). The Messiah was foreseen by Isaiah as "a great light" (Isaiah 9:2). In John's Gospel, Jesus is "the light [that] shines in the darkness" (John 1:5). He is the "true light that gives light to everyone" (1:9).

God provides illumination to help a believer find the way along the path of life. Anyone who claims to share in the eternal life provided by God through Christ, but walks in darkness (practices unrighteousness), is a liar.

John was likely thinking of the gnostic teachers here (1 John 1:6). They held that for the one who is enlightened by knowledge, one's moral conduct does not matter. To be saved, in the gnostic view, individuals needed mental illumination, not forgiveness. John calls sin, *sin*. One's walk, one's daily life, determines whether a person is walking in the light and in the fellowship.

The atoning blood of Jesus purifies in an ongoing process. Purifying requires the confession of sin. The person who will not or does not recognize sin and confess it cannot continue in fellowship with God, for the person makes God out to be a liar. God is light; that is, God is completely holy. Those who have fellowship with God must be holy too. God has made it possible for sinful individuals to be purified and made holy so that they can have fellowship with God.

Christians who walk in the light can see the way along which they are going, and they can constantly reaffirm, through confession and forgiveness, the fellowship they enjoy.

1 John 2:1-6. Sin hampers fellowship. Sin is rebellion against God's will. In 2:1, John indicates that another purpose of his letter is to help Christians deal with the problem of sin in their lives.

What John writes is in direct opposition to the gnostic view. Rather than seeing sin for what it is—evil—they saw it as a misfortune for which the individual was not really responsible. To Gnostics, knowledge of God was the real issue of life; and this knowledge was obtained through mental activity apart from the physical part of life. What the mind knew was essential; what the body did was unimportant.

Christian doctrine sees the problem of sin in both the mind and the flesh. Jesus said, "The things that come out of a person's mouth come from the heart [mind], and these defile them. For out of the heart come evil thoughts—murder, adultery, sexual immorality, theft, false testimony, slander" (Matthew 15:18-19). He also taught that as a person thinks, so is that person. Paul called on believers to "not conform to the pattern of this world, but be transformed by the renewing of your mind. Then you will be able to test and approve what God's will is—his good, pleasing and perfect will" (Romans 12:2).

So the Christian must not make sin (rebellion against God's commandments) a way of life. A person may slip and fall into sin along the road of life, however, threatening the fellowship with God. If that happens, the fellowship is not broken; for the committed believer has an advocate (defense attorney) before God. That advocate is Jesus Christ. He is called "the Righteous One" (1 John 2:1), reflecting the idea in Hebrews 4:14-16.

Jesus is also the atoning sacrifice for sins. That is, Jesus is the means by which all sins are forgiven. The just penalty of sin is death; and Hebrews 2:9 tells us that by the grace of God, Jesus tasted death for everyone.

One who is both a defense lawyer and the means by which our sins are forgiven is worth knowing. How can a person be assured of knowing Jesus Christ? A person can know Jesus Christ by keeping his commandments. Knowing and doing are identical, as far as John is concerned. This view is in line with the words of Jesus: "Why do you call me 'Lord, Lord' and do not do what I say?" (Luke 6:46).

To say "I know him" as the Gnostics did, and then to ignore Christ's commandments is to be a liar. To know Christ is to have fellowship with him. To obey him is to show love for God. Mature, complete love for God is shown by keeping God's word. Jesus is a perfect example of love for God and obedience to God's will. Walk in Jesus' footsteps; follow his example.

1 John 2:7-11. The "old command" (v. 7) is to love one another. Jesus taught that all the commandments are summed up in love of God and love for neighbor as oneself (Matthew 22:34-40). The "new command" is, "As I have loved you, so you must love one another" (John 13:34). Love is proven by sharing, as an expression of Christian fellowship. The darkness of sinfully hating and ignoring others who are in need is passing away. The light of the example of God's Son is shining. Jesus Christ gave his life for us out of love. Out of love we ought to share our life with others.

1 John 2:12-17. Those addressed by John in 2:12-14 include all groups of Christians in fellowship with God. Fellowship with God (knowing God) provides powerful benefits: forgiveness of sins, power to overcome the evil one, sustaining strength, and "the sword of the Spirit, which is the word of God" (Ephesians 6:17).

The testimony of the gospel is based on historical realities, not on the philosophical imaginings of would-be teachers like the Gnostics. John commends those in whom the Word of God remains. They will not be confused by the evil one, the devil.

All Christians who share in the benefits of fellowship with God are urged by John not to love the world. *World* does not refer to the natural creation; God considered that "very good" (Genesis 1:31). The word here refers to people who are governed by lusts, ambition, and jealousies. They are under the rule of the evil one (John 14:30) and in bondage to human desires. The world loves its own and hates God's own (John 15:19). The world is dominated by the three base motivations mentioned in 1 John 2:16. These motivations are not of God; they are of the evil one (5:19).

The world of selfish desires will pass away, but the person in fellowship with God, the Eternal One, will abide forever. That One has the eternal life John mentions in 1:2 and 2:25.

1 John 2:18-29. To continue in fellowship with God, God's Son, and God's people, believers need to be able to identify the antichrists and to remain in Christ. Since the last hour has arrived, these actions are essential.

Antichrist means one "against Christ, an opposer of Christ." One can oppose Christ by impersonating him, by teaching against him, or both. Jesus warned of those who would come in his name claiming to be Christ (Matthew 24:4-5). He also warned that many would be led astray in the last days.

In a real sense, the last hour occurs for each of us in our lifetime. Since time is measured in this life but not after this life, we all live in the last hour as far as our earthly existence is concerned. The time between death and the resurrection is, in that sense, but the twinkling of an eye.

These antichrists, surprisingly, were once a part of the fellowship (2:19). So the antichrists were not ungodly pagans. They were false teachers, along with their followers, who had arisen in the midst of the faithful. We assume John was speaking of the gnostic teachers.

These persons had been identified as apostates by their teachings. The false teachings are mentioned in 2:22-23a. They denied that Jesus is the Messiah, the Christ, the Anointed One of God. To deny the Son and his role as Messiah is to deny the Father, for God bore testimony to Jesus that he was God's Son (Luke 3:21-22; John 5:30-47).

The Gnostics claimed special knowledge of the truth, but they were really liars who denied the Son. Those believers to whom John wrote actually possessed the true testimony about Jesus (1 John 2:20-21). Further, they had the anointing of the Holy Spirit that Jesus promised the night before his crucifixion (John 15:26-27; 16:7-14).

All that the faithful believers were required to do was to remain in the truth that they had heard from the beginning (1 John 2:24). If they did this, then they would abide in Christ. The fellowship with God and Jesus Christ would remain unbroken throughout eternity.

To emphasize the fact that they had the truth and needed enlightenment from no one, especially from liars who did not have the truth, John repeated in 2:26-27 what he said in 2:18-25.

1 John 2:28-29. The last verses of our lesson appeal to the readers to remain in Christ. His coming is certain. The Second Coming has been an essential doctrine of Christianity from the very beginning of the church. The call is to remain in the fellowship with God, Jesus Christ, and the faithful followers like John. Those who do can have confidence at his appearing.

Some persons will be ashamed at Christ's coming. The ashamed will be those who did not remain in Christ but who believed the lies of the antichrists. To follow such teachings is to live a life of unrighteousness. Those who do right not only maintain the fellowship but also give living evidence that they are the children of God. To be "born of [God]" is a common expression in John's writings (John 1:13; 1 John 3:9; 4:7; 5:4, 18).

DIMENSION THREE:
WHAT DOES THE BIBLE MEAN TO ME?

1 John 2:6—Walk in the Footsteps of Jesus

A modern expression that is the equivalent of "to walk" is *lifestyle*. Our lifestyles are the expression of our beliefs about self, about others, about the world in which we live, and about spiritual realities. These ideas motivate us to do what we do in the ways that we do them.

For Christians who have believed the testimony of Scripture and the Christian witness of others, lifestyle ought to be determined by a sincere desire and effort to keep God's commandments. Jesus summed up the commandments with the word *love*. We are to love God with our total being and to love our neighbor as we love ourselves.

Exactly what this means in terms of the lifestyle of each of us will be determined by how we understand what Jesus did and taught. We cannot follow in his footsteps unless we trace them. We will have to be learners (disciples) to know how he thought about himself, others, the world, and spiritual realities. What we will look for in the incidents of the life of Jesus are examples of how to relate to God, others, and the world.

Then we must apply our understanding of Jesus' walk to the circumstances of our lives. This is a part of the adventure of living a Christian life. The process is ongoing and unique to each of us. We must be careful not to condemn one another, because each one's walk is unique. As we walk, we should do so with thanks that we have our defense attorney in the courts of heaven to justify us before God when we slip and fall along the way.

1 John 2:16—Lust and Pride

We need to explore the meaning of *lust*. The word was used in ancient times to mean "pleasure." By the time the Bible was translated into English, the word had developed the meaning we have today, "a strong desire to possess and enjoy," usually in a sexual sense.

Another way to gain a sense of the word in the context of 1 John 2:16, is to compare translations of the verse in several versions.

God created us with desires of the flesh that are not inherently evil. Without the sex drive, for example, there would be no human race. We are, however, to control and channel our natural desires. Paul stated it this way, "I strike a blow to my body and make it my slave so that after I have preached to others, I myself will not be disqualified for the prize" (1 Corinthians 9:27).

The renewing of our minds as Christians requires that we control what our eyes see. Jesus taught that if your eye causes you to sin, you should pluck it out and throw it away; it is better to enter eternal life with one eye than to be cast into the burning junk heap of eternity with both eyes (Matthew 18:9).

In the same chapter, Matthew recorded Jesus' words on humility (18:1-4). Humility is the opposite of pride. Whoever humbles himself or herself like a little child is the greatest in the kingdom of heaven. There is no place for overweening pride in the Christian. The Christian has been bought with a price and is not her or his own. Any praise goes to God.

Everyone who believes that Jesus is the Christ is born of God, and everyone who loves the father loves his child as well. (5:1)

11

FELLOWSHIP IN THE FAMILY OF GOD

1 John 3–5

DIMENSION ONE:
WHAT DOES THE BIBLE SAY?

Answer these questions by reading 1 John 3

1. What two things can God's children be sure of when Christ appears? (3:2b)

   We know that when Christ appears "we shall be like him" and "we shall see him as he is."

2. How can the children of God be distinguished from "the children of the devil"? (3:7-10)

   The children of God do right. "Children of the devil are: Anyone who does not do what is right" and "anyone who does not love their brother and sister."

3. In what practical way can Christians show love "with actions and in truth"? (3:17-18)

   A Christian who has material possessions can provide for a "brother or sister in need." That is love "with actions and in truth," not "with words or speech."

4. What are the two basic commands of God to Christians? (3:23)

   "This is his command: to believe in the name of his Son, Jesus Christ, and to love one another."

Answer these questions by reading 1 John 4

5. How can we determine who has the Spirit of God and who has the spirit of the antichrist? (4:2-3)

   Whoever has the Spirit of God "acknowledges that Jesus Christ has come in the flesh." Those who do not acknowledge Jesus have "the spirit of the antichrist."

6. What two things did God do that show God's love for us? (4:9-10)

   God showed love for us by sending "his one and only Son into the world that we might live through him" and by sending "his Son as an atoning sacrifice for our sins."

7. Why is love a valid test of the love a person has for God? (4:20-21)

   "Whoever claims to love God yet hates a brother or sister is a liar." The person who "does not love their brother and sister, whom they have seen, cannot love God, whom they have not seen."

Answer these questions by reading 1 John 5

8. What is the content of the faith that overcomes the world? (5:4-5)

   The faith that overcomes the world is the belief that "Jesus is the Son of God."

9. What three witnesses testify that God gave us eternal life in Jesus Christ? (5:6-8)

   "There are three that testify: the Spirit, the water and the blood; and the three are in agreement."

10. John describes the two types of sin. What does he call these two types? (5:16-17)

    John calls the two types: "sin that does not lead to death" and "sin that leads to death."

11. If "the whole world is under the control of the evil one," why is the one born of God not in the power of the evil one? (5:18-19)

    The one born of God is not in the power of the evil one because "anyone born of God (Jesus) does not continue to sin; . . . God keeps them safe, and the evil one cannot harm them."

12. Of what temptation in particular does John warn Christians at the end of his letter? (5:21)

    John warns Christians to keep themselves from idols.

DIMENSION TWO:
WHAT DOES THE BIBLE MEAN?

In our first lesson on First John, we discovered how the theme of *fellowship* ties the varied parts of the letter together in a loose way. The testimony of Jesus' apostles provides the basis for the fellowship. Although that much is clear from the opening verses of the letter, nothing in the letter gives any details on the testimony, except that Jesus was the Messiah (Christ) and that he came in the flesh. John assumes that his readers have the information about Jesus from the Gospel of John.

The Gospels do not give a complete history of Jesus, and each Gospel writer had a particular audience and purpose in mind when writing. While each is somewhat different from the other, together they give a composite picture of the main events in the life and ministry of Jesus.

John's Gospel is quite distinct from the Synoptic Gospels, the collective name used for Matthew, Mark, and Luke. (They are called *Synoptic* because they are fairly similar to one another.) Luke indicates that his Gospel was written for Theophilus (friend of God) "that you may know the certainty of the things you have been taught" (Luke 1:4). Luke also indicates that many others had undertaken to compile a narrative of the things that had been accomplished in relationship to Jesus (Luke 1:1).

John wrote his account for a specific purpose as well. He stated it this way: "Jesus performed many other signs in the presence of his disciples, which are not recorded in this book. But these are written that you may believe that Jesus is the Messiah, the Son of God, and that by believing you may have life in his name" (John 20:30-31). So the readers of the letter had heard the testimony, believed, and received that life in his name that is described as "eternal life" in 1 John 1:2.

The conditions of the fellowship "with the Father and with his Son, Jesus Christ" (1 John 1:3) were presented in lesson 10. To review briefly, they were (1) to walk in the light, (2) to walk in the footsteps of Jesus, (3) to pass the test of brotherly love, (4) to know God and keep God's commandments, and (5) to shun the antichrist and to remain in Christ. In this lesson, we will read of the fellowship described in terms of a family relationship. Toward the close of the letter, John spotlights a number of facets of the fellowship.

1 John 3:1-3. The opening verse of this section is filled with the sense of amazement and appreciation that John experienced as he thought about the relationship to God that he and other believers had in Jesus. They are called children of God because it is true.

This idea is a continuation of an expansion on the thought in 2:29, "You know that everyone who does what is right has been born of him." The word *born* means "begotten" in this context. John 1:12-13 helps explain this idea: "Yet to all who did receive him, to those who believed in his name, he gave the right to become children of God—children born not of natural descent, nor of human decision or a husband's will, but born of God."

Paul calls Christians "children of God" in Romans (8:14) and Galatians (3:26; 4:6-7) and "God's children" in Romans 8:16. Romans 8:14 is particularly helpful because it states that "those who are led by the Spirit of God are children of God." This statement agrees with 1 John 3:1, where it is clear that the blessing of being God's children comes at the initiative of God. And it agrees with John 1:12. To the one who receives Christ, that is, believes in his name, God gives power to become God's child. Later in First John, the readers are told that "everyone who believes that Jesus is the Christ is born of God" (5:1).

In 1 Peter 1:3, God is praised because "in his great mercy he has given us new birth into a living hope through the resurrection of Jesus Christ from the dead." This new birth is "not of perishable seed, but of imperishable, through the living and enduring word of God" (1 Peter 1:23). Again in 1 Peter 2:2, believers are urged "like newborn babies, [to] crave pure spiritual milk." Two other New Testament writers use related expressions. Titus 3:5b uses the word *renewal*, the equivalent of "new birth"; and in James 1:18, we read that "he chose to give us birth through the word of truth."

All these expressions are evidence of God's great love. The initiative has been God's from the beginning, "for God so loved the world that he gave his one and only Son, that whoever believes in him shall not perish but have eternal life" (John 3:16). God is not some uncaring deity who is so removed from the world that God has no concern for it, as some of the Gnostics would have it.

That the world did not recognize Jesus, in fact rejected him, was discussed by Jesus in the upper room (John 15:18–16:4a). He clearly indicated to his disciples that the world would hate them as it hated him.

In 1 John 3:2-3, John clarifies what it means to be a child of God. It is, first, a present reality. But this family relationship also has tremendous potential for the future. The future will bring the fulfillment of all that God has prepared for those who love God. The future will be realized when Jesus Christ appears again (as in 2:28). A certain mystery is involved in this, but believers can have confidence that they will be like him when he appears. Jesus Christ is the firstborn of God; believers are children of God by grace. The genetic relationship between the firstborn and the lately born will be evident when he appears: "we shall be like him" (v. 2). Since purity is a characteristic of the family of God, those who hope in Christ will purify themselves (by the cleansing blood, 1:7).

1 John 3:4-10. The "everyone" of 3:4 is the opposite of the "All" in 3:3. The Greek verb used here indicates the "habit of sinning" and "practice of sinning." It is the opposite of doing what is right (2:29).

"Sin is lawlessness" (v. 4). The Gnostics thought themselves above the moral law. They considered themselves enlightened, but they turned freedom into license. They claimed superior fellowship with God and taught as though they had authority. The Gnostics may have been those who said, "we have not sinned'" making God a liar (1:10). Lawlessness is disobedience to God's commandments, and that is sin. Perverting God's commandments is equivalent to disobeying them.

Jesus is the subject of 3:5. Second Corinthians 5:21, Hebrews 4:15, and 1 Peter 2:22 state clearly that Jesus was without sin. He came to take away sins. "He has appeared once for all at the culmination of the ages to do away with sin by the sacrifice of himself" (Hebrews 9:26b). Those who have received the testimony of the apostles have a relationship with Jesus that does not allow for living a life of sin. The family connection means that one who "lives in him" (v. 6) "must live as Jesus did" (2:6). The child of God practices doing right.

Devil is the English word for Greek *diabolos*, "accuser, slanderer." In the Greek version of the Old Testament, *diabolos* was used to translate the Hebrew *Satan*. In the New Testament, *devil* and *Satan* are essentially the same.

Jesus spoke of the devil as the enemy (Matthew 13:39), the evil one (Matthew 13:38), the prince of this world (John 14:30), a murderer, a liar, and the father of lies (John 8:44). We do not have a complete picture of the devil from Scripture. His origins as a rebellious, fallen angel are hinted at but not detailed in the Bible. He is the personification of the evil influences and activities in the world.

The devil has his offspring too (3:8, 10). They have their identifying characteristics. They practice sin, which is lawlessness. They do not practice righteousness. The children of the devil show their genetic relationship. The devil has sinned from the beginning. Sinning as a way of life is the major characteristic of those in Satan's family.

The main mark by which the children of God can be distinguished from the children of the devil is their deeds. Children of God do right and practice family love. Children of the devil sin and do not show unselfish love for others.

1 John 3:11-18. Verse 11 reminds us of 2:7-11. Love between members of the family of God is not an option; it is essential. The tone of the relationships in the family is set by the nature of God: God is love (4:8).

From the very beginning, family members were expected to love one another. In the first family, however, hatred, the opposite of love, lurked in the heart of Cain. He murdered his brother "because [Cain's] own actions were evil and his brother's were righteous" (3:12). Cain can be identified as a child of the devil by his murderous deed. As Jesus said, "By their fruit you will recognize them" (Matthew 7:16).

Cain's murder of Abel is another example of the way in which the world of sin and selfishness treats the children of God. A similar thought is expressed in 3:1c. The way of the world is death; it is passing away; it will die (2:17). In sharp contrast to the hatred and resulting murder that is the way of the world, the family of God has passed out of death into life (3:14). Eternal life is an essential part of the fellowship that John mentions at the beginning of the letter (1:2).

To love the other members of the family of God is to pass out of death into life. One who loves the world, of course, cannot love God (2:15) or the family of God. To fail to love the family is to remain in death, because the opposite of love is hate. Hate results in murder, either actual murder or that committed in the heart (Matthew 15:19). The hater/murderer cannot possess an abiding eternal life. Revelation 21:8 makes this fact even clearer: "Murderers . . . they will be consigned to the fiery lake of burning sulfur. This is the second death."

It is not enough for John to draw this sharp contrast between love and hate in general terms. He provides clear and specific teaching on what the true nature of love is (3:16-18). Earlier, as we noted, he indicated that one of the conditions of sharing in the fellowship is to walk in the same way that Jesus walked (2:6). Here he gives a specific example of what that requires. Jesus laid down his life for us. He suffered death on the cross on our behalf. We were in desperate need of forgiveness of sin; he satisfied that need. That deed of Jesus is a perfect definition of what the word *love* means.

Jesus acted selflessly, in sharp contrast to Cain, who acted selfishly. Love is selfless action to meet the need of another member of the family of God. This love requires a willingness to lay down one's life for the other. Here, one's life includes the "material possessions" (v. 17) that one has. That is easy to understand. A part of one's life is invested in obtaining the necessities of life.

One with material possessions acts selfishly when seeing a brother or sister in Christ in need and closing up the heart to compassion . That is the way the children of the devil act. The love of God abides in the hearts of God's children. True love is shown in deed and in truth, not in word or speech alone.

Examples from the early church of people who spoke but did not do are Ananias and Sapphira (Acts 5:1-11). They apparently pledged to give all the proceeds from the sale of a property into the common treasury of the Jerusalem church. This treasury was used to provide for the necessities of widows (Acts 6:1) and perhaps for the needs of others. Ananias and Sapphira acted selfishly, however, withholding some funds rather than giving all, as they had said.

1 John 3:19-24. The word *this* (v. 19) refers to loving "with actions and in truth" (v. 18). The believer who normally shows that kind of love can know that he or she "belong[s] to the truth" (v. 19). To belong to the truth includes accepting the testimony about God and Christ and accepting the validity that sincere believers are children of God.

Belonging to the truth is not a matter of guessing that one is in God's grace. To love in actions and in truth is proof positive that this is so. Faith rests not on feelings but on historical facts and the promises of God. God's promises can reassure a person if and when one's heart may condemn that person.

Faithful followers of Christ may be conscience stricken at times, knowing that, "If we claim we have not sinned, we make him out to be a liar and his word is not in us" (1:10). But even though the heart may condemn, God does not: "If we confess our sins, he is faithful and just and will forgive us our sins and purify us from all unrighteousness" (1:9).

In Hebrews 10:35, believers are encouraged: "So do not throw away your confidence; it will be richly rewarded." Paul assures Christians that "neither death nor life, neither angels nor demons, neither the present nor the future, nor any powers, neither height nor depth, nor anything else in all creation, will be able to separate us from the love of God that is in Christ Jesus our Lord" (Romans 8:38-39).

Believers ought to approach God confidently (1 John 3:21-22). The writer of Hebrews urged, "Let us then approach God's throne of grace with confidence, so that we may receive mercy and find grace to help us in our time of need" (4:16). Jesus taught his followers to approach God with the words "Our Father." Being a part of the family of God makes that possible. What the Christian asks will also reflect the family connection.

Sincere believers can have confidence in the abiding relationship that has been established by receiving the testimony. They can know that they abide in God by keeping God's commandments. Those commandments are summarized in 3:23. Believers can also know that God abides in the person of faith. God has given the Holy Spirit to them for this purpose.

This section has close connections with the discourse of Jesus to his disciples in the upper room on the night before his crucifixion. John 13:34 and 15:12-17 contain the commandment to love one another. John 14:15-26; 15:26-27; and 16:7-13 deal with the promised coming of the Holy Spirit.

The Holy Spirit came in power on the day of Pentecost (Acts 2:1-4). As a result, Peter preached to those present. He closed his sermon by urging them to repent and be baptized for the forgiveness of sins. They were then to receive the gift of the Holy Spirit (Acts 2:38). The Holy Spirit is the indwelling presence of God in the lives of God's children.

Another way of expressing God's presence in the lives of believers is "Christ in you" (Colossians 1:27). Paul also spoke of the body of Christians as "temples of the Holy Spirit" (1 Corinthians 6:19). At the same time, he could speak of being "in Christ" (2 Corinthians 5:17).

This mutual abiding is another way to express the idea of the fellowship that exists for those in the family of God. The indwelling presence of the Spirit blesses believers with assurance.

1 John 4:1-6. The mention of the Spirit in 3:24 opens the way for John to warn about false teachers. The false prophets (teachers) have gone out into the world (from the church). They were the same as the antichrists mentioned in 2:18-20. They had gone out of the church, but they were apparently still teaching and preaching in the region.

John insists that God's children test the spirits. The way to discern between teachers who have the Spirit of God and those who have false spirits is simple. Those who confess that Jesus Christ was a fully human person have the Spirit of God. Those who do not confess the historical reality of Jesus as "a man accredited by God to you by miracles, wonders and signs, which God did among you through him" (Acts 2:22) are not of God. Those who teach that the Christ-Spirit descended on an already existing man, like the Gnostics teach, do not confess the historical Jesus. They are "the spirit of antichrist" (1 John 4:3).

John's readers are a part of the family of God (v. 4). They have fellowship "with the Father and with his Son, Jesus Christ" (1:3). Jesus said, "In this world you will have trouble. But take heart! I have overcome the world" (John 16:33). God's faithful children share in the family victory over the false teachers.

The false teachers are of the world. The source of their teaching is "the one who is in the world" (1 John 4:4). Naturally the worldly minded would be drawn to them. But God's children share God's Spirit. They listen to "us" (v. 6), the apostolic witness. They can discern between the two spirits.

1 John 4:7–5:21. John never tires of discussing the subject of love. Knowing the correct doctrine is one thing, but it is not enough. Correct doctrine without the inspiration and warmth of love can be very unattractive.

1 John 4:7-21. God is the source of the love that a Christian is to reflect in life. Love comes from God; God is love. That God is love is shown by the evidence of God's love for individuals (vv. 9-10). These verses reflect the truths found also in John 3:16.

A major facet of the fellowship, then, is love. Because God is love, God's children ought also to love. As John states later, 'We love because he first loved us" (4:19).

First John 4:12 expresses the same idea in almost the identical words of John 1:18: "No one has ever seen God, but the one and only Son, who is himself God and is in closest relationship with the Father, has made him known." Jesus said, "Anyone who has seen me has seen the Father"

(John 14:9b). The idea in our verse is probably this, however: God is invisible. You cannot expect to see the invisible God abiding in a person. The evidence of God abiding in a person is the presence of love in that person, since God's nature is love. When we love one another, love exists as God intended it to be.

John returns in 4:13 to the subject of the Holy Spirit, as in 3:24. By the power of the Holy Spirit within them, the apostles testified to what they had seen. They had not seen God, but they witnessed that God sent Jesus as the Savior of the world. The persons who accept and confess that testimony have the basis for a lasting relationship with God (4:14-15).

The family relationship of God's children to God is again highlighted in 4:16. The love of God is both an experience ("know") and a matter of faith ("rely on"). A result of the perfection of love within a child of God is confidence. The Day of Judgment is not to be feared by Christians. You have no need to fear punishment when you possess the very nature of the Judge: love. Perfect love harbors no suspicion and no dread (1 Corinthians 13).

The perfection of God's love in believers is shown by their love for the other members of the family of God (1 John 4:19-21). We have no option on whether or not to love the other members of the family. Love for one another is commanded. From this we can see that love is not an emotion; it is an action. Love is not expressed by how one feels toward another; it is expressed in deed and in truth (3:18).

1 John 5:1-5. Faith and love have a vital relationship. The word *everyone* in verse 1 leaves no room for exceptions. Faith in Jesus as both the Christ and the Son of God (v. 5) is the basis for being a part of the family of God. It is not enough to believe only that he is the Messiah foretold in the Old Testament. Nor is it enough to believe only in his divine nature. Belief in both is necessary.

Jesus testified that he had overcome the world. Those who are a part of God's family have also overcome the world. The world is that selfish way of thinking and living that is the opposite of loving the children of God and meeting their needs. Christians are engaged in spiritual warfare against worldly ideas and practices. Properly outfitted (Ephesians 6:10-17), victory is certain. Faith is a shield that can quench all the flaming darts of the ruler of this world, the evil one.

1 John 5:6-12. The power to overcome the world comes by faith in Jesus, the Son of God. Three witnesses provide a basis for faith in Jesus Christ: the water (of his baptism, John 1:19-34), the blood (of his atonement, John 19:34), and the Spirit (of truth, John 15:26). The ministry of Jesus began with his baptism, which was marked by the coming of the Holy Spirit on him. At the cross, blood and water gushed forth when the spear was thrust into his side. "It is finished," Jesus said (John 19:30). The water and the blood testify to the humanity of Jesus, against the gnostic teachers. The Holy Spirit bore witness that Jesus was from God, for no one could do the things Jesus did unless God was with him.

God has testified through God's power in the life of Jesus. God has also provided the testimony of eyewitnesses like John. The one who believes also has the testimony within. The eternal life that God gives to the person of faith is a living testimony to the truth of the gospel. Their testimony is something akin to what Paul said of the Christians in Corinth: "You yourselves are our letter, written on our hearts, known and read by everyone" (2 Corinthians 3:2).

1 John 5:13-21. Verse 13 echoes the main ideas in 1:1-4. Those to whom John wrote had believed the apostolic testimony. That testimony was rooted in the witness of God. The apostolic testimony was the testimony of believers in God. It was the source of eternal life, the fellowship with God "the Father and with his Son, Jesus Christ" (1:3b).

John wants his readers to be confident of this fellowship. That confidence is expressed in an active prayer life. God's children, of course, will ask according to the will of God (Matthew 6:10). They will pray for one another. The prayer of a righteous person has great power in its effects. The prayer of faith will save the sick, and if that person has committed sins, they will be forgiven (James 5:13-16).

John mentions sin that is beyond the power of prayer but does not give a description by which such a sin can be identified. Perhaps this is the sin against the Holy Spirit about which Jesus taught (Mark 3:29). The human heart can harden. People can live in such a state of sin that they call evil good and good evil (Isaiah 5:20). Or, John may have in mind the apostate, as in Hebrews 6:4-6.

But John is confident that among his beloved readers are only those who are in the family of God, and they have overcome the world and the evil one. They do not practice sin (5:18-19). John's confidence in God's children is based on the fact that they have received his testimony about God and Jesus Christ. He and they know the truth about Jesus. They understand and have no need of instruction from false prophets. John and his readers experience a fellowship with God and God's Son Jesus Christ, which can be described only as eternal life (5:20).

An idol is any substitute for the true God. An idol can even be the false ideas about God that the gnostic teachers held. They worshiped a creation of their own imaginations rather than the true God, whom the only Son made known. The closing thought of the aged apostle: Be on your guard against every false god.

DIMENSION THREE:
WHAT DOES THE BIBLE MEAN TO ME?

1 John 3:17-18—Help for Human Needs

The question posed in the participant book is a difficult problem that each Christian has to resolve in good conscience. Here are some ideas to explore in thinking about the problem:

1. We have a primary responsibility to meet the needs of those God has placed in our immediate care. "Anyone who does not provide for their relatives, and especially for their own household, has denied the faith and is worse than an unbeliever" (1 Timothy 5:8).

2. A distinction ought to be made between *needs* and *desires*. Living in an affluent society, Christians can easily convince themselves to spend all their resources for their or their family's desires, leaving nothing to meet the needs of others.

3. Paul gave instructions: "As we have opportunity, let us do good to all people, especially to those who belong to the family of believers" (Galatians 6:10).

4. Those who have an opportunity to work and are able to work ought to do so and "not be dependent on anybody" (1 Thessalonians 4:11-12).

Response to First John

The following ideas in First John increased my joy in Christ and my appreciation of God:

1. We are, in fact, the children of God (3:1);

2. We shall be like Christ when he appears (3:2);

3. Remaining in God (2:24-27): how important this idea was to John; how important remaining in God is to me;

4. I can overcome the world, every worldly tendency that threatens my ability to act in love (5:4);

5. John has given me an example of what, by God's grace, I can be as an elderly person.

Encourage participants to share with one another the messages from First John that have spoken to them.

[T]his is love, that we walk in obedience to his commands. (2 John 6)

12

TWO PERSONAL LETTERS FROM JOHN

2 John and 3 John

DIMENSION ONE: WHAT DOES THE BIBLE SAY?

Answer these questions by reading Second John

1. How does the writer identify himself? (v. 1)

    The writer calls himself "the elder."

2. Identify the main word used by the writer in the salutation. (vv. 1-3)

    The main word used in the salutation is truth.

3. Why was the author joyful about news he received concerning the "lady chosen by God and . . . her children"? (v. 4)

    He was joyful because he found that some of them were following the truth, "just as the Father commanded us."

4. Above all else, what did the writer want the readers to do? (vv. 5-6)

    He wanted the readers to "love one another," which is following Jesus' commands.

5. What is the identifying mark of a deceiver and the antichrist? (v. 7)

    The deceivers and antichrist "do not acknowledge Jesus Christ as coming in the flesh."

6. Why shouldn't a Christian receive into the house nor greet someone who does not continue in the teachings of Christ? (vv. 10-11)

   To do so would be to share in "their wicked work."

7. Why is this letter so short? (v. 12)

   The elder hopes to talk to the chosen lady face to face.

Answer these questions by reading Third John

8. How did the elder know that all was well with the soul of Gaius? (vv. 2-3)

   The elder knew that it was well with the soul of Gaius because some believers arrived and testified to the truth of his life.

9. In the elder's opinion, what is an especially worthy thing for a Christian to do? (vv. 5-6)

   It is a loyal thing to render any service "for the brothers and sisters, even though they are strangers" and "to send them on their way" in God's service.

10. What specific things did Diotrephes do that the elder condemned? (vv. 9-10)

    Diotrephes (1) liked to put himself first, (2) did not acknowledge the authority of the elder, (3) gossiped maliciously against the elder, (4) refused "to welcome other believers," (5) stopped those who wanted to welcome them, and (6) put those who wanted to welcome the believers out of the church.

11. Why did the elder commend Demetrius? (v. 12)

    The elder commended Demetrius because everyone, including the elder, spoke well of him.

12. Why is the elder's letter to Gaius so brief? (vv. 13-14)

    The elder hoped to see him "face to face."

DIMENSION TWO:
WHAT DOES THE BIBLE MEAN?

Before we investigate the text of Second John and Third John, we will look at the relationship of the two letters to First John. Then we will note the similarities and differences between letters two and three.

The Writer. We discussed the authorship of First John in lesson 10. There we concluded that the writer of the letter was likely the writer of the Gospel of John also. This opinion is held by many scholars who have investigated the letters in great detail.

The writer of the Gospel of John did not name himself, and neither did the writer of First John. From hints within the text of the Gospel, however, it seems evident that "the disciple whom he [Jesus] loved" (John 19:26) was the writer. He has been identified as John, the son of Zebedee.

First John contains many similarities to the Gospel of John. The vocabulary, the style, and several of the emphases are alike. That is why the apostle John is also believed to be the writer of First John.

The writer of Second John and Third John did not name himself either. He used the word *elder* in referring to himself. The question is, does the elder refer to the apostle John or to some other person?

The word *elder* means an "older person." In Bible times, the elders of a community were respected and honored for their wise counsel and leadership. So the word *elder* came to have an overtone of dignity and authority.

A council of elders guided each Israelite community. In Numbers 11:16, God instructs Moses, "Bring me seventy of Israel's elders who are known to you as leaders and officials among the people."

Israelite elders are mentioned in Joshua 24:31. When Boaz arranged to marry Ruth, ten of the elders of Bethlehem were witnesses to the proceedings (Ruth 4).

In Jesus' time, a great council of elders called the Sanhedrin controlled the religious affairs of the Jews in Jerusalem. Wherever Jewish synagogues were built, the elders of the communities had the chief seats of honor (Matthew 23:6; Luke 11:43). It is likely that the "leaders of the synagogue" in Acts 13:15 were a group of elders.

A similar pattern of leadership was used in the early church. The church in Jerusalem was first guided by the apostles and elders (Acts 11:30; 15:2, 4, 6, 22-23; 16:4; 21:18). Paul and Barnabas appointed elders in the churches that they established on their first missionary journey (Acts 14:23). Christian elders are mentioned in Paul's letters to Timothy and Titus. The title also appears in James and in First Peter. In Revelation 4:4, elders are pictured in heaven, seated around the throne of God.

Would John the apostle have called himself "the elder"? It's quite likely. We know that in First Peter 5:1, the expression *fellow elder* is used of Peter. According to tradition, John was the last survivor of the apostles. He may have lived as late as the end of the first-century AD. The same tradition places him as a leader in the church in Ephesus during the latter part of his life, so he would have been an elder in both senses of the word: in age and in authority.

If the apostle John was not the elder and the writer of the letters attributed to him, then another John, a church leader (elder), might have written them. But the tradition appeared early that the letters and the Gospel were written by John in Ephesus when he was an old man. Irenaeus, who died about AD 200, reported that when he was just a boy he heard from the lips of Polycarp, bishop of Smyrna, about John in Ephesus. (Polycarp lived from about AD 69 to AD 155.)

First, Second, and Third John are similar in style and expression. They express different emphases because they were written for different purposes. Second and Third John are applied to particular situations. The interweaving of expressions, style, and somewhat of content suggests that the same person wrote all three letters.

Date of Second John and Third John. First John seems to reflect expressions and ideas found in the Gospel of John. The Gospel was probably written toward the end of the first-century AD. Then followed the letters, but we do not know in what order they were written. They are arranged in the present order on the basis of length and relationship to the longest letter. In other words, the content of Second John is more closely related to First John than Third John, so Second John follows the longest letter.

Concerns of Second John. This letter is a brief, personal note "to the lady chosen by God and to her children." The purpose of the letter is to encourage the readers to be ruled by love. Love is equivalent to following the commandments of God. The letter also has a warning to be careful not to assist deceivers by providing them with hospitality.

Outline of Second John

I. Salutation (1-3)
II. Follow truth and love (4-6)
III. Beware false teachers (7-11)
IV. Conclusion (12-13)

2 John 1-3. We do not know where the writer was when he wrote, but we propose that it was Ephesus. The basis for that proposal is simply tradition.

We also do not know to what place the letter was sent. The letter is addressed "to the lady chosen by God and to her children," but the writer gives no indication of where they were living. Some suggestions of the letter's first destination are Rome, Ephesus, or the Roman province of Asia.

Many interpreters understand the *lady chosen by God* to refer to an excellent lady of upper social rank and superior character who supported the church with her wealth and influence. The expression may, however, refer to a church rather than an individual. Or, it may refer to the church at large. The letter was understood as a general letter to the churches, which is the reason it is in the group called the General Letters (Hebrews, James, First and Second Peter, First, Second, and Third John, and Jude). But more likely than simply being addressed to the church at large is the view that it was addressed to the churches in a particular region.

That the letter is addressed to a church or churches rather than a person also seems likely because of some statements within the letter. In verse 13, mention is made of a chosen sister. The children of the chosen sister, rather than the sister herself, send greetings. In verse 4, reference is made to "some of your children walking in the truth." That sounds like a church in which some members remain steadfast while others stray rather than a close-knit Middle Eastern family.

The use of female imagery to represent God's people Israel is well-known in the Bible, as in Jeremiah 31:21c, for example, where the nation is called "O Virgin Israel." In Revelation 18 and 19, both the church and its enemy (Babylon) are depicted as women.

The word *chosen* is used in the New Testament to refer to Christians. Paul asked, "Who will bring any charge against those whom God has chosen?" (Romans 8:33). First Peter 1:2 uses the expression "chosen according to the foreknowledge of God the Father." The King James Version translates that phrase "elect according to the foreknowledge of God the Father." And in 2 Peter 1:10, believers are urged to "make every effort to confirm your calling and election."

For our study, then, we will assume that the letter was written to a church whose members were thought of as children by John. This assumption is in line with his frequent expression "dear children" in these letters, even when it is clear that he is writing to adults. Although written to a church, the letter was intended for circulation to other churches, because it was not addressed to a particular church in a particular place.

John loved the church "in the truth." The phrase may mean "truly," indicating in reality or in a genuine manner. The phrase can also be understood as "in the truth" of God revealed in Christ Jesus. John loved those to whom he wrote because they shared that truth. To love in the truth, then, is to love those who have heard and obeyed the truth. They are the members of the household of faith.

John was not the only one who loved the church—the chosen lady—but all those who knew the truth loved her. Every sincere Christian loves the church because it is the body of Christ. To love the church is to follow in the footsteps of Jesus, who "loved the church and gave himself up for her" (Ephesians 5:25).

This truth that motivated John's love and the love of all others for the church lives in believers and will remain with them forever. In 1 John 2:14b, the word of God is described as that which "lives in you." Jesus taught, "If you remain in me and my words remain in you, ask whatever you wish, and it will be done for you" (John 15:7). The enduring nature of the truth and those in the truth is emphasized in 1 John 2:17: "The world and its desires pass away, but whoever does the will of God lives forever."

John assures his readers that "grace, mercy and peace . . . will be with us" (2 John 3), both readers and writer. He uses a form of the greeting found in most New Testament letters. Usually, only *grace* and *peace* are used. Sometimes one or both of the usual expressions are joined to *love* or *mercy*. Verse 3 is the only place in the writings of John where *mercy* is used. The word *grace* is used in the writings of John only here and in the beginning of the Gospel (John 1:14, 16, 17). *Peace* is found here, in 3 John 14b, and in the sections of the Gospel that deal with the Last Supper and the Resurrection (John 14:27; 16:33; 20:19, 21, 26).

The source of grace, mercy, and peace is "God the Father and . . . Jesus Christ, the Father's Son" (2 John 3). *Grace* is the free gift of salvation and God's favor, as in John 3:16. *Mercy* is God's willingness to forgive all sins and trespasses because the penalty of sin (death) has been paid by "Jesus Christ the Father's Son." *Peace* is the result of the mercy and grace of God and of

Jesus Christ. When we are reconciled to God through Jesus Christ, "the peace of God, which transcends all understanding" (Philippians 4:7) is ours.

2 John 4-6. John was joyful because he found that some of the Christians to whom he was writing followed the truth. We do not know how he found this out. It may have been during a personal visit sometime in the past. We can assume that John visited churches as did Paul. It could be that he heard about their faithful Christian walk from a visitor from the congregation. Or he could have received a letter from them.

John was joyful because these "children" were following the truth. They were living life in an authentic way, living honestly before God and others. God had so commanded his children: "Whoever claims to live in him must walk as Jesus did. Dear friends, I am not writing you a new command but an old one, which you have had since the beginning. This old command is the message you have heard" (1 John 2:6-7).

That command is to love one another. Jesus said, "My command is this: Love each other as I have loved you. Greater love has no one than this: to lay down one's life for one's friends. You are my friends if you do what I command" (John 15:12-14). First Peter 1:22 urges, "Love one another deeply, from the heart."

John's joy must have been reduced somewhat because only "some of your children" (v. 4) were following the truth. In the context, it seems evident that those who were not following the truth were not walking in love. The true measure of love is following Jesus' commandments. Although "commands" is in the plural (v. 6) rather than the singular form, they all can be covered by the word *love*. To follow Jesus' commands is to follow the way of love. Love was the message of Jesus from the beginning of his ministry, and it remains the core of true Christian teaching. "Whoever says 'I know him,' but does not do what he commands is a liar, and the truth is not in that person" (1 John 2:4).

2 John 7-11. Apparently some of the chosen lady's children were not following the truth. They were either among the deceivers or were deceived by them. The warning about these deceivers is identical to that in 1 John 2:18-27 and 4:1-6. The word *deceivers* denotes "wandering, roving." Instead of following love, these deceivers have "gone out into the world" (v. 7). First John 4:1 also emphasizes that "many false prophets have gone out into the world."

First John 2:18-19 points out that "many antichrists have come. . . . They went out from us, but they did not really belong to us. For if they had belonged to us, they would have remained with us; but their going showed that none of them belonged to us."

The deceivers were in the company of the believers, but they went out into the world. They departed from the company of the faithful. They left the church because that they would not acknowledge the coming of Jesus Christ in the flesh.

The deceivers did not reject the second coming of Christ. They rejected the Incarnation, the humanity of Jesus. Again, this is similar to 1 John 4:2. These heretical teachings were a part of Gnosticism. Gnostics taught that the Christ did not actually come in the flesh; he only seemed to do so. The gnostic philosophy held that matter was evil and spirit was good. The good Messiah, then, would never have stooped to taking on evil flesh, for flesh is matter. This view undercuts the atoning death of Jesus and makes the Resurrection unnecessary.

To the Gnostics, salvation came through secret knowledge. The knowledge was available only to those who would seek it from special teachers who possessed it. Salvation was by knowledge rather than by faith through the grace of God. Such teaching undercut the historical foundations of the gospel. It transformed the gospel for all into the privilege of the few.

With antichrists like this, who had gone out of the congregation, but who apparently still had contact with some of the congregation, more believers were in danger of being deceived by the deceivers. John therefore warns his readers: "Watch out that you do not lose what we have worked for" (v. 8). The idea is that they should not be gullible. They should watch so that they are not taken in by the false teaching of the deceivers.

Anyone who follows this new, deceptive teaching will lose the reward. That person will be going ahead, away from the doctrine of Christ. That person, desiring to be with God, will be without God. Instead of the full reward that the faithful follower of truth and love will receive, the person who follows the antichrist will lose all that the apostles of Jesus worked for and all that the individual hopes for.

The correct teaching is the way of love and truth. That way acknowledges the doctrine of Christ. He has come in the flesh. This doctrine is so true and so essential that hospitality must not be shown to anyone who comes to you without this truth.

The persons who might come to the church and be offered hospitality were wandering prophets and teachers. Congregations in the early days of the church met in homes, and Christian teachers who were passing through were housed and fed by the young congregations. The visitors would teach in return for their room and board. From this letter, we can see that in the latter part of the first Christian century some of these traveling teachers were deceivers. John warns his readers against such antichrists. To offer them hospitality would be to share in their wicked work.

2 John 12-13. The writer had used up approximately one sheet of papyrus, the paper of the day, for his letter. He chose not to write a longer letter. Instead, he hoped to visit his readers soon. And although he had considerable joy when he heard of the faithful who followed the truth (v. 4), there would be greater joy for visitor and visited when he could "talk with you face to face" (v. 12).

The last verse of the letter suggests that the greeting is from the church of which the writer was a part. The greeting is from the "children" of the chosen sister. Both they and the "children" of the receiving congregation are the chosen.

The Third Letter of John. We have discussed the date and authorship of Third John above. Second John and Third John have several similarities. For example, the openings of the letters use expressions that are alike. But Third John is written to an individual and is more personal than First John or Second John.

Gaius may have had a church in his house. While John expresses interest in Gaius as a friend, the main concern of the letter is that Christian visitors to the church be shown appropriate hospitality. Diotrephes is condemned for failing to do this. However, Demetrius is commended for doing good. This may imply that Demetrius is a model of a Christian host to visiting preachers and teachers.

Outline of Third John

I. Salutation (1-4)

II. In praise of Gaius (5-8)

III. Warning against Diotrephes (9-10)

IV. Commendation for Demetrius (11-12)

V. Conclusion (13-14)

3 John 1-4. We do not know who Gaius was. Three of Paul's friends were named Gaius: Gaius of Corinth (1 Corinthians 1:14), Gaius of Macedonia (Acts 19:29), and Gaius of Derbe (Acts 20:4). The name seems to have been a popular one.

Just as in Second John, the one or ones receiving the letter are dear to the writer. John loves all who are followers of the truth.

John expresses a prayerful wish that Gaius will prosper in body as he has in spirit. To be in Christ is to be spiritually made whole. John had heard from visiting believers that Gaius was flourishing spiritually. He was following the truth. And, as in 2 John 4, the writer could not have heard news that would make him happier. John had the heart of a Christian shepherd.

3 John 5-8. John addresses Gaius as a *dear friend*. Gaius was a dear friend because he acted loyally toward visiting missionary-teachers, and that was exactly what John wanted Christians to do. Of course, as we have seen in Second John, those who were to be shown hospitality were loyal to Christ and not deceivers.

Gaius is commended because he was hospitable even though the visiting teachers were strangers. John knew about Gaius's loyalty to traveling Christian teachers because some of them had visited John. They had told (the church in Ephesus) of Gaius's helpful care when they visited him.

The writer commends Gaius for such service. Not only was it the right thing to do, but it was also good to "send them on their way" (v. 6). This means that Gaius was to provide the travelers with what they needed for the journey to their next stop. The idea appears also in Acts 15:3; Romans 15:24; 1 Corinthians 16:6, 11; 2 Corinthians 1:16; Titus 3:13.

Christians should support those in God's service in this way. Christian workers should not have to seek support from nonbelievers. Those Christians who are hospitable toward brothers and sisters in Christ who are traveling in God's service are counted as fellow workers in the truth. The truth, of course, is the truth of the gospel message of salvation through Jesus Christ.

3 John 9-10. John had written a letter to a church, but we do not know what he wrote. Diotrephes was apparently a leader in that church. He did not accept the authority of John in the matter with which the letter dealt. In other words, Diotrephes sought to put himself first in authority over the church.

Besides failing to acknowledge the authority of John, Diotrephes refused to show hospitality to "the believers." These may have been traveling teachers sent by John. This would have been another rejection of John's authority. Diotrephes also refused to permit other Christians in the church in which he was a leader to show hospitality to the visitors. Those who did show such hospitality Diotrephes excommunicated from the congregation. These were extremely highhanded actions.

John did not accuse Diotrephes of being a deceiver. The charge was not acknowledging proper authority.

Apparently Gaius was a member of the congregation over which Diotrephes put himself first, or Gaius knew the people and the circumstances. Since John wrote to Gaius and commended his hospitality, Gaius may have been one of those put out of the church by Diotrephes.

John hoped to visit the church. On the proposed visit, he planned to address both issues: what Diotrephes was doing (in refusing hospitality to visiting missionary teachers) and what Diotrephes was saying against John. Gossiping is "malicious nonsense" (v. 10). While these activities are not uplifting at any time, Diotrephes worsened them by what he gossiped about. He slandered the faithful witnesses.

3 John 11-12. Again the writer addresses Gaius with the familiar expression of endearment, *dear friend*. He urges Gaius not to imitate the evil that is so evident in the deeds and words of Diotrephes. Rather, Gaius should imitate good.

Just as Diotrephes was an example of evil, John had an example of good ready at hand. We know nothing of Demetrius other than what John testifies about him in this letter. But Demetrius had the testimony of "everyone," including the writer, that he was good; he also had testimony from "the truth itself" (v. 12). This last testimony is probably the testimony of his life and witness, based on the saving truth that made him a Christian. In other words, his life was a true testimony to his goodness.

Gaius probably did not know Demetrius. He may have been the visiting missionary who carried the letter from John to Gaius. John urged Gaius to receive Demetrius. Diotrephes would not have done so. But Gaius had established a reputation as a faithful host to God's traveling servants. He had been a fellow worker in the truth with others in times past (v. 8), and now Gaius had the opportunity to host the good Demetrius in the face of the opposition and example of Diotrephes.

3 John 13-14. As in 2 John 12, the writer explains why the letter is not long; he hopes to visit Gaius and to speak with him face to face. In light of the letter, one of the topics that would be discussed further probably was the case of Diotrephes.

"Peace to you" (v. 13) is patterned after the Hebrew *shalom*, which can serve as either a greeting or a farewell.

This letter to Gaius was written by a man who had a circle of supporters whom he called friends. They also sent their greetings to Gaius. They would have known the problem that the writer addressed in the letter. There were a group of disciples like Gaius in his community. They would have counted John and his friends as their friends. They likely were hospitable to traveling teachers and evangelists, as was Gaius.

DIMENSION THREE: WHAT DOES THE BIBLE MEAN TO ME?

2 John 7-9—The Doctrine of Christ: The Coming of Jesus in the Flesh

What we believe about Jesus may have two sources: (1) We may absorb the ideas and viewpoints of other, usually older, Christians. Then the ideas we absorb may be modified by our experiences. (2) We may go back to the historical source of our faith in Jesus, the Gospel accounts and the apostolic teaching concerning Jesus. As we mature, we need to lean less on what others tell us about Jesus and more on the biblical testimony and our personal exploration and understanding of the Bible as the basis for what we believe.

That our Savior was fully human is an essential doctrine of the Christian faith. As we noted in Hebrews 2:17-18, because Jesus was tempted in every respect as we have been, he is able to help those who are tempted. His atoning death was a genuine suffering on our behalf. It was not an illusion perpetrated on unsuspecting humans by God.

We have "new birth into a living hope through the resurrection of Jesus Christ from the dead" (1 Peter 1:3b). If Jesus had not really come in the flesh, the Resurrection would not be a reality for us. John assured his readers that he had touched the human Jesus. Jesus was no phantom (1 John 1:1).

As the truth about Jesus is the basis for our individual salvation, so it is the basis for the existence of the church. The survival of the church depends on the testimony of the eyewitnesses to the gospel events being transmitted faithfully from one generation to the next.

3 John 5-7—Christian Hospitality

Hospitality practices vary from region to region. One tendency in modern American society that hinders easy hospitality is the sense that our homes must be show places when we have guests. Yet the greatest benefit that guests and hosts alike derive from hospitality is the personal contact, the fellowship of kindred souls. The experience of sharing food and faith will be remembered by our guests long after any details or our housekeeping skills have faded from the memory. As Christians, we should learn to appreciate one another for what we are rather than what we have. Our homes are not hotels. Nor are they to be facades of economic status. They are to reflect our love for Christ and for one another as members of the family of God.

The local church should make every effort to encourage the members to be hospitable to visiting Christians. Often traveling choirs, youth groups, and visiting missionaries need hospitality. Opening your church doors or even homes to these visiting groups is a way to show Christian hospitality and to encourage and support the work of others for God's kingdom.

But you, dear friends, build yourselves up in your most holy faith . . ., keep yourselves in God's love. (Jude 20-21)

13

THE BOOK OF JUDE

Jude 1-25

DIMENSION ONE: WHAT DOES THE BIBLE SAY?

Answer these questions by reading Jude.

1. How does Jude describe his relationship to Jesus and to James? (v. 1)

Jude is "a servant of Jesus Christ and a brother of James."

2. What three words describe the people to whom Jude writes? (v. 1)

They are called, loved, and kept.

3. What three blessings does Jude pray for his readers? (v. 2)

He prays that they will have mercy, peace, and love.

4. What is the specific reason Jude writes to his Christian readers? (v. 3)

He writes to appeal to them "to contend for the faith that was once for all entrusted to God's holy people."

5. What two actions are the godless persons guilty of? (v. 4)

The godless persons are guilty of perverting the grace of God into immorality, and they are guilty of denying Christ.

6. In verses 5-7, Jude reminds his readers of God's judgment on three groups who were unbelieving and immoral. Who are these groups?

    The three groups are: (1) those God saved out of Egypt who did not believe, (2) the angels who abandoned their proper dwelling, and (3) the people of Sodom and Gomorrah.

7. The people mentioned in verse 8 are guilty of three acts worthy of condemnation. List those acts.

    They "pollute their own bodies, reject authority and heap abuse on celestial beings."

8. What act have these people committed that even Michael the archangel would not commit? (vv. 9-10)

    They have reviled "whatever they do not understand."

9. What examples from nature does Jude use to describe the people he condemns? (vv. 12-13)

    He describes them as waterless clouds, fruitless trees, wild waves of the sea, and wandering stars.

10. According to Enoch, why is the Lord to execute judgment on the godless? (vv. 14-16)

    The Lord is coming to judge the godless for their acts and for their harsh words "spoken against him."

11. Of what particular prediction of the apostles does Jude remind his readers? (vv. 17-18)

    He reminds them that the apostles said, "In the last times there will be scoffers who will follow their own ungodly desires."

12. What action words does Jude use to urge his readers on in the faith? (vv. 20-21)

    He urges them to build themselves up, pray, keep themselves in the love of God, and wait for mercy.

13. What actions does Jude recommend toward weak Christians? (vv. 22-23)

    He urges his readers to save some and to have mercy on some.

DIMENSION TWO:
WHAT DOES THE BIBLE MEAN?

Jude is the last of the General Letters and reflects the general characteristics of the works we have been studying. Jude shows a concern for the spiritual health of the early church. Whenever anything genuine appears, a substitute usually follows, claiming to be better than the original. Spiritually speaking, this describes the situation that brought forth this letter.

Ungodly people had joined the church. They were corrupting the morals of many in the church, and they were teaching false and unscriptural doctrines. Jude offers guidance for dealing with these godless people.

Writer and Date. The writer identifies himself as "Jude, a servant of Jesus Christ and a brother of James" (v. 1). Jesus had a brother named Jude (Judas) and another named James (Matthew 13:55). The brothers of Jesus did not accept him as the Messiah during his ministry (Matthew 13:57; Mark 6:4). Yet, after Jesus' death, burial, resurrection, and ascension, they were found among the disciples in the upper room, awaiting the promised coming of the Holy Spirit (Acts 1:14). Paul refers to James as "the Lord's brother" in Galatians 1:19. There can be little doubt that the writer of our book is identifying himself not only as the brother of James but also of Jesus.

The writer does not identify himself as the brother of Jesus, only of James. But Clement of Alexandria (last decade of the second-century AD) thought that, like James, Jude would not call himself the brother of Jesus. That might infer he was claiming too much authority.

Some scholars attribute the letter to a later person, writing under the pseudonym of Jude. The reason for suspecting that the letter was written after the time of Jude the brother of Jesus is some expressions in the book that suggest a later date. He speaks of "the faith that was once for all entrusted to God's holy people" (v. 3) and asks his readers to "remember" the words of the apostles (v. 17). However, we do not know how much younger Jude was than Jesus. Jesus was Mary's firstborn, and Jude could have been born fifteen to twenty years after Jesus. He could easily have been alive in the last quarter of the first-century AD.

No one knows precisely who wrote the book. The weight of tradition and the testimony of Scripture suggest that the writer was Jude, the younger brother of Jesus.

We have no definite indication of the date the letter was written. In some respects, the letter is quite similar to Second Peter. The writer of Second Peter apparently drew on Jude as he wrote. The two books probably date to about the same time. But the dating for both is disputed. Jude is dated as early as before the death of Peter, around AD 64 to AD 68, and as late as AD 125 to AD 150 by various scholars.

The church in general did not accept Jude as revelation from the apostolic era until after the time of Eusebius. He was a church historian in the time of Constantine and died about AD 339. Eusebius mentioned that not all the churches accepted the apostolic authorship of the book. Jude was recognized as an authentic book for the use of the church at the Council of Carthage in AD 397. Acceptance indicated that the book was widely known and used by many congregations long before the Council of Carthage.

The First Readers. The letter is addressed to "those who have been called" (v. 1). This reference is too general to identify them. From the many references to Old Testament history, Jude was either intended for Jewish Christians or for Gentile converts who were well acquainted with the biblical stories. Like some of the other General Letters, Jude was probably addressed to the church in general rather than to a specific congregation or individual. The book's teachings and warnings are certainly applicable to Christians of every time and place.

Outline of Jude.

I. Salutation (1-2)

II. Purpose of the letter (3-4)

III. Judgment on the ungodly element in the church (5-16)

      A. Examples of punishment of unbelievers (5-13)

      B. Enoch prophesied judgment on the ungodly (14-16)

IV. Adhere to the true faith (17-23)

V. Benediction (24-25)

Jude 1-2. As with the opening of the Letter of James, Jude calls himself a servant. This frequently used word in the New Testament is more accurately rendered "bond-servant" or "slave."

The people to whom Jude writes are "the called." This is a frequently used expression referring to Christians. The expression is used in 1 Peter 2:9: "him who called you out of darkness into his wonderful light." In 2 Thessalonians 2:13, Paul explains that God called the Christians in Thessalonica through the gospel to "be saved through the sanctifying work of the Spirit and through belief in the truth."

The idea of "kept for Jesus Christ" may seem peculiar at first glance. Christians have been "bought at a price" (1 Corinthians 6:20). Jesus will return to receive those who are his own, who have been kept for him by their love for him.

The words *called*, *loved*, and *kept* indicate the powerful forces at work in the believers' relationship to God. As Paul insisted, "neither death nor life, neither angels nor demons, neither the present nor the future, nor any powers, neither height nor depth, nor anything else in all creation, will be able to separate us from the love of God that is in Christ Jesus our Lord" (Romans 8:38-39).

Jude's desire is that those who read his letter will experience more and more of God's mercy, the peace that comes from reconciliation to God and other people, and love.

Jude 3-4. The writer states that he actually had intended to write "about the salvation we share" (v. 3). Because of the more immediate and pressing problem addressed in his letter, we can only speculate about what additional insights about the common salvation Jude might have shared with his first readers (and us).

As it is, Jude appealed to his readers to "contend for the faith" (v. 3), the faith once and for all time delivered to the saints. The faith is for all time, for all circumstances, for all purposes, and for all people. It is universal. That faith is, no doubt, the facts to be believed, the commands to be obeyed, and the promises to be received that make up the gospel.

God's holy people, of course, are all sincere Christians. The people of the faith, the church, are the living repository of the faith. The Bible cannot defend itself; only those who believe its truths will come to its defense.

The word *contend* refers to a vigorous verbal defense of the gospel. Paul charged Timothy to "fight the good fight of the faith. Take hold of the eternal life to which you were called when you made your good confession in the presence of many witnesses" (1 Timothy 6:12).

Jude's concern was for the influence in the church of some who had secretly gained admission. The Greek word used here has the idea of slipping in, as through a side door. These people appeared to have accepted the faith once for all delivered when they were converted, but they began to pervert the faith.

Jude states that these "ungodly people" were long ago designated for this condemnation. The word *condemnation* may refer to Jude's condemnation in the letter. More likely it is the idea that the wicked were known to God long ago and destined for condemnation.

What had these so-called Christians been doing that so endangered the church? They had perverted the grace of God into licentiousness. But more than this, these ungodly people were denying "Jesus Christ our only Sovereign and Lord" (v. 4). Jude had called himself a servant of Jesus Christ. He knew who his only Master was. As we have seen earlier in our study of these letters, God calls God's people to be holy. Immoral activity is a direct denial of Christ's lordship over a person.

Jude 5-16. The heart of the letter of Jude is contained in this section. Jude has identified the problem and will attack it by reminding his readers of the way in which God has dealt with the ungodly in the past (vv. 5-8). Then he vividly describes what these ungodly people do in the church and what will be their destiny (vv. 9-13). Jude draws parallels between them and other perverters of the faith in the Old Testament. He also reminds his readers of the prophecy of Enoch, which he sees fulfilled in the ungodly of his time.

Jude 5-7. Jude tells his readers that they already know what he now stresses: the God who saves can also destroy. They know examples of that fact. He mentions three: the unbelieving Israelites who perished in the wilderness, the rebellious angels who came under judgment, and the destruction of Sodom and Gomorrah.

We are well aware of the reason that almost all that generation who left Egypt perished in the wilderness. The cause was unbelief, and this was stressed in our study of Hebrews (3:12-19). The events are recorded in Numbers 13–14.

We also know the story of the destruction of Sodom and Gomorrah (Genesis 19:1-28). This illustration fits well the concern of sexual immorality with which Jude charges the ungodly. The point of the illustration is the type of destruction that befell those notorious places. It was punishment by fire.

The fire is described as "eternal" (v. 7). Jesus used the expressions "the fire of hell" (Matthew 5:22c) and the "eternal fire prepared for the devil and his angels" (Matthew 25:41). In the Book of Revelation "the lake of fire" (20:14-15) is the place into which death and Hades are cast, as well as anyone whose name is not found written in the book of life. This is likely the idea expressed by "eternal fire" in Jude.

What we find most puzzling is the reference in verse 6 to the angels who "did not keep their positions of authority." The first readers would have known exactly what Jude was talking about, but we have no such incident recorded in the Bible.

The story of the fallen angels is recorded in the Book of Enoch. This intertestamental book is a collection of stories and moral teachings that date from the second-century BC to the beginning of the first-century AD. Jesus said, "I saw Satan fall like lightning from heaven" (Luke 10:18); and we have noted the Matthew 25:41 reference to the "eternal fire prepared for the devil and his angels." So, even though we have only a nonbiblical reference (Enoch) to the revolt in heaven, evidently the story was well known in pre-Christian Judaism and in the early church.

Jude's reason for mentioning the fallen angels was that their rebellion brought certain punishment. How horrible a contrast to go from being angels of light to bound prisoners of utter darkness! Jude intended to shock his readers into a realistic awareness of the danger of the godless in their midst.

Jude 8-11. Despite the general knowledge of examples of the sure punishment of God for ungodliness and immorality, these people "pollute their own bodies, reject authority, and heap abuse on celestial beings" (v. 8). All this is the result of their "dreams." They may have induced trances and claimed special revelations or inspiration, then claimed the right to be free from the demands of normal decency.

Jude addresses particularly the abuse of celestial beings. Exactly what the celestial beings are is unclear. Abuse basically means to cheapen. To abuse is to address with shameful language. In contrast to the activities of godless humans (who are, remember, in the church), the archangel Michael, in a situation where he might have slandered the devil, refrained from doing so.

Again we have no biblical reference to this contention between Michael and Satan over the body of Moses. The story comes from another Jewish book of the intertestamental period called The Assumption of Moses.

These godless people act like "irrational animals." They slander what they do not understand and thereby set themselves up for judgment.

Woe is a familiar biblical expression. The English word comes from an old Anglo-Saxon expression meaning "pain, misery, affliction." The woe these ungodly ones can expect is like that of Cain (Genesis 4:3-16), Balaam (Numbers 22–24; 31:8), and those Israelites who died as the result of joining Korah's rebellion (Numbers 16). All these came to an evil end after rebelling against the authority of God or God's servant.

Jude 12-13. Here are a series of word pictures Jude has drawn from nature to describe the destructive character of the godless people in the church. "Blemishes at your love feasts" is more accurately translated "hidden rocks in your love feasts." These immoral church members were like reefs (rocks) hidden just beneath the surface of the sea, ready to bring the disaster of immoral conduct into the gathering of God's unsuspecting saints. They set a crass example, boldly carousing together, looking after themselves rather than having a sincere love of their brothers and sisters in Christ.

Waterless clouds give the promise of rain but produce no rain. Fruitless trees give the appearance of producing, but they have no mature fruit in the time of harvest. They are uprooted by the owner. They are twice dead: producing no new life and being uprooted. These people are like wandering stars, to be lost in space. In the context of first-century culture, stars should remain fixed points of light. (This word picture likely refers to comets.)

Jude 14-16. Jude again calls attention to the Book of Enoch and quotes from it. (The "holy ones" (v. 14) are the heavenly host of angels around the Almighty. Jude uses the quotation to show that this type of ungodliness was prophetically foretold long ago, and it has now appeared. Again, the words of Enoch point to the coming judgment on the ungodly.

The people who soil the church are grumblers and faultfinders. The words of Christians are to minister grace to the hearers (Ephesians 4:29). Christians are to be content (Hebrews 13:5). The ungodly follow their own desires; lust controls them. Christians are to control sinful desires (1 Peter 2:11). These people are boasters of self and flatterers of others, flattering for personal gain. Humility is required of Christians (James 4:10; 1 Peter 5:5b; and the example of Jesus, Philippians 2:8). Flattery was forbidden by Jesus. He insisted, "All you need to say is simply 'Yes or 'No'; anything beyond this comes from the evil one" (Matthew 5:37; James 5:12).

Jude 17-23. Not only does Jude provide examples of God's judgment on the godless from the Old Testament and from other traditions, he says Jesus' apostles also predicted that ungodly scoffers would appear "in the last times" (v. 18). We have no record of this prediction, other than this mention of it by Jude. Christians have been living in the last times since the ascension of Jesus and the days of the apostles.

The scoffers, those driven by fleshly rather than spiritual desires, are the ones who cause disunity among God's people. Worldly people are by definition devoid of the Spirit. The Spirit is a gift to repentant, baptized believer (Acts 2:38). The unity of believers was a matter of prayer for Jesus (John 17:20-21). "There is one body and one Spirit, just as you were called to one hope when you were called; one Lord, one faith, one baptism; one God and Father of all, who is over all and through all and in all" (Ephesians 4:4-6).

Rather than be influenced by the divisive, ungodly element, Jude urges his readers actively to build up the protective walls of their faith. They can build themselves up through praying in the Holy Spirit, abiding in the love of God, and waiting (patiently and confidently) for the fulfillment of the promises that are in the Lord Jesus Christ.

Not only are the readers to look after their own faith, they are commanded to save whomever they can. Each group of those fellow Christians whose commitment is weak must be addressed in a different way. Doubters need to be convinced by the example and the testimony of the faithful. Those closer to the brink of hellfire must be snatched out. Others need mercy while letting them know that you fear for them. Let your disgust at their past, lustful deeds show; but showing concern for them may save some.

Jude 24-25. Jude's benediction expresses great confidence in God's power to save. Even in the midst of a situation like that on which he has focused in this letter, Jude assures his readers that God can save, and save a person unblemished. That is possible because the blood of Jesus Christ, our Savior, cleanses the repentant and committed from all sin and unrighteousness. It is possible to be saved, even in a polluted church, and to enter the presence of God rejoicing.

The marvelous power of God to save those who come to him through Christ is evidence that to God is the "glory, majesty, power and authority" (v. 25). They are God's in the past, the present, and the future. The godless are but for a moment. They may trouble the church, but the Savior reigns forever.

DIMENSION THREE: WHAT DOES THE BIBLE MEAN TO ME?

Jude 3—Contending for the Faith

To contend for the faith refers to a strenuous, verbal defense of what has been divinely revealed for Christians to believe. You may want to ask a pastor or professor to share some insights about what the essentials of the faith are.

Another source that you can consult is the entry on *faith* in a Bible dictionary. You cannot contend for the faith unless you can define it.

With a good understanding of the faith once for all delivered to the saints, help group members explore modern times and circumstances. How is our society different from the first century?

The point of Jude's letter was to contend for the faith against that element in the church that followed godless desires. Grumblers, malcontents, boasters, those who cause divisions and the like, were weakening the faith of weaker church members. Do we have persons like that still in our churches today? How can dedicated, faithful Christians counteract such individuals or such tendencies?

Verses 20-23 likely provide the means by which to combat ungodliness and ungodly people in Christian circles. The call is to build up your faith, to pray in line with what the Holy Spirit lays on your heart (the concerns of the living God), to remain in the love of God by being conscious of that love (being aware of God's blessings and guidance), and to look for the return of the Lord Jesus Christ. An optimistic outlook is a powerful testimony of faith.

Contending for the faith means persuasively presenting your testimony to those who doubt (v. 22). Presenting your testimony is simply telling the doubters what great things God has done for you. The purpose is to save some, snatching them from the fire; so a genuine concern for them is essential.

Jude 16-19—Handling Our Sinful Desires

Perhaps the biggest conflict we have in developing into mature Christians is overcoming our tendency to consider self first and others last. Sinful desires can refer to lust. The sexual drive is a normal part of being human, but it must be controlled lest it lead to adultery and abuse. The key to controlling ourselves is to "offer your bodies as living sacrifices" (Romans 12:1). That is, we are to willfully determine to serve God. Rather than be conformed to the norms of a society that is hardly Christian, we are to be transformed by the renewing of our minds. By setting our mind on things that are above, we can control our thoughts and our bodies. We can control what we allow to enter our minds through our senses.

The human sinful desires include other drives as well, for example: envy, coveting, anger, malice, and revenge. Ephesians 4:17–5:4 provides wise counsel on handling sinful desires like these. Humility, a genuine concern for the welfare of others, trust in the provisions of God to meet one's needs, and especially modeling one's life after that of the Master are powerful tools for transforming our base tendencies into godliness.

Made in the USA
Middletown, DE
19 December 2020

SCHWETZ MOL DEITSCH!

An introductory Pennsylvania Dutch course

Joshua R. Brown and Douglas J. Madenford

Published by the
Center for Pennsylvania German Studies at Millersville University
with the support of the *Max Kade Foundation*

Editors:

C. Richard Beam
Professor Emeritus
Millersville University of Pennsylvania

Alice Spayd
Instructor of Pennsylvania Dutch

Lee Thierwechter
Instructor of Pennsylvania Dutch

Published by the
Center for Pennsylvania German Studies at Millersville University
with the support of the *Max Kade Foundation*

2009

Library of Congress Number: 2009936917
International Standard Book Number: 978-1-60126-203-5

* Cover fraktur image courtesy of the Muddy Creek Farm Library, Ephrata, Pennsylvania.

For our earliest Pennsylvania Dutch teachers:

Josh's grandmother, **Emma M. Gaugler**

and

Doug's grandparents, **Joseph & Arlene Bauer** *and*
Ray & Alma Madenford

Preface from the Publisher:

The *Center for Pennsylvania German Studies at Millersville University of Pennsylvania* takes great pleasure in publishing *Schwetz mol Deitsch!* by Joshua R. Brown, who holds a Bachelor's degree in German from Millersville University, and Douglas J. Madenford, who holds a Master's degree in German from Millersville University. Millersville University, the oldest of the fourteen state universities in the commonwealth has been preparing teachers for 150 years. In the twentieth and twenty-first centuries, it has prepared many of the German teachers in southeastern Pennsylvania.

The establishment of the *Center for Pennsylvania German Studies at Millersville University* was in 1986, the same year that the Director's article "A Century of Pennsylvania German Plays, 1880-1985" was published in *Annals Five: Probleme, Projekte, Perspectiven --- Symposium 1985* in Montreal, Quebec. Another landmark in 1986 was the publication of M. Ellsworth Kyger's three-volume dictionary: *An English-Pennsylvania German Dictionary: A Working Manuscript*. Since that time, the Director's latest article, "Pennsylvania German Lexicography: Past and Present," appeared in the *Yearbook of German-American Studies* in 2003 and the Director and Co-editors have published 18 volumes of Pennsylvania Dutch dictionaries and books of folklore, including the eleven volumes of *The Comprehensive Pennsylvania German Dictionary* (2004-2007).

Since 1971, the Center has participated in the weekly dialect broadcast over WLBR in Lebanon, Pennsylvania; since 1975, the Director has been writing a weekly dialect column in the Sugarcreek (Ohio) *Budget* and since 1980 in the *Ephrata Shopping News*. The Center's Journal, a quarterly publication, currently in Volume 15, has been appearing since 1989.

At present, the Center is engaged in the publication of Ernest Waldo Bechtel's Pennsylvania German writings. For 18 years, from January 1970 to 1988, Ernest Waldo Bechtel (1923-1988) wrote a weekly Pennsylvania German column in *The Ephrata Review*.

In recent years the field of Pennsylvania German studies has seen the publication of Isaac R. Horst's *Separate and Peculiar* (*Bei sich selwer un ungwehnlich*) (2001), *Mit Pennsylvaanisch-Deitsch darich's Yaahr* (2006), Peter Fritsch's *Der Haahne Graeht* (2006), *Schlaf, Boppli, Schlaf* (2006) by David and Sylvia Troyer, and *Pennsylvania*

Dutch Holiday Poems (2008) by Gerry Kerschner. The German "Edition Tintenfass" during this period has republished *The Night Before Christmas*, *Mammi Gans*, *Hans un Yarick* (*Max and Moritz*) and *Der Glee Prins* all in Pennsylvania German.

Millersville's Center for Pennsylvania German Studies is honored to be able to publish this latest Pennsylvania German textbook. The text is traditional in its analysis of dialect grammar, yet refreshingly up-to-date in its use of Pennsylvania German prose and poetry.

In the years 2004 and 2005, Joshua R. Brown served as Co-editor with C. Richard Beam of *The Comprehensive Pennsylvania German Dictionary*. "Yossi" Brown was also the Co-Editor with Leroy T. Hopkins, Jr. of *Preserving Heritage: A Festschrift for C. Richard Beam* (2006). In the year 2008, he co-edited the restored edition of *Rosanna of the Amish* and currently conducts research among Anabaptists in Northern Appalachia. Douglas J. Madenford is an accomplished high school German teacher. He has established himself as a regular correspondent for the journal *Hiwwe wie Driwwe*. He teaches all levels of German language courses at Keystone Central School District.

C. Richard Beam, Director
Center for Pennsylvania German Studies
Millersville University
July 2009

Willkumm!

Welcome to an exciting language and culture! As the title, *Schwetz mol Deitsch!* suggests, you will become familiar with a language that mirrors today's communication needs. By being exposed to numerous real-life situations you will be able to better relate to your own surroundings and make comparisons between the cultures of Pennsylvania Dutch-speaking areas and your own.

"Why should I learn Pennsylvania Dutch (PD)? Isn't it a dead language?" you may ask yourself. Did you know:

- PD has been continuously spoken in America since 1648.
- Up to 400,000 people in more than 20 states and one Canadian province speak PD.
- PD speakers can communicate with about 1,000,000 Germans who live the Palatinate region.
- You can find lots of PD resources on the Internet.
- There is a wealth of literature written and published in PD.

You will learn skills that will help you to communicate on many topics. As you begin learning PD, you will initially listen, and then gradually learn to speak about topics that interest you. Don't be afraid to express yourself. It's natural to make mistakes, but your language skills and cultural understanding will gradually become stronger each time you use PD. In short time your confidence will increase as you experience success communicating in PD.

Schwetz mol Deitsch! uses naturalistic texts and dialogues, realia, vocabulary and grammar in context and presents the learner and the instructor with both an accessible and effective tool for Pennsylvania Dutch language instruction. It stresses the competencies of foreign language learning: interpretation, expression, and negotiation. Additionally, the integration of technology enhances the learning options for the student and pronounces the role of the Pennsylvania Dutch in the 21st century.

Building upon very limited teaching resources for Pennsylvania Dutch, we have produced this volume in the hope of receiving much feedback from both the instructor and the student. Producing the "perfect" textbook is both impossible and unrealistic, but we are confident that this book will provide the necessary stepping stone for Pennsylvania Dutch pedagogy in the 21st century.

Although this textbook is the result of years of effort and careful editing by our editors, we are certain that there are some errors in the text. The authors assume full responsibility for those errors and welcome your corrections. Although a significant contribution of this textbook is the incorporation of communicative activities and considerably lessened reliance on the audio-lingual method, we hope to expand the scope of the exercises in future editions by incorporating even more communicative activities for newer learners of Pennsylvania Dutch.

We are also aware that the grammar and forms presented in this text are not used by all Pennsylvania Dutch speaking groups throughout North America. As language teachers --- and language users --- we know that language changes... and we embrace those changes. While this textbook is fairly conservative in its presentation of grammar, we do draw the students' and teachers' attention to the variation within the Pennsylvania Dutch speaking world --- most notably the differences between sectarians and non-sectarians. Although non-sectarians have retained the dative case, for example, while sectarians have not, its presentation in this text should prove no hindrance, nor great communicative difficulty between speakers. Non-sectarians and sectarians frequently speak to each other in Deitsch without marring the fluidity of conversation on the basis of a case discrepancy.

We hope that future editions of this book will seek to address these variations. Until then, we welcome your comments and suggestions.

We wish you a lot of success and a lot of fun!

Viel Glick un viel Schpass!

Chapter	Topics	Communicative Functions	Grammar	Culture
1 "Wie bischt du?"	Greetings. Introductions. Identifying People. Where a person lives. Alphabet. Numbers 0-20.	Greetings. Introducing oneself. Telling where one lives. Giving a telephone number. Addition and Subtraction.	Personal Pronouns. Alphabet. Nominative Case. Definite Articles.	What is PD?
2 "In der Schul"	School Expressions. Numbers 20 – Above. Present Tense Verbs. Question Words. Telling one's age. Telling Time. Days of the Week.	Telling one's age. Telling time. Forming Questions. Yes/No Questions.	Indefinite Articles. Present Tense Verb Forms. Question Words. HAWWE. Possessive Adjectives.	Two-Room Country Schoolhouse.
3 "Mei Familye"	Family members. Likes and Dislikes. Genealogy.	Describing your family. Describing Likes and Dislikes. Forming Questions.	gleiche / net gleiche. Accusative Case. Accusative Pronouns. Plural Nouns. WISSE / KENNE.	PD Folk Art: Fraktur.
4 "Uff em Land"	The Farm. Animals. Months, Seasons of the Year. Weather.	Describing rural life. Describing various times of the year. Describing the weather.	SEI. ES GEBT. Compound Nouns. Irregularly conjugated verbs. Present Progressive. Diminutive	The PD and Farming

	Vocabulary	Functions	Grammar	Culture
5 "Kumm esse"	Foods. Beverages. Eating Establishments. Colors.	Choosing from a Menu. Offering something to eat and drink. Making requests.	Modal Auxiliaries. Future Tense. Negation.	PD Cuisine.
6 "Gehne mir eikaafe"	Grocery Shopping. Articles of Clothing. Rooms of the House. Furniture.	Making suggestions. Asking about prices. Describing and choosing clothing items. Talking about a department store.	Dative Case. Dative Prepositions. Dative Verbs. Dative Pronouns.	The Sectarians.
7 "Mei Daag"	Body Parts. Health and Hygiene. Daily Routine. Music.	Describing a daily routine. Describing musical preferences. Describing how you feel.	Words used for emphasis. Separable prefix verbs. Reflexive Verbs. Genitive	PD Music.
8 "Feierdaage"	Birthdays. Weddings. Holidays. Parties.	Inviting someone to an occasion. Telling and describing a birthday. Giving and receiving presents. Planning a party.	Meege. Adjective Endings. Adjectives as Nouns. Comparative and Superlative.	Der Belsnickel.
9 "Freizeit"	Hobbies. Leisure-Time Activities. Sports.	Describing a hobby. Describing what you do in your free time. Describing athletic activities.	Present Perfect Tense – Irregular Verbs. Present Perfect Tense – Regular Verbs. Two-Way Prepositions.	Groundhog Lodges and Versammlings.

10 "Um die Schtadt"	Giving / Asking Directions. Places in Town.	Giving/Asking for Directions. Telling someone to do something.	Commands. Coordinating Conjunctions. Subordinating Conjunctions.	PD Place Names.
11 "En Rees"	Describe / Plan a trip. Ask for Information. Means of Transportation.	Describing / Planning a trip. Asking / Giving Information. Describing means of transportation. Telling what language one speaks.	Passive Voice.	Hex Signs.
12 "Sell Macht Schpass"	PD Prose. PD Poetry. Reading / Writing a Letter. The Pledge of Allegiance. Lord's Prayer.	Describing a past event. Describing Hypothetical Situations. Writing a Letter / Email. Describing a Poem.	Preterite of SEI Subjunctive Mood.	PD in the 21st Century.

Table of Contents

Kabiddel 1 –

"Wie bischt du?"

In this chapter you will be able to:

- Greet and say farewell to someone
- Ask and tell someone's name
- Introduce yourself
- Give telephone numbers
- Ask and tell how things are going
- Ask where someone lives

Guder Daag!

Mark:	Guder Daag!
John:	Guder Daag!
Mark:	Was is dei Naame?
John:	Mei Naame is John. Un dei Naame?
Mark:	Mark. Wu wuhnscht du, John?
John:	Ich wuhn in Barricks Kaundi. Un du?
Mark:	Ich kumm vun Lechaa Kaundi.
Mark:	John, wie bischt du heit?
John:	Gut, un du?
Mark:	Aa gut, denkyaa.

1. *Was weesscht du vun dem Dialog?* Answer the following questions based on the above dialog:

    1. What is a way of saying hello in PD?

    2. Was is dei Naame?

    3. Wu wuhnscht du?

Schprooch

Griesse – Greetings:

Guder Daag.	Hello, Good day.
Guder Mariye.	Good morning.
Guder Nummidaag.	Good afternoon.
Guder Owed.	Good evening.
Guti Nacht.	Good night.
Mach's gut.	Good-bye.
Sehn dich schpeeder.	See you later.

Mach dich bekannt! – Introduce yourself!

The following phrases are ways of introducing yourself, describing how you are doing, telling where you live and explaining where you come from.

Was is dei Naame (Familyenaame)?
    Mei Naame (Familyenaame) is _____.

Was is sei / ihr Naame?
    Sei / Ihr Naame is _____.

Wer is sell?
    Sell is _____.

Wie bischt du?
    Ich bin gut / schlecht / zimmlich gut / zimmlich schlecht.

Wu wuhnscht du?
    Ich wuhn in _____.

Wu kummscht du bei?
    Ich kumm vun _____.

Rolleschpiel

Carry on a brief conversation with the person next to you asking such questions as: *Was is dei Naame? Wie bischt du? Wer is sell? Was is sei / ihr Naame? Wu wuhnscht du? Wu kummscht du bei?*

Schprooch

Es Alphabet – The alphabet:

The PD Alphabet contains the same letters as the English alphabet. Below are the letters and their pronunciation:

A	ah	N	enn
B	beh	O	oh
C	tseh	P	peh
D	deh	Q	kuh
E	eh	R	err
F	eff	S	ess
G	geh	T	teh
H	hah	U	oo
I	ee	V	fau
J	yot	W	veh
K	kah	X	ix
L	ell	Y	ipsilon
M	emm	Z	tset

2. *Wie schreibt mer sell?* Spell the following words using the PD Alphabet:

1. Diefenderfer

2. Kutzeschteddel

3. Distelfink

4. Bottboi

5. struwwelich

6. Schnitzelbank

7. Faasnacht

8. Wunnerfitz

Practice pronunciation!
Using the alphabet that you just learned, the pronunciation guide in the reference section, and your instructor's cues, read through the following poem:

Es Deitsch Ah-Beh-Tseh
by Gladys S. Martin

A schteht fer **Amschel**, er singt laut mit Freed.
B schteht fer **Bauer**, er blugt un er maeht.
C schteht fer **Caesh**, es glingelt in de Seck.
D is fer **Drauwe**, **Dischdle** und **Dreck**.
E is fer **Ecke-Balle**, as die yunge Kalls schpiele,
wann en Vendu als is: Seller Kall kann gut ziele.
F schteht fer **Fensemaus**, freindlich un froh.
G is fer **Grott**, feierlich un groh.
H schteht fer **Hanswascht**, er is immer so lappich.
I is fer **Ieme**, mit Hunnich so bappich.
J schteht fer **Jammer**, des findt aller Mensch.
K is fer **Katz**, er singt uff der Fens.
L schteht fer **Lebkuche**, gewaerzich un siess.
Mer esst sie viel liewer as Obscht odder Gemiess.
M is fer **Maed**, un die sin aa siess.
Sin Zucker un Gewaerz vun ihr Kepp zu ihr Fiess.
N schteht fer **Nixnutz**, er waar so gebore ---
Voll Gschpass un mutwillich, mit Gnepp hinnich de Ohre.
O schteht fer **Offe**, fer **Obscht**, un fer **Oier**.
P schteht fer **Parre**, mit en Schtimm wie en Groier.
Q schteht fer **Quallefleesch**, was schmackt des so gut.
R is fer **Rumleefer** mit en zottlicher Hut.
S is fer **Seideschpeck** mit **Schunke** debei.
Hen mir net alles gut gesse uff der alt Bauerei?

T schteht fer **Trommel**, **Taxe**, un **Tee**, fer
Tannebaum, **Teekessel**, un aa noch viel meh.
U is fer **Unbennich**, was hasse mir die.
Deel Leit sin so unbennich, as en Schtall wilde Vieh.
V is fer **Veggel**, sie singe so siess
Un fresse die Keffer vun unser Obscht un Gemiess.
W is fer **Weschpe**, **Wanse** und **Warem**,
So Dinger wie die, sehne kens vun uns gaern.
X is fer **X-Beine**, is sell net en fremm Watt?
Y is fer **Yaahre**, sie schleiche so fatt.
Z is fer **Zidder**, mit Myusick blessierlich;
schteht aa fer **Zidderli** un **Zucker** nadierlich.

The German A B C's

A is for robin, he sings loudly with joy.
B is for farmer, he plows and mows.
C is for cash, that jingles in pockets.
D is for grapes, thistles and dirt.
E is for corner ball, that the young boys play
when there is a sale: That young man can aim well.
F is for chipmunk, friendly and happy.
G is for toad, solemn and grey.
H is for clown, he is always so silly.
I is for bees, with sticky honey.
J is for misery, each of us will find it.
K is for cat, who sings on the fence.
L is for sugar cookies, spicy and sweet,
we'd much rather eat them than fruit or vegetables.
M is for girls, and they too are sweet.
They are sugar and spices from their head to their feet.
N is for scamp, he was born so ---
full of fun and playful with lumps behind his ears.
O is for stove, for fruit and for eggs.
P is for parson, with a voice like an auctioneer.
Q is for dried beef, that tastes so good.
R is for hobo, with a tattered hat.
S is for bacon, with ham also.
Didn't we eat well on the old farm?
T is for Jew's harp, taxes and tea.
Also for fir tree, tea kettle, and more.

U is for rowdy, how we hate these.
Some folks are as a rowdy as a pen of wild cattle.
V is for birds, that sing so sweetly,
and eat the bugs from our fruit and vegetables.
W is for wasps, bed bugs, and worms.
Things like this we do not see gladly.
X is for bow-legged. Isn't that an odd word?
Y is for years, they slip away.
Z is for zither, with such pleasant music;
also for souse and sugar, of course.

[Reprinted with permission from: Martin, Gladys S. <u>Kumm laaf mit mir: A collection of PA German poetry with English translation</u>. Gordonville, PA: S.K. Typing, 2005.]

Schprooch

Die Nummer – The Numbers

0 - null	1 - eens	2 - zwee	3 - drei	4 - vier
5 - fimf	6 - sex	7 - siwwe	8 - acht	9 - nein
10 - zehe	11 - elf	12 - zwelf	13 - dreizeh	14 - vatzeh
15 - fuffzeh	16 - sechzeh	17 - siwwezeh	18 - achtzeh	19 - neinzeh
		20 - zwansich		

3. *Was is dei Fonnummer?* Give your telephone number using the PD numbers:

  * 359 – 4303 =

  drei – fimf – nein – vier – drei – null – drei

4. *Was is dei Zip Code?* Give the Zip Code using the PD numbers:

18049 – Emmaus

18103 – Allentown

19601 – Reading

19550 – Rehrersburg

5. *Was is die Nummer? Wu is sell?* Look at the following advertisements; give the phone number and street address with zip code, *in Deitsch!*

BIRD-IN-HAND FAMILY ***Restaurant & Smorgasbord***	***STRASBURG RAIL ROAD***

2760 Old Philadelphia Pike Bird-in-Hand, PA 17505 717-768-1500	Route 741, P.O. Box 96 Strasburg, PA 17579 717-687-7522

6. Wie viel is...?

* 2 + 10 =

Zwee un zehe is zwelf.

* 8 + 5 =

Acht un fimf is dreizeh.

* 3 – 1 =

Drei un eens wennicher losst zwee.

1. 8 + 11 =

2. 13 – 1 =

3. 5 + 2 =

4. 20 – 6 =

5. 16 – 5 =

6. 7 + 9 =

Saag eppes!

Wu wuhnscht du?

datt driwwe

in Lebanon

graad um's Eck rum

in der Elmschtross

net weit weck

do

dehinner

middes in der Schtadt

Schprooch

The Definite Article – Nominative Case

In PD there are four variations of the definite article 'the' in the nominative case, *der, die, es* and *die*. The nominative case is used to identify the subject.

Der Bu *is siwwezeh.* – The boy is seventeen.

Die Fraa *wuhnt in Lebanon.* – The woman lives in Lebanon.

Es Buch *is gross.* – The book is big.

Note that all nouns in PD (including names and places) are capitalized. It is extremely important to learn the articles that accompany the individual nouns. We refer to these as masculine *(der)*, feminine *(die)*, neuter *(es)* and plural *(die)*. Be aware, however, that the nouns associated with either of the four articles are not necessarily "masculine" or "feminine" or "neuter" by nature – for example, the article for a girl *(es Meedel)* is neuter.

	Masculine	Feminine	Neuter	Plural
Nominative	**der**	**die**	**es**	**die**

Plurals – In English, plurals are typically marked with an "s" (the book – the books). PD marks the plural in two ways:

- With the article – the plural article in PD is *"die"*

- With the ending – there are several plural endings; these should be learned with the nouns.

der Daag – die Daage

die Nacht – die Nechde

es Buch – die Bicher

Geb Acht!

PD Pronunciation

PD Pronunciation differs from English in certain respects. Take note of these three situations:

1. *ei - ie*

> "ei" in PD makes an "eye" English sound. – *bei, gleich, sei, Deiwel*

> "ie" in PD makes an "ee" English sound. – *die, Kieh, biede, Glieder*

2. *–ch*

> If "ch" follows: i, ei or ie – it is pronounced like the initial "h" sound in the English word "huge" – *Bicher, gleich, rieche*

> If "ch" follows: a, o or u – it is pronounced by making a guttural sound like in the English/Scottish word "loch" – *Dach, noch, suche*

3. *"g"* between two vowels

> If there is a "g" between two vowels – the "g" is pronounced like the "y" in the English word "yes" – *Daage, rege, saage*

Schprooch

Personal Pronouns

Singular		Plural	
ich	*I*	mir	*we*
du	*you*	dihr	*you (plural)*
er, sie, es	*he, she, it*	sie	*they*

Personal Pronouns are pronouns that are used as substitutes for proper or common nouns.

Der Josh *wuhnt in State College.* – **Er** *wuhnt in State College.*

Die Susan *kummt vun Reading.* – **Sie** *kummt vun Reading.*

Es Buch *is gross.* – **Es** *is gross.*

Die Heather un die Kelly *sin Meed.* – **Sie** *sin Meed.*

7. *Was meehnscht?* Using the two columns below, match a noun from column one with an adjective from column two to create six sentences in PD. Then replace the nouns with personal pronouns.

- Der Mann is dumm. – Er is dumm.

es Buch	gscheit
die Zeiding	alt
der Karebet	schee
die Fraa	yung
die Uhr	unfreindlich
es Wedder	gschpassich

Kuldur

What is Pennsylvania Dutch?

Pennsylvania Dutch is a language that resulted from the leveling of several southwestern German dialects in 18th century colonial America. Originally, the language was spoken among non-sectarian, church people (Lutherans, Reformed) and sectarians (Amish, Mennonites) in southeastern Pennsylvania. Since then the language has spread, mostly due to new Amish and Mennonite settlements in Canada and the mid-west. Today, Pennsylvania Dutch is spoken by over 250,000 Amish alone.

There is some contention over the terminology for the language: Pennsylvania German or Pennsylvania Dutch. Many assume Pennsylvania Dutch to be a misapplication of the term "Deutsch" to the German immigrants of Pennsylvania. However, at their time of immigration the notion of "Deutsch" was not a common concept. At the time of their immigration, "Dutch" was the common and acceptable term used in English for anyone from central Europe. As such, the term Pennsylvania Dutch is not a misnomer or false translation, but an accurate description of the people's place of origin at the time of immigration. Current use of the word "Dutch," though, should not lead to confusions that these people originated in the Netherlands.

Pennsylvania Dutch originated from several German dialects, so its relationship to standard German is of course evident. However, centuries of contact with English and displacement from Germany has lead to several innovations and changes in the language of the Pennsylvania Dutch. It is important to note, though, that their language is not simply "incorrect German" or "German with a lot of English." Pennsylvania Dutch is a fully functional language. Even borrowings into the language from English are conformed to Pennsylvania Dutch grammar. For example, nouns are assigned a gender.

Several differences between the Pennsylvania Dutch of the Amish and Mennonite, on the one hand, and the Lutherans and Reformed, on the other, do exist. Whereas most sectarians have lost the dative case in Pennsylvania Dutch, nonsectarians still maintain the dative case. It will be introduced in this text. Some word differences, e.g. *ausleere* vs. *ausschidde* and diminutive differences are discussed. It is important to note that Pennsylvania Dutch does have minor differences from region to region. This textbook strives to introduce a Pennsylvania Dutch that is most manageable among several regions.

Further reading:

- Klees, F. The Pennsylvania Dutch. New York: Macmillian. 9th printing in 1964.
- Kuhns, Oscar. The German and Swiss settlements of colonial Pennsylvania. New York: Holt. Reprint by Aurand Press, 1945.
- Parsons, W. T. The Pennsylvania Dutch: A persistent minority. Boston: Twayne. Reprint by Chestnut Books, 1986.

Rickguck

8. *Eppes paerseenlich.* Answer the following questions *in Deitsch!*

> 1. Was is dei Naame? Was is dei Familyenaame?
>
> 2. Wu wuhnscht du?
>
> 3. Wu kummscht du bei?
>
> 4. Was is dei Fonnummer?

9. *Eppes zu lese.* Read the following short selections and then answer the questions *in Deitsch!*

Sell is die Mary Schneider. Sie wuhnt in Ellsdaun. Ihr Fonnummer is 797-4860. Sie hot drei Kinner. Ihrem Mann sei Naame is Mark. Der Mark kummt vun Barricks Kaundi bei Reading.

> 1. Was is der Fraa ihre Naame?
>
> 2. Wu wuhnt sie?
>
> 3. Wu kummt ihr Mann bei?
>
> 4. In weller Kaundi is Reading?

Guder Mariye, mei Naame is Nate Dunkel. Ich bin zimmlich gut. Ich kumm vun Nei Yarick. Nei Yarick is net in Pennsylfaania. Nau wuhn ich in Easton. Mei Zip Code is 01237.

> 1. Is es Owed odder Mariye?
>
> 2. Was is dem Nate sei Famillyenaame?
>
> 3. Wie is der Nate?
>
> 4. Wu kummt er bei?
>
> 5. Wu wuhnt er nau?

Was weesscht du?

This section is intended to check your general understanding of this chapter. All of your responses should be in PD.

- Say hello and good-bye to your classmate and your teacher.

- Ask a classmate these questions and listen to the answers. Then reverse roles:

    a. What is your name?

    b. Where do you live?

    c. Who is that?

    d. Where do you come from?

- Count from 0 to 20. Count by even numbers and then again with the odds.

- Give the Definite Article for the following nouns:

    Fraa, Mann, Meedel, Buch, Eck, Schtadt

- With a partner spell each other's names in PD.

Waddelischt

alt – old
aus – from
beikumme – to come from
es Buch (Bicher) – the book, *n*
der Bu (-we) – the boy, *m*
datt driwwe – over there
der Daag (-e) – the day, *m*
dehinner – behind
dihr – you (plural)
do – there
du – you (singular)
dumm – dumb
eppes – something
er – he
es – it
der Familyenaame – the last name, *m*
die Fraa – the woman, Mrs. *f*
die Fonnummer – the phone number, *f*
graad ums Eck – right around the corner
gross – big
gscheit – smart
gschpassich – fun
gut – good
ich – I
ihr – her
in – in
der Karebet – the carpet, the rug, *f*
die Kinner – the children, *pl*
kumme– to come
Mach's gut – take care
der Mann – the man, husband, Mr. *m*

der Mariye – the morning, *m*
es Meedel (Meed) – the girl, *n*
middes in der Schtadt – downtown
mir – we
der Naame (Naeme) – the name, *m*
die Nacht (-e, Nechde) – the night, *f*
nau – now
net weit weck – not far away
die Nummer (-e) – the number, *f*
der Nummidaag (-e) – the afternoon, *m*
der Owed (-e) – the evening, *m*
schee – pretty
schlecht – bad
schpaeder – later
sehne – to see
sei – his
sell – that
sie – she, they
die Uhr (-e) – the clock, *f*
unfreindlich – unfriendly
vun - from
was – what
es Wedder – the weather, *n*
wie – how, what
Wie bischt du? – How are you?
wu – where
wuhne – to live
yung – young
die Zeiding (-e) – the newspaper, *f*
zimmlich – reasonably, rather

Kabiddel 2 ~

"In der Schul"

In this chapter you will be able to:

- Ask what time it is
- Ask and tell someone's age
- Talk about school
- Ask for and give information

Wer is gscheit?

Elizabeth:	Dummel dich!
Sarah:	Langsam! Langsam! Die Schul beginnt aerscht um acht.
Natalie:	Mir hen graad Deitsch. Die Klaess is so hatt.
Elizabeth:	Net fer die Sarah. Sie grickt allsfatt en A.
Sarah:	Yawell, ich mach aa mei Schularewet, un dihr?
Natalie:	Mir brauche net. Du hoscht yo alle Antwatte.
Sarah:	Un wer is waericklich gscheit?

1. *Falsch!* The following statements are incorrect. Provide the correct statements *in Deitsch*.

    1. Die Sarah grickt in Deitsch en B.

    2. Die Elizabeth un die Natalie hen alle Antwatte fer Deitsch.

    3. Die Deitschklaess beginnt um siwwe.

    4. Die Natalie macht die Schularewet fer Deitsch.

Was is daheem?

James:	Hoscht du dei Rechelbuch?
Andrew:	Ya, in der Schulsack. Mir brauche der Calculator.
James:	Oh, der is daheem.
Andrew:	Du hoscht doch en Nootbichli un en Kopp.
James:	Es Nootbichli hab ich, awwer mei Kopp is leer.
Andrew:	Na, du hoscht Druwwel.
James:	Du hoscht recht. In Rechelklaess geb's allsfatt "Problems"!

2. *Antwadde selle Froget!*

    1. Wu is dem Andrew sei Rechelbuch?

    2. Wer braucht der Calculator?

    3. Wu is dem James sei Calculator?

    4. Hot der James en Nootbichli?

    5. Was gebt's allsfatt in Rechelklaess?

3. *In Deitsch, sei so gut!* Answer the following questions affirmatively in PD.

    1. Do you have all of the answers?

    2. Is the class difficult?

    3. Does the PD class being at 8?

    4. Is Robert smart?

    5. Does he always get an A?

4. Try to ask your neighbor a question in PD!

Schprooch

Present Tense Verb Forms

In the present tense in English, there are basically two different verb forms for all persons. For example, "live" is used for all persons, except after "he", "she" or "it" where it is "lives". In PD, however, the verb has more forms, as can be seen in the chart below.

To use the proper form, you need to know the infinitive of the particular verb. The infinitive of the English verb forms "said" or "says" is "to say". The infinitive of a PD verb ends with –e as in *wuhne, kumme* or *saage*. The infinitive is a combination of the stem of the verb and the ending (infinitive = stem + ending).

When the stem of a verb is known, you need to know the appropriate ending for the particular singular or plural form. The chart below shows the conjugation of the verb *saage*:

Singular	ich	**saag + *(no ending)***	I say, I am saying, I do say
	du	**saag + *scht***	You say, You are saying, You do say
	er		He says, He is saying, He does say
	sie	**saag + *t***	She says, She is saying, She does say
	es		It says, It is saying, It does say
Plural	mir	**saag + *e***	We say, We are saying, We do say
	dihr	**saag + *t***	You say, You are saying, You do say
	sie	**saag + *e***	They say, They are saying, They do say

Note: Certain spelling changes are necessary in the present tense of some verbs.

- All verbs whose stem ends in *s, ss* or *sch* drop these letters before the ending of the second person singular: *esse* - to eat = *du escht.*

21

- All verbs having a single long *e, o* or *u* before a single consonant in the infinitive, double this vowel throughout the singular and second person plural if the ending *–t* is used there: *lese* – to read

ich	lees	*mir*	lese
du	leescht	*dihr*	leest
er, sie, es	leest	*sie*	lese

- All verbs whose stem ends in *w*, change this letter to *b* throughout the singular and in the second person plural when the ending *–t* is used there: *liewe* – to love

ich	lieb	*mir*	liewe
du	liebscht	*dihr*	liebt
er, sie, es	liebt	*sie*	liewe

- Verbs whose infinitive ends in the *–ye*, have the stem ending *–ig* throughout the singular and in the second person plural when it ends in *–t*: *folye* – to follow, obey

ich	folig	*mir*	folye
du	foligscht	*dihr*	foligt
er, sie, es	foligt	*sie*	folye

5. Fill in the blank with the appropriate form of the verb in parenthesis:

1. Der Joe un die Michelle _____ (wuhne) in Yarrick.

2. Ich _____ (gehe) in die Schtadt.

3. _____ (kumme) er heem?

4. Dihr _____ (liewe) mei Schweschder.

5. Du _____ (kenne) die Fraa.

6. Translate the following sentences into PD:

    1. I am reading the book.

    2. He loves math class.

    3. We obey the English teacher.

    4. You guys are talking at school.

    5. She knows the boy.

    6. They live in Reading.

    7. I am coming home.

7. Create full PD sentences using the information given. Don't forget to conjugate the verbs and add the appropriate *der* words where necessary.

    1. Der Mike / lese / Buch

    2. Du / schreiwe / uff es Babier

    3. Mr. Stolz / liewe / Rechelklaess

    4. Dihr / folye / Schulmeeschdern

    5. Er / gehe / zu Schul

Eppes zu wisse

Es Klaesschtubb – Here are various objects you might find in a classroom:

die Uhr	*the clock*
der Waddefresser	*the computer*
die Landkaart	*the map*
der Disch	*the table*
der Schtul	*the chair*
die Schulsack	*the schoolbag*
die Fedder	*the pen*
der Bleipensil	*the pencil*
es Babier	*the paper*
der Ausreiwer	*the eraser*
es Nootbichli	*the notebook*
es Buch	*the book*
die Greid	*the chalk*
die Daafel	*the chalkboard*
der Schulmeeschder	*the teacher (male)*
die Schulmeeschdern	*the teacher (female)*

Wu is dei Buch? In der Schuldutt.

Wu is dei Schulsack? Do.

Wer is dei Deitschschulmeeschder? Mr. Miller.

Un dei Rechelschulmeeschdern? Fraa Grower.

Schprooch

Formation of Questions

To form a question you must use the so-called inverted word order. The subject and the verb of the sentence are interchanged.

Statement: *Du kummscht frieh.* You are coming early.

Question: *Kummscht du frieh?* Are you coming early?

- *Wuhnt Mr. Smith in Lengeschder?* Does Mr. Smith live in Lancaster?
- *Hemmer Zeit?* Do we have time?
- *Weesscht du die Antwatt?* Do you know the answer?

You can readily see that the formation of questions in PD is simpler than in English where most questions use the form of "to do" (do you?, does he?, etc.) The inverted word order is also used with such question words as those listed below:

- *Wie?* How? What? *Wie schpot is es?* How late is it? What time is it?
- *Wu?* Where? *Wu wuhnscht du?* Where do you live?
- *Was?* What? *Was is sell?* What is that?
- *Wer?* Who? *Wer is sell?* Who is that?
- *Wie viel?* How much? *Wie viel is drei un fimf?* How much is three plus five?

8. John is quite inquisitive. He asks you lots of questions. Answer affirmatively *in Deitsch!*

1. Is die Monica vatzeh?
2. Kummscht du schpaeder?
3. Is die Jennifer daheem?
4. Wuhnscht du weit weck?
5. Is es elf Uhr?

9. Ask John questions and have a classmate speculate on the answers.

25

10. Ask questions about the italicized items.
   * Ihr Naame is *Lauren*.
   * Was is ihr Naame?

   1. Der *Derek* kennt der Mark arig gut.

   2. Sell is *die Anne*.

   3. Mr. Jones wuhnt *in Lebanon*.

   4. Vier un nein is *dreizeh*.

   5. Die Tina is *in der Kich*.

   6. Der Peter un der Jim hen *Zeit*.

11. *Was? Wie? Wu?* odder *Wer*?

   1. _____ alt bischt du?

   2. _____ wuhnt dei Freind?

   3. _____ schpot is es?

   4. _____ kummt schpaeder?

   5. _____ is Pittsbarrig?

   6. _____ is sei Naame?

   7. _____ viel is achtzeh un nein wennicher?

   8. _____ is der Karen ihre Schweschder?

12. *Verbinne*…Choose one item from each column to form a question:

I	II	III
Kennt	Fraa Kreider	achtzeh
Is	du	dei Schweschder
Bischt	Jeremy	daheem

26

Geb Acht!

Present Tense of *hawwe*

Ich hab en Buch. – Sie hen Bicher. – Du hoscht en Buch.

What do you notice about the verb? Does it follow the normal pattern?

Singular	ich	**hab**	I have
	du	**hoscht**	you have
	er		he has
	sie	**hot**	she has
	es		it has
Plural	mir	**hen**	we have
	dihr	**hett**	you (plural) have
	sie	**hen**	they have

Note: The Question word order of the 1st person singular is *hawwich* (have I). The inverted word order of the first person plural is *hemmer* (have we).

Hoscht du Zeit? – Do you have time?

Ya, ich hab Zeit. – Yes, I have time.

Hett dihr en Buch daheem? – Do you have a book at home?

Ya, mir hen en Buch daheem. – Yes, we have a book at home.

13. *Wer hot heit Zeit?* You are asking who has some time today. Luckily, everyone does.

      * *Hot die Natasha heit Zeit?*
      * *Ya, sie hot heit Zeit.*

    1. Hoscht du heit Zeit?

    2. Hett dihr heit Zeit?

    3. Hen der Steve un der John heit Zeit?

    4. Hemmer heit Zeit?

Schprooch

Die Nummer – 10 and above:

10	20	30	40	50
zehe	zwansich	dreissich	vatzich	fuffzich

60	70	80	90	100
sechzich	siwwezich	achtzich	neinzich	hunnert
				ee hunnert

1,000

dausend

ee dausend

21	22
een un zwansich	zwee un zwansich

Telling one's age:

Wie alt bischt du? – Ich bin _____ Yaahr alt.

Wie alt is er / sie? – Er / Sie is _____ Yaahr alt.

14. Answer the following questions *in Deitsch!*

    1. Wie alt bischt du?

    2. Wie alt is dei Daadi?

    3. Wie saagt mer 152 in Deitsch?

    4. Wie viel is fimf un fuffzich un zwee un zwansich?

    5. Wie alt is Amerikaa?

    6. Was is dei Hausnummer?

Schprooch

What Time Is It?

One of the most important phrases to know in any language is "What time is it?" In PD, you need to be able to ask someone for the time. The most common ways to ask the time are *Was Zeit is es?* or *Wie schpot is es?* Here are some examples of expressing time in PD:

10:00 = Es is zehe Uhr.

8:00 = Es is acht Uhr.

3:30 = Es is drei Uhr dreissich. (Es is halwer vier.)

8:15 = Es is acht Uhr fimfzeh. (Es is Vaddel nooch acht.)

12:45 = Es is zwelf Uhr fimf un vatzich. (Es is Vaddel eb eens.)

9:33 = Es is nein Uhr drei un dreissich.

15. *Was Zeit is es?* Complete each time expression by providing the missing words.

1. 12:38 = Es is zwelf Uhr _____.

2. 6:30 = Es is _____ siwwe.

3. 2:52 = Es is _____ Minutte eb drei.

4. 10:45 = Es is _____ eb elf.

5. 4:10 = Es is _____ nooch vier.

Schprooch

Die Daage vun der Woch – The Days of the week

Sunndaag	Mundaag	Dinschdaag	Mittwoch	Dunnerschdaag	Freidaag	Samschdaag

Weller Daag is heit? – Heit is Mundaag.

Weller Daag is mariye? – Mariye is Dinschdaag.

16. *Weller Daag is mariye? Antwadde selle Froge!*
    * *Heit is Freidaag. Un mariye?*
    * *Mariye is Samschdaag.*

    1. Heit is Dunnerschdaag. Un mariye?

    2. Heit is Dinschdaag. Un mariye?

    3. Heit is Samschdaag. Un mariye?

    4. Heit is Mittwoch. Un mariye?

17. *Was hoscht du um _____ Mariye?*

    With a partner, ask what they are doing at a certain or on a certain day of the week.

Schwetz glee bissel!

Wann kummt…? Your teacher is organizing an all-day trip. Not everyone can come at the same time. Form groups of three to five. Write your name and the time that you can come on a piece of paper. Then pass your paper to another student in the group. One student in each group is the recorder and asks each group member, *Wann kummt (name of person)?* The person holding the paper with that name responds *(name of person) kummt um _____ Uhr.* The recorder makes a complete list of names and times and reports the information to the class.

Eppes zu wisse

En Schtunndeplan

	Mundaag	Dinschdaag	Mittwoch	Dunnerschdaag	Freidaag
8:00 – 8:20	Heemschtubb				
8:25 – 9:20	Rechelklaess	Myusick	Rechelklaess	Myusick	Rechelklaess
9:25 – 10:20	Englisch	Tschimm	Englisch	Tschimm	Englisch
10:25 – 11:20	Wisseschaft	Study Hall	Wisseschaft	Study Hall	Wisseschaft
11:20 – 12:05	Middaagesse				
12:10 – 1:05	Kunscht	Baend	Kunscht	Baend	Kunscht
1:10 – 2:05	Deitsch	Computers	Deitsch	Computers	Deitsch
2:10 – 3:05	Gschicht	Gsundheit	Gschicht	Gsundheit	Gschicht

- Was fer Klaess hot er? Er hot…
- Was fer en Klaess hot sie um zehe nooch zwelf am Mundaag? Um zehe nooch zwelf hot sie Kunscht.
- Weller Klaess hoscht du gaern? Ich hab…gaern.
- Is Deitsch leicht? Nee, Deitsch is hatt.
- Wann hot er Gschicht? Er hot am Mundaag, Mittwoch un Freidaag Gschicht.
- Was fer en Marick grickt sie? Sie grickt en B.

Schprooch

Indefinite Article – Nominative Case

	Masculine	Feminine	Neuter
Nominative	**en**	**en**	**en**

The indefinite articles are called indefinite because they do not specifically identify the noun they are associated with. All articles you have learned so far, i.e., *der, die* and *es* are *der-* words (definite articles). In English the indefinite article is either "a" or "an".

en Bu (der) - en Fraa (die) - en Buch (es)

En Bu wuhnt in sell Haus. – A boy lives in that house.

En Fraa kummt vun der Schul. – A woman is coming from the school.

En Buch is wichdich fer Rechelklaess. – A book is important for math class.

Saag eppes!

Wie is die Klaess?

arig laut   ruhich   langweilich

leicht   inderessant   freindlich

gschpassich   hatt

33

Schprooch

Possessive Adjectives

A possessive adjective is used as an adjective to indicate who owns the noun that follows it. It replaces the article in front of the noun. The table below shows the adjectives and their appropriate endings:

	Masculine	Feminine	Neuter	Plural
ich	mei			
du	dei			
er	sei			
sie	ihre			
es	sei			
mir	unser			
dihr	eier			
sie	ihre			

Mei Mudder schwetzt gut Deitsch.

Was is der Naame vun **dei** Schulmeeschder?

Sell is **sei** Buch.

Sie schreibt **ihre** Schularewet.

Unser Haus is zu glee fer **ihre** Familye.

18. Complete the following sentences with the phrases in parentheses.

    1. Sell is _____ (my female teacher).

    2. Ich hab _____ (your pencil).

    3. Er leest _____ (their homework).

    4. Mir gehne nooch _____ (his school).

Kuldur

The Two-Room Country Schoolhouse
Alice Spayd

Most if not all Pennsylvania Dutch youths prior to the 1950s attended a one-room country schoolhouse. You attended the nearest schoolhouse to your home or farm. It was also common for most students to only attend through the eighth grade. Following is an account of my experience at a two-room country schoolhouse in Schuylkill County, PA.

In 1950 I started first grade in a 2-room country schoolhouse in Pleasant Valley, Pine Grove Township, Pennsylvania. There were 4 grades in each room. While the teacher worked with one grade, the other three grades were quietly reading, writing, or doing some assignment that they had been given, or just listening to the class that was in session. The floors were wooden and each Friday we would take turns sweeping them. The chalkboards were black and went all across the front of the room. Each week we took turns washing them. The large, pot-bellied coal stove was in the right back corner of the room. Apparently the teacher had to arrive at school early to start the fire. Some desks were for 1 student and others for 2. They had inkwells and we had handwriting once a week using special pens.

The art teacher and the music teacher came once a week to each room - isn't this more efficient than having all the students move from room to room! We made special things in art for the holidays and I remember especially liking Thanksgiving because of making the cap, face and shoulders of the pilgrims and then also a garland of circles made from construction paper to hang up for Christmas.

We had to carry out lunches to school in a metal lunchbox. Occasionally a student would forget his or her lunch and the teacher would then always give an apple or orange from his own lunch. The toilets were outside toilets. Imagine the cruelties we suffered! But Tanny Dubb's store was practically next-door and was on the same side of the road. We could go there for Green Spot ice cream, chips, pretzels and candy - all sorts of luscious goodies!

In the fall of 1951, I started attending school at Oak Grove. At Oak Grove there was a stream right next to the school and there was that wonderful woodland where we played at recess and lunch. More than once someone slipped and got a little too wet, but there was that wonderful large, pot-bellied stove to dry, boots, shoes, sock, mittens and coats. There was a huge fallen tree that served as a train, bus, horse, or whatever for numerous kids could sit on it. We could play up on the "commons", and occasionally could talk the teacher(s) into taking a walk far to the rear of the school crossing over the railroad bed and down to see what was on the other side.

We could also walk to Fidler's store - quite a distance. The teacher that I had in 3rd and 4th grade at Oak Grove was Mr. Haggerty from, I think, the Hazleton or Scranton area. He was not PA Dutch. I know this because one day in history he said, "the grandparents of all of you in this room were from the Old Country, only the American Indians were here." He would have known that the PA Dutch were here much longer than that!

Even though most of the students could speak Pennsylvania Dutch, the dialect was never used in school. Certain words that were accepted into English were used however i.e. *struwwelich* or *rutsch*.

For grades 5 and 6 it was back out to Pleasant Valley school and then after that in 1956 to the new Junior/Senior High School that had just been built - a cafeteria, indoor bathrooms, but too many kids, too many teachers, too much commotion! I do not think that we learned any better or easier than we did in country school.

For further information:

- Kaufmann, Henry. The American One-Room Schoolhouse. Masthof Press. 1997.
- The Pennsylvania German Cultural Heritage Center in Kutztown, PA has a completely restored one-room schoolhouse that is open for tours. More information can be found at:
  http://www.kutztown.edu/community/pgchc/

Rickguck

19. *Eppes paerseenlich.* Answer the following questions *in Deitsch!*

    1. Wie viele Klaess hoscht du?

    2. Um was Zeit hoscht du Deitsch?

    3. Is Wisseschaft leicht?

    4. Was is der Naame vun deim Deitschschulmeeschder?

    5. Welli Klaess gleichscht du? Fer was?

20. Provide the appropriate PD word to complete the sentences:

    1. Um was Zeit (begins) _____ die Schul?

    2. Um (half) _____ acht.

    3. Hemmer am Mittwoch (science) _____?

    4. Nee, am (Thursday) _____.

    5. Ich (have) _____ heit viel Schularewet.

    6. Fer (PD) _____?

    7. Ya, un aa fer (history) _____.

    8. Dennot hoscht du heit (afternoon) _____ ken Zeit.

    9. Nee, awwer (tomorrow) _____.

    10. Gut. Ich (come) _____ mariye niwwer.

21. *Mei Klaess.* Complete Julia's observations about her class by using the words provided. You will not need all of the words.

hatt	beginnt	braucht	Klaess	griege
Mr.	Zeit	is	Buwe	allsfatt

1. Frau Eckenroth is um Vaddel nooch siwwe in der _____.

2. Die Meed un _____ kumme um fimf eb acht.

3. Die Rechelklaess _____ pinktlich.

4. Die Klaess _____ vun 7 Uhr 55 bis 8 Uhr 35.

5. Nooch der Rechelklaess kummt _____ Hoffman.

6. Die Klaess is net _____.

7. Es gebt awwer _____ viele Schularewet.

8. Ich _____ in Rechelklaess guti Maricke.

22. *Mir gehne zur Schul.* Describe (in narrative and/or dialog style) the following sequence, using the cues merely as a guideline.

You are walking to school...picking up your friend on the way...waiting several minutes before he or she comes out of the house...greeting him or her...talking about several items concerning school...arriving at school...hurrying because the first class begins soon.

Was weesscht du?

This section is intended to check your general understanding of this chapter. All of your responses should be in PD.

- *Zur Schul.* On your way to school with your friend, you ask about several things. Write five questions that you would like to have answered.

- Point to at least seven classroom objects and identify them including the articles (*der, die, es*).

- Prepare a class schedule of the subjects that you or your child are taking including days of the week and times.

- *En Interview.* Talk to a classmate, asking questions and using the question words, *wer un was*.

- Describe your daily school routine, starting with the time you leave home until you return home.

Waddelischt

aa – also
aerscht – first
allsfatt – always
die Antwatt (-e) – the answer, *f*
arig – very
awwer – but
es Babier – the paper, *n*
die Baend – the band, *f*
beginne – to begin
der Bleipensil – the pencil, *m*
brauche – to need
der Daadi – the father, *m*
die Daafel – the chalkboard, *f*
daheem – at home
Deitsch – PD
dennot – then
der Disch – the table, *m*
sich dummle – to hurry oneself
die Englisch – English, *f*
es gebt – there is, there are
die Fedder – the pen, *f*
fer was - why
folye – to follow
frieh – early
gehe – to go
glee – small
graad – right away, now
die Greid – the chalk, *f*
griege – to get, receive
die Gschicht – the history, story, *f*
die Gsundheit – the health, *f*

halwer – bottom of the hour
hatt – difficult
hawwe – to have
die Heemschtubb – the homeroom, *f*
heit – today
inderessant – interesting
ken – not, any, none
kenne – to know
die Klaess – the class, *f*
es Klaessschtubb – the classroom, *n*
der Kopp (Kepp) – the head, *m*
die Kunscht – the art class, *f*
die Landkaart – the map, *f*
langsam – slow, slowly
langweilich – boring
laut – loud
leer – empty
die Leibsklaess – favorite class, *f*
leicht – easy
lese – to read
liewe – to love
mache – to make, to do
die Marick (-e) – the grade, *f*
mariye – tomorrow
es Middaagesse – the lunch, dinner, *n*
die Minutt (-e) – the minute, *f*
die Myusick – the music, *f*
net – not
niwwer - over

es Nootbichli – the notebook, *f*
pinktlich – punctual
die Rechelklaess – the math class, *f*
ruhich – quiet
saage – to say
schpaeder – later
schpot – late
der Schtul (Schtiel) – the chair, *f*
die Schul – the school, *f*
die Schularewet – the homework, *f*
der Schulmeeschder – the male teacher, *m*
die Schulmeeschdern – the female teacher, *f*
die Schulsack (-e) – the school bag, *f*
schwetze – to speak
der Tschimm – gym class, *m*
die Uhr (-e) – the clock, *f*
um – at
Vaddel eb – quarter of
Vaddel nooch – quarter after
verbinne – to combine
was fer – what kind of
weller – which
wichdich – important
wie viel – how much
waericklich – really
die Wisseschaft – the science, *f*
die Woch – the week, *f*
die Zeit – the time, *f*
zu – too

Kabiddel 3 ~

"Mei Familye"

In this chapter you will be able to:

- Describe people
- Point out family members
- Express likes and dislikes

Ich heer gaern Myusick

Tom:	Guder Mariye, Alex.
Alex:	Tom! Wie bischt!
Tom:	Was fer Myusik heerscht du gaern?
Alex:	Ich gleich Classical, wie Mozart un Bach.
Tom:	Ugh. Ich gleich selli Myusik gaar net.
Alex:	Fer was?
Tom:	Mozart un Bach sin langweilich!
Alex:	Sell mehnt mei Bruder aa!
Tom:	Dann gleich ich sei Gschmack mit Myusik.
Alex:	Was denkscht du vun Rockmyusik?
Tom:	Rockmyusik heere ich allsfatt gaern. Die is so wunnerbaar! Was denkscht du?

1. Answer the following questions based on the dialog.

   1. Was fer Myusick gleicht der Alex?

   2. Fer was gleicht der Tom Classicalmyusick net?

   3. Was fer Myusick gleicht der Tom?

   4. Fer was gleicht der Tom Rockmyusick?

Wer gleicht Boi?

Abby:	Mark! Do bischt du yo!
Mark:	Guder Daag, Abby!
Abby:	Wu is dei Mudder? Ich hab en Boi vun meinre Grossmudder fer sie.
Mark:	Was fer en Boi?
Abby:	Sell is en Kascheboi.
Mark:	Ya, mei Mudder gleicht Kascheboi...un mei Daadi duht aa.
Abby:	Mir hen zu viel Kasche daheem. Mei Grossdaadi gleicht sie net un mei Eldre esse ken Boi.
Mark:	Fer was esse dei Eldre ken Boi?
Abby:	Mei Mudder mehnt, Boi hot zu viel Zucker. Mei Daadi gleicht der Deeg net.
Mark:	Well, mir duhne der Boi gaern esse! Hattyee, Abby!

2. *Was weesscht du vun dem Dialog?* Answer the following questions based on the above dialog:

    1. Was hot Abby fer dem Mark sei Mudder?

    2. Was fer Obscht gleicht der Abby ihr Grossdaadi net?

    3. Wer kann ken Boi esse? Fer was?

Schprooch

Present Tense of *wisse*

The verb *wisse* (to know) has irregular forms when it is used with *ich, du* and *er, sie, es*. The plural forms are regular.

Singular	ich	**weess**	I know
	du	**weesscht**	you know
	er		he knows
	sie	**weess**	she knows
	es		it knows
Plural	mir	**wisse**	we know
	dihr	**wisst**	you guys know
	sie	**wisse**	they know

Note that both words (in some PD speaking communities), *kenne* and *wisse*, mean "to know". However, *kenne* means "to know a person, a place or a thing," whereas *wisse* means "to know something" (as a fact).

Kennscht du der James? Do you know James?

Weesscht du, wer der James is? Do you know who James is?

Mir kenne Harrisbaerrick. We know Harrisburg.

Kennscht du sell Buch? Do you know this book?

Wisse sie, wu sell Buch is? Do they know where that book is?

3. Fill in the blanks with the appropriate forms of *wisse*.

    1. Die Gloria _____ die Antwatt.

    2. Der Robert un die McKenzie _____, wu mei Haus is.

    3. Ich _____ mei Naame.

    4. _____ dihr, wu Erie is?

    5. _____ die Heidi mei Fonnumner?

    6. Mir _____, wer sei Bruder is.

4. *Kenne* odder *Wisse*? Provide the correct form of the appropriate verb.

    1. _____ sie, was Zeit as der Brian kummt?

    2. Ich _____ die Molly. Sie is mei Schweschder.

    3. _____ du Fraa Hamm?

    4. _____ dihr, was der Ralph un der Walter heit mache?

    5. _____ die Christina die Antwatt?

    6. Mir _____, wu Mr. Beam wuhnt.

    7. _____ dihr Fraa Dreibelbis ihre Dochder?

    8. Die Hannah _____ die Rachel gut.

Eppes zu wisse

Die Familye

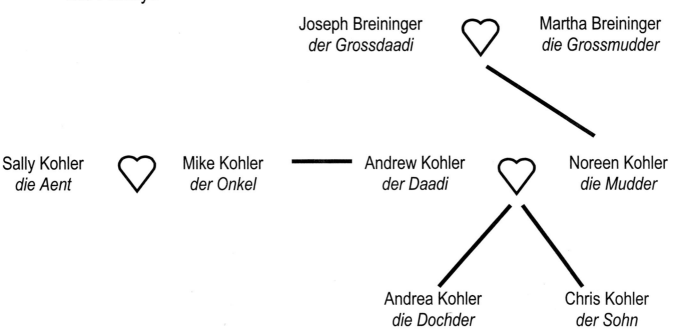

Der Andrew Kohler is der Andrea ihr Daadi.
Die Noreen Kohler is der Andrea un dem Chris ihre Mudder.
Der Andrew un die Noreen Kohler sin der Andrea un dem Chris ihre Eldre.
Die Andrea is dem Chris sei Schweschder.

Der Chris is der Sohn vun dem Andrew un der Noreen Kohler.
Die Andrea is die Dochder vun dem Andrew un der Noreen Kohler.

Der Joseph Breininger is der Andrea un dem Chris ihr Grossdaadi.
Die Martha Breininger is der Andrea un dem Chris ihre Grossmudder.
Der Joseph un die Martha Breininger sin der Andrea un dem Chris ihre Grosseldre.

Der Mike Kohler, der Bruder vun dem Andrew Kohler, is dem Chris sei Onkel.
Die Sally Kohler is der Andrea ihre Aent.

* A note about possession: In English, possession is shown with ('s), e.g. John's book. In PD, possession is expressed differently: with "vun" (from) or one of the possessive adjectives (see chapter 2), e.g. *dem John sei Buch* = John's book. You will fully learn about possession in a later chapter.

5. *Schreib en Antwatt fer selli Froget!* Use the family tree given on the previous page.

    1. Wer is dem Chris sei Schweschder?

    2. Wie heesst der Andrea ihre Aent?

    3. Wie heesst der Noreen Kohler ihr Daadi?

    4. Wer is dem Chris sei Grossmudder?

    5. Wer is dem Mike Kohler sei Bruder?

    6. Wie heesst dem Andrew Kohler sei Sohn?

6. *Dei Familye.* Talk with a classmate about his or her family members. Then, reverse roles and talk about your family.

7. *Mach en Familyebaam* (family tree). Label all of your relatives using the PD words. Put a star next to the people on your tree that could speak PD.

8. Describe your favorite TV family in PD.

9. Bring in family photos and describe them to your classmates.

Schprooch

gleiche un net gleiche

To express likes and dislikes in PD, use the verb *gleiche* (to like). It is a regular verb and conjugates normally.

> *Ich gleich Baseball schpiele.* – I like to play baseball.

> *Ich gleich net Baseball schpiele.* – I don't like to play baseball.

10. *Was gleicht er/sie odder Was gleicht er/sie net*? Using the sentences provided, tell what the person likes or doesn't like to do:

* Der Tom hot viele CDs.

* Er gleicht Myusik heere.

1. Der Robert sammelt altes Geld.

2. Die Cindy schpielt die Glapperbax alli Daag vun der Woch.

3. Die Samantha esst all die Gaardesache awwer ken Selleri.

4. Der Andy hot viele Bicher.

5. Der Matt hot zwee Katze un ken Hund.

11. *Was gleichscht du?* Answer the following questions about yourself.

1. Gleichscht du Baseball? Football?

2. Gleichscht du Myusik? Was fer Myusik?

3. Gleichscht du lese? Was fer Bicher?

4. Gleichscht du eppes sammele? Was sammelscht du?

5. Gleichscht du Movies? Was fer Movies?

6. Was nooch?

Saag eppes

Was denkscht du vun _____?

To ask what you think of something or how you find something, use the phrase "*Was denkscht du vun _____*"

> *Was denkscht du vun dem Bresident?*
>
> *Ich denk der Bresident is en guter Mann.*

12. *Was denkscht du vun...?* Using the adjective below (or others) answer the following questions completely.

gut	schlecht	bleed	wunnerbaar	langweilich
net so gut	inderessant	bissel zu hatt	dumm	zu gross
gutguckich	hesslich	zu laut	zu langsam	zu glee

1. Was denkscht du vun Deitsch?

2. Was denkscht du vun Rock-myusik?

3. Was denkscht du vun Classical-myusik?

4. Was denkscht du vun Gaardesach?

5. Was denkscht du vun deim Deitschschulmeeschder?

6. Was denkscht du vun der Schtadt Nei Yarrick?

7. Was denkscht du vun Barricks Kaundi?

8. Was denkscht du vun Deitschland?

9. Was denkscht du vun deinre Familye?

10. Was denkscht du vun deine Kichli?

11. Was nooch?

13. Interview a partner using the questions above (or others). Present the results to another classmate. Discuss similar opinions with the whole class.

Schprooch

The Accusative Case

As we learned in chapter 1, the nominative case identifies the subject of a sentence. The accusative case is used to identify the direct object of a sentence.

Die Andrea kaaft es Buch. – *Andrea* is the subject (nominative), *kaaft*, the verb and *es Buch* the direct object.

Kennscht du der Onkel? Do you know the uncle?

Ich heer die Myusick. – I am listening to the music.

Mir lese der Brief. – We are reading the letter.

Definite Articles:

	Masculine	Feminine	Neuter
Nominative	**der**	**die**	**es**
Accusative	**der**	**die**	**es**

From the chart, you can see that the *der* words for both nominative and accusative cases do not change.

14. Fill in the blanks with the appropriate *der* word.

1. _____ Meedel kaaft _____ Bleipensil.

2. _____ Daadi leest _____ Buch.

3. _____ Mudder bringt _____ Calculator.

4. _____ Schulmeeschder schreibt _____ Brief.

Personal Pronouns:

Nominative	Accusative
ich	**mich**
du	**dich**
er	**en**
sie	**sie**
es	**es**
mir	**uns**
dihr	**eich**
sie	**sie**

Indefinite Articles:

	Masculine	Feminine	Neuter
Nominative:	**en**	**en**	**en**
Accusative:	**en**	**en**	**en**

15. Definite Articles, Indefinite Articles or Personal Pronouns.

1. Kennscht du _____ (the) Schulmeeschder?

2. Kaafe mir _____ (a) Haus?

3. Die Susan kennt _____ (us).

4. Mir lese _____ (the) Buch.

5. Wann beginnt _____ (the) Klaess?

6. Ich kenne _____ (him).

7. Ich brauche _____ (a) Fedder.

8. Die Susan schpielt _____ (the) Glapperbax.

9. Is es Geschenk fer _____ (me)?

51

Schprooch

Accusative Prepositions

The Accusative case always follows these prepositions:

bis	*until, till, by*
darrich	*through*
fer	*for*
geeich	*against*
gege	*against*
um	*around*
unne	*without*
wedder	*against*

Darrich der Daag duh ich viel.

Es Buch is **fer mich**.

Der Hund laaft **um der** Gaarde.

These accusative prepositions and articles are contracted as long as there is no special emphasis on the article.

darrich + es =	**darrich's**
fer + es =	**fer's**
geeich + es =	**geeich's**
um + es =	**um's**
wedder + es =	**wedder's**

Ich geh **um's** Haus.

Der Bu schpielt **geeich's** Maedel.

Geb Acht!

Irregular Plural Nouns

As discussed in Kabiddel 1 there are different ways of forming the plural of PD nouns. There are some nouns in PD that are considered irregular, meaning that their plural form is quite different from their singular form. Below are just a few of these nouns. Always check a PD dictionary when forming the plural of nouns that you are not familiar with.

Singular	Plural
der Bu	die Buwe
die Fraa	die Weiwer, die Weibsleit
es Meedel	die Meed
der Mann	die Mannsleit

Der Bu singt en Lied. - Die Buwe singe en Lied.

Die Fraa kocht gaern. - Die Weibsleit koche gaern.

Es Meedel laaft schnell. - Die Meed laafe schnell.

Der Mann gleicht Boi esse. - Die Mannsleit gleiche Boi esse.

Kuldur

Pennsylvania Dutch Fraktur Folk Art

Pennsylvania Dutch folk art had its high point in the second half of the eighteenth century and first half of the nineteenth century. The use of vivid colors and decoration of utilitarian objects (e.g. pie plates, cookie cutters, dough trays, tombstones, etc.) characterize Pennsylvania Dutch folk art.

The Pennsylvania Dutch adopted European art traditions of manuscript illumination. Of all the Pennsylvania Dutch folk art, possibly the most impressive is the fraktur art, decorating birth and baptismal certificates, bookplates, and Vorschriften. Fraktur describes the writing style used. Predominately the colors used for this paper artwork were reds, yellows, greens, and blues; the most familiar motifs included tulips and hearts. Typically an itinerant fraktur artist would go from home to home with samples of his artistry as Vorschriften and then be commissioned to decorate birth and baptismal certificates for the household.

The writing used on the fraktur art is typically in standard German, with passages from hymns or Bible verses. Since the emphasis on fraktur art is on tradition, there is rarely extreme departure from standard texts or standard designs.

The Amish and Mennonites also practice fraktur folk art. Possibly the most prominent Amish folk artist was Barbara Ebersol, who designed book plates among other things. The Amish and Mennonites typically do not have baptismal certificates in fraktur style. The most prominent Mennonite folk artist was Christopher Dock, a schoolteacher in southeastern Pennsylvania, who presented his students with fraktur rewards for good merit.

Further reading:

- Shelley, D. A. The fraktur writing or illuminated manuscripts of the Pennsylvania Germans. Allentown, PA: 1961.
- Schlechter's. Lichten, F. Folk art of rural Pennsylvania. New York: Scribner. 1946.

- Weiser, F. S. & Howell J. H. <u>The Pennsylvania German fraktur of the Free Library of Philadelphia</u>. Pennsylvania German Society & Free Library of Philadelphia. 1976.
- Yoder, D. <u>The Pennsylvania German broadside</u>. University Park, PA: Penn State Press. 2005.

An example of fraktur folk art from the collection at the Muddy Creek Farm Library, Ephrata, Pennsylvania

Rickguck

16. Fill in the blank with the appropriate form of either *wisse* or *kenne*:

    1. Ich _____ die Antwatt.

    2. Die Andrea _____ es Meedel vun Allentown.

    3. _____ dihr, was ich heit ess?

    4. Der John _____ die Eve arig gut.

    5. Mir _____ wu die Smiths wuhne.

17. *Was gleicht dei Partner?* Using the questions from exercise number 9 and others that you have formulated, ask a partner what he/she likes and does not like. Report your findings to the class.

18. Fill in the blanks with the appropriate definite articles, indefinite articles or personal pronouns.

    1. Kennt er _____ (a) Mann vun Harrisbaerrick?

    2. Dihr kaaft _____ (the) Buch.

    3. Du kennscht _____ (her).

    4. Wer gleicht _____ (the) Boi esse?

    5. Der Schulmeeschder kennt _____ (us) gut.

19. Using the questions below, tell what you think each person thinks of the item associated with them.

    1. Was denkt en Amerikaaner vun Freiheit?

    2. Was denke die Amische vun Leckdrick?

    3. Was denkt en Bauer vun gutem Wedder?

    4. Was denkt en Schulmeeschder vun Schularewet?

    5. Was denkt en Grossdaadi vun Rockmyusick?

Was weesscht du?

This section is intended to check your general understanding of this chapter. All of your responses should be in PD.

- Tell your classmates about four family members or relatives and indicate their names and ages and where they live.

- Describe where you live, who else lives there and what time you are usually at home.

- Count in fives from 0 to 100.

- Describe the difference between *wisse* and *kenne*. Create sentences using both verbs.

- Look through a grocery store flier. With a partner, point to various objects and say if you like them or if you dislike them.

- Say in PD:
  a. How old your friend is.

  b. Where he or she lives.

  c. That your friend's brother or sister is good.

Waddelischt

die **Aent** – the aunt, *f*
der **Amerikaaner** – the American, *m*
die **Amische** – the Amish, *pl*
der **Bauer (-e)** – the farmer, *m*
bissel – a little
bleed – shy
der **Boi** – the pie, *m*
der **Bresident (-e)** – the president, *m*
der **Brief** – the letter, *m*
bringe – to bring
der **Bruder (Brieder)** – the brother, *m*
der **Daadi** – the father, *m*
der **Deeg** – the dough, *m*
denke – to think
die **Dochder (Dechder)** – the daughter, *f*
dumm – dumb
die **Eldre** – the parents, *pl*
esse – to eat
der **Familyebaam** – the family tree, *m*
fer – for
die **Freiheit** – the liberty, the freedom, *f*
gaar – absolutely
es **Gaardesach (-e)** – the vegetables, *n*
es **Geld** – the money, *n*
es **Geschenk (-e)** – the present, gift, *n*
die **Glapperbax (-e)** – the piano, *f*
gleiche – to like
der **Grossdaadi** – the grandfather, *m*
die **Grosseldre** – the grandparents, *pl*
die **Grossmudder** – the grandmother, *f*

der **Gschmack** – the taste, *m*
gutguckich – good looking
heere – to hear
hesslich – ugly
der **Hund** – the dog, *m*
kaafe – to buy
die **Kasch (-e)** – the cherry, *f*
die **Katz (-e)** – the cat, *f*
es **Kichli (-n)** – the cookie, *n*
koche – to cook
laafe – to walk
die **Leckdrick** – the electricity, *f*
es **Lied (-er)** – the song, *n*
mehne – to be of the opinion
die **Mudder (Midder)** – the mother, *f*
der **Onkel** – the uncle, *m*
die **Rockmyusick** – the rock music, *f*
sammle – to collect
schnell – quickly
schpiele – to play
schreiwe – to write
die **Schweschder (-e)** – the sister, *f*
der **Selleri** – the celery, *m*
singe – to sing
der **Sohn (Seh)** – the son, *m*
viel – much
vun – of, from
wisse – to know a fact
wunnerbaar – wonderful
der **Zucker** – the sugar, *m*

Kabiddel 4 –

"Uff em Land"

In this chapter you will be able to:

- Describe rural life
- Describe various times of the year
- Describe the weather

In der Gaarde

Chris:	Daniel!
Daniel:	Guder Mariye, Chris!
Chris:	Was machscht du do?
Daniel:	Ich bin an meim Gaarde blanse.
Chris:	Is sell hatt?
Daniel:	Net so hatt...awwer mei Gaarde is aa net so gross.
Chris:	Was musschst du so mache?
Daniel:	Ich blans die Gaardesach, wesser die Blanse un ropp's Umgraut...
Chris:	Sell is en bissel zu viel Arewet fer mich!
Daniel:	Awwer dann kann ich die Gaardesach roppe. Ich gleich frische Aerbse, Grummbiere, un Gehlriewe esse.
Chris:	Well, ich gleich aa frischi Gaardesach... awwer ich hab kee Zeit... ich kaaf mir sie mol im Schdor!

1. *Was weesscht du vun der Dialog?*

   1. Was macht der Daniel?

   2. Was macht mer in der Gaarde?

   3. Was gleiche der Chris un der Daniel?

   4. Was macht der Chris?

En Klaessreis uff re Bauerei.

Schulmeeschdern:	Well, Kinner, ich bin arig froh, as mir all do uff der Bauerei sin! Mir kenne viel vun de Gediere und de Blanse lanne.
Alex:	Was is sell?!?!
Schulmeeschdern:	Sell is die Sau. Ihr Schwans is net so graad un sie is arig dick.
Melanie:	Un sell is es Hinkel, gell?
Schulmeeschdern:	Ya, sell is es Hinkel. Wisst dihr was mir vun em Hinkel esse?
Alex:	Oier!
Schulmeeschdern:	Sell is recht, Alex. Un guck mol! Datt is en Gans un en Ent!
Rebecca:	Ich gleich die Ent. Sie yammert net so viel wie die Gans.
Schulmeeschdern:	Un datt is en Gaul.
Melanie:	Er is awwer gross un schee.
Rebecca:	Kenne mir der Gaul reide?
Schulmeeschdern:	Ich denk, der Gaul is bissel zu gross fer eich Kinner.
Alex:	Guck mol! Datt is en Gees. Mei Mudder saagt, die Gees duhne es Graas fresse... verleicht sette mir eener daheem hawwe, no brauch mei Daadi es Graas nimmi maehe!

2. *Was weesscht du vun seller Dialog?*

      1. Wu is die Klaess heit?

      2. Wie guckt die Sau?

      3. Was esse mir vun em Hinkel?

      4. Gleicht die Rebecca die Gans? Fer was odder fer was net?

      5. Reide die Kinner der Gaul? Fer was odder fer was net?

      6. Fer was braucht der Alex en Gees?

Schprooch

Present Tense of *sei*

The forms of *sei* (to be) are irregular; they do not follow the same pattern as regular verb forms.

Singular	ich	**bin**	I am
	du	**bischt**	you are
	er		he is
	sie	**is**	she is
	es		it is
Plural	mir	**sin**	we are
	dihr	**seid**	you (plural) are
	sie	**sin**	they are

Special Note: When saying "it is" – "*es is*" it is commonly said and written as: *'sis* (contraction of es + is).

Wie alt bischt du?   *Der Rob un der Jason sin schunn do.*

Ich bin neinzeh Yaahre alt.   *'Sis en scheener Daag*

3. Pretend you are interested in learning about several people at a party. Ask some questions using the cues.

    * Der Zach un der Ryan / net do
    * Sin der Zach un der Ryan net do?

    1. Die Emma un der Will / gscheit

    2. Der Scott / en Bauer

    3. du / der Kate ihr Freind

    4. dihr / in Deitsch gut

Eppes zu wisse

Uff der Bauerei! As we know, farming was a very important part of the Pennsylvania Dutch culture and history. Therefore it is important to learn various vocabulary words associated with the farm and farming.

die Gediere	the Animals
die Kuh	Cow
der Gaul	Horse
die Sau	Pig
der Hund	Dog
die Katz	Cat
es Hinkel	Chicken
der Haahne	Rooster
die Gluck	Hen
der Welschhaahne	Turkey
die Gans	Goose
die Ent	Duck
der Gees	Goat
es Schof	Sheep

Um der Scheierhof	Around the Barnyard
die Scheier	*Barn*
es Bauerehaus	*Farmhouse*
der Schopp	*Shed*
die Fens	*Fence*
es Fenschder	*Window*
der Traktor	*Tractor*
der Waage	*Wagon*
der Blug	*Plow*
es Feld	*Field*
der Gaarde	*Garden*

Annere Wadde	Other Words
blanse	*to plant*
picke	*to pick*
drenke / wessere	*to water an animal / plant*
roppe	*to weed, to pluck*

die Blanse	The Plants
es Welschkann	Corn
die Grummbier	Potato
es Tomaet	Tomato
die Aerbs	Peas
die Gehlrieb	Carrot
die Buhn	Bean
die Rotrieb	Red Beet
es Schtroh	Straw
der Weeze	Wheat
es Hoi	Hay
der Hawwer	Oat
es Graas	Grass
es Umgraut	Weed

> Brainstorm in a group farming vocabulary not found in the list.

4. *Weller Gediere is sell?* Tell which animal is being described.

  1. Gebt uns Millich.

  2. Mir esse sell fer Dankfescht.

  3. Gebt uns Oier.

  4. Fliegt Sudd im Winder.

  5. Gebt uns Woll.

  6. Is dem Mann sei beschter Freind.

  7. Gleicht in dem Dreck lege.

5. Using vocabulary from the previous pages, discuss with a partner things found on a farm, favorite animal or vegetable.

Schprooch

Irregular Verbs

You have already learned that some verbs in the present tense are conjugated irregularly (see Chapter 2). In addition to those earlier, here are two more to learn:

Griege is 'to get' and is irregular in the singular forms:

ich grick	mir griege
du grickscht	dihr griegt
er grickt	sie griege

Geh is 'to go' and is irregular in the plural forms by adding an 'n' between the root and the endings. Note that other verbs, like '*schtehe*' (to stand) and '*duh*' (to do, make) follow the same pattern.

ich geh	mir gehne
du gehscht	dihr gehnt
er geht	sie gehne

6. Fill-in the correct verb form.

    1. Mir _____ (go) in die Karich.

    2. Der Sam _____ (gets) der Ball.

    3. Ich _____ (stand) bei der Scheier.

    4. Der Tom un du _____ (stand) unnich em Fenschder.

    5. Der David _____ (does) sei Arewet.

    6. Der David un der Mark _____ (do) nix alli Daag.

7. Fill-in the following text with correct verb forms.

Heit _____ (sei) ich mei Buch am lese. Ich _____ (hawwe) aa nooch so viel zu duh. Mei Mudder un ich _____ (geh) in der Schdor und mir _____ (kaafe) Aerbse un Grummbiere. Dennoh _____ (gucke) ich bissel in die Guckbax. Vielleicht _____ (schpiele) mei Schweschder aa nooch der Glapperbax. Sell _____ (gleiche) ich.

Schprooch

Es Gebt

The phrase "*es gebt*" in PD translates to "there is" or "there are" in English. English speakers have a tendency to want to say "*datt is*" or "*datt sin*". Do not make this error in your speaking and writing.

Es gebt en Gaul in dem Feld.

Gebt es viel Wasser fer der Hund zu saufe?

Eppes zu lese

Practice reading the poem aloud. Try composing your own poem in PD.

Umgraut Roppe
Peter V. Fritsch

Rausroppe! Rausziehe!
Des wieschderli Graut!
Des hot mir mei ganzer Gaarde versaut!

Do schtreng ich der Buckel,
Un schwitz noch dazu.
Fer schee Gaarde halde, grickt mir ken Ruh.

Umleitliche Bledder,
Sie glitze vun Hand!
Odders Watzel brecht ab, graad wie es kann!

So widderlich Umgraut!
So schtowwerich Schteck!
Verfluchdichni Blanse, zum Deiwel geh weck!

[Reprinted with permission from: Fritsch, Peter V. <u>Der Haahne greht</u>. Morgantown, PA: Masthof Press, 2006.]

Eppes zu wisse

Die Munet un Yaahreszeite

Yenner	Hanning	Matz	Abrill
Winder	Winder	Friehyaahr	Friehyaahr
Moi	Tschunn	Tschulei	Aaguscht
Friehyaahr	Summer	Summer	Summer
September	Oktower	Nofember	Diesember
Schpotyaahr	Schpotyaahr	Schpotyaahr	Winder

8. *Im Friehyaahr, Summer, Schpotyaahr odder Winder?* Relate the months to the seasons.

   * *Yenner - Yenner is im Winder.*

   1. Tschulei

   2. Oktower

   3. Diesember

   4. Moi

9. *Weller Munet is sell?* Determine the month in which each event takes place.

   1. Dankfescht

   2. Valentine's Day

   3. Independence Day

   4. Your birthday

   5. Memorial Day

   6. Halloween

Schprooch

Es Wedder

When asking about the weather in *Deitsch*, use the phrase: *"Wie is es Wedder?*
Below are various ways of describing the weather.

Die Sunn scheint.	The sun is shining. / It is sunny.
Es reggert.	*It is raining.*
Es schneet.	*It is snowing.*
Es dunnert.	*It is thundering.*
'Sis schee.	*It is nice out.*
'Sis schlecht.	*It is nasty out.*
'Sis kalt.	*It is cold.*
'Sis kiehl.	*It is cool.*
'Sis warm.	*It is warm.*
'Sis hees.	*It is hot.*
'Sis windich.	*It is windy.*

Saag eppes

Here are some more weather words:

drieb – *cloudy*

darr, drucke – *dry*

suddlich – *drizzling*

newwlich – *foggy*

schmodich – *humid*

feicht – *damp*

eisich – *icy*

10. *Wie is es Wedder in Gettysburg?* Using the forecast given, describe the weather for each day. All of your answers should be *in Deitsch*.

Wednesday	Thursday	Friday	Saturday	Sunday
Cloudy	Thunderstorms	Rain	Rain	Cloudy
41° | 34°	61° | 44°	60° | 40°	51° | 34°	56° | 37°

1. Mittwoch

2. Dunnerschdaag

3. Freidaag

4. Samschdaag

5. Sunndaag

11. Describe the weather in Pennsylvania for the following months *in Deitsch*.

1. Aaguscht

2. Yenner

3. Abrill

4. Nofember

5. Diesember

12. How is the weather today? What is your favorite type of weather and why?

Schprooch

Present Progressive

You have already learned how to form the present tense in Deitsch. However, similar to English, Deitsch has two present tense forms:

(a) Sarah plays the piano.

(b) Sarah is playing the piano.

In (a) there is a sense of repetition; Sarah plays the piano *every Friday*, for example. In (b) there is a sense of present action; *At this very moment in time* Sarah is playing the piano. You have been working with verb conjugations like the first example:

(a) Sarah plays the piano.

   Die Sarah schpielt die Glapperbax.

But if you need to express an action that is happening at that moment in conversation, then use:

(b) Sarah is playing the piano.

   Die Sarah **is** die Glapperbax **am schpiele**.

The form of the present progressive involves the helping verb '*sei*' and '*am + infinitive of the verb.*' The '*am + infinitive*' is generally placed at the end of the sentence.

13. Insert an appropriate form of a verb into the blanks below.

    1. Ich _____ mei Taxe am ausfiggere.

    2. Du _____ der Guckbax am gucke.

    3. Mir _____ am naehe.

    4. Er is sei Katz _____.

    5. Die Tina is die Fenschder _____.

    6. Sie sin die Aerbse _____.

14. Change the following sentences from regular present tense into the present progressive.

    1. Der Mark wessert die Blanse.

    2. Der Tim roppt der Gaarde.

    3. Der Mark un die Sarah picke es Welschkann.

    4. Sie esse die Grummbiere.

    5. Er butzt es Fenschder.

    6. Dihr faahrt der Traktor.

15. *Die Ausrette* (excuses). You are on the phone with a friend who wants to go to the movies. You aren't able to join her at the moment, because you are in the middle of something. Give excuses from the list below or use your own.

    1. Buch lese

    2. Myusik heere

    3. Gleeder wesche

    4. Haus butze

    5. Owedesse esse

    6. Kuche backe

    7. ???

Geb Acht!

You may have noticed that sometimes physical gender corresponds to grammatical gender:

der Mann	the (*m*) man
die Fraa	the (*f*) woman
der Bu	the (*m*) boy
der Daadi	the (*m*) dad
die Mudder	the (*f*) mother

However, *Maedel* 'girl' is neuter, **es Maedel**. The reason that *Maedel* is neuter is because of the *–el* ending, which always requires the noun to be neuter. That ending is called a "diminutive ending" and it makes the noun "smaller." This is similar to the –ette ending in English, e.g. kitchenette, Paulette, etc.

In the Pennsylvania Dutch speaking areas, there are two distinct diminutive endings, *-che* and *–li / -el*. The *–che* ending is predominately found in the northeastern counties of the core Pennsylvania Dutch speaking area (Berks, Lehigh, Northampton etc.), while *–li* is found in the southern counties (Lancaster, York, Lebanon etc.) and among all Mennonite and Amish speakers in other parts of Pennsylvania, the Midwest, and Canada.

By adding one of these endings to the noun, you will make it smaller...so a small piece of paper (*Babier*) is called either a *Babierche* or a *Babierli*. In either case, the gender is neuter!

Note that some vowels may change when you add the diminutive ending...so *Kapp* becomes *Keppli*.

16. Create diminutives of the following words.

1. Babiersack

2. Fuuss

3. Blans

4. Blumm

5. Hutsch

Schprooch

Compound Nouns

Sometimes two nouns can come together and make one word in Deitsch, just as in English, e.g. wallpaper.

In Deitsch the second noun in the compound determines both the plural ending and the gender of the entire compound, so *der Hawwer* (oat) + *es Mehl* (flour) = *es Hawwermehl* (oatmeal).

17. Use nouns from list I and combine them with nouns from list II to create new words (use a dictionary if necessary). Remember to mark the gender of the new word:

I	II
der Regge	die Yacht
der Blohbier	die Schissel
die Haase	der Graut
die Suppe	es Wasser
die Hexe	die Wascht
der Summer	der Tee

18. Scan written PD Texts for compound nouns. Try with a partner to figure out their meanings.

Kuldur

Pennsylvania Dutch Farming

It seems that Pennsylvania Dutch and farming are linked together. As we know, the vast majority of Pennsylvania Dutch were farmers throughout southeastern Pennsylvania. Not only were they farmers, but the Pennsylvania Dutch are considered among the greatest farmers in American history. Many of their agricultural traditions have shaped American farming practices that are still used today. In Oscar Kuhns' book <u>The German and Swiss Settlements of Colonial Pennsylvania</u>, he illustrates why and how the PD farmers were successful: "their prosperity was largely due to their earnestness, frugality and consummate agricultural skill." Other reasons for the PD farming successes was the limestone soil in southeastern Pennsylvania and crop rotation practices.

PD farming practices were brought to America as the PD emigrated from the Palatinate and Rhineland areas of Germany. Most PD farmers were completely self-sufficient, especially in canning their harvested vegetables and fruits for use throughout the winter.

In order to accommodate the farm, the PD built one of their most lasting legacies to the Pennsylvania landscape: the Bank Barn. A Bank Barn or Pennsylvania Barn is a style of barn noted for its accessibility, at ground level, on two separate floors. Often built into the side of a hill (bank) both the upper and the lower floors area could be accessed from ground level. Many still survive today.

Life on the farm centered around planting, harvesting etc. and was planned accordinly to advice found in yearly agricultural almanacs, containing weather forecasts, planting charts, astronomical data, recipes. Agricultural almanacs are still published today, the most famous is <u>Baer's Agricultural Almanac</u> published in Lancaster.

A typical PD farm would include a farm house (usually stone, but not always) with a summer kitchen, a bank barn, a smoke house, a root or cold cellar for the storing of canned goods, an orchard, a vegetable garden, and plenty of fields.

Consider visiting the *Landis Valley Museum* located just outside of Lancaster. The Landis Valley Museum is a living history village and farm. Another good place to visit is the *Pennsylvania German Heritage Center* located in Kutztown. The Center is located on a 30-acre 19th century farmstead with restored buildings and a library.

For more information about Pennsylvania Dutch Farming please consider these titles:

- Richman, Irwin. <u>Pennsylvania German Farms, Gardens and Seeds: Landis Valley in Four Centuries</u>. Schiffer Publishing. 2007.
- Ensminger, Robert F. <u>The Pennsylvania Barn: Its Origin, Evolution and Distribution in North America</u>. Johns Hopkins University Press. 2003.
- Fegely, H. Winslow. <u>Farming Always Farming</u>. Pennsylvania German Society. 1987.

Also these websites:

- *Landis Valley Museum*: http://www.landisvalleymuseum.org
- *Pennsylvania German Heritage Center*: http://www.kutztown.edu/community/pgchc/index1.htm

Rickguck

19. Supply the correct forms of *sei*.

    1. Wie viel Uhr _____ es nau?

    2. Die Melanie un die Sonja _____ in der Schtadt.

    3. _____ du um acht Uhr daheem?

    4. Dihr _____ allsfatt so schpot.

    5. Ich _____ Maryie net do.

    6. Ohio _____ net weit vun do.

    7. _____ er Mr. Kreider?

    8. _____ dihr um siwwe do?

    9. Wer _____ es Meedel?

    10. Die Arewet _____ leicht.

20. *Gedier, Blans odder Munet.* Tell which category the following words fall into.

    1. Moi

    2. Hoi

    3. Gaul

    4. Welschkann

    5. Matz

    6. Katz

    7. Tschulei

    8. Gees

    9. Grummbier

21. Describe the weather in Pennsylvania for the following seasons:

    1. Summer

    2. Winder

    3. Schpotyaahr

    4. Friehyaahr

22. Change the following sentences from the present progressive to regular present tense.

    1. Der Josh is die Blumme am wessere.

    2. Die Lauren is es Umgraut am roppe.

    3. Der Bill un die Tina sin die Grummbiere am ausmache.

    4. Dihr seid der Gaul am reide.

    5. Du bischt es Fenschder am butze.

Was weesscht du?

This section is intended to check your general understanding of this chapter. All of your responses should be in PD.

- Describe *in Deitsch* what you have in your garden. Also describe what you have to do to maintain your garden.

- *Was gebt's alles uff re Bauerei?* Select three things you would find on a farm and write at least two sentences about each one.

- Imagine that you and your friend are visiting a local Amish farm. Create a dialog describing your visit.

- Visit **http://www.weather.com** and find the weather forecasts for the following cities. Then describe the weather *in Deitsch.*

  a. Reading

  b. Philadelphia

  c. Lancaster

  d. Scranton

  e. Mainz, Germany

Waddelischt

die **Aerbs (-e)** – the pea, *f*
ausfiggere – to figure out
ausmache – to dig potatoes
es **Bauerehaus (-heiser)** – the farmhouse, *n*
die **Bauerei** – the farm, *f*
blanse – to plant
der **Blug (Blieg)** – the plow, *m*
die **Buhn (-e)** – the bean, *f*
butze – to clean
darr - dry
dernoh - afterwards
der **Dreck** – the dirt, *m*
drenke – to water (animals)
drieb – cloudy, overcast
duh – to do
dunnere – to thunder
eisich – icy
die **Ent (-e)** – the duck, *f*
feicht - damp
es **Feld (-er)** – the field, *n*
die **Fens (-e)** – the fence, *f*
es **Fenschder (-e)** – the window, *n*
fliege – to fly
fresse – to eat (animals)
frisch – fresh
der **Fuuss (Fiess)** – the foot, *m*
die **Gaarde** – the garden, *f*
der **Gans (Gens)** – the goose, *m*
der **Gaul (Geil)** – the horse, *m*
es **Gedier (-e)** – the animal, *n*
der **Gees** – the goat, *m*

die **Gehlrieb (-riewe)** – the carrot, *f*
Gell? – Right?
die **Gluck** – the hen, *f*
es **Graas** – the grass, *n*
griege – to get
die **Grummbier (-e)** – the potato, *f*
gucke – to look, to see, to watch
der **Guckbax** – the television, *m*
der **Haahne** – the rooster, *m*
hees - hot
es **Hinkel** – the chicken, *n*
es **Hutsch** – the colt, *m*
kalt - cold
die **Karich (-e)** – the church, *f*
kiehl - cool
die **Kuh (Kieh)** – the cow, *f*
es **Land (Lenner)** – the land, country, *n*
lege – to lay
maehe – to mow
die **Millich** – the milk, *f*
naehe – to sew
newwlich - foggy
es **Oi (-er)** – the egg, *n*
es **Owedesse** – the evening meal, supper, *n*
picke – to pick
reggere – to rain
reide – to ride
roppe – to pick
die **Rotrieb (-riewe)** – the red beet, *f*
die **Sau (Sei)** – the pig, *f*

saufe – to drink (animals)
der **Schdor (-e)** – the store, *m*
die **Scheier (-e)** – the barn, *f*
der **Scheierhof** – the barnyard, *m*
scheine – to shine
schmodich - humid
schnee-e – to snow
es **Schof** – the sheep, *n*
der **Schopp** – the shed, *m*
schtehe – to stand
es **Schtroh** – the straw, *n*
schunn - already
der **Schwans** – the tail, *m*
sei – to be
der **Sudd** – the south, *m*
suddlich - drizzling
die **Sunn** – the sun, *f*
es **Tomaet (-s)** – the tomato, *n*
der **Traktor (-s)** – the tractor, *m*
uff – on
es **Umgraut** – the weed, *n*
der **Waage (Wegge)** – the wagon, *m*
warm - warm
der **Weeze** – the wheat, *m*
der **Welschhaahne (-hinkel)** – the turkey, *m*
es **Welschkann** – the corn, *n*
wesche – to wash
wessere – to water plants
windich - windy
die **Woll** – the wool, *f*
yammere – to make noise

Kabiddel 5 –

"Kumm esse"

In this chapter you will be able to:

- Offer something to eat or drink
- Order from a menu
- Make requests

Ich gleich koche!

Beth:	Oh, sell guckt awwer appeditlich!
Alicia:	Denki...sell is meinre Memm ihre Reseet. Mir esse allsfatt daheem Grummbiere mit Schpeck.
Beth:	Was is drin?
Alicia:	Well, ich schneid Zwiwwele und Schpeck. Ich hitz Eel uff em Offe un schmeiss die Zwiwwele un der Schpeck nei. Sie koche en bissel. Dennoh schael ich die Grummbiere un schneid die aa. Die Grummbiere misse aa in em Eel koche, bis sie weech sin.
Beth:	Ken Sals odder Peffer?
Alicia:	Ich sals un peffer am End.
Beth:	Was kannscht du damit esse?
Alicia:	Ich gleich Selaat mit gudi Selaatbrieh. Vielleicht kannscht du Hinkelfleesch odder Kiehfleesch dezu esse. Gleichscht du aa koche?
Beth:	Nee...gaar net. Ich verbrenn alles!
Alicia:	Oh nee!
Beth:	Ich will dir gaern mit em Owedesse helfe...awwer leider bin ich damit net so begaabt.
Alicia:	Ich koch die Grummbiere mit Schpeck und es Hinkelfleesch aa. Du kannscht der Selaat uffrischde...sell kannscht du gaar net verbrenne!

1. *Was weesscht vun sell Dialog?* Answer the following questions *in Deitsch!*

    1. Wie kocht mer Grummbiere mit Schpeck?

    2. Was esst mer mit Grummbiere un Schpeck?

    3. Gleicht die Beth koche? Fer was odder fer was net?

    4. Was rischdet die Alicia zum Owedesse uff? Un die Beth?

Im Essblatz

Frank:	Nau welle mir awwer gut esse!
Sarah:	Mehnscht du net, as es en bissel deier is?
Frank:	Der Essblatz is en bissel deier, awwer es Esse is so gut un appeditlich. Es Fleesch is so zaart.
Sarah:	Kannscht du eppes aarode?
Frank:	Hmmm.... die Ent mit Abrigosbrieh is wunnerbaar! Sell nemm ich.
Sarah:	Ich weess net... ich gleich Abrigose net.
Abwaardern:	Kann ich eich eppes zu drinke bringe?
Frank:	En guder Wei!
Sarah:	Yuscht Wasser.
Abwaarden:	Gut...un zu esse?
Frank:	Ich nemm die Ent mit Abrigosbrieh.
Sarah:	Ich nemm der Seimaage mit Grummbiere un Griehbuhne.
Abwaarden:	Ya... nooch eppes?

Sarah:	Kenne mir eppes Brot hawwe? Un hoscht du aa en bissel Lattwarick un Schmierkaes in der Kich?
Abwaardern:	Ich muss mol schaue... noch eppes?
Frank:	Ich mehn net.
Sarah:	Nee, denki.
Frank:	Fer was nemmscht du Seimaage?!?! Un Lattwarick?!?! Sell kannscht du net in en four-star Essblatz esse! Sell kenne mir daheem esse!
Sarah:	Ich weess, awwer mei deitscher Maage gleicht so feini Ess-Sach gaar net!

2. *Was weesscht du vun sell Dialog?* Answer the following questions *in Deitsch*!

1. Fer was is der Essblatz so gut?

2. Was drinkt der Frank un die Sarah?

3. Was esse der Frank un die Sarah?

4. Fer was nemmt die Sarah es feini Ess-Sach net?

Schprooch

Modal Auxiliaries

There are seven verbs in *Deitsch* which are used in conjunction with other verbs to express modality and are called modal verbs. Each verb has an exact equivalent in English: *brauche* (to need to), *daerfe* (to be allowed to), *kenne* (to be able to, can), *meege* (to like to), *misse* (to have to, must), *solle* (to be supposed to), *wolle* (to want to). The conjugations of each verb are given below, because they are irregular:

	brauche	daerfe	kenne	meege	misse	solle	wolle
ich	**brauch**	**daerf**	**kann**	**maag**	**muss**	**soll**	**will**
du	**brauchscht**	**daerfscht**	**kannscht**	**maagscht**	**musscht**	**sollscht**	**witt**
er sie es	**braucht**	**daerf**	**kann**	**maag**	**muss**	**soll**	**will**
mir	**brauche**	**daerfe**	**kenne**	**meege**	**misse**	**solle**	**wolle**
dihr	**braucht**	**daerft**	**kennt**	**meegt**	**misst**	**sollt**	**wollt**
sie	**brauche**	**daerfe**	**kenne**	**meege**	**misse**	**solle**	**wolle**

Each of these verbs can be used with another verb. The modal verbs are conjugated and placed in the second position in the sentence. The second verb is always placed at the end of the sentence in its infinitive form:

> *Ich schpiel Baseballe.* – I am playing baseball.
>
> *Ich kann Baseballe schpiele.* – I can play baseball.
>
> *Ich will Baseballe schpiele.* – I want to play baseball.

3. *Was kannscht du duh?* Answer the following questions appropriately.

Was kannscht du im Essblatz duh?

Im Essblatz kenne mir esse.

1. Was kannscht du in re Bicherschtubb duh?

2. Was kannscht du in re Schtadt duh?

3. Was kannscht du uff re Bauerei duh?

4. Was kannscht du im Gaarde duh?

5. Was kannscht du im Supermarrick duh?

6. Was kannscht du im Cafe duh?

4. Fill in the following dialogue with the correct verb forms.

Mudder: Schloof gut, Sam!

Sam: Wann _____ (misse) mir mariye uffschteh?

Mudder: Recht frieh! Du _____ (kenne) net lenger als 8 Uhr
schloofe.

Sam: Ok... _____ (daerfe) ich mei Comic-Bicher mitnemme?

Mudder: Ya. Awwer du _____ (solle) mer aa im Schdor helfe.

Sam: Was _____ (wolle) du datt kaafe?

Mudder: Mir brauche Oier, Zellerich, Millich, Mehl un viel meh.

Sam: Ok... _____ (kenne) du mich mariye uffwecke?

Mudder: Ya... schloof gut!

Sam: Du aa.

5. Create your own questions based on the dialog from exercise 4. Exchange your questions with a partner.

Eppes zu wisse

Die Esszeit – the meals

Can you think of any food items not listed?

Generate a list of things with your classmates.

	der Kaffi	*Coffee*
	der Tee	*Tea*
	gebaeht Brot	*Toast*
es Mariye-Esse	gebrodne Oier	*Fried eggs*
	gebrodne Grummbiere	*Home fries*
	der Schpeck	*Bacon*
	die Millich	*Milk*
	der Sandwich	*Sandwich*
	die Supp	*Soup*
es Middaagesse	der Kaes	*Cheese*
	die Chips	*Chips*
	es Bretzel	*Pretzel*
	die Pizza	*Pizza*
	der Fisch	*Fish*
	greeschde Fleesch	*Roast Beef*
	gemaeschde Grummbiere	*Mashed Potatoes*
es Owedesse	die Brieh	*Gravy*
	es Brot	*Bread*
	es Noochesse	*Dessert*
	der Kuche	*Cake*

Was witt du zu Mariye-Esse? Ich will Kaffi un gebrodne Oier hawwe.

Was esscht du fer Owedesse? Fer Owedesse ess ich reeschde Fleesch.

6. *Was esse mir selle Woch?* Tell what is being eaten for each day using the information given:

Sunndaag / ich / Schunkefleesch

Am Sunndaag ess ich Schunkefleesch.

1. Mundaag / du / en Pizza

2. Dinschdaag / mir / Fisch mit Grummbiere

3. Mittwoch / er / en Hambariger mit Chips

4. Dunnerschdaag / dihr / Kaes

5. Freidaag / ich / Wascht mit gebrodne Grummbiere

6. Samschdaag / sie / Rickmeesel un Siessgrummbiere

7. Design *en Esszeddel* (menu). Break the menu into the three different meals. Make sure to include prices. Have your friends order from the menu and then tell them how much they owe *in Deitsch!*

Schprooch

Negation

In Deitsch, there are two words for negation: *net* and *ken* (or *kee*). *Net* is placed before the word that is being negated.

>Sell is *net* deier.
>Sell is *net* gross.

Net can also be placed at the end of the sentence to negate the whole sentence:

>Ich kaaf sell *net.*
>Mir lese es Buch *net.*

Ken is placed before nouns to negate them:

>Esse mir Grummbiere zu Owedesse?
>Nee, mir esse *ken* Grummbiere.

8. Ask a partner the following questions.

>1. Hoscht du en Henkeglaas?
>
>2. Kaafscht du viel Gleeder?
>
>3. Leescht du efders die Zeiding?
>
>4. Butzscht du es Haus alli Woch?
>
>5. Hockscht du gaern im Cafe?
>
>6. Gehscht du oft in der Essblatz?
>
>7. Schpielscht du Kaarde mit annere?

9. Try creating questions that your partner will answer negatively.

Eppes zu wisse

Die Farewe – The Colors

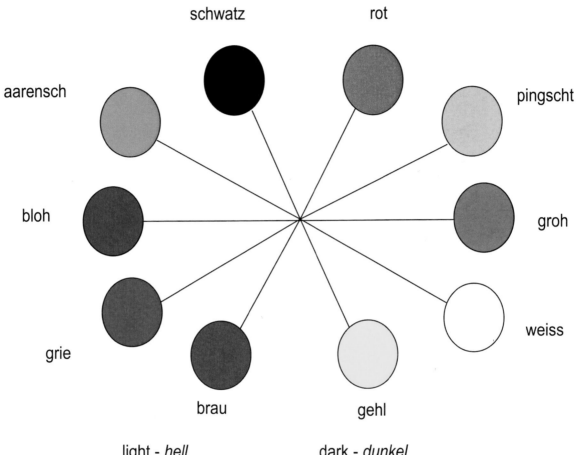

schwatz rot

aarensch pingscht

bloh groh

grie weiss

brau gehl

light - *hell*   dark - *dunkel*

Welle Fareb hot die Kasch? – Sie is rot.

Un die Karebs? – Sie is aarensch.

10. *Beschreib dei Klaess-schtubb!* (Describe your classroom). Look around your classroom and identify at least five objects, including their colors.

Do is en Disch. Er is brau.

Do is en Buch. Es is gehl.

Schprooch

Future Tense

In expressing events that will take place at any time after the present, we may use the future tense.

Ich waer / zaehl en Hambariger kaafe. – I will buy a hamburger.

Similar to the modal auxiliaries, *waerre* acts as a helping verb and requires a second verb in the infinitive form. This verb is usually found at the end of a clause or sentence.

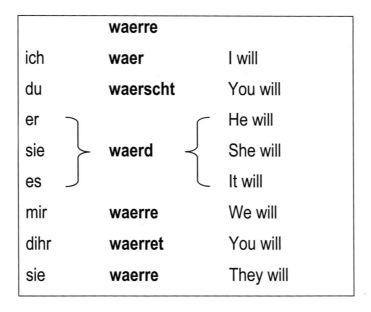

	waerre	
ich	waer	I will
du	waerscht	You will
er		He will
sie	waerd	She will
es		It will
mir	waerre	We will
dihr	waerret	You will
sie	waerre	They will

Should the content of the conversation or description imply future events, the present tense often with an adverb of time (mariye, heit) is used.

Mir schpiele mariye Baseballe.

　　　We'll play baseball tomorrow.

Im Friehyaahr gehne mir noch Kanadaa.

　　　In the spring we'll be going to Canada.

93

11. *Was waerre / zaehle sie nooch der Schul mache?* Describe what the following people will be doing after school.

Der Tom / Umgraut roppe.

Der Tom waerd /zaehlt Umgraut roppe.

1. Der John un der Frank / Myusik heere

2. Mir / Schularewet mache

3. Die Anne / mit em Daniel uff em Telefonn schwetze

4. Die Sally / en Brief schreiwe

5. Dihr / eppes esse un drinke

6. Mr. Smith / en Buch lese

7. Du?

8. Dei Freind?

12. *Wann waerd / zaehlt sell sei?* Indicate when the various events take place.

Mir gehne in die Pizzeria. (heit Owed)

Mir waerre / zaehle heit Owed in die Pizzeria geh.

1. Die Alice bsucht ihre Freind. (am Sunndaag)

2. En Baend schpielt in der Schtadt. (in zwee Daage)

3. Mir gehne in der Essblatz. (heit Nummidaag)

4. Der Bill un die Tina faahre nooch Harrisbaerrick. (im Winder)

5. Mei Schulmeeschder kummt en Schtund schpaeder. (mariye)

6. Ich kaaf Gaardesach. (am Freidaag)

Kuldur

Pennsylvania Dutch Cuisine

Much of PD cuisine comes from the regions of Germany from which most PD families came. It has since developed into a distinct cuisine after contact with earlier American cuisines.

Most meals incorporate the fresh produce and simple ingredients. Unfortunately, though, as good and rich as it may taste, a lot of PD food is not very healthy with heavy uses of butter, starches and fatty meats.

Below is a list of just some of the food you might find at a PD table:

Lattwarick (*Apple Butter*): a condiment often used instead of (and sometimes on top of!) butter. You will find this often served with cottage cheese.

Chow-Chow: a mixture of pickled vegetables such as cabbage, carrots, beans, cauliflower and peas. It is served cold.

Pannhaas (*Scrapple*): a "meat-loaf" made of meat, cornmeal (or cereal) and mixed with various herbs and spices. It is then cut into slices and fried. It can be eaten with ketchup, apple butter or table syrup.

Bott Boi (*Pot Pie*): a stew, usually made from chicken, ham or beef with square egg noodles, potatoes, celery, and carrots. Saffron is common addition in southern Pennsylvania.

Seimaage (*Stuffed Pig Stomach*): a wintertime tradition in PD country, a cleaned pig's stomach stuffed with smoked sausage, potatoes, and vegetables. It is then sewn shut and boiled or baked until done.

Faasnachts (*Doughnuts*): deep-fried potato dough that is either left plain or coated in sugar. Faasnachts tend to be square-shaped or triangular-shaped. They are traditionally eaten on Faasnacht (*Fat Tuesday*) in preparation of Faschtzeit (*Lent*).

Melassichriwwelkuche (*Shoofly Pie*): a traditional favorite among the PD as well as many tourists, consisting of molasses, brown sugar, water and butter. There are two common varieties: wet-bottom with a layer of moist, gooey molasses beneath a crumb topping and dry-bottom with a cake-like consistency.

The above list is in no way complete. There are many other traditional PD foods that are not mentioned. As you travel throughout Pennsylvania Dutch country, you will find many restaurants that still offer traditional PD cuisine.

For more information on Pennsylvania Dutch Cuisine check out the following texts:

- Frederick, J. George. <u>Pennsylvania Dutch Cook Book</u>. Dover Publications. 1971.
- Groff, Betty. <u>Betty Groff's Pennsylvania Dutch Cook Book</u>. BBS Publishing Corporation. 1996.
- Weaver, William W. <u>Sauerkraut Yankees: Pennsylvania Dutch Food and Foodways</u>. Stackpole Books. 2002.

Rickguck

13. *Ich gleich…esse.* Tell one of your classmates what you usually eat for breakfast, lunch and dinner. Reverse roles by asking your classmate what he or she likes to eat. *Was gleichscht du Mariye-Esse, Middaagesse un Owedesse esse?*

14. *Was daerfe mer mache?* Using the street signs below, indicate what you are allowed to and not allowed to do.

rechts net abdrehe	60 mph faahre	parke
stoppe	kaempe	langsam faahre

15. *Was muss der Tom mache?* Tom is a very strange boy. He rarely bathes, never does his schoolwork, eats like a pig, and never has fun outside. He sits in front of the television and when his parents ask him to help out around the house, he refuses. Give Tom some suggestions to be more clean, upstanding, and respectful.

16. You are with several friends in the city for the day. Each one is being polite and not outwardly telling you what they want to do. They have hinted at their desires. From the information given, indicate what your friends want to do.

Die Ruth kaaft Gleeder gaern.
Die Ruth maag Gleeder kaafe, so sie will in der Gleeder- Schdor geh.

1. Die Sandy esst Ice-Cream gaern.

2. Die Beth schpielt die Geig.

3. Der Mark seht Movies gaern.

4. Der Allen schlooft gaern.

5. Der Alex laaft gaern.

17. Interview a partner and determine what she / he doesn't have at home.

Hoscht du en Schwetzkaschde?

Ya, ich hab en Schwetzkaschde. / Nee, ich hab ken Schwetzkaschde.

Guckbax	Scheier
Glapperbax	Poschtbax
Computer	Gaarde
Waddebuch	Baam
Essdisch	Bortsch
Schreibdisch	Aeddick / Schpeicher

18. Fill in the appropriate form of *waerre / zaehle*.

1. Der Mike _____ die Blumme wessere.

2. _____ mir in der Essblatz gehe?

3. Dihr _____ en neie Computer kaafe.

4. Ich _____ eppes siess esse.

5. _____ du en Koppche Kaffi drinke?

6. Die Kuh _____ glee bissel Wasser hawwe.

7. Sie _____ uff em Glapperbax schpiele.

Was weesscht du?

- Identify five items in your classroom, including their colors.

   Beischpiel: Datt is en Disch. Er is brau.

- *Was waerrscht du mache?* Discuss at least three activities that you will do in the near future. Use *waerre / zaehle.*

- Create a dialog that takes place in a local restaurant. Make sure to include in your situation at least one customer ordering a meal.

- *Was esscht un drinkscht du zum Mariye-esse, Middaagesse un Owedesse?* Name at least one item that you eat and drink at breakfast, lunch and dinner.

- Respond to each of these questions:

   a. Was gleichscht du drinke?

   b. Was fer Ice Cream witt du esse?

   c. Was daerfscht du am Sunndaag odder am Samschdaag mache?

   d. Gleichscht du in der Essblatz geh? Fer was? Fer was net?

   e. Was fer Pizza gleichscht du esse?

- Complete each of the following sentences:

   a. Heit Nummidaag maag ich…

   b. Ich will…

   c. Weesscht du, wann…

   d. Mariye muss ich…

   e. Ich ess…

   f. Zum Owedesse drink ich…

Waddelischt

die **Abrigos** (-e) – the apricot, *f*
der **Aeddick** – the attic, *m*
annere – others
appeditlich – delicious
aufschtehe – to wake up
der **Baam** (Beem) – the tree, *m*
begaabt – talented
die **Bortsch** – the porch, *f*
brauche – to need
brenne – to burn
es **Bretzel** – the pretzel, *n*
die **Brieh** – the gravy, *f*
es **Brot** – the bread, *n*
butze – to clean
daerfe – to be allowed to
deier - expensive
drinke – to drink
dunkel - dark
es **Eel** – the oil, *n*
efders – often
esse – to eat
der **Essblatz** – restaurant, *m*
es **Ess-sach** – the food, *n*
die **Fareb** (Farewe) – the color, *f*
der **Fisch** – the fish, *m*
es **Fleesch** – the meat, *n*
gebrode - fried
gemaeschde – mashed
die **Geig** (-e) – the violin, *f*
die **Gleeder** – the clothes, *pl*
die **Grienebuhne** – the green beans, *f*
helfe – to help
hell - light
es **Henkeglaas** – the mug, *n*
hitze – to heat
hocke – to sit
der **Hambariger** – the hamburger, *m*
kaempe – to camp
der **Kaffi** – the coffee, *m*
kenne – to be able to, can
die **Kich** – the kitchen, *f*
koche – to cook
der **Lattwarick** – the apple butter, *m*

der **Maage** – the stomach, *m*
es **Mariye-esse** – the breakfast, *n*
meege – to like to
meh – more
mehne – to think
mer – one, as in a person
es **Middaagesse** – the lunch, *n*
misse – to have to, must
mitnemme – to take along
noch eppes – something else
es **Noochesse** – the dessert, *n*
der **Offe** (Effe) – the stove, *m*
es **Owedesse** – the supper, *n*
der **Peffer** – the pepper, *m*
es **Poschtbax** – the mail box, *n*
reeschde – roasted
die **Reseet** – the recipe, *f*
es **Rickmeesel** – the pork chop, *n*
es **Sals** – the salt, *n*
schaele – to peel
schaue – to check, to look
schloofe – to sleep
der **Schmierkaes** – the cottage cheese, *m*
schneide – to cut
der **Schpeck** – the bacon, *m*
es **Schunkefleesch** – the ham, *n*
der **Schwetzkaschde** – the radio, *m*
der **Selaat** – the salad, the lettuce, *m*
die **Selaatbrieh** – the salad dressing, *f*
solle – to be supposed to
der **Supermarrick** – the supermarket, *m*
die **Supp** – the soup, *f*
der **Tee** – the tea, *m*
uffrischde – to prepare a meal
uffwecke – to wake up
es **Waddebuch** (-bicher) – the dictionary, *n*
waerre - will
die **Wascht** – the sausage, *f*
weech – soft
der **Wei** – the wine, *m*
wolle – to want to
zaart - tender
die **Zwiwwel** (-e) – the onion, *f*

Kabiddel 6 –

"Gehne mir eikaafe"

In this chapter you will be able to:

- Ask about prices
- Describe and choose clothing items
- Talk about shopping excursions
- Identify rooms and furniture

In dem Ess-sach-Schdor

Joe:	Was welle mir heit kaafe?
Rob:	Mir brauche Millich un Oier.
Joe:	All recht... welli Satt Percent drinkscht du?
Rob:	Mitaus fett. Un wieviel Oier?
Joe:	Nur sechs...der Dokder meehnt, ich sett net alli Daag en Oi esse.
Rob:	Ich muss der Robin Yoghurt kaafe.
Joe:	Wu is dei Fraa die Woch?
Rob:	Sie is bei ihre Maemm.
Joe:	Was fer Yoghurt gleicht sie? Mit Obscht drin?
Rob:	Ya, ich kaaf re allsfatt Aerbeer... sie gleicht sell.
Joe:	Do is die Schokolaad!
Rob:	Oh nee... der Dokder gleicht sell net... es gebt zu viel Zucker drin.
Joe:	Oh kumm! Du kannscht dir en gleeni Schtick kaafe.
Rob:	Well, all recht...
Joe:	Rob! Sell is die grosse Dutt!
Rob:	Was?
Joe:	Du saagscht awwer, der Dokder …
Rob:	Nee, nee... nadierlich geb ich de Kinner eppes Schokolaad!
Joe:	Du gebscht ihne nix vun deinre Schokolaad. Ich weess, wie schokolaad-suchtich du bischt!
Rob:	Ya, ya... was brauche mir nooch? Mir misse uns dummle... ich muss der Schokolaad uffesse, bevor die Robin heem kummt!

1. *Was weesscht du vun dem Dialog?* Answer the following questions based on the above dialog.

    1. Was fer Millich drinkt der Rob?

    2. Was fer Yoghurt gleicht die Robin?

    3. Fer was soll der Rob ken Schokolaad esse?

    4. Wer esst der Schokolaad?

In dem Mall

Sarah:	Maemm, ich muss awwer schee fer der Dans aussehne!
Maemm:	Sell weess ich!
Sarah:	Kannscht du mir en farewicher Halsduch kaafe?
Maemm:	Ich muss dir nooch en Duch kaafe?!? Ich kaaf dir schunn en scheener Frack!
Sarah:	Awwer en Frack mitaus em farewich Halsduch guckt en bissel langweilig.
Maemm:	En seidiches Duch odder eens aus Baawoll?
Sarah:	Die Dicher aus Seide sin so weech un scharmand.
Maemm:	Sell kann ich awwer schunn mit dem Preis sehne.
Sarah:	Oh, Maemm, sei nett so geizich! Do is der Schmuck.
Maemm:	Ich kaaf dir kee Schmuck, du hoscht so viel Leftsschdifte un Ohrringe.
Sarah:	Un Schuhe!
Maemm:	Oh nee!
Sarah:	Die Amy hot neie Schuhe letscht Woch grickt...
Maemm:	Sie helft awwer allidaag mit em Esse.
Sarah:	Sell kann ich aa duh! Ich verschprech es dir.

Maemm:	Welli Greess?
Sarah:	Siwwe... un du waerscht neine, so kaaf sechs un du kannscht die vun mir auslehne!

2. *Was weesscht du vun dem Dialog?* Answer the following questions based on the dialog.

1. Wu geht die Sarah hie?
2. Was braucht die Sarah?
3. Fer was will die Maemm es seidich Duch net kaafe?
4. Fer was braucht die Sarah ken Schmuck?
5. Fer was kaaft die Maemm der Sarah Schuhe in Greess sechs?

Eppes zu wisse

Die Gleeder – Articles of Clothing

der Hut	*the hat*	der Rock	*the coat*
es Hemm	*the shirt*	der Schtock	*the skirt*
es Swedder	*the sweater*	es Kittel	*the blouse*
die Hosse	*the pants*	der Frack	*the dress*
es T-Shirt	*the T-Shirt*	die Schtrimp	*the stockings*
der Schtrump	*the sock*	die Iwwerhosse (Jeans)	*the jeans*
der Suit	*the suit*	die Katzhosse	*the shorts*
der Wammes	*the jacket*	es Halsduch	*the scarf*
die Hensching	*the gloves*	es Swettschirt	*the sweatshirt*
die Schtiwwel	*the boots*	die Schuh	*the shoes*

Was fer Gleeder draagt die Jenn?
Die Jenn draagt en scheener Frack un weisse Schuh.

Was waert die Fraa?
Die Maria waert en Halsduch.

Wie basst / gfallt dir die Hosse?
Sie sin zu lang

Is der Wammes zu gross?
Nee, er is zu glee.

In Winder draag ich allsfatt en Halsduch un Hensching.

Welle Fareb hot em Mike sei T-Shirt?
Dem Mike sei T-Shirt is dunkelbloh.

3. *Was draage alle?* With a classmate discuss what others in the class are wearing. Your conversation should include euch questions as: *Was draagt...? Wie is...? Welle Fareb hot...?*

4. In groups, play the roles of shoppers *(Eikaafer)* with a $1,000 budget, salespeople *(Verkaafer)*. The *Eikaafer* are to spend as close to the $1,000 as possible. Some useful words and expressions are: *Wie viel koschdt ...? Kann ich dir helfe? Was witt du kaafe?*

Schprooch

The Dative Case

In the sentence *Ich kaaf en Buch*, you know that *Ich* is the subject, *kaaf* is the verb and *en Buch* is the direct object (accusative case).

Now, consider this sentence: *Ich kaaf dem Freind en Buch*. In this sentence *dem Freind* is called the indirect object or dative. Whereas *en Buch* is directly connected with the action of the verb, *dem Freind* is indirectly connected with the verb and therefore called the indirect object. The easiest way to identify the indirect object is to determine if "to" or "for" can be put before the noun. In the above example, it would be "I am buying a book **for** the friend." (Or: I am buying the friend a book.)

	Masculine	Feminine	Neuter	Plural
Nominative	der	die	es	die
	en	en	en	
Accusative	der	die	es	die
	en	en	en	
Dative	**dem**	**der**	**em**	**de**
	me	**re**	**me**	

Ich schick **dem** Schulmeeschder en Brief.

Der Bu schreibt **der** Mudder en Poschtkaart.

You have already learned the meaning of the possessive adjectives (*mei*/my, *dei*/your, *sei*/his, *ihr*/her). These possessive adjectives take the same endings as those of the indefinite article.

Ich schick **meim** Schulmeeschder en Brief.

Der Bu schreibt **deinre** Mudder en Poschtkaart.

107

5. *Wem soll ich es denn schicke?* You have several items that you are supposed to mail. Can you take care of it?

    * Onkel / es Pickderbuch

    * Schick yuscht dem Onkel en Pickderbuch

    1. Freind / Kaart

    2. Schweschder / CD

    3. Schulmeeschdern / Buch

    4. Fraa / Hosse

    5. Grosseldre / Brief

6. *Wem kaafscht du selle Dinger?* Indicate for whom you are buying the various items.

    * mein Freind / en Fedder

    * Ich kaaf meim Freind en Fedder.

    1. sei Bruder / en Bleipensil

    2. mei Daadi / en DVD

    3. ihre Schweschder / en Swedder

    4. dei Friend / en Paar Hensching

    5. mei Aent / een Halsduch

    6. sei Onkel / en Geschenk

Schprooch

Dative Personal Pronouns

Like English, PD has special personal pronouns for the dative case:

He gives **her** the newspaper. – *Er gebt **re** die Zeiding.*

The following are the PD dative personal pronouns:

ich	-	**mer**
du	-	**der**
er	-	**ihm**
sie	-	**re**
es	-	**em**
mir	-	**uns**
ihr	-	**eich**
sie	-	**ihne**

7. Insert the correct dative pronouns into the sentences below.

   1. Ich kaaf _____ (her) sell Buch.

   2. Der Tom kaaft _____ (them) scheeni Gleeder.

   3. Der Craig schreibt _____ (him) en Briefli.

   4. Fraa Schneider geht mit _____ (us) eikaafe.

   5. Nee, mir gehne mitaus _____ (her).

   6. Die Karen wuhnt noch bei _____ (them).

   7. Alli Woch schreibt mei Bruder _____ (me) en Brief.

8. In pairs, talk about the following:

Was schenkscht du deim Vadder fer sei Gebottsdaag? Un dei Mudder? Dei Fraa / Mann? Dei Kinner? Un fer Grischtdaag?

*** Ich schenk ihm en Maschien fer sei Gebottsdaag.

9. Match the following objects with the person. Write out a complete question and answer for each, then take turns asking questions and answering in partners.

Was gheert zu dem Parre?

Es Biewel gheert zu ihm.

Nodel	Klaess-schtubb	Scheier
Waegli	Brot	Messer

1. der Becker

2. der Butscher

3. der Dokder

4. die Schulmeeschdern

5. der Bauer

6. die Amische

Now ask the class what object belongs to other professions.

Eppes zu wisse

Es Haus – the house

die Kich – *the kitchen*		die Baadschtubb – *the bathroom*	
die Schpielbank	*the sink*	es Briwwi	*the toilet*
die Kiehler – die Eisbax	*the refrigerator*	der Baadzuwwer	*the bathtub*
der Offe	*the stove*	die Waschbank	*the sink*
die Microwave	*the microwave*		
es Gscharrmaschine	*the dishwasher*		
die Bettschtubb – *the bedroom*		**die Wuhnschtubb**- *the living room*	
es Bett	*the bed*	der Schtul	*the chair*
der Deppich	*the bedspread*	es Sofe	*the sofa*
die Weckeruhr	*the alarm clock*	die Guckbax	*the TV*
der Schreibdisch	*the desk*	der Stereo	*the stereo*
der Schenk	*the closet*	der Buchlaade	*the bookshelf*
es Licht	*the lamp*	die VCR/DVD-Schpieler	*the VCR/DVD-player*

Here are few other parts of the house with their PD words:

es Fenschder - *window*

die Dier - *door*

es Dach - *roof*

der Schannschtee - *chimney*

die Gratsch - *garage*

die Poschtbax - *mailbox*

10. *Was ich alles in meinre Schtubb hab.* Describe at least five objects that you have in your living room or in your own room. What do you need to buy or what could other people buy for you?

Hei, diddel, diddel

Hei, diddel, diddel!
Die Katz mit de Fiddel,
Die Kuh schpringt iwwer der Muun.
Es Hundelche lacht
Un weddelt un blafft;
Die Schissel un Leffel,
Die schpringe um's Effel,
Wie ewwe so Schussliche duhn.

[Reprinted with permission from: Sauer, Walter, ed. Mammi Gans: Mother Gooose's Nursery Rhymes, translated and adapted by John Birmelin. Neckarsteinack: Edition Tintenfass, 2003.]

Schprooch

Dative Prepositions

The Dative case always follows these prepositions:

aus	*out of*
bei	*at the house of, at, by*
in Blatz vun	*instead of*
mit	*with*
mitaus	*without*
noch	*to, toward, after*
vun	*from, of, by*
weeich	*on account of*
wege	*on account of*
zidder	*since*
zu	*to, at*

Die Tina kummt um halwer zwee **aus** der Schul.

Kummscht du **mit** deinre Fraa?

Zidder em Yaahr wuhn ich do.

Weeich em Wedder schpiel ich ken Baseball.

Ich kann **mitaus** meinre Schuh net laafe.

In Blatz vun meinre Mudder kummt mei Daadi.

These dative prepositions and articles are contracted as long as there is no special emphasis on the article.

bei + dem = beim
vun + dem = vum
vun + me = vumme
zu + dem = zum
zu + me = zumme

*Ich wuhn **beim** Schdor. - Der Bauer kummt **vumme** Feld.*

11. Translate the following sentences into PD:

    1. They are buying milk from a farmer.

    2. They are reading a letter from the male teacher.

    3. He must go to the house.

12. Provide the proper preposition for each sentence. There may be more than one possible preposition in some sentences.

    1. Loss dei Bicycle _____ dem Haus.

    2. Fer was kummt dihr so schpot _____ der Schul?

    3. Ich waer en Kaart _____ meinre Schweschder griege.

    4. Die Monica geht _____ ihrem Freind.

    5. Mr. Smith is _____ Tschulei nimmi daheem.

    6. Wuhnscht du weit _____ Riggelweg?

    7. _____ seinre Mudder, kummt sei Daadi zum Footballschpiel.

    8. Sie waarde _____ dem Schtor.

    9. Was macht dihr _____ dem Gebottsdaag?

    10. Gehne mir schunn um acht Uhr _____ der Party?

Kuldur

The Sectarians

The Amish and Mennonites are Christian groups, which emerged as part of a Radical Reformation in 16th century Switzerland. Known early on as the Swiss Brethren or Anabaptists, they believed in separation of church and state, adult baptism, pacifism, and nonconformity to the world. In 1693, Jacob Amman, who grew dissatisfied with the increasing worldliness of the Swiss Brethren created a splinter group later known as the Amish.

Today, there are no Amish in Europe, but Mennonites do exist there. There are over 250,000 Amish today living in the United States and Canada. Both Amish and Mennonites have clergy, nominated by lot, formally untrained, and serving for life. There are many types of Amish and Mennonites with the most familiar being the Old Orders, who use horse-and-buggy transportation. However, the most numerous are the mainstream Mennonites, who do not have clothing proscriptions or transportation restrictions. There are also Amish-Mennonites and Black-Bumper Mennonites, who dress plainly but may own cars for transportation.

The Old Order groups each have their own specifications on dress-style, hair length, prayer covering type, and technological restrictions. No Old Order may own television or radio, though Old Order Mennonites can own telephones, while some Old Order Amish may have telephones outside of the house.

The Old Orders also operate their own parochial schools, typically housed in a one-room schoolhouse and not exceeding grade eight. After that, Old Orders work on the farm with their parents, or complete vocational training.

Further reading:
- Hostetler, J. A. Amish society. Baltimore: Johns Hopkins. 1993.
- Kraybill, D. & Bowman, C. D. On the backroad to heaven. Baltimore: Johns Hopkins. 2001.
- Kraybill, D. & Hurd, J. P. Horse-and-buggy Mennonites. University Park, PA: Penn State Press. 2006.
- Amish Studies at Elizabethtown College: http://www2.etown.edu/amishstudies

Rickguck

13. *Wu findt mer alles? In der Wuhnschtubb? In der Bettschtubb? In der Kich? In der Baadschtubb?* Indicate where you may find these items, some of which could be found in more than one room.

* *der Schreibdisch*
* *Der Schreibdisch is in der Bettschtubb.*

1. der Buchlaade

2. es Briwwi

3. der Offe

4. der Deppich

5. die Guckbax

6. es Bett

7. die Waschbank

14. *Was macht Sinn?* (What makes sense?) From the list below, find the words that best complete the phrases.

drinke	gehe	hawwe	bleiwe
schreiwe	esse	koschde	draage

1. en Wascht

2. en Wammes

3. eppes Geld

4. zwee Daage

5. en Glaas Millich

6. daheem

7. viel Glick

8. en Brief

15. *Eppes paerseenlich*

1. Du hoscht $200. Was witt du kaafe?

2. Was draagscht du heit? Welle Farewe hen dei Gleeder?

3. Wu kannscht du in deinre Schtadt Gleeder kaafe?

4. Kaafscht du viel bei *Walmart*? Fer was? Fer was net?

16. Imagine you are employed in a department store and have to assist a customer (*Kunne*). Complete the following two dialogs with meaningful sentences.

Du:

Kunne: Ich will en Hemm.

Du:

Kunne: Bloh odder rot. Sin selle Jeans zu lang?

Du:

Kunne: Wie viel koschde sie?

Du:

Kunne: Sell is verninfdich. Ich kaaf sie.

Kunne: Wu sin die Kittel?

Du:

Kunne: Ach, die Waahl is gross.

Du:

Kunne: Selle Kittel is zu katz.

Du:

Kunne: Wunnerbaar. Die basst. Is die Kittel deier?

Du:

Was weesscht du?

- *Gleeder.* Identify three clothing items and indicate their colors, whether or not you like them and why.

- *Ich draag...* Tell your classmate what you are wearing today. Give as many details as possible.

- *Was soll ich kaafe?* Pretend that you just moved into a house or apartment. Your room is completely empty. List the five most important items that you would like to have in your room.

- *Dei Schtubb.* Describe to a classmate what is all in your room. Have them then in turn describe their room at home.

- *Dei Haus.* Draw a floor plan of your house. Label all of the rooms and furniture *in Deitsch!*

Waddelischt

aus – out of
auslehne – to borrow
die Baadschtubb – bathroom, *f*
der Baadzuwwer – bathtub, *m*
die Baawoll – cotton, *f*
der Becker – baker, *m*
bei – at the house of, by
es Bett (-er) – bed, *n*
die Bettschtubb (-schtuwwe) – bedroom, *f*
es Briwwi – toilet, *n*
der Buchlaade – bookshelf, *m*
der Butscher – butcher, *m*
es Dach (Decher) – roof, *n*
der Dans (-e) – the dance, *m*
der Deppich – bedspread, *m*
die Dier (-e) – door, *f*
draage – to carry, to wear
der Eikaafer – customer, *m*
die Eisbax - refrigerator, *m*
es Fenschder (-e) – window, *n*
der Frack (-e) – dress, *m*
der Gebottsdaag (-e) – birthday, *m*
geizich – frugal
gheere zu – to belong to
die Gratsch – garage, *f*
die Greess – size, *f*
es Halsduch (-dicher) – scarf, *n*
es Hemm (-er) – shirt, *n*
die Hensching – gloves, *pl*
hie – hither
die Hosse – pants, *pl*
der Hut (Hiet) – hat, *m*
in Blatz vun – in place of
die Iwwerhosse – jeans, *pl*
die Katzhosse – shorts, *pl*
die Kich (-e) – kitchen, *f*
die Kiehler – refrigerator, *f*
es Kittel – blouse, *n*
der Leftsschdift (-e) – lip stick, *m*
die Licht (-e) – light, lamp, *f*
die Maschien (-e) – car, *f*
mitaus - without
nadierlich - naturally

die Nodel (-e) – needle, *f*
der Offe (Effe) – oven, *m*
der Ohrring (-e) – earring, *m*
der Parre – pastor, *m*
die Poschtbax – mailbox, *n*
der Preis – price, *m*
der Riggelweg – railroad, *m*
der Rock (Reck) – coat, *m*
die Satt (-e) – sort, type, *f*
der Schannschtee – chimney, *m*
scharmand - elegant
der Schenk – closet, *m*
der Schmuck – jewelry, *m*
die Schokolaad – chocolate, *f*
die Schpielbank (-benk) – sink, *f*
der Schreibdisch – desk, *m*
es Schtick (-er) – piece, *n*
die Schtiwwel – boots, *pl*
der Schtock (Schteck) – skirt, *m*
der Schtrump (Schtrimp) – stocking, *m*
der Schtuhl (Schtiehl) – chair, *m*
die Schuh – shoes, *pl*
der Seide – silk, *m*
seidich – silken
es Sofe – sofa, *n*
suchtich – addicted
der Suit – suit, *m*
es Swedder – sweater, *n*
es Swettschirt – sweatshirt, *n*
der Verkaafer – salesman, *m*
verninfdich - reasonable
verschpreche – to promise
die Waahl – selection, *f*
waere – to wear
der Wammes – jacket, *m*
die Waschbank – sink, *f*
die Weckeruhr – alarm clock, *f*
weeich – on account of
wege – on account of
die Wuhnschtubb – living room, *f*
zidder – since
zu – to, at

Kabiddel 7 ~

"Mei Daag"

In this chapter you will be able to:

- Describe your daily routine
- Describe musical preferences
- Describe how you feel
- Identify parts of the body

Ich muss gut aussehne

Yunger Mann:	Guder Mariye!
Aldi Fraa:	Du weesscht, as ich in mei Bed & Breakfast allsfatt um siwwe Uhr es Mariye-Esse hab.
Yunger Mann:	Ya, ich weess...
Aldi Fraa:	Was machscht du datt drowwe? Fer was bischt du so schpot?
Yunger Mann:	Well, ich weck mich um siwwe Uhr aerschtmol uff. No muss ich mich balwiere un baade.
Aldi Fraa:	Fer sell braucht mer net meh as en halb Schtunn!
Yunger Mann:	No muss ich mich schtraele un mich aaduh.
Aldi Fraa:	Die yunge Leit misse sich schee gucke mache... ken Wunner as es dich so viel Zeit nemmt.
Yunger Mann:	Mir misse gut aussehne fer die annere yunge Leit.
Aldi Fraa:	Sell macht nix aus... die yunge Leit dummle sich so viel. Sie hen ken Zeit annri aazugucke.
Yunger Mann:	Dann un wann muss mer sich schee aaduh, gell net? Vielleicht hoscht du ya en neier Frack in deim Gleederkemmerli...
Aldi Fraa:	Ich hab yuscht mei Sundaagsgleeder.
Yunger Mann:	Vielleicht kannscht du dei Sundaagsgleeder uff en Muundaag draage?
Aldi Fraa:	Un wann soll ich dei Mariye-Esse rischde, wann ich mei ganzi Mariye vorme Schpiggel rumbring? Vielleicht kannscht du es selwert rischde... dihr yunge Leit dummle eich zu viel ennihau...

1. *Was weesscht du vun selle Dialog?*

   1. Wann gebt es Mariye-Esse?

   2. Was muss der yung Mann mariyets mache?

   3. Was denkt die alt Fraa iwwer yunge Leit heidesdaags?

   4. Was schlackt die alt Fraa dem yunge Mann vor?

En schlechti Woch

Cindy:	Andy! Mei Mann hot gsaat, as du net gut bischt.
Andy:	Ya, ich hab en schlechti Woch.
Cindy:	Saag mol, was bassiert is!
Andy:	Well, mei Finger dutt weh… Finger un Hammer basse net so gut mitennaner.
Cindy:	Waar sell bei der Arewet geschehe?
Andy:	Ya.
Cindy:	Du duhscht dich allsfatt weh bei der Arewet!
Andy:	Ya, es is gut, as ich Insurance hab. Ich bring awwer viel zu viel Zeit im Grankehaus rum.
Cindy:	Es is gut, as du nau daheem bischt. No kann dei Maem gut achtgewwe uff dich.
Andy:	Nee, sie greischt zu viel an mich aa.
Cindy:	Fer was?
Andy:	Well, der Hammer hot net yuscht mei Finger gedroffe, awwer aa es Fenschder in ihre Schlofschtubb!
Cindy:	Ohh…
Andy:	Mei Maem mehnt, as sie sich ball verkelde daede mit en offeni Fenschder…

Cindy: Sell dutt mir leed... awwer du musscht es Fenschder bessere... ich wott aa net in en kaldi Schtubb schloofe!

2. *Was weesscht du vun selle Dialog?*

     1. Was is der Andy bassiert? Un wu?

     2. Was mehnt em Andy sei Maem?

     3. Wie kann sei Maem sich verkelde?

     4. Was mehnt die Cindy iwwer es Fenschder?

3. *Wie gut kannscht du zeichne?* Choose one of the two previously read dialogs and create a comic strip retelling the story. Be creative with your own dialog in speech bubbles – do not just rely on the text.

Schprooch

Verbs with Separable Prefixes

You can combine verbs with prefixes and thus change their meaning. In most cases such prefixes are prepositions, just as in English (to stand – to understand)

The prefixes, which you can add or eliminate, are called separable. The prefixes are separated from their verbs and placed at the end of the sentence.

(aakumme) – *Die Draen kummt um 2 Uhr aa.*

The train is arriving at 2 o'clock.

(eilaade) – *Der Steve laadt der Bill zu der Party ei.*

Steve is inviting Bill to the party.

(ausmache) – *Wie machscht du heit aus?*

How are you doing today?

These are some verbs with separable prefixes:

aahawwe	datthiegehe	herkumme	eikaafe
mitbringe	ausgewe	mitkumme	eilaade
aakumme	ausmache	aafange	uffbasse

4. *Was is denn alles bei dem James los?* Today is James' birthday. Summarize everything that is going on.

    * sei Aent / am Nummidaag aus Reading / aakumme

    * Sei Aent kummt am Nummidaag aus Reading aa.

    1. Sei Daadi / Sache fer die Gebottsdaagparty / eikaafe

    2. Sei Mudder / die Grosseldre / eilaade

    3. Sei Freind / um vier Uhr / datthiegehe

    4. Sei Eldre / viel Geld / fer dem James sei Party / ausgewe

5. *Antwadde selle Frooge!*

    * Was bringt die Tina mit? (Pickderbuch)

    * Sie bringt en Pickderbuch mit.

    1. Was hot die Elizabeth heit aa? (en Frack)

    2. Wer kummt in die Movies mit? (alli-epper)

    3. Wie mache der Peter un der Mike am Owed aus? (schlecht)

    4. Um wie viel Uhr kaaft Mr. Dreibelbis in der Schtadt ei? (um drei Uhr)

    5. Wie viele Buwe laade die Tanya zu der Party ei? (fimf)

    6. Wu kummt Fraa Hoch aa? (im Aerport)

    7. Wann fangt es Movie aa? (um sechs Uhr)

6. Plan your own birthday or party. Be as descriptive as possible.

Eppes zu wisse

Es Kareberdeel

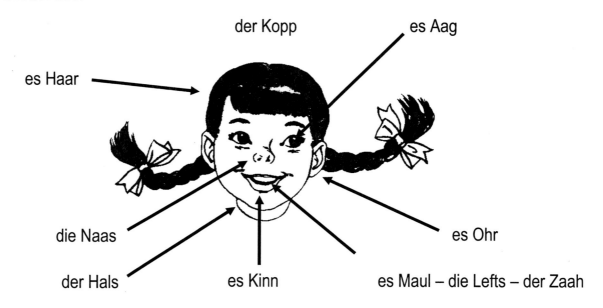

der Kopp

es Aag

es Haar

die Naas

es Ohr

der Hals

es Kinn

es Maul – die Lefts – der Zaah

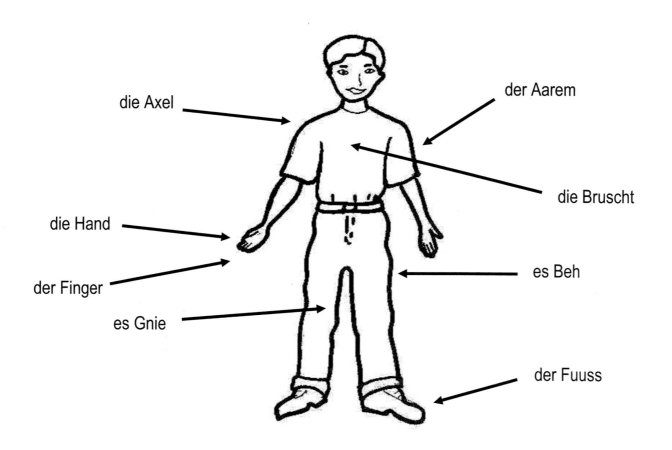

die Axel

der Aarem

die Bruscht

die Hand

der Finger

es Beh

es Gnie

der Fuuss

Schprooch

Reflexive Verbs

Certain verbs in Deitsch need pronoun objects which refer back to the subject; they are called reflexive verbs and sometimes are best translated in English as "myself" etc. or not at all.

The reflexive pronouns are the same as the accusative pronouns, except third person singular and plural (he, she, it, they – er, sie, es, sie) are '**sich**.'

Here are the reflexive pronouns:

ich	**mich**	*mir*	**uns**
du	**dich**	*dihr*	**eich**
er, sie, es	**sich**	*sie*	**sich**

Here are some common reflexive verbs:

to get dressed – sich aaduh	*to comb* – sich schtraele
to dress up – sich uffbutze	*to sit down* – sich annehocke
to shave – sich balwiere / sich rasiere	*to catch a cold* – sich verkelde
	to bathe – sich baade
to wash oneself – sich wesche	*to hurry* – sich dummle
to injure onself – sich wehduh	*to wake up* – sich uffwecke

Ich <u>duh mich</u> mariyets <u>aa</u>, eb ich mei Mariye-Esse hab.

Sie <u>dutt sich</u> allsfatt <u>weh</u>, wann <u>sie sich</u> so <u>dummelt</u>!

<u>Mir</u> misse <u>uns</u> alli Daag die Haar <u>schtraele</u>.

<u>Die yungi Leit butze sich</u> graad nau <u>uff</u> fer der Dans.

7. Fill in the correct reflexive pronoun

    1. Du musscht _____ annehocke, wann die Bus faahrt.

    2. Ich weess, as es schpot is... mir dummle _____!

    3. Um siwwe Uhr weck ich _____ allsfatt uff.

    4. Kann ich _____ verkelde, wann ich mit nassi Haare nausgeh?

    5. Mei Mann dutt _____ alli zwee Daage balwiere.

    6. Dihr kennt _____ wesche in der Baadeschtub.

8. Using the following pictures, tell what each person is doing.

1. Simone

2. Jason

3. Mr. Smith

4. Mason

9. Tell a classmate about your own morning routine. Then have your partner retell it to the class.

Saag Eppes

Was far en Myusickinstrument schpielscht du? – Ich schpiel…

der Trompet

die Gitarre

es Glaffier

die Klarinet

die Geig

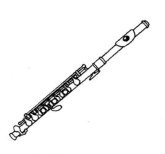

die Floete

es Schlaggding

129

9. *Froog epper!* Ask someone in your class the following questions:

    1. Was fer en Myusickinstrument schpielscht du?

    2. Wie viel koscht selle Myusickinstrument nei?

    3. Wu schpielscht du es?

    4. Wie lang schpielscht du schunn?

    5. Wer in deinre Familye schpielt en Myusickinstrument?

    6. Was is der Naame vun deinre Leibsbaend odder Leibssaenger?

    7. Nooch eppes?

Saag eppes

Wie is die Myusick? – Sie is…

zu schnell   zu ruhich   romantisch

altmodisch   waerecklich gut   blessierlich

11. How would you describe the following bands, singers or genres of music? *In Deitsch!*

    1. The Beatles

    2. Madonna

    3. Frank Sinatra

    4. Rap

Schprooch

The Genitive Case – Possession

Just like English, Deitsch has a way to mark nouns which possess. In English we do this with *'s*:

> That is John**'s** house.

In this sentence, John is the possessor and the house is the object being possessed; John owns the house.

In Deitsch, a special construction is used to show possession. The possessor is placed in the dative case, followed by the object being possessed with a possessive adjective:

> That is John's house. →   Sell is **dem John sei Haus**.

→ Please refer to the Schprooch section of Kabiddel 2 "Possessive Adjectives"

12. In the following exercise, mark the possessor.

> 1. Sell is dem Andy sei Hemm.
>
> 2. Sell is dem Daadi sei Bensil.
>
> 3. Sell is der Amy ihre Frack.
>
> 4. Dem Mark sei Bu is datt drowwe.

13. In the following exercise, fill in the appropriate missing word from the possessive construction.

> 1. _____ Robert sei Gaarde is schier gaar verwaxe.
>
> 2. Der Maem _____ Kich is ordentlich sauwer.
>
> 3. Ich muss _____ David sei Dochder mit der Hausarewet helfe.
>
> 4. Mir kenne _____ Eldre ihre Schlofschtubb butze.
>
> 5. Dem Nochber _____ Scheier waar geschder am brenne.

Geb Acht!

Words used for Emphasis

A number of PD words are used for emphasis: *awwer, yuscht, mol* and *ya*. These words cannot be translated literally.

Du bischt gscheit.

> You're smart.

*Du bischt **awwer** gscheit!*

> **Aren't** you smart!

Er hot die Antwatt.

> He has the answer.

*Er hot **yuscht** die Antwatt.*

> He **just** has the answer

Bring dei nei CD mit.

> Bring your new CD along.

*Bring **mol** dei nei CD mit!*

> Why **don't** you bring your new CD along!

Du weesscht, mir wuhne in Lebnen.

> You know, we live in Lebanon.

*Du weesscht **ya**, mir wuhne in Lebnen.*

> You know **very well**, we live in Lebanon.

Kuldur

Pennsylvania Dutch Secular Folk Music

Pastor Fredrick Weiser in his accompanying word to Albert Buffington's <u>Pennsylvania German Secular Folk Songs</u> states: "Singing is part of every culture. It is often the vehicle of expression for the emotions of a people. Unwittingly, unconsciously a people tells us what they think of themselves, of life in the songs they spin and enjoy."

Much of the secular music of the PD is full of frivolity… sung from barrooms to schnitzing parties to other fests throughout the PD community. A type of folk song is the "question and answer song," in which one person asks a question and in the same verse another person answers. The song we have included which falls under this category is: "Maedli witt du heire" or "Girl do you want to marry." In this song, the father is asking the daughter whom she wants to marry. In each verse the daughter answers and gives a reason why she doesn't want to marry a certain type of man.

The other song that we included is the popular song "Ich bin der Doktor Eisenbaart" or "I am Doctor Ironbeard." In this song Dr. Eisenbaart tells how he cures various types of people of their illnesses. Some of the traditional Pennsylvania Dutch instruments include the guitar, banjo, autoharp and the mountain dulcimer.

For more information on Pennsylvania Dutch Music:

- Buffington, Albert F. <u>Pennsylvania German Secular Folk Songs</u>. The Pennsylvania German Society. Breinigsvillle. 1974
- Toad Creek Music – Keith Brintzenhoff's Website http://www.keithbrintzenhoff.com

32. Ich bin der Dockder Eisenbaart
Version (a)

1. Ich bin der Dock-der Ei-sen-baart, Zwill-i, will-i, wie kumm

bumm! Ich keyur die Leit noch mein-re Aart, Zwill-i, will-i, wie kumm

bumm! Zumm-e Hei-rens-daag, zumm-e Hei-rens-daag, Zwill-i will-i,

wie kumm bumm! Zumm-e Hei-rens-daag, zumm-e Hei-rens-daag,

Zwill-i, will-i, wie kumm bumm!

2. Ich mach die Laahmen, dass sie gehen,
Zwilli, willi, wie kumm bumm!
Ich mach die Blinde, dass sie sehe,
Zwilli, willi, wie kumm bumm!

Refrain:

Translation: 1. I am Dr. Ironbeard; Zwilli, willi, wie kumm bumm! I cure the people in my own way, etc. 2. I make the lame that they walk, etc. I make the blind that they see, etc.

[Reprinted with permission from the Pennsylvania German Society: Buffington, Albert F. <u>Pennsylvania German Secular Folk Songs</u>. Breinigsville, PA: The Pennsylvania German Society, 1974.]

42. Meedli, witt du heiere?
Version (a)

1."Meed-li, witt du hei-e-re?" "Ya, Vaa-der, ya!" "So
hei-erscht du en Bau- er." "Nein, Vaa-der, nein! Bau-er hei-e-re
will ich net; Kieh-schtall mischd-e gleich ich net. Nein, Vaa-der,nein!"

2. "Meedli, witt du heiere?"
   "Ya, Vaader, ya!"
   "So heiersch du en Parre."
   "Nein, Vadder, nein!
   Parre heiere will ich net;
   Windle wesche gleich ich net.
   Nein, Vaader, nein!"

3. "Meedli, witt du heiere?"
   "Ya, Vaader, Ya!"
   "So heierscht du en Dockder."
   "Nein, Vaader, nein!
   Dockder heiere will ich net;
   Leit vergifde gleich ich net.
   Nein, Vaader, nein!"

[Reprinted with permission from the Pennsylvania German Society: Buffington, Albert F. Pennsylvania German Secular Folk Songs. Breinigsville, PA: The Pennsylvania German Society, 1974.]

135

Rickguck

14. *Kannscht du selle Sentences faddich mache?*

      1. Ich schwetz mit dem _____.

      2. Ich schreib mit der _____.

      3. Ich denk mit dem _____.

      4. Ich deid (point…to) mit dem _____ uff die Landkaart.

      5. Ich heer mit dem _____.

      6. Ich riech (smell) mit der _____.

      7. Ich hawwe _____ uff dem Kopp.

      8. Ich kann mit dem _____ sehe.

15. *Welle Wadde gehne zammer?* Match each word with one of these three categories: *Kareberdeel, Myusickinstrument, Esszeddel.*

      1. Beh

      2. Geig

      3. Kaes

      4. Wascht

      5. Axel

      6. Glapperbax

      7. Grummbier

      8. Schlaggding

      9. Naas

      10. Gaardesach

16. Form sentences using the following elements.

    1. Bauer / Kuh / grank

    2. Parre / Karich / weiss

    3. Nochber / Fraa / Elizabeth

    4. Kind / Gschenk / unnich dem Grischtdaagsbaam

    5. Mr. Smith / Onkel Walter

    6. Schulmeeschder / Buch / alt un gross

    7. Hund / Haus / aus Hols gmacht

    8. Lisa / Gaarde / mitaus Umgraut

Was weesscht du?

- *Was fer Kareberdeel hot en Person? En Person hot...* In your description, give such answers as *En Person hot zwee Aage.* Then ask a partner or in a group the question *Fer was braucht man Aage? (Antwadde: Fer sehne.)* Here are some additional useful words for your answers: *denke* (to think), *rieche* (to smell). Others that you already know are: *heere, schwetze, esse, laafe, schmecke.*

- *Wer schpielt en Myusickinstrument?* Name four people and describe what musical instrument they play.

- Describe your daily routine, starting with the time you wake up until you leave the house for work or school.

- *Selle Baend odder Seller Saenger gleich ich viel.* Identify a band or singer that you like. In your description include such details as how many are in the band, how old they are, what instruments the various band members play and anything else you know about them.

Waddelischt

sich aa/duh – to get dressed
aa/fange – to start
es Aag (e) – the eye, *n*
aa/greische – to yell at
aa/gucke – to look at
aa/hawwe – to have on
aa/kumme – to arrive
der Aarem – the arm, *m*
aa/schreie – to scream at
aerschtmol – at first
sich anne/hocke – to sit down
aus/gewe – to spend
aus/mache – to matter
aus/seh – to look like
die Axel – the shoulder, *f*
sich baade – to bathe oneself
sich balwiere – to shave oneself
bassiere – to occur, happen
es Beh – the leg, *n*
die Bruscht – the breast, chest, *f*
die Bus – the bus, *f*
dahie/geh – to go there
die Draen – the train, *f*
sich dummle – to hurry oneself
ei/laade – to invite
ennihau - anyhow
der Finger – the finger, *m*
die Floete – the flute, *f*
der Fuuss (Fiess)– the foot, *m*
die Geig – the violin, *f*
geschehe – to occur

die Gitarre – the guitar, *f*
die Glapperbax / es Glaffier – the piano, *f,n*
es Gleederkemmerli – the closet, *n*
es Gnie – the knee, *n*
es Haar (e) – the hair, *n*
der Hals – the neck, *m*
die Hand – the hand, *f*
her/kumme – to come from
es Kinn – the chin, *n*
die Klarinet – the clarinet, *f*
der Kopp – the head, *m*
die Lefts – the lips, *pl*
es Maul (Meiler) – the mouth, *n*
mit/bringe – to bring with
mit/kumme – to come with
die Naas (Nees) – the nose, *f*
nass - wet
naus/geh – to go outside
es Ohr (e) – the ear, *n*
rum/bringe – to spend time
es Schlaggding – the drums, *n*
der Schpiggel (e) – mirror, *m*
sich schtraele – to comb oneself
der Trompet – the trumpet, *m*
uff/basse – to pay attention
sich uff/wecke – to wake up
sich verkelde – to catch a cold
sich weh/duh – to hurt oneself
die Wunner – the wonder, *f*
der Zaah (Zaeh) – the tooth, *m*

Kabiddel 8 –

"Feierdaage"

In this chapter you will be able to:

- Invite someone to a party
- Describe holidays and traditions
- Offer and accept gifts
- Congratulate someone

Was fer en Gschenk hot der Steve?

Steve:	Am Freidaag hot die Samantha en Gebottsdaag. Sie waerd fuffzeh.
Heather:	Hoscht du schunn en Gschenk fer sie?
Steve:	Ya, ich schenk ihr en DVD. Un du?
Heather:	Ich weess net. Vielleicht kaaf ich ihr en Buch odder Ohrringe.
Steve:	Sie leest gaar net so oft. Ohrringe hot sie awwer allsfatt gaern.
Heather:	En Gebottsdaagkaart brauch ich aa nooch.

1. *Was fehlt?*

    1. Der Steve _____ der Samantha en DVD.

    2. Die Samantha hot _____ gaern.

    3. Am Freidaag hot die Samantha _____.

    4. Die Samantha is heit _____ Yaahre alt.

    5. Die Heather waerd der Samantha Ohrringe _____.

    6. Die Samantha _____ net so oft.

2. *Antwadde selle Frooget!*

    1. Wann hot die Samantha Gebottsdaag?

    2. Wie alt waerd sie dann?

    3. Was schenkt der Steve der Samantha?

    4. Welle Gschenke will die Heather vielleicht kaafe?

    5. Fer was will die Heather ken Buch kaafe?

    6. Was fer en Kaart braucht die Heather noch?

Wer geht zu der Party?

Joe:	Wann hot der Matt die Party?
Mike:	Am Samschdaag Nummidaag. Kummscht du?
Joe:	Aye gewiss. Die Martha kummt aa.
Mike:	Kennscht du sie schunn lang?
Joe:	Yuscht zidder Tschulei. Solle mer Gschenke mitbringe?
Mike:	Der John macht sell. Er kaaft en T-Shirt un en Halsband fer alli-epper.
Joe:	Wann fangt die Party aa?
Mike:	Baut halwer vier Uhr.

3. *Falsch!* These statements are incorrect. Provide the correct statements *in Deitsch.*

1. Die Party is am Sunndaag.

2. Der Joe hot die Party.

3. Der Joe kennt die Martha seit Tschunn.

4. Alli-epper kaaft en T-Shirt un en Halsband.

5. Die Party fangt um vier Uhr dreissich aa.

Geb Acht!

Meege – the verb meege can be used when saying "would like". It is used like a modal auxiliary (meege + infinitive at end of sentence). Below is the conjugation of meege:

meege – to like (would like)			
ich	**meecht**	mer	**meechte**
du	**meechtscht**	dihr	**meechte**
er,sie,es	**meecht**	sie	**meechte**

Ich meecht en Buch kaafe.

> I would like to buy a book.

Du meechtscht en DVD schenke.

> You would like to give a DVD.

Was meechtscht du fer dei Gebottsdaag griege?

> What would you like to get for your birthday?

4. *Gschenke fer der Erica ihre Gebottsdaag.* Erica's friends are planning a surprise birthday party. Prior to the party, they all get together and decide what each one should give Erica.

> * *Jason - Sweatshirt*
> * *Der Jason meecht en Sweatshirt schenke.*

> 1. Ray - Buch

> 2. Leroy un Robert – Halsband

> 3. Susan – Reggeschaerm

> 4. Mer – DVD

> 5. Du – Tennisschlagger

5. What would you like to get for your birthday? What would you like to give someone?

Eppes zu wisse

Feierdaage – Holidays

The Pennsylvania Dutch celebrate all of the common American holidays. However the traditions they practice during these holidays sometimes are different from traditional American practices. More about the PD holiday traditions will follow.

Below is a list of the major holidays throughout the year with their corresponding PD word:

New Year's Day	Neiyaahrsdaag	*Ascension Day*	Himmelfaahrtsdaag
Groundhog Day	Grundsaudaag	*Pentecost*	Pingschde
Valentine's Day	Feldi	*Memorial Day*	Gedechtnisdaag
Shrove Tuesday	Faasnacht	*Father's Day*	Daadisdaag
Ash Wednesday	Aschermittwoch	*July 4th*	Freiheitsdaag
Palm Sunday	Pallemsunndaag	*Halloween*	Schpuckdaag
Good Friday	Karfreidaag	*All Saint's Day*	Allerheilichi
Easter	Oschder	*Thanksgiving*	Dankfescht
May Day	Moidaag	*Advent*	Advent
Mother's Day	Muddersdaag	*Christmas*	Grischtdaag

Here are some typical PD holiday wishes / greetings:

Ich winsch dir en hallich, frehlich glicklich Nei Yaahr! –

I wish you a happy, joyful and prosperous New Year!

Frehlicher Oschder! – Happy Easter!

En frehlicher Grischtdaag! – Merry Christmas!

En hallicher Grischtdaag! – Merry Christmas!

144

Schprooch

Adjective Endings

In English as in PD, adjectives are used to describe a noun. In English, adjectives are generally used after linking verbs or immediately before nouns.

After a linking verb = The house is **big**. - The house is **small**.

Immediately before a noun = a **big** house - a **small** house

In PD, adjectives that follow linking verbs do not take endings:

*Es Haus is **gross**. - Es Haus is **glee**.*

However, adjectives that precede nouns take special endings, known as adjective endings. There are three categories of endings. Please study the following the adjective ending tables.

Weak Adjective Endings are used when the adjective follows a Definite Article (-der word):

Weak Adjective Endings – following a Definite Article				
	Masculine	Feminine	Neuter	Plural
Nominative and Accusative	der **yung( )** Mann	die **yung( )** Fraa	es **yung( )** Kind	die **yunge** Menner
Dative	dem **yunge** Mann	der **yunge** Fraa	em **yunge** Kind	de **yunge** Menner

*Der **yung** Mann schreibt der **yunge** Fraa en Brief.*

*Die **gross** Schul is graad um's Eck rum.*

Mixed Adjective Endings are used when the adjective follows an Indefinite Article (-en word):

Mixed Adjective Endings – following an Indefinite Article				
	Masculine	Feminine	Neuter	Plural
Nominative and Accusative	en yung**er** Mann	en yung**i** Fraa	en yung**es** Kind	ken yung**e** Menner
Dative	me yung**e** Mann	re yung**e** Fraa	me yung**e** Kind	ken yung**e** Menner

*En **yunger** Mann schreibt re **yunge** Fraa en Brief.*

*En **grossi** Schul is graad um's Eck rum.*

Strong Adjective Endings are used when the adjective does NOT follow a Definite Article or an Indefinite Article:

Strong Adjective Endings – not following a DA or IA				
	Masculine	Feminine	Neuter	Plural
Nominative and Accusative	yung**er** Mann	yung**i** Fraa	yung**( )** Kind	yung**e** Menner
Dative	yung**em** Mann	yung**er** Fraa	yung**em** Kind	yung**e** Menner

***Yunger** Mann, wu kummscht du bei?*

***Dicke** Kinner solle wennicher esse un meh schpiele!*

146

Geb Acht!

Here are a few important points to remember when adding adjective endings:

The following rules apply to adjectives:

- Final B becomes W:

  *Der Hund is **lieb**. – Der is en **liewer** Hund*

- Final T becomes D:

  *Der Hund is **gut**. – Der is en **guder** Hund.*

- schee and glee (and other adjectives that end in –e) add –n before endings:

  *Die **schee** Fraa is do. – En **scheeni** Fraa is do.*

- Two or more adjectives modifying the same noun have the same endings:

  *En **scheeni gudi** Katz schloft in re Scheier.*

6. Fill in the appropriate adjective and adjective ending:

    1. Der _____ (old) Schulmeeschder is am lese.

    2. Die _____ (smart) Katz fangt die

        _____ (dumb) Maus.

    3. Es _____ (tall) Kind schpielt Basketball.

    4. Die _____ (small) Blumme brauche meh Wasser.

    5. Es _____ (pretty) Maedel danst mit dem _____

    (short) Bu.

    6. Ich les en _____ (long) Buch.

7. Fill in the appropriate adjective and adjective ending:

    1. En _____ (slow) Kuh drinkt Wasser.

    2. En _____ (fast) Gaul laaft in die Wies.

    3. Mit me _____ (new) Computer geht es besser.

    4. En _____ (rich) Fraa kaaft me _____ (poor)

    Mann en _____ (warm) Rock.

    5. En _____ (skinny) Fisch schwimmt in en

    _____ (cold) Wasserloch.

8. Fill in the appropriate adjective and adjective ending:

    1. Es Buch is voll mit _____ (long) Wadde.

    2. _____ (good) Maed liege net!

    3. _____ (warm)Kaffi schmeckt gut mit Millich un Zucker.

    4. _____ (old) Schuhe sin net so gut wie _____ (new)

    Schuhe.

Schprooch

Adjectives as Nouns

Adjectives in PD can be used as nouns. They must then be capitalized and must retain their appropriate endings:

> *der Alt – en Alder* : the old man, an old man

When these adjectives turned nouns follow *eppes* or *nix*, they are always given the ending **–es**:

> *eppes Neies, nix Deieres* : something new, nothing expensive

More Adjective Ending Rules:

- PD speakers do not always use adjective endings on *neegscht* (next) and *letscht* (last) when they are followed by time expressions

  neegscht Woch, neegschdi Woch, letscht Woch, letschdi Woch

- If an adjective ends in **–er** or **–el**, then e is often dropped when endings are added:

  *es Haus is deier - es is en **deires** Haus*

  *die Nacht is dunkel - es is en **dunkli** Nacht.*

9. With a partner, create a dialog or skit that has adjectives being used as nouns *in Deitsch*. Be as creative as possible!

Schprooch

Comparative and Superlative Forms

In English, the ending *–er* is normally added to the end of an adjective to form the Comparative:

> small – smaller, great – greater

In PD the Comparative is formed by *–er* as well:

> *reich - reicher,   langsam – langsamer*

In English, the ending *–est* is normally added to the end of an adjective to form the Superlative:

> small – smallest, great – greatest

In PD the Superlative is formed by adding the ending *–scht* and placing an **es** in front of the superlative:

> *nei – es neischt,   dumm – es dummscht*

Don't forget about special adjective rules previously covered in this chapter:

		Comparative	Superlative
B to **W**	lieb (dear)	liewer	es liebscht
T to **D**	laut (loud)	lauder	es laudscht
One **S** is dropped before -*scht*	heess (hot)	heesser	es heesscht
An **E** before **L** or **R** may be dropped before -*er*	deier (expensive)	deirer	es deierscht

Some PD adjectives not only add endings to form the Comparative and the Superlative, but also change stem vowels:

	Comparative	Superlative
alt (*old*)	elder	es eldscht
kalt (*cold*)	kelder	es keldscht
lang (*long*)	lenger	es lengscht
waarem (*warm*)	weeremer	es weeremscht
schpot (*late*)	schpeeder	es schpeedscht
hoch (*high*)	heecher	es heechscht
gross (*large, big*)	greesser	es greesscht
yung (*young*)	yinger	es yingscht

Some adjectives completely change in the Comparative and Superlative Forms. These are known as Irregulars. Here are two examples:

	Comparative	Superlative
gut (*good*)	besser	besscht
viel (*much, many*)	meh, mehner	menscht

To form the phrase *as _____ as* (as tall as) in PD, use the phrase *so _____ as*.

> *Mei Bruder is **so gross as** ich*

To continue this phrase in the Comparative, drop the *so*:

> *Mei Bruder is **greesser as** ich.*

To continue this phrase in the Superlative:

> *Mei Bruder is **es greesscht**.*

Don't forget that Comparative and Superlative Forms still require the appropriate Adjective Endings!

10. Fill in the blank with the appropriate Comparative Form of the adjective:

    1. Mei Grossmudder ihre Kuche is _____ (sweeter) as dei Grossmutters.

    2. Der Winder is _____ (colder) as Friehyaahr.

    3. Die Katie is allsfatt _____ (later) as ihre Schwester.

    4. Europe is _____ (older) as Nordamerika.

    6. Der Nile Rewwer is _____ (the longest).

    7. Rockmyusick is _____ (the loudest).

    8. Mer kann _____(the most expensive) Sache in Nei Yarick Schtadt kaafe.

11. Translate the following sentences into PD:

    1. The barn is bigger than the house.

    2. The Empire State Building is the highest.

    3. July is warmer than December.

    4. Water is good, tea is better but coffee is the best.

    5. Math homework is harder than PD homework.

    6. His dog is faster than the chicken.

12. Come up with five of your own sentences using the Comparative and Superlative forms. Than share them with the class and see if they agree with you or not.

13. Compare people in your classroom. Use as many adjectives as possible.

More adjectives!

Read the following poem aloud and then describe people, situations, and places using some of the adjectives.

28 Similies in Deitsch
Gladys S. Martin

So alt wie die Hiwwle.	As old as the hills.
So bidder as Gall.	As bitter as gall.
So dief wie der See.	As deep as the sea.
So bleech as en Schpuck.	As pale as a ghost.
So hatt as en Felse.	As hard as a rock.
So graad as en Schnur.	As straight as a line / stretched cord.
So grumm as en Hund sei hinner Beh.	As crooked as a dog's hind leg.
So wiescht as en Heckefens.	As ugly as a brush fence.
So weiss as Schnee.	As white as snow.
So dinn as en Booneschtiel.	As thin as a broomstick.
So runzlich as en Gwetsch.	As wrinkled as a prune.
So dick as Fleh uff em Hund.	As think as fleas on a dog.
So fett as en Sau.	As fat as a pig.
So faul as er schtinkt.	So lazy that he stinks.
So schtowwerich as en Esel.	As stubborn as a mule.
So bees as en Baar.	As cross as a bear.
So bees sie hot net Buhne gsaat.	So angry she couldn't say beans.
So glatt as en Ool.	As smooth as an eel.
So dumm as en Ox.	As dumb as an ox.
So aarm as en Karichemaus.	As poor as a church mouse.
So schtolz as en Pohaahne.	As proud as a peacock.
So langsam as Melassich in Yenner.	As slow as molasses in January.
So schwatz as en Grapp.	As black as a crow.
So ruhich as en Maus.	As quiet as a mouse.
So schlau as en Fux.	As sly as a fox.
So deitsch as Sauergraut.	As German as sauerkraut.
So schtofflich as en Ox.	As block-headed as an ox.

[Reprinted with permission from: Martin, Gladys S. 2005. <u>Kumm laaf mit mir: A collection of PA German poetry with English translation</u>. Gordonville, PA: S.K. Typing.]

153

Eppes zu lese

Die Sarah hot en Gebottsdaag

Samschdaag, der zwelft Tschulei, is fer die Sarah Dreibelbis en abaddicher Daag. Am seller Daag hot sie en Gebottsdaag. Sie will en paar Schulfreinde eilaade. Deswege schwetzt sie mit ihrer Mudder. Hoffentlich waerd sie en Kuche backe.

Sarah:	Maem, ich meecht fer mei Gebottsdaag en paar Schulfreinde eilaade. Is sell allrecht?
Mudder:	Wie viele solle kumme?
Sarah:	Fimf odder sechs. Ich weess noch net, wer kumme kann.
Mudder:	Sarah, bis zu deim Gebottsdaag is es bloss fimf Daage. Hemmer net viel Zeit. Ruf deine Freind graad uff!
Sarah:	Sell duh ich. Kannscht du en Kuche backe?
Mudder:	Fer schur. Wollt dihr draus feiere?
Sarah:	Ya, do is meh Blatz as in meire Schtubb.
Mudder:	Soll ich nooch en Picknick vorbereide?
Sarah:	Ya!
Mudder:	Helf mer awwer mit der Arewet!
Sarah:	Sell duh ich!

Die Sarah ruft ihre Schulfreinde aa. Vier zaehle kumme – die Katie, der Jason, die Dolly un die Michelle. Sie schickt alli-epper en Eilaading mit dem Email. Sie weesscht, as ihre Mudder alles ganz schee vorbereide waerd. Deswege helft die Sarah ihr aa mit der Arewet.

Endlich is der Daag do. Ihre Schulfreinde kumme pinktlich. Die Sarah, ihr Daadi, ihre Mudder un ihr Bruder begegne die Schulfreinde. Der Sarah ihre Schulfreinde bringe Gschenke mit un winsche ihr en "Hallicher Gebottsdaag." Alli-epper geht in der Hinnerhof. Die Sarah will graad ihre Gschenke sehe. Was fer Geschenke waerd sie griege? Der Jason gebt ihr en Buch vun Geil. Vun der Michelle grickt sie en CD un vun der Dolly en neie T-Shirt. Dennot grickt sie noch en Softballmitt vun der Katie. Die Katie saagt, "Sell is en aabaddiches Gschenk. Nau kannscht du besser Softball schpiele. Vielleicht waerscht du nau der Balle fange." Alli-epper lacht.

Baut vier Uhr bringt Fraa Dreibelbis der Gebottsdaagkuche. Der schmeckt arig gut. Alli-eipper schwetzt wege Schul, Freind, Sports un abaddich, was sie im Summer duhe waerre. Schpeeder schpielt Mr. Dreibelbis Softball mit de Kinner. Noch zwee Schtun rischdet Fraa Dreibelbis der Disch. Aus der Kich bringt sie die Picknick Ess-sache mit Hotdogs, Grummbieresalaat, Gummere, Kaes un Lemonade. Noch dem Picknick hocke sie um en Caempfeier. Um halwer zehe geht alli-epper heem. Die Sarah bedankt ihre Schulfreinde nochemol fer die scheene Gschenke.

14. *Was kummt neegscht?* Place the sentences in the proper sequence according to what happened in the story.

1. Fraa Dreibelbis saagt ihre Dochder, sie soll ihr helfe.

2. Fraa Dreibelbis bringt der Kuche.

3. Sie esse Picknick Ess-sache.

4. Die Dreibelbises begegne der Sarah ihre Schulfreinde.

5. Fraa Dreibelbis rischdet der Disch.

6. Fraa Dreibelbis saagt ihre Dochder, as sie en Kuche backe waerd.

7. Fraa Dreibelbis will wisse, wie viele zum Gebottsdaag kumme.

8. Die Michelle gebt der Sarah en CD.

9. Um 9 Uhr 30 gehne der Sarah ihre Schulfreinde heem.

10. Die Sarah will ihre Schulfreinde eilaade.

11. Alli-epper geht in der Hinnerhof.

12. Die Kinner un Mr. Dreibelbis schpiele Softball.

13. Die Sarah ruft ihre Schulfreinde uff.

15. *Antwadde selle Frooget!*

1. Wann hot die Sarah en Gebottsdaag?

2. Fer was schwetzt sie mit ihrer Mudder?

3. Was soll die Sarah graad duh?

4. Fer was waerde sie draus un net in der Sarah ihr Schtubb feiere?

5. Wer kummt zu der Sarah ihre Gebottsdaag?

6. Was fer Geschenke grickt sie vun der Michell un dem Jason?

7. Fer was gebt die Katie der Sarah en Softballmitt?

8. Was bringt der Sarah ihre Mudder um vier Uhr?

9. Was esst alli-epper schpaeder?

10. Was duht alli-epper noch em Esse?

Kuldur

Der Belsnickel

Der Belsnickel (sometimes pronounced *Belschnickel*) in the PD tradition replaces the Santa Claus figure that we are all familiar with.

It would be hard for Americans to imagine a non-jolly gift giver at the holiday season, but that is exactly what the Pennsylvania Dutch are accustomed to. Der Belsnickel was a scary fur-clad man with a beard. He carried a bag of treats in one hand and a switch or whip in the other. Prior to entering the house, he would try to scare the children of the house by rattling his sticks over the windowpanes.

Once in the house, he would ask all of the children to gather around and recite a *Grischtdaag Schtick* (a memorized poem for presentation at the Sunday School Christmas festival). Once the children had recited their poem, der Belsnickel would give them candy, nuts and sometimes small toys. However, der Belsnickel would use his switch to whip the bad children while the good children went after the treats.

The man who played the role of der Belsnickel was usually a local farmer, but sometimes younger boys filled the role of "*belsnickeling*".

For more information on der Belsnickel and other Pennsylvania Dutch Christmas celebrations please read:

- Delong, Solomon and Zimmerman, Thomas C. <u>Die Nacht vor der Grischtdaag</u>. Edition Tintenfass. 2005.
- Shoemaker, Alfred L. <u>Christmas in Pennsylvania: A Folk-Cultural Study</u>. Stackpole Books. 1999.

Rickguck

16. Fill in the appropriate form of *meege*:

    1. Ich _____ en paar Schulfreinde eilaade.

    2. Was _____ du kaafe?

    3. Mir _____ meh zu drinke.

    4. Der Jeff _____ der Jessica en Camera schenke.

    5. Wie viel Kuche _____ dihr hawwe?

17. Put these holidays in the correct order, according to when they happen throughout the year.

Grischtdaag	*Feldi*	*Faasnacht*	*Schpuckdaag*
Muddersdaag	*Oschder*	*Daadisdaag*	*Neiyaahrsdaag*

18. Fill in the blanks with the appropriate adjectives:

    1. Der _____ (young) Parre kann gut breddiche.

    2. En _____ (fat) Katz fresst en Maus.

    3. Mit re _____ (new) Maschien geht es besser.

    4. Ich schreib _____ (long) Briefe.

    5. Der _____ (rich) Man kaaft en Boot.

19. Translate the following sentences into *Deitsch*.

    1. Mr. Smith is older than Mrs. Smith.

    2. Nine o'clock is later than 7 o'clock.

    3. John F. Kennedy is our youngest President.

    4. Is the Susquehanna longer than the Schuylkill river?

    5. He has the most.

Was weesscht du?

- *Was mache mir zum Gebottsdaag?* You want to give your friend a surprise birthday party. Discuss this with a classmate. Your conversation should include such details as: the age of your friend, the day and time you would like to have the party, whom to invite, what to have to eat and drink, what to do at the party, etc.

- *Was fer en Gschenk solle mir kaafe?* You would like to buy a gift for someone who has a special occasion coming up. Describe what and when this occasion is, how much money you want to spend, what and why you want to buy a certain gift. Be as creative as possible.

- Ask at least five of your classmates when their birthdays are (including the day and the month). Then put the dates in chronological order, writing out the dates. (Example: *Der Robert hot am sechste Moi Gebottsdaag.*)

- Ask someone you know how they celebrated the holidays listed in the Feierdaage section of this Kabiddel. Report your findings back to the class.

- Describe how you will celebrate your next birthday.

Waddelischt

aa/fange – to start, to begin
alli-epper - everyone
baut – about (in time reference)
bloss - only
es Boot (s) – the boat, *n*
Dankfescht – Thanksgiving, *m*
danse – to dance
deier - expensive
dennot - then
deswege - therefore
draus – outside
drum – about (a thing, fact)
dunkel - dark
ei/laade – to invite
die Eilaading – the invitation, *f*
endlich - finally
Faasnacht – Shrove Tuesday, *f*
fange – to catch
feiere – to celebrate
Feldi – Valentine's Day, *m*
der Gebottsdaag (e) – the birthday, *m*
es Gschenk (e) – the present, *n*
gewiss - indeed
griege – to get
Grischtdaag – Christmas, *m*

Grundsaudaag – Groundhog Day, *m*
die Gummer (e) – the pickle, *f*
es Halsband – the necklace, *n*
heess – hot
der Hinnerhof (-hef) – the back yard, *m*
hoch – high
hoffentlich - hopefully
die Kaart (e) – card, *f*
langsam - slow
laut - loud
meege – would like to
Neiyaahrsdaag – New Years, *m*
Oschder - Easter
der Reggeschaerm – the umbrella, *m*
der Rewwer – the river, *m*
rischde – to set the table
schenke – to give a gift
Schpuckdaag – Halloween, *m*
der Tennisschlagger – the tennis racquet, *m*
vorbereide – to prepare
es Wasserloch (-lecher) – the pond, *n*
winsche – to wish
zidder - since
zwelft – twelfth

160

Kabiddel 9 ~

"Freizeit"

In this chapter you will be able to:

- Describe a hobby
- Describe what you do in your free time
- Describe athletic activities

Sie schpiele Tennis

John:	Witt du mit uns Basketballe schpiele?
Erica:	Net heit. Um zwee Uhr schpiele die Anne un ich Tennis.
John:	Mir brauche noch zwee Schpieler.
Erica:	Ruf mol die Lauren un der Bill uff. Sie schpiele allsfatt mit.
John:	Die Lauren is arig schportlich. Awwer mit dem Bill is es oft net so gut. Er is zu langsam un net arig schportlich.

1. *Was basst zamme?*

1. Die Lauren is _____

2. Die Erica un die Anne schpiele _____

3. Der Bill is _____

4. Der John braucht _____

5. Der John soll _____

6. Die Erica will _____

   a. die Lauren un der Bill uffrufe   d. Tennis

   b. zu langsam   e. schportlich

   c. heit net Basketballe schpiele   f. noch zwee Leit

Erica:	Was is los mit em Beh?
Anne:	Es is heit arig schteif. Awwer mit em Tennis schpiele waerd es los.
Erica:	Kumm, gehne mir!
Anne:	Loss uns mit der Maschien faahre, schunscht nemmt es zu lang.
Erica:	Sehnscht du der Tennisschlagger do? Der is yuscht nei.
Anne:	Wunnerbar! Heit hoscht du en gudi Gelegeheit. Mei Schlagger is alt un ich bin aa net in guder Form.

2. *Recht odder Falsch?* Determine whether the following statements are correct or incorrect. If they are incorrect, provide a correct statement *in Deitsch*.

1. Der Erica ihre Beh is arig schteif.

2. Die Anne will mit em Bicycle faahre.

3. Der Erica ihre Schlagger ist net alt.

4. Die Anne waerd heit wedder die Erica en guti Gelegeheit hawwe.

Anne:	Ich hoff mir griege en Tennisblatz.
Erica:	Um zwee Uhr is net viel los.
Anne:	Du hoscht recht. Datt schpiele yuscht zwee Leit.
Erica:	Hoscht du en Paar Balle?
Anne:	Ya, die do sin alt. Fer lewing sin sie awwer gut genunk.
Erica:	Es Netz is wennich zu hoch.
Anne:	Sell macht nix aus. Es is en Vaddel fer mich.

3. *Was fehlt do?*

    1. Die Anne _____ en Paar alte Balle.

    2. Um zwee Uhr _____ net viel Leit.

    3. Es _____ nichts aus, as es Netz zu hoch is.

    4. Die Erica un die Anne _____ noch en Tennisblatz.

    5. Der Anne ihre Balle _____ alt.

    6. Fer die Anne _____ es en Vaddel, wenn es Netz zu hoch is.

4. *Antwadde selle Frooget!*

    1. Fer was kann die Erica heit net Basketballe schpiele?

    2. Fer was waerd die Erica heit en gudi Gelegeheit wedder die Anne hawwe?

    3. Sin viel Leit uff em Tennisblatz?

    4. Fer was will der John net, as der Bill Basketballe schpielt?

    5. Fer was faahre die Erica un die Anne mit de Bicycles zum Tennisblatz?

    6. Fer was soll der John die Lauren un der Bill uffrufe?

    7. Fer was glaabt die Anne, as sie en Vaddel hot?

    8. Was hot die Anne mit em Beh?

Schprooch

Two-Way Prepositions

A number of prepositions use the dative or the accusative case, depending on the particular situation. These prepositions are as follows:

an	*at, on*
g'schwischich	*between*
hinnich	*behind*
in	*in, into*
iwwer	*over, above, past, after, across*
newe	*next to, near*
newich	*next to, near*
uff	*on, upon*
unnich	*under*
var	*before, in front of, ago, of (telling time)*

These prepositions require the DATIVE CASE when used with a verb that DOES NOT indicate motion into or out of a place. The dative case can be determined by asking the question, Where? (*Wu?*)

These prepositions require the ACCUSATIVE CASE when used with a verb that DOES indicate motion toward a specific point or direction. The accusative case can be dertermined by asking the question, Where to? or, In which direction? (*Wu anne?*)

Wu? (Dative)	Wu anne? (Accusative)
Er wuhnt am Eck.	Er geht an's Eck.
He lives at the corner.	*He goes to the corner.*
Der Kaschde schteht g'schwischich der Dier un dem Eigang.	Er schteckt der Kaschde g'schwischich die Dier un der Eigang.
The box is standing between the door and the entrance.	*He is putting the box between the door and the entrance.*
Die Maschien schteht hinnich em Haus.	Er faahrt die Maschien hinnich es Haus.
The car is behind the house.	*He drives the car behind the house.*
Wuhnscht du in der Schtadt?	Gehscht du in die Schtadt?
Do you live in the city?	*Are you going to town?*
Es Luftschiff is iwwer em Airport.	Es Luftschiff fliegt iwwer es Airport.
The airplane is over the airport.	*The airplane is flying over the airport.*
Sie schtehe newe (newich) der Maschien.	Sie parke die Maschien newe (newich) es Haus.
They are standing next to the car.	*They are parking the car next to the house.*
Der Deller schteht uff dem Disch.	Sie schtellt der Deller uff der Disch.
The plate is on the table.	*She places the plate on the table.*
Es Kind is unner dem Disch.	Es Kind laaft unner der Disch.
The child is under the table.	*The child is running under the table.*
Die Schieler waarte var der Schul.	Der Schulmeeschder bringt die Schieler var die Schul.
The students are waiting in front of the school.	*The teacher takes the students in front of the school.*

* NOTE: Some of the prepositions can be contracted with definite articles and indefinite articles. These contractions are used more frequently in spoken *Deitsch*.

Dative Contractions	Accusative Contractions
am = (an + dem)	an's = (an + es)
amme = (an + me)	hinnich's = (hinnich + es)
im = (in + dem)	in's = (in + es)
imme = (in + me)	iwwer's = (iwwer + es)
varm = (var + dem)	newich's = (newich + es)
	uff's = (uff + es)
	unnich's = (unnich + es)
	var's = (var + es)

5. *Wu is alles im Haus? Saag, wu all selle Sache sin!* Use a definite article on each blank.

1. Die Schulsack legt uff _____ Bett.

2. Der Brief is hinnich _____ Guckbax.

3. Die Maschien schteht var _____ Haus.

4. Der Buchlaade schteht in _____ Eck.

5. Der CD-Schpieler is in _____ Wuhnzimmer.

6. Die Uhr is uff _____ Schreibdisch.

6. *Der Ralph laadt seine Freinde ei. Er hot net viel Blatz in seinem Haus un saagt alli-epper, wu anne sie sich hocke solle.* Use a definite article on each blank.

    1. Christa, hock dich uff _____ Schtuhl!

    2. Ronald, hock dich an _____ Disch!

    3. Heidi, hock dich var _____ Licht!

    4. Monica, hock dich newe _____ Schrank!

    5. Sally, hock dich var _____ Fenschder!

    6. Tim, hock dich hinnich _____ Computer.

    7. Peter, hock dich uff _____ Sofe.

7. *Mach selle Sentences faddich!* Use a definite article on each blank.

    1. Fer was parkscht du deine Maschien net var _____ Haus?

    2. Der Bus schtoppt hinnich _____ Schul.

    3. Er schtellt sei Bicycle g'schwischich _____ Maschien un _____ Scheier.

    4. Mir schwimme iwwer _____ Wasserloch.

    5. Gehne mir uff _____ Baseballeschpiel?

    6. Die Leit hocke an _____ Disch.

    7. Bleibscht du bis drei Uhr in _____ Schul?

    8. Die Zeiding liegt unner _____ Schtul.

    9. Die Tourists versammle sich var _____ Karrich.

    10. Um wie viel Uhr gehne sie in _____ Theater?

    11. Sehnscht du es Bild iwwer _____ Glapperbax?

    12. Der Poschtmann schteht var _____ Dier.

Eppes zu wisse

Was fer en Hobby hoscht du?

Ich harich em
Schwetzkaschde.

Ich schpiel es Glaffier.

Ich schpiel Schach.

Ich schpiel Kaarte.

Ich guck an die
Guckbax.

Ich les Bicher.

Ich sammel Briefmarke.

Ich laaf.

Ich nemm Pickders ab.

Schprooch

Present Perfect Tense

The Present Perfect Tense is used in Deitsch to express the past tense. It is formed with an auxiliary verb and the past participle. The two auxiliary verbs used in Deitsch are *hawwe* and *sei*. *Sei* is only used in situations where there is a change of position or condition.

Ich hab Deitsch gelannt. – I learned Deitsch.

In this sentence *hawwe* is the auxiliary verb and *gelannt* is the past participle.

REGULAR VERBS – The past participle is formed by:

- Dropping the –e on the infinitive
- Adding "ge" to the front of the stem
- Adding "t" to the end of the stem

$$ge + \quad stem + \quad t = \quad Past\ Participle$$

mache = ge + mach + t = gemacht

IRREGULAR VERBS – The past participle is formed by:

- Dropping the –e on the infinitive
- Adding "ge" to the front of the stem
- Adding "e" to the end of the stem

*** In most irregular verbs, the stem changes spellings, hence they are irregular verbs.

$$ge + \quad stem + \quad e = \quad Past\ Participle$$

lese = ge + les + e = gelese

Ich hab en Buch gelese. – I read the book.

Mir sin in die Schul geloffe. – We ran to school.

170

There are some rules in Deitsch when forming past participles:

- Regular verbs ending in a consonant + LE (rechle), drop the final E and add an E before the L, then add the ending T: *rechle = gerechelt*

- Regular verbs whose stems end in D (*deide*) change the D to T: *deide = gedeit*.

- Regular verbs whose stems end in DD (*andwadde*) change the DD to TT: *andwadde = geandwatt*.

- Verbs that begin with the letters H, F and S only take a G instead of GE to form the past participle: *heesse = gheese, fuule = gfuult, sitze = gsotze, schwetze = gschwetzt* * the GH is pronounced like a K.

- The prefix GE is dropped altogether before some stems beginning with G: *gewwe = gewwe, geh = gange, griege = grickt* (*kumme* also follows this rule).

- No GE is added to a verb with an inseparable prefix: *verschteh = verschtanne, bezaahle = bezaahlt*.

- If a verb has a separable prefix, the prefix is simply attached to the front of the past participle; the entire construction is then written as one word: *uffschteh = uffgschtanne, rumlaafe = rumgeloffe*.

Common Regular Verbs with their Past Participles

Infinitive	Past Participle	English
frooge	gfroogt	*to ask*
hawwe	ghatt	*to have*
heere	gheert	*to hear, listen*
hocke	ghockt	*to sit*
lanne	gelannt	*to learn*
saage	gsaat	*to say*
schaffe	gschafft	*to work*
schpiele	gschpielt	*to play*
schwetze	gschwetzt	*to speak*
sei	gewest	*to be*
wisse	gewisst	*to know a fact*
wuhne	gewuhnt	*to live*
yuuse	geyuust	*to use*

Ich hab der Schulmeeschder gfroogt.

Was hoscht du gsaat?

Er is zwee Woche in Deitschland gewest.

Wu hen Mr. un Fraa Smith gewuhnt?

Der Bauer hot der Traktor geschder geyuust.

Common Irregular Verbs with their Past Participles

Infinitive	Past Participle	English
bleiwe	gebliwwe	to stay
drinke	gedrunke	to drink
duh	geduh	to do
esse	gesse	to eat
geh	gange	to go
heesse	gheesse	to be called
helfe	gholfe	to help
kumme	kumme	to come
laafe	geloffe	to run
lese	gelese	to read
nemme	genumme	to take
schreiwe	gschriwwe	to write
schteh	gschtanne	to stand
sehne	gsehne	to see
sitze	gsotze	to sit

Der Tom hot drei Koppche Kaffi gedrunke.

Was hot dei Familye letscht Freidaag gesse?

Mir sin heem gange.

Hoscht du die Regel verschtanne?

8. Place the following situations in full sentences in the present perfect tense:

- *Die Shirley / ihr Daadi frooge*

- *Die Shirley hot ihr Daadi gfroogt.*

1. Der Steve / daheem schaffe

2. Die Cortney un die Heather / mit Freinde uff der Telephone schwetze

3. Der Chris / mit seiner Mannschaft Basketballe schpiele

4. Die Mary / die Antwatt wisse

5. Die Kinner / Hochdeitsch lanne

6. Mr. un Fraa Eckenroth / viele Diere hawwe

9. Provide the appropriate past participle of the following verbs on the blanks:

1. Ich hab meine Mudder viel in der Kich _____ (help).

2. Der Belsnickel is am Grischtdaag _____ (come).

3. Mir hen viel in der Museum _____ (see).

4. Der Onkel is zu lang bei uns _____ (stay).

5. Hot der Steve viele Pickders _____ (take).

6. Die Emily is fimf Meil _____ (run).

7. Der Ray is zum Dokder _____ (go).

8. Uff em Picknick hen die Kinner viel Lemonade _____ (drink).

10. Go back to the opening dialog of this chapter and re-write it in the present perfect tense.

11. Provide the correct form of *hawwe* or *sei*.

1. Wann _____ dihr heem kumme?

2. Die Kinner _____ Tennis gschpielt.

3. Die Amy _____ viel fer uns geduh.

4. Es Luftschiff _____ von Philadelphia nach Los Angeles gflogge.

5. _____ du die Movie gsehne?

6. Der Bill und die Tina _____ drei Yaahr do gewuhnt.

7. Dihr _____ der Computer geyuust.

8. Er _____ uff em Schtul ghockt.

Saag Eppes

Welle Schport schpielscht du?

Ich schpiel Tennis.

Ich schpiel Basketballe.

Ich schpiel Baseballe.

Ich schpiel Golf.

Ich geh Bowling.

Ich schpiel Fuussballe.

12. Translate the following sentences into *Deitsch*!

    1. Michelle plays tennis.

    2. We play basketball.

    3. My friend plays football.

    4. Scott and Cory play golf.

    5. Cathy's sister bowels.

    6. I play baseball.

13. *Was macht die Karen im ganze Munet Tschulei?* Karen is planning various activities during the month of July. Describe each one. Begin your description with all of the Monday activities for the month followed by all the activities for each of the other four days.

Tschulei				
Mundaag	Dinschdaag	Mittwoch	Dunnerschdaag	Freidaag
2 golf with Peter	3	4	5	6
9	10	11 Allentown football	12	13
16	17	18	19 cards with my uncle and aunt	20
23	24	25	26	27 basketball with friends
30	31 tennis with my brother			

* *Am Mundaag, der zwett Tschulei, schpielt die Karen mit dem Peter Golf.*

177

Eppes zu lese

En Baseballe Schpiel

Der Issac Dissinger schpielt Baseballe fer en Mannschaft vun Reading. Der Mannschaft sei Naame is die Reading Aadler.

Der Issac is der Star in der Mannschaft vun Reading. Alle Mundaag un Dunnerschdaag iebt er mit seinre Mannschaft aus. Eemol die Woch schpielt seiner Mannschaft gege en annere Mannschaft. Selle Yaahr is dem Issac seine Mannschaft arig gut. Sie schteht an zwett Schtelle in der League. Mariye waerd seine Mannschaft gege die beschde Mannschaft in Lebnen schpiele. Heit am Dunnerschdaag iewe er un die annere Schpieler der Mannschaft zwee Schtunde. Der Coach schwetzt lang mit seinen Schpieler. Er gebt de Schpieler Tips fer es Schpiel am naegscht Daag.

Endlich is der grosse Daag do. Der Coach un sei Mannschaft faahre mit em Bus noch Lebnen. In der Bus schwetze ee paar iwwer es Schpiel, annere heere Myusick. Noch 40 Minutte kumme sie in Lebanon aa. Viele Reading Fans sin aa schunn do. En halwer Schtund eb em Schpiel laafe all die Schpieler uff es Feld. Deel schmeise Balle, annere schlagge Balle.

Es Schpiel fangt um ee Uhr aa. Allebeed Mannschafte schpiele heit arig gut. Noch nein Innings is es nooch null zu null. All die Reading Fans wisse, as sie in der letscht Inning, eppes gut duh misse. Die erschte zwee Reading Batters hen nix gmacht. Nau is der Issac der naegscht Batter. Der Lebnen Schmeisser hot zwee Balle gschmisse. Beim naegschte Balle hot der Issac en Homerun gschlagge. Alli-epper hot gegrische un sin hallich gewest.

14. Provide the correct verb forms from the list below.

faahre	schlagge	sei	iewe
laafe	aafange	gewwe	

1. Es Baseballe Schpiel _____ um ee Uhr _____.

2. Der Coach _____ de Schpieler en paar Tips.

3. Eb es Schpiel _____ die Schpieler uff es Feld.

4. Sell Yaahr _____ dem Issac sei Mannschaft gut.

5. Der Issac _____ alle Mundaag.

6. Der Isaac hot en Homerun _____.

7. Die Mannschaft is mit der Bus noch Lebnen _____.

15. *Antwadde selle Frooget!*

1. Fer welli Mannschaft schpielt der Issac heit?

2. Wie oft iewt der Issac mit seinre Mannschaft?

3. Wie gut is dem Issac seine Mannschaft sell Yaahr in seine League?

4. Gege wen schpiele die Reading Aadler mariye?

5. Was gebt der Coach seinre Mannschaft fer es grosse Schpiel?

6. Wie kummt alli-epper vun Reading noch Lebnen?

7. Was mache die Schpieler eb es Baseballe Schpiel?

8. Um wie viel Uhr fangt es Schpiel aa?

9. Was macht der Issac in der letschde Inning?

Kuldur

Grundsau Lodtsche un Versammlinge
Dr. William Donner

In 1933, twelve men met at the Keystone Trail Inn in Allentown to form an organization that would help celebrate the Pennsylvania Dutch language and culture, and also provide an opportunity to have fun. They decided to choose the groundhog's weather predicting ability as a theme around which to develop their organization. A key member of that group was William Troxell, who wrote a popular Pennsylvania Dutch language column for the Allentown Call under the pen name of "Pumpernickle Bill." The following year, the first full Grundsau Lodge meeting was held in Allentown with over 300 in attendance. Except for a few years during World War II, this lodge has held annual meetings every year since 1934. Other lodges were established--often with the help of Troxell--until a total of 17 were formed, and all but one continue to meet annually. (The only defunct lodge was formed at Temple University in Philadelphia in 1938; it was eventually disbanded, probably in the early 1970s.) In addition, numerous Versammlinge, or "gatherings" were established, often modeled on the general content of the Grundsau Lodge meetings, but without specific references to the groundhog. These continue to meet throughout the Pennsylvania Dutch regions of southeastern Pennsylvania and beyond. During the first decade of the 21st century, the Berks County Versammling (founded in 1937) still draws almost 1,000 people to its annual meetings in Leesport, Pennsylvania. Women cannot attend the Grundsau meetings, which are for men only; but Versammlinge are open to both sexes. There is one "Weibsleit Grundsau" lodge in Upper Perkiomen, Pennsylvania, which is only for women.

At the meetings of all these organizations, only the Pennsylvania Dutch language should be spoken and traditionally there are fines for speaking in English. Meetings usually begin with a prayer, the pledge of allegiance, and the singing of patriotic songs (such as *America*), all in Pennsylvania Dutch. There are announcements, jokes, speeches, sometimes skits, and more songs. At the Grundsau meetings, there is a report about whether or not the groundhog saw his shadow with a prediction about whether there will be more winter. The songs are usually popular English songs ("America," "Nellie," "Adoline") that are translated into Pennsylvania Dutch, although there is usually a rendition of the popular Schnitzelbank. The skits are written and performed by lodge members and often include some commentary on contemporary social events presented with humor and sarcasm. The main speeches

(*Feschtrede*) are humorous, sometimes racy, but they also usually include a moral message for the listeners (many of the Grundsau speakers are from the clergy), often with references to the importance and strengths of traditional Pennsylvania Dutch cultural practices.

Don Yoder once described three types of Pennsylvania Dutch in terms of their attitude towards their ethnicity and interests: first, the Germanizing approach which emphasizes German heritage and origins; second, the Americanizing approach which encourages assimilation into the national society and the use of English; and finally the "dialectizing" approach who celebrate Pennsylvania Dutch culture and language as part of a distinctive American identity.

He notes that the Grundsau meetings and Versammlinge are representative of this third movement and ethnic identity.[1]

The Grundsau lodges and their related Versammlinge represent the development of a self-conscious pride in Pennsylvania Dutch identity and language that began in the 1930s and continues to the present. Although attendance at many of the meetings is dwindling, most still remain active. The motto of the Grundsau Lodges sums up their purpose:

Liewer Gott im Himmel drin

Loss uns Deitche was mer sin;

Un erhalt uns alle Zeit

Unser Deitschi Freelichkeit

---

[1] Don Yoder, "The Pennsylvania Germans: Three Centuries of Identity Crisis", pages 41-65 in Frank Trommler and Joseph McVeigh, editors, *American and the Pennsylvania Germans: An Assessment of their Three-Hundred-Year History, Volume I: Immigration, Language, Ethnicity* (University of Pennsylvania Press, 1985).

Rickguck

16. *Eppes Paerseenlich*. Answer the following questions *in Deitsch*!

    1. Weller Schport schpielscht du?

    2. Weller Schport guckscht du deelmol an die Guckbax?

    3. Welle Kareberdeel yuust mer in selle Schport?

    4. Fer was hoscht du seller Schport gaern?

    5. Was machscht du in schtatz Schport aa gaern?

    6. Welle Mannschafte gebt es bei dir daheem?

    7. Ask a classmate these questions. Report back to the class with your findings.

17. Provide the appropriate DER Word.

    1. Es Kind schpielt var _____ Haus.

    2. Musscht du in _____ Schtadt faahre?

    3. Hockt dich uff _____ Schtuhl.

    4. Er schteht g'schwischich _____ Buwe un em Maedel.

    5. Der Schulmeeschder hot die Klaess an _____ Bus gebrocht.

    6. Hoscht du es Buch uff _____ Zeiding gelegt?

    7. Es Luftschiff fliegt iwwer _____ Land.

    8. Kannscht du hinnich _____ Gaarde waarde?

    9. Der Traktor is newe _____ Scheier.

18. *Mach sell faddich!* Complete the following sentences with an appropriate past participle.

esse	*fliege*	*wuhne*	*kaafe*
schpiele	*schreiwe*	*drinke*	*frooge*

1. Mir hen geschder Fuussballe _____.

2. Die Becky hot en neie Maschien _____.

3. Was hoscht du der Schulmeeschder _____?

4. Mr. un Fraa Deisher hen in Quarryville _____.

5. Der Schpieler hot en halwer Galluun Wasser _____.

6. Die Veggel sin schunn noch dem Sudd _____.

7. Der William Shakespeare hot viele Schpiele _____.

8. Uff em Danksfescht hot der Jim zu viel _____.

Was weesscht du?

- Describe a sport you are participating in or that you like to follow on TV or in a newspaper. Your description should include the name of the sport, some observations on how the sport is played and when (during the year) the sport is played. *In Deitsch*!

- *Was machscht du gaern?* Write a paragraph about one or two activities or hobbies that you like. List the activity or hobby and give reasons why you like to do it.

- *Mir hen viel Schpass.* Conduct a survey on sports and hobbies to see what your classmates are involved in. Begin by making a survey sheet with five columns where you will note the responses of five of your classmates. Ask your classmates the following questions:

  1. Weller Schport schpielscht du? Was fer en Hobby hoscht du?
  2. Fer was hoscht du seller Schport / Hobby gaern?
  3. Wu schpielscht du odder wu machscht du selle Hobby?
  4. Wann schpielscht du seller Schport odder wann machscht du selle Hobby?
  5. Wie oft schpielscht du odder wie oft machscht du dei Hobby?
  6. Wie gut schpielscht du seller Schport odder wie gut machscht du dei Hobby?
  7. Wer macht alle mit?
  8. Nooch eppes?

As each classmate responds to your questions, record his or her responses in the appropriate column.

After you have finished, turn in your survey sheet so that the results can be tallied. Your teacher may choose to conduct a survey orally. If so, be ready to respond.

Waddelischt

aa/fange – to begin, to start
aa/kumme – to arrive
ab/nemme – to take pictures
allebeed - both
an – at, on
der Balle – the ball, *m*
die Briefmark (-e) – the stamp, *f*
der Buchlaade – the bookcase, *m*
dauere – to last
en Paar – a few
es Feld (-er) – the playing field, *n*
die Freizeit – the free time, *f*
der Fuussballe – the football, *m*
die Galluun (-e) – the gallon, *f*
die Gelegeheit – the possibility, *f*
greische – to scream, cheer
g'schwischich - between
der Held – the hero, *m*
hinnich – behind
iewe – to practice
in – in, into
in guder Form – in good shape
die Iewing – the practice, *f*
iwwer – over, above, past, after, across
die Kaart (-e) – the card, *f*
die Kareer – the career, *f*
los - loose

losse – to let
die Mannschaft (-e) – the team, *f*
die Maschien (-e) – the car, *f*
es Netz (-e) – the net, *n*
newe – next to, near
newich – next to, near
parke – to park
sammele – to collect
es Schach – chess, *n*
schlagge – to hit
der Schlagger – racquet, club, *m*
schmeisse – to throw
der Schpieler – the player, *m*
der Schport – the sport
schportlich – sporty, athletic
schteif – stiff
die Schtelle – the place, the standing, *f*
schtoppe – to stop
der Schwetzkaschde – the radio, *m*
der Tennisblatz – the tennis court, *m*
uff – on, upon
unnich - under
es Vaddel – the advantage, *n*
var – before, in front of, ago, of (telling time)
versammle – to collect
die Versammling (-e) – the meeting, *f*

Kabiddel 10 ~

"Um die Schtadt"

In this chapter you will be able to:

- Give commands
- Describe various places in a town or city
- Give and ask for directions

Do kummt die Poscht

Alle Mariye bringt der Poschtmann gschwischich elf un zwelf Uhr die Poscht. Er draagt en grosser Sack voll Briefe. Die Fraa Dietrich kann schunn vun ihrem Wuhnschtubb aussehne, wann der Poschtmann kummt. Oft begegnet sie ihn vanne am Haus.

Fraa Dietrich:	Guder Mariye, Mr. Binkley! Wie allsfatt bischt du wider uff rechdi Zeit.
Poschtmann:	Sell muss ich duh. An daere Zeit waarde viel Leit uff ihre Poscht.
Fraa Dietrich:	Bischt du net schunn faddich mit deinre Arewet?
Poschtmann:	Noch net. In zwee Schtunde gehn ich erscht heem. Wie du weesscht, es is allsfatt Mariyets viel zu duh.
Fraa Dietrich:	Geschder hoscht du mir nix Abaddiches gebrocht. Ich hoff, heit hoscht du eppes Gudes.
Poschtmann:	Dattdruff hab ich leider ken Eifluss.

1. *Welle Watte fehle do?*

   1. Die Fraa Dietrich _____ der Poschtmann vanne am Haus.

   2. Der Poschtmann hot geschder nix Abaddiches _____.

   3. Die Fraa Dietrich _____ der Poschtmann vum Fenschder aus.

   4. Der Poschtmann _____ ken Eifluss, was fer Poscht die Leit griege.

   5. Der Poschtmann _____ die Fraa Dietrich ihre Poscht gschwischich elf un zwelf Uhr.

Poschtmann:	Erscht grickscht du selle Magazine.
Fraa Dietrich:	Sell macht mich arig froh alli Munet. Drin gebt's allsfatt guti Reseete. Viele davun browier ich mit meinem Mann.
Poschtmann:	Ich weess, as du en gude Koch bischt. Dei Nochber, die Fraa Eisenhauer, hot mir sell ausgelegt.
Fraa Dietrich:	Weesscht du, fer mich is es yuscht en Hobby.
Poschtmann:	Do is ihre Zeiding.
Fraa Dietrich:	Die will ich bletzlich lese. Bei *Boscov's* soll es mariye en Sale gewe. Mei Mann hot am Sunndaag sei Gebottsdaag un ich will ihn mit enner Digital Camera iwwerfalle.
Poschtmann:	Is dei Mann denn en guter Abnemmer?
Fraa Dietrich:	Nee, gewiss net. Awwer ich meecht in unserem Ferien net alles abnemme.

2. *Vun wem schwetzt man do? Selle Paerson…*

1. kocht arig gaern un gut.

2. hot am Sunndaag sei Gebottsdaag.

3. bringt en Zeiding.

4. lest oft die Reseet in den Magazine.

5. is ken abaddich guder Abnemmer.

6. lest, wer am naegschde Daag Sales hot.

Fraa Dietrich:	Hoscht du eppes schunnscht?
Poschtmann:	Ya, do sin zwee Briefe un en grosser Briefumschlag.
Fraa Dietrich:	Was heesst Briefe? Die sin fer schurr Rechling odder Advertisements. Die kennscht du gaern widder mitnemme.
Poschtmann:	Ya, ich kann net alli Daag gude Nei-ichkeede bringe.
Fraa Dietrich:	Nau waard mal! Sell hab ich zu frieh gsaat. Do is en Brief vun meinre Schweschder in Marrland. Sie will uns im Schpotyaahr bsuche. Ich denk es schteht alles im Brief.
Poschtmann:	Du hoscht en Schweschder in Maryland?
Fraa Dietrich:	Sie wuhnt bei ihrer Dochder un ihrem Dochdermann. Ihr Mann is letschde Yaahr gschtarewe. Mir sin froh, as sie en paar Woche zu uns kummt.
Poschtmann:	Mei Fraa un ich hen vor, naegschd Munet noch Baltimore zu faahre. Mir hen Freindschaft datt.
Fraa Dietrich:	Iwwer sell Zeit kummt die Poscht wennich schpaeder?
Poschtmann:	Ich glaab sell net. En Mithelfer macht schurr, as die Poscht uff Zeit kummt. Yawell, bis mariye, Fraa Dietrich!

3. Was fehlt do?

1. Wann en Mensch eppes schreiwe will, dann schickt mer en

   _____ mit der Poscht.

2. Wann mer die Cable fer sei Guckbax hot, dann muss mer bezaahle. Eemol

   im Munet kummt en _____.

3. Wann ich en Onkel odder en Cousin hab, dann sin sie _____ vun mir.

4. Wann en Kumpanie en Sale hot, dann seht mer oft die _____ in

   der Zeiding.

5. Es is dem _____ sei Arewet, as Briefe un Peck an die rechte

   Wohnet kumme.

6. Mer schteckt en Brief in en _____ un bringt ihn zur Poscht.

7. Wann mer eppes Abaddiches koche will, dann braucht mer vielleicht en

   _____. Es findt man im Kochbuch.

4. Anwadde selle Frooget!

1. Was macht der Poschtmann, wann er vun eem Haus zu annere geht?

2. Was macht die Fraa Dietrich vor ihrem Haus?

3. Gege wie viel Uhr is der Poschtmann alle Daag mit seinre Arewet faddich?

4. Wie oft grickt die Fraa Dietrich en Magazine?

5. Was lest sie gaern in der Magazine?

6. Was hot die Fraa Eisenhower der Poschtman gsaat?

7. Fer was lest die Fraa Dietrich die Sales in der Zeiding?

8. Vun wem hot die Fraa Dietrich en Brief grickt?

9. Wu anne faahrt der Poschtmann naegschd Munet?

Eppes zu wisse

Was gebt's in re Schtadt?

die Poschtaffis

die Baenk

der Ess-sach-Schdor

die Polies

die Feier Kumpanie

es Grankehaus

es Essblatz

die Karich

die Gas-Schtaetion

5. *Wu schwetzt mer davun?* Tell which place around town is being described.

    1. Der Steve hot Geld un will es sicher mache.

    2. Mr. Long sei Maschien geht nimmi.

    3. Die Fraa Bechdel hot Hunger un will net koche.

    4. Die Jessica will en Brief schicke.

    5. Der Tim hot sei Aarem gebroche.

    6. Dem John sei Bu will eppes vun Gott lanne.

    7. Der Bill un die Jane hen nix daheem zu esse.

    8. Die Dorothy muss en Raawerei berichde.

    9. Die Lauren hot viel Schmok in ihre Kich.

6. *Schreib eppes!* Write a short paragraph in the present perfect tense describing the various places you might go when running errands. Be as creative as possible. When you are finished, share your paragraph with your teacher and fellow classmates.

Schprooch

The Command Form

1. Familiar Command

To form commands in English, the speaker simply takes the infinitive without "to", e.g., "go," "run," or "write." In PD, the familiar command form in the singular is constructed by eliminating the "-e" from the infinitive, i.e., by maintaining the stem.

> Geh! (geh(e)) *Go!*

> Schreib! (schreiw(e)) *Write!*

When you address more than one person, the familiar (plural) is as follows:

> Kummt zu mir! *Come to me!*

> Schpielt mit em Balle! *Play with the ball!*

It is helpful to remember that the familiar plural command is the same as the *dihr*-form but without the *dihr.*

2. The *mir*-Command Form (Let's…)

The *mir*-command form is used when asking for some action in the sense of Let's (do something)…!

> Gehne mir! *Let's go!*

> Singe mir en Lied! *Let's sing a song!*

*One might also hear or see the construction: *Loss uns* _____ (verb)!

> Loss uns geh! *or* Loss uns en Lied singe!

7. You have invited several of your friends to a birthday party. You instruct each friend what to do before and during the party.

der Disch rischde – Rischt der Disch!

1. en Kuche kaafe

2. mit der Sally iwwer die Party schwetze

3. en Kaart schreiwe

4. mit de Freinde danse

5. wennich frieher kumme

6. bis acht Uhr bleiwe

8. Mr. Klotz saagt seinre Klaess, was sie mache solle. Mr. Klotz, the PD teacher, is telling several of his students what they are supposed to do.

Die Jenny un die Reese / heem gehe

Jenny un Reese, geht heem!

1. Der Paul un der Jason / die Schularewet mache

2. Die Tina un die Ann / Glapperbax schpiele

3. Die Andrea un der Spencer / es Deitschbuch lese

4. Der Kyle un der Tyler / en Brief schreiwe

5. Die Kayla un die Chelsea / net so laut schwetze

6. Der Matt un der Josh / die Myusick heere

9. Provide the appropriate command forms.

(rufe) _____ mir die Polies! – Rufe mir die Polies!

1. (kumme) _____ her, John!

2. (mache) _____ schnell, Sarah un Janelle!

3. (bsuche) _____ mir die scheene Schtadt!

4. (esse) _____ dei Brot!

5. (schenke) _____ Aent Mary en Kiddel, Justin un Wes!

6. (lese) _____ es Buch fer Freidaag, Stephanie!

7. (gehe) _____ mir am Sunndaag in die Karich!

10. One of your friends is very messy. Tell them what they should do to clean up!

Saag Eppes

Giving and Asking for Directions

There are three main ways of asking for directions:

Wie kumm ich zu _____? – *How do I get to _____?*

Wu is _____? – *Where is _____?*

Kannscht du mir saage, wu _____ is? – *Can you tell me where _____ is?*

When giving directions, you can give them in command form:

Dreh mol rechts uff der Elm Schtrooss! – *Turn right on Elm Street!*

Geh mol graad bis zur Poschtaffis! – *Go straight ahead until the post office!*

Here are some important words in PD in regards to directions:

gehe	*to go*	rechts	*right*
drehe	*to turn*	links	*left*
hinner	*behind*	graad	*straight ahead*
newe	*next to*	iwwer vun	*across from*
uff dem Eck	*on the corner*	net weit weg	*not far away*

11. Using the map provided, give directions from point A to point B.

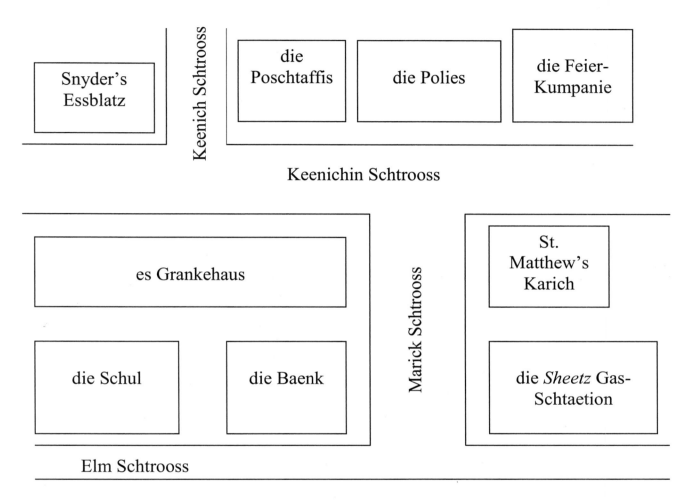

Wie kumm ich vun der Schul an Grankehaus?

Geh mol graad uff der Elm Schtrooss! Dreh mol links uff der Marick Schtrooss! Dreh mol links uff der Keenichin Schtrooss.

1. Wie kumm ich vun der Baenk an Snyder's Essblatz?

2. Wie kumm ich vun St. Matthew's Karich zu der Poschtaffis?

3. Ich bin bei die Feier-Kumpanie. Wie kumm ich zu der Schul?

4. Ich bin in der Poschtaffis. Ich will zu der Baenk.

5. Wie kumm ich vun der *Sheetz* Gas-Schtaetion zu der Polies?

Schprooch

Conjunctions

Coordinating Conjunctions

Coordinating Conjunctions are used to connect two words, phrases or clauses. The addition of a coordinating conjunction does NOT affect the word order of the two main clauses joined together. The coordinating conjunctions are:

awwer	*but*
odder	*or*
un	*and*

Ich will laenger bleiwe, <u>awwer</u> ich hab ken Zeit.

> *I want to stay longer, but I don't have the time.*

Fliegscht du noch Waschington <u>odder</u> faahrscht du mit der Maschien?

> *Are you flying to Washington or driving?*

Der Tom grickt en Buch <u>un</u> der Bill grickt en CD.

> *Tom is getting a book and Bill is getting a CD.*

Subordinating Conjunctions

Subordinating conjunctions are used to connect a main clause and a dependent clause. A subordinating conjunction does not affect the word order in English, but in PD it does. In a sentence beginning with the main clause, the main verb of the dependent clause appears at the end of the dependent clause or the complete sentence. Clauses are separated by commas.

Mir gehne in der Essblatz, <u>weil</u> mir hungrig sin.

> *We are going into the restaurant because we are hungry.*

In a sentence beginning with the dependent clause (the conjunction is at the beginning of the sentence), the conjugated verb of the dependent clause appears at the end of the dependent clause (before the comma) and the inverted word order is applied.

<u>Wann</u> ich Zeit hab, zaehl ich eppes kaafe.

If I have time I will buy something.

The most common subordinating conjunctions in PG are:

as	*that*
bis	*until, till, by the time*
eb	*before, whether*
so as	*so that, in order that*
vun wege as	*because, because of the fact*
wann	*when, if*
weil	*because*
wie	*when, how*
zidder as	*since*

NOTE: When the conjunction *wann* (when, if) is followed by *mir* (we), the two are contracted to *wammer*. Ex: *wammer Zeit hen – if we have time.*

12. *Verbinne selle Sentences!*

Die Carla geht heem. Mir gehne zu die Movies. (un)

Die Carla geht heem un mir gehne zu die Movies.

1. Der Mr. Seiber drinkt Kaffi. Die Fraa Seiber drinkt Tee. (awwer)

2. Die Kinner faahre zum Essblatz. Sie gehe zum Wattshaus. (odder)

3. Mir esse Pizza. Mir addere Kuche. (odder)

4. Mei Schweschder fliegt noch Texas. Ich flieg noch Kalifornia. (awwer)

5. En Klaess faahrt mit em Draen. Die annere Klaess faahrt mit em Bus. (un)

13. *Verbinne selle Sentences!*

Ich schpiel Tennis. Es is waarem.

Ich schpiel Tennis, wenn es waarem is.

1. Ich drink die Lemonade. Es is faddich.

2. Sie schreibt. Der Walter will lenger in Ohio bleiwe.

3. Er kaaft en nei-i Maschien. Er hot viel Geld.

4. Die Lauren is im Grankehaus. Sie hot en Operation.

5. Ich les es Buch. Ich hab Zeit.

6. Der Kurtis geht in die Schul. Er will viel lanne.

7. Der Riggelweg faahrt noch Reading. Es faahrt noch Laengeschder.

8. Die Katz hot en Wund. Sie hot mit en annere Katz gfochde.

Eppes zu lese

Bei dem Doktor

Die Katie hot schunn zidder zwee Daage Halsweh. Den Mariye is sie uffgwacht un het gaar net schlucke kenne. Ihre Eldre hen ihre gsaat, as sie zum Doktor Burkey, ihrem Doktor, geh soll. Ihre Mudder ruft frieh am Mariye. Die Katie hot Glick. Sie kann schunn um acht Uhr zum Doktor Burkey varbeikumme.

Bei der Reception saagt sie ihre Naame. En Fraa schreibt ihre Naame uff en Lischt und saagt die Katie, sie sell sich in die Waardeschtubb hocke. Es dauert yuscht zehe Minudde, bis sie ihre Naame heert. Sie schteht graad uff un folgt en yungi Fraa in die Doktorschtubb.

Der Doktor:	Guder Mariye, Katie! Was is nau los?
Katie:	Ich hab en greislich Halsweh. Es hot vargeschder aagfange un scheint aa net besser zu waerre. Un Fieber hawwich aa.
Der Doktor:	Yawell, dann messe mir erscht eemol dei Blutdruck. Leg dei Aarem arig los uff der Disch!
Katie:	Un wie is mei Blutdruck?
Der Doktor:	All recht. Nau noch der Puls messe. Ya, der is aa gut. Mach yuscht mol dei Maul uff un saag "Aah!"
Katie:	Aaaah! Ich glaab, mei Driese sin rot.
Der Doktor:	Net yuscht sell. Sie sin aa eppes gschwolle. Du hoscht en Halsinfektion. Un nau die Ohre. Dei Ohre sehne awwer glaar aus.

Katie:	Mir hen noch bis Mittwoch Ferien. Dann fangt die Schul widder aa.
Der Doktor:	Ich kann dir heit noch net saage, wann du widder in die Schul geh kannscht.
Katie:	Allerdings muss so eppes in mei Ferien gschehe! Mir wolle mariye schwimme geh.
Der Doktor:	Sell darfscht du nadierlich net. Bleib drei Daage daheem un ruh dich aus. Hoffentlich fiehlscht du viel besser in paar Daage. Wann net, dann kumm widder do zerick

Der Doktor Burkey schreibt en Preskription un saagt die Katie, as sie die naegschde zehe Daage daeglich zwee Pille nemme soll. Er glaabt, as sie viel besser bis Mittwoch fiehlt.

Der Doktor:	Arewet is die beschde Arznei. Wann du die Schul gaern hoscht, dann bischt du gschwinder gsund.
Katie:	Wer will denn noch der katze Ferien widder in die Schul geh? Waericklich frei ich mich, weil ich in zwee Woche mit meine Freinde kaempe geh will.
Der Doktor:	Bis sell Zeit waerscht du widder gsund sei. Mit re Halsinfektion darfscht du nadierlich net im Zelt schloofe.
Katie:	Yawell, ich browier mei Beschtes.
Der Doktor:	Sell heer ich arig gaern. Gude Bessering!
Katie:	Denki!

14. *Was geht do am beschte?*

1. Die Katie hot	a. sich in Waardeschtubb hocke sett
2. Den Mariye kann	b. en Preskription
3. Sie gebt	c. rot aus
4. Die Katie soll	d. net besser zu waerde
5. Sie folgt	e. zidder zwee Daage Halsweh
6. Die Halsweh scheint	f. mariye schwimme geh
7. Der Doktor messt	g. der Blutdruck
8. Die Driese sehe	h. sich uff naegschde Wochend
9. Die Ohre sin	i. bei der Reception ihre Naame
10. Die Katie wollt	j. sie net schlucke
11. Der Doktor Burkey schreibt	k. en yungi Fraa in die Doktorschtubb
12. Die Katie freit	l. glaar

15. *Antwadde selle Frooget!*

1. Was kann die Katie den Mariye net duh?

2. Was hen ihre Eldre gsaat?

3. Was hot en Fraa an der Reception geduh?

4. Muss die Katie lang in der Waardeschtubb waarde?

5. Was macht der Doktor Burkey aerscht?

6. Wie sin die Driese?

7. Wann is der Katie ihre Ferien varbei?

8. Was darf die Katie mariye net duh?

9. Was soll sie duh, wann sie in een paar Daage net besser fiehlt?

10. Wie viele Pille muss die Katie in die naegschde zehe Daage nemme?

Kuldur

Pennsylvania Dutch Place Names

Residents of Pennsylvania's Dutch Country are often amazed when they encounter strange street signs and place names, which record the history of the German-American settlement in the area. Driving through Lancaster County, one stumbles across Katze Boucle Weeg (Cat's Back Road) and Schtee Bruch Weeg (Stone Quarry Road) in West Earl Township.

Lehigh County, particularly the northwestern end around Lynn Township, is full of odd street names: Haasadahl Road (Rabbit Valley Road), Eile Dahl Road (Owl Valley Road), Herrnhutter Strass Road (Moravian Street Road), Allemaengel Road (All-Want Road) and Hoffadeckel Court (Crockpot Cover Court). We do have some Dutch place names in southern Lehigh County, too. Hosensack (Pant's Pocket) is a small village, whose name is often attributed to the fact that the surrounding valley is closed at one end, like a pant's pocket. Other local lore attributes the name to the earliest settlers, who arrived in the dead of night --- the darkness of the valley making them think that they were in a pant's pocket.

To the north in Northampton County is the infamous site of powwowing and Pennsylvania Dutch supernatural happenings: Hexenkoph (Witch's Head). Although the area is increasingly being built up, the road circling the mountain is still called Hexenkoph Road... not too far from Wassergass (Water Alley) in Williams Township. These street signs and place names, which are easily found on contemporary maps, are just the tip of the iceberg compared to the local Dutch names applied to fields or places. Many of these have been lost over time; some have fortunately been recorded and exemplify the creativity of language-play of our ancestors.

The German-Pennsylvanian Association located in Ober Olm, Germany and headed by President Dr. Michael Werner is currently involved in a Pennsylvania Dutch Place Name project. Their goal is to have bilingual street and place name signs erected throughout the Pennsylvania Dutch speaking counties.

For more information on their project and the association, please visit:

- http://dpak.wordpress.com

Rickguck

16. Translate the following sentences *in Deitsch*!

    1. Go to the post office! (singular command)

    2. Call the fire company! (plural command)

    3. Let's go to the church!

    4. Ralph, eat at the restaurant!

    5. Jeremy and Austin, buy something at the grocery store!

    6. Jeff, get some gas at the gas station!

    7. Jane, send your sister to the hospital!

    8. Don't go to the bank! (singular command)

    9. Park in front of the police! (plural command)

17. Give someone directions!

With a partner, describe the inside of your house. Give them directions from room to room. Make sure you visit each room of your house.

    Geh in der vedderscht Dier. Nau bischt du in der Kich. Dreh mol rechts un geh graad, nau bischt du in der Wuhnschtubb…

18. Lead a blindfolded student out of the classroom.

19. Translate the following sentences *in Deitsch!*

1. I drink root beer but my friend drinks cola.

2. Since July he is living in Lebanon.

3. I am buying the new CD or a new DVD.

4. We will play cards when Mr. Wert comes.

5. Susan is writing a letter and Lee is playing baseball.

6. Tim is eating broccoli because of the fact that it is healthy.

7. She says that the president is on TV.

8. John is learning a song so that he can sing in church.

9. He is taking medicine until he feels better.

10. Before I can go home, I have to finish my homework.

11. He is sick because he slept outside.

Was weesscht du?

- Create a dialog with a partner. Your dialog should be about a trip to the post office. You are getting ready to send out your Christmas cards and you need to buy some stamps. Be as creative as possible. Feel free to write your dialog in either present tense or present perfect tense. When you are finished share the dialog with your teacher and act it out in front of the class.

- *In Deitsch* describe what is all found in your hometown. Also describe where the various businesses and offices are located in reference to each other.

- Play *"der Simon saagt"* in Deitsch. Come up with a list of commands that you can ask your classmates to perform. Remember that they only count if *"der Simon saagt"*!

- *Wie kumm ich…*Using a map of Pennsylvania. Give directions from one town or city to another.

  Reading ⟶ Allentown

  Vun Reading bis Ellsdaun muss mer uff der 61 Nord faahre noch Hambarrig. In Hambarrig dreh mol rechts uff der 78 Ost. Geh mol 25 Meile uff der 78 Ost noch Ellsdaun.

Waddelischt

Ab/nemme – to take pictures
der Abnemmer – the photographer, *m*
allerdings – above all, by all means
die Arznei – the medicine, *f*
as - that
aus/lege – to explain
awwer - but
baddere – to worry about
die Baenk – the bank, *f*
begegne – to meet
bletzlich – right away
der Blutdruck – the blood pressure, *m*
der Briefumschlag – the envelope, *m*
bringe – to bring
browiere – to try out
daeglich - daily
der Dochdermann – son-in-law, *m*
draage – to carry
die Driese – the glands, *pl*
eb – before, whether
der Eifluss – the control, *m*
fechde – to fight
die Ferien – vacation, *f*
die Fieber – the feaver, *f*
fiehle – to feel
die Freindschaft – the relatives, *f*
die Gas-schtation – the gas station, *f*
glaar - clear
es Grankehaus – the hospital, *n*
greislich - terrible
gschehe – to happen, to occur
gschwinder – more quickly
gschwolle - swollen
gsund - healthy

die Halsweh – the sore throat, *f*
iwwerfalle – to surprise
kaempe – to camp
der Kumpanie – the company, *m*
messe – to measure
der Mithelfer – colleague, *m*
nadierlich - naturally
die Nei-ichkeede – the news, *f*
der Nochber (-e) – the neighbor, *m*
odder - or
der Pack (Peck) – the package, *m*
der Pill (-e) – the pill, *m*
die Polies – the police, *pl*
die Poscht – the mail, *f*
die Poschtaffis – the post office, *f*
der Poschtmann – the mailman, *m*
der Puls – the pulse, *m*
die Raawerei – the robbery, *f*
die Rechling – the bill, *f*
scheine – to appear
schlucke – to swallow
der Schmok – the smoke, *m*
schtarewe – to die
schtecke – to place
so as – so that, in order that
vun wege as – because, because of the fact
die Waardeschtubb – the waiting room, *n*
wann – when, if
waericklich – really
weil – because
die Wund – the wound, *f*
der Zelt – the tent, *m*
zidder as - since

Kabiddel 11 –

"En Rees"

In this chapter you will be able to:

- Describe and Plan a Trip
- Ask for and Give Information
- Describe Means of Transportation
- Tell what Language one Speaks

Am Airport

Der Chris un die Diane sin en Munet lang darich Deitschland gereest. Sie sin in Rheinland-Pfalz gewest. Sie hen viel vun ihrer Familye ihr Heemet gelannt. Sie hen viel Familye-Unnersuch geduh. Heit geht's widder noch Pennsylfaania zerick.

Diane: Mir hen waerecklich viel Peck.

Chris: Yawell, mir sin yuscht mit me Suitcase driwwekumme. Es sin all die Gschenke fer unsere Freinde un Blutsfreinde.

Diane: Du hoscht recht. Mir kumme ya net alle Yaahr nooch Deitschland.

Chris: Kumm, gehne mir zum Monitor!

1. *Eppes is net recht. Kannscht du die richdiche Antwatte gewe?*

   1. Die Diane un der Chris sin in Berlin gewest.

   2. Sie sin en Woch darich Deitschland gereest.

   3. Sie reese heit nooch Deitschland.

   4. Im Pack sin Gschenke fer der Chris un die Diane.

   5. Die Diane schteht var me Monitor.

Chris: Do is es: Flug 64 nooch Atlanta, vaddel noch 10 Oweds.

Diane: Wann kumme mir aa?

Chris: Mariye um 12 Uhr 35. Dennot misse mir zwee Schtunde waarde. Unser Luftschiff fliegt um 14 Uhr 30 noch Philadelfi ab un kummt zwee Schtunde schpaeder aa.

Diane: Wu sin unsere Passports?

Chris: Die hawwich do mit unsere Flugkaarte. Mir misse aerscht zum Counter.

2. *Mach selle Sentences faddich!*

1. Wu _____ der Diane und dem Chris ihre Passports?

2. In Atlanta misse allebeed zwee Schtunde _____.

3. Sie _____ Mariye gege halwer eens in Atlanta aa.

4. Der Chris un die Diane _____ aerscht zum Counter.

5. Vun Atlanta _____ sie um halwer drei noch Philadelfi.

6. Uff em Monitor _____, vun weller Gate sie abfliege.

Allebeed geh zum Counter. Do schtehne schunn viel Leit. Es dauert awwer net lang, bis en Counter frei is. Der Chris gebt dem Schaffmann die Flugkaarte. Der Schaffmann will aa die Passports sehne. Er gebt sie ihm. Es Luftschiff is heit arig voll. Der Chris un die Diane hen Glick. Sie hen schunn ihre Hockbletz. Sie gewwe dem Schaffmann ihre Peck un griege vun ihm die Boarding Passes. Dennot geh sie zum Gate.

Diane:	Ich verschteh gaar net, fer was im Tschulei so viel Leit noch Amerikaa fliege.
Chris:	Du weesscht, darich selli Yaahreszeit is es oft in Amerikaa abaddich schee. Es gebt dann viele Feschte – im Pennsylfaania un im Kutzeschteddel gebts Die Pennsylfaanisch Deitsch Volklewe Fescht.
Diane:	Du hoscht recht. Hoscht du gheert, was der Schaffmann gsaat hot?
Chris:	Fer schurr, er hot der Flug annebschtellt. In en paar Minudde kenne mir neischteige.
Diane:	Ich bin froh, as ich en Buch mitgebrocht hab.
Chris:	Lese meecht ich net. Es soll en wunnerbaare Movie gewwe.

3. *Was geht do am beschde?*

1. Im Tschulei fliege   a. ihre Boarding Passes.

2. Die Diane is froh, as   b. in en paar Minudde neischteige.

3. Der Schaffmann will   c. arig voll.

4. In Amerikaa gebt   d. sie en Buch mitgebrocht hot.

5. Sie griege   e. der Schaffman die Peck.

6. Es Luftschiff is   f. die Passports sehne.

7. Sie kenne   g. viel Leit nooch Amerikaa.

8. Sie gewwe   h. es im Summer viel Feschte.

4. *Antwadde selle Frooget!*

1. Fer was hen der Chris un die Diane viel Peck?

2. Mit wie viel Suitcases sin sie noch Deitschland kumme?

3. Wu anne fliege sie um vaddel nooch zehe Oweds?

4. Wann kumme sie in Philadelfi aa?

5. Was muss der Chris dem Schaffman gewwe?

6. Fer was hen der Chris un die Diane Glick?

7. Was brauche allebeed am Gate?

8. Wie lang misse sie in Atlanta waarde?

9. Was hot der Schaffmann annebschtellt?

10. Was waerd die Diane im Luftschiff duh?

5. Talk about a trip that you have gone on!

213

Eppes zu wisse

Means of Transportation – *Wege fer Faahre*

es Boot

es Schiff

es Luftschiff

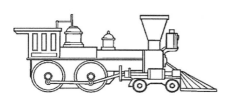

der Draen

der Bus

die Maschien

der Motorcycle

der Bicycle

Wie kumme sie noch Ellsdaun?	Der Peter faahrt mit der Maschien. Ich faahr mit dem Bus.
Laafscht du in die Schtadt?	Nee, ich faahr mit dem Bicycle.
Faahrscht du mit em Schiff noch Europe?	Nee, ich flieg mit em Luftschiff.
Was machscht du uff em Wasserloch?	Ich faahr mit em Boot.

6. *Wie kummt mer am beschde dohin?* Select the most appropriate phrase for each situation described. Use only one of these phrases: *laafe, mit em Schiff, mit der Maschien, mit em Luftschiff.*

1. Die Mary wuhnt in Pottsville un will im Summer noch Deitschland reese.

2. Mr. Long geht gaern zum *Dairy Queen*. Es is yuscht en Eck vun seim Haus.

3. Der Kyle un der Spencer wolle vun Nei Yarrick Schtadt noch England reese. Die Rees dauert sechs Daage.

4. Die Emily grickt zu ihrem Gebottsdaag naegschd Woch en Bicycle. Alle Daag geht sie nau noch mit ihrer Freind um halwer acht in die Schul.

5. Die Jonses wolle im Winder mit der ganze Familye in die Poconos skiing geh. Vun Reading noch Ost-Schtroudsburg is es 80 Meil.

6. Die menschde Tourists fliege noch Europe, awwer deel wolle en lengeri Rees mache.

Schprooch

The Passive Voice

The Passive Voice means that the subject of the sentence is not doing the action of the verb, but rather the action of the verb is being done to the subject of the sentence. English uses *is/are being* + *past participle* to form passive sentences. Take, for example, the following sentence:

A new house is being built on our street.

In this sentence it is not important who is doing the building, but rather that a house is being built.

To form the passive voice in PD, you use the forms of *waerre* + *the past participle* of the verb.

Die Maschien waerd gwesche. – *The car is being washed.*

Die Bicher waerre glese. – *The books are being read.*

Although passive sentences need not indicate who performs the action of the verb, some passive sentences include an "agent". When there is an agent in the sentence, PD uses the preposition *vun* before it. Remember that *vun* is followed by the dative case.

Es Haus waerd vun meim Noochber widderhergschtellt. –

The house is being restored by my neighbor.

7. Place the following active sentences into the passive!

> * *Mei Daadi kaaft en Maschien.*

> * *En Maschien waerd vun meim Daadi kaaft.*

1. Der Bu schreibt en Brief.

2. Der Hund beisst der Poschtmann.

3. Die drei Tourists aus Deitschland mache en Rees.

4. Der Schportler schmeisst en Balle.

5. Dei Onkel schtreicht es Haus aa.

6. Der Schulmeeschder lest en Buch vum Shakespeare.

7. Der Joe un die Michelle singe en Lied.

8. *Was waerd gmacht?* Combine the three processes with the following sentences and place them in the correct order. The three processes are:

A. *Party vorbereide*   B. *Essay schreiwe*   C. *en nei-i Maschien suche*

1. Die beschde Maschien waerd kaaft.

2. Es Ess-sach waerd gekocht.

3. Der Disch waerd grischt.

4. Die Sentences waerre nooch eemol glese.

5. Die Maschiene waerre aageguckt.

6. Die Guests waerre eigelaade.

7. Die Advertisements in der Zeiding waerre noochgeguckt.

8. Der Verkaafer waerd gerufe.

9. Die Kerze waerre uff der Disch geschtellt.

10. En Plan waerd gemacht.

11. Information waerre gsammlet.

12. Die Arewet waerd gschriwwe.

217

Eppes zu wisse

Sack un Peck – Luggage

der Beidel

es Ricksack

der Briefcase

der Suitcase

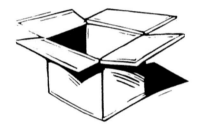

der Kaschde

es Eikaafssack

Was draagscht du?

Ich draag en Eikaafssack fer Ess-sach.

Ich draag mei Ricksack fer mei Bicher.

Er draagt en Suitcase fer sei Rees nooch Kanadaa.

9. *Was schwetzt mer davun?* Select the most logical items for each situation.

1. Der Andrew schickt seinre Freind zum Gebottsdaag en

   _____.

2. Mr. un Fraa Sellers brauche fer ihre Rees nooch Austria zwee

   _____.

3. Alle Mariye geht der Josh mit seim _____ in die Schul.

4. Fraa Kreider hot ihr Geld in dem _____.

5. Die Samantha wandert mit ihre Freinde in der Busch. Sie draagt en

   _____.

6. Die Heather muss noch schnell Brot, Millich, Kaes un Wascht eikaafe. Sie

   hot en _____ mitgebrocht.

7. Der Schulmeeschder bringt die Schularewet in seim _____.

Saag eppes

Wer schwetzt welle Schprooch in selle Lenner?

Amerikaa - Englisch

Kanadaa – Englisch un
Franzeesisch

Deitschland -
Hochdeitsch

Mexiko - Schpanisch

Frankreich – Franzeesisch

Italy - Italeenisch

Japan - Japaneesisch

China - Chieneesisch

Egypt - Arabisch

In Amerikaa schwetzt mer Englisch.

In Deitschland schwetzt mer Hochdeitsch.

10. *Weesscht du, welle Schprooch mer in selle Schtedt odder Lenner schwetzt?*

    * Mexiko

    * In Mexiko schwetzt mer Schpanisch.

1. Toronto	5. Vienna
2. Buenos Aires	6. Rome
3. Madrid	7. Tokyo
4. Paris	8. Berlin

11. *Weesscht du welle Lenner die sin un was die Haaptschtedt sin?*

    * Eiffel Tower

    * Sell is in Frankreich. Die Haaptschtadt is Paris.

1. Coloseum	4. The Pyramids
2. Big Ben	5. The Great Wall
3. Niagra Falls	6. Mayan Pyramid

Eppes zu lese

Die Meyer Familye faahrt uff en Ferien

Mr. un Fraa Meyer wuhne mit ihre drei Kinner in Bernville, en gleeni Schtadt in Barricks Kaundi. Alle Yaahr faahre sie zwee Woche uff en Ferien. Des Yaahr welle sie in Huntingdon in Huntingdon Kaundi en Ferien mache. Selli Schtadt legt am Raystown Lake, net weit weg vun Altoona. Dohie kumme alle Yaahr viel Tourists net yuscht aus Pennsilfaania, awwer aa vun Marrland, Ohio un West Virginia.

Endlich is der Daag der Rees datt. Die Meyers hen schunn frieh am Mariye die Sack un Peck gepackt. Uff em Weg wolle sie en Picknick in Belleville mache. Deswege hot Fraa Meyer Brot, Kaes, Schunkefleesch, Lemonade un Obscht mitgnumme. Mr. Meyer guckt noch ee mol in der Maschien, as aa alles do is. Dennot geht's los.

Noch baut zwee Schtund mache sie net weit vun Belleville en Picknick. Es gebt do Greenwood Furnace State Park. Belleville is en gleeni Schtadt im Grosse Daal. Die Meyers hocke sich am Picknick Disch, esse un drinke eppes. Sie gucke aa die Gegend aa. Es gebt viel Amische un gleene Schtors in Grosse Daal. Die Eldre kaafe gaern ei un die Kinner aa.

Am Nummidaag kumme sie in Huntingdon aa. Do waerde sie die naegschde zwee Woche in en Bed un Breakfast bei der Lane Familye wuhne un aa ihre Mariye-Esse und Owedesse griege. Die Lanes bewillkumme ihre Guests un zeige sie graad ihre Schtubb. Um halwer sechs Uhr hocke die Meyers un die Lanes am Disch uff der vedderscht Bortsch, schwetze mitenanner un esse dennot wennich schpaeder ihre Owedesse.

Noch zwee Woche kumme die Meyers widder heem. Darich der Ferien waar es Wedder arig schee. Es regert yuscht en Daag. Deswege hen alle viel Schpass ghatt. Die Meyers hen viel Zeit uff em Raystown Lake verlebt. Sie hen en Boot glehnt un hen viel geangelt. Sie mache aus, naegschd Yaahr widder datthie zu geh.

12. *Was geht do?*

1. Alle hocke   a. sie en Picknick

2. Es regert   b. die Sack un Peck

3. Huntingdon legt   c. sie uff em Ferien

4. Uff em Weg mache   d. die Gegend aa

5. Viel Amische wuhne   e. yuscht en Daag

6. Alle Yaahr faahre   f. in Grosse Daal

7. Fraa Meyer packt   g. net weit weg vun Altoona

8. Sie gucke sich   h. uff der vedderscht Bortsch

13. *Antwadde selle Frooget!*

1. Wie viel Daage gehne die Meyers uff en Ferien?

2. In welle Kaunty faahre sie des Yaahr?

3. Was nemme die Meyers fer en Picknick?

4. Was mache sie net weit vun Belleville?

5. Wu waerde die Meyers alle Daag in Huntingdon esse?

6. Wu hocke alle frieh Oweds?

7. Wie waar es Wedder darich de Meyers ihre Ferien?

8. Was kann mer uff Raystown Lake duh?

Kuldur

Hex Signs

The hex sign, barn star, or barn sign is perhaps the most noticeable feature of the Pennsylvania Dutch farmstead. Hex signs are circular and geometric designs painted on the front of the barn's forebay. Although the term Hex means witch or spell in PD, these symbols have nothing to do with protection from witchcraft. Most scholars agree that barn stars were for decoration.

Designs on barn stars can be found elsewhere in PD folk art. There are two major categories of Hex Signs: Geometric and Folk. Geometric Hex signs are based on a geometric shape, normally a star (usually more than five points). Folk Hex signs use other PD symbols, such as hearts or the Distelfink.

Current attempts are underway to preserve hex signs and tours can be arranged with tourist bureaus.

Further reading:
- Shoemaker, A. L. <u>Hex marks! But who says so?</u> The Pennsylvania Dutchman. 1949.
- Yoder, D. & Graves, T. <u>Pennsylvania Dutch barn symbols and their meaning.</u> Stackpole. 2000.

Example of a Geometric Hex Sign: found first on the farm of Charles H. Madenford located in Kirbyville, Berks County, PA.

Rickguck

14. *Eppes Paerseenliches!*

1. Wu anne meechtescht du uff en Ferien geh? Fer was?

2. Bischt du schunn bei em State Park gewest? Wann waar sell, un wu waarscht du?

3. Welle Schprooch kann mer in deinre Schul lanne?

4. Machscht du gaern en Picknick? Wu kann mer bei dir en Picknick mache?

15. Translate the following sentences *in Deitsch*!

1. The book is being read by the boy.

2. The bread is being eaten by the goat.

3. The milk is coming from the cows.

4. The presents are being bought by my mother.

5. The lunch in being prepared by the old ladies.

6. The car is being washed by his grandfather.

7. The horse is being ridden by the young girl.

16. *Welle Wadde gehne do?*

nein	Luftschiff	Woche	fliegt
dauert	Kaes	gepackt	Eldre
fliege	zerick	wisse	Montreal
Daage	kummt	State Park	bringt

1. Mir wolle in der _____ en Picknick mache.

   Was _____ ihr dennot mit?

   Brot, Lemonade un _____.

2. Mir _____ naegschde Woch nooch Kanadaa.

   Hett dihr dennot eier Sack un Peck schunn _____?

   Ya, schunn zidder viel _____.

   Wu anne _____ dihr?

3. Wie lang _____ die Rees aus?

   Acht Schtund mit dem Bus awwer nur zwee Schtund mit em

   _____.

   Wer _____ dennot mit?

   Mei _____ un mei Schweschder.

4. Wie viele _____ waerret dihr in der Bed un Breakfast iwwer

   Nacht bleiwe?

   Fer schurr _____.

   Wann kummt dihr widder _____?

   Des _____ mir nooch net.

Was weesscht du?

- *Was soll ich uff en Rees mitnemme?* You've decided to travel with one of your classmates. Indicate the destination of your trip since this may change what you will take along. For example, you would take different items to Florida or to Alaska. Prepare a list of items that you intend to take along. Then compare your list with those of your classmates. Limit your list to the most necessary items. Discuss why you should or should not take along certain items.

- *Selli Rees hen mir arig gegliche.* Describe a vacation trip that you have taken in the past, or one that you would like to take. Your description should include the following information: time of year and place you traveled to, how long you stayed, who came along, some of the activities you did and when you returned home.

- *Wuhie kumme sie un welli Schprooch schwetze sie?* Undoubtedly, you know some people from your school or neighborhood who speak other languages besides English. Make a list of these people including where they or their parents or grandparents came from and which languages they speak.

  Example: *Fraa Perez kummt aus Mexiko. Sie schwetzt Schpanisch.*
  Mr. Wong kummt aus China. Er schwetzt Chineesisch.

- *Was ich gaern uff em Ferien duh meecht.* Imagine that you have two weeks and enough money to go on vacation. List five items that indicate where you would go, whom you would take along, what you would have to buy before your departure and what you would like to do once you get there, and so on.

- *Sell meecht ich gaern sehne.* Pick one area of Germany, Austria, Switzerland or Pennsylvania that you would like to see. From the Internet or some other source describe in English and PD what is so unique about this area and when you would like to visit it.

- *Wer is do gewest?* Someone you know undoubtedly went on a trip (camping, bus, train, plane) during the past year. Find out a few details and then write at least six sentences *in Deitsch* about this person's experience.

Waddelischt

aa/gucke – to look at
aa/kumme – to arrive
aa/schtreiche – to paint
ab/fliege – to take off
allebeed – both
angle – to fish
anne/bschtelle – to announce
aus/mache – to plan
der Beidel – the purse, the handbag, *m*
beisse – to bite
bewillkumme – to greet
der Blutsfreind (-e) – the relative, *m*
es Boot (-e) – the boat, *n*
dauere – to last
deswege - therefore
driwwe/kumme – to come over
es Eikaafsack – the shopping bag, *n*
es Fescht (-er) – the festival, *n*
fliege – to fly
die Flugkaart (-e) – the airplane ticket, *f*
Franzeesisch - French
die Gegend – the area, *f*
es Glick – the luck, *n*

die Haaptschtadt (-schtedt) – the capital, *f*
die Heemet – the home, *f*
Hochdeitsch - German
der Hockblatz (-bletz) – the seat, *n*
der Kaschde – the box, the package, *m*
die Kerz (-e) – the candle, *f*
mitnemme – to take with, along
neischteige – to board
der Pack (Peck) – the luggage, *m*
packe – to pack
die Rees (-e) – the trip, *f*
reese – to travel
es Ricksack – the back pack, *n*
der Schaffmann (-menner) – the employee, *m*
es Schiff (-e) – the ship, *n*
die Schprooch (-e) – the language, *f*
suche – to look for, to search
die Unnersuch – the research, *f*
verlewe – to spend time
wandere – to hike
zeige – to show

Kabiddel 12 ~

"Sell macht Schpass!"

In this chapter you will be able to:

- Describe a past event
- Describe Hypothetical Situations
- Write a letter / E-Mail

Gehne mir danse

Joe:	Guder Daag, Becky! Hoscht du die Grace gsehne?
Becky:	Du hoscht waericklich ken Aage! Sie schteht graad do un schwetzt mit der Maria.
Joe:	Weesscht du, was Zeit as sie am Samschdaag zum Dans geht?
Becky:	Hoscht du noch net mit ihr gschwetzt?
Joe:	Nee, geht sie dann net mit dem Dylan?
Becky:	Sell glaab ich net. Er hot doch en Freind.

1. *Was geht do?*

1. Die Becky glaabt net, as   a. mit der Becky.

2. Der Joe hot   b. die Grace graad do.

3. Der Dylan hot   c. net mit dem Dylan zum Dans geh.

4. Die Becky seht   d. net mit der Grace gschwetzt.

5. Die Grace waerd   e. die Grace mit dem Dylan zum Dans geht.

6. Der Joe schwetzt   f. schunn en Friend.

Joe:	Gehscht du am Wochend zum Dans?
Grace:	Nee, ich will net. Ich bin es letschde Mol datt gewest. Die Baend hot net gut geschpielt.
Joe:	Die neie Baend aus Oley soll awwer arig gut sei. Un du, Becky? Was machscht du?
Becky:	Die Maria un ich geh fer schur. Kummscht du aa?
Joe:	Ya. Mir kenne ya alle drei zamme datthiegehe.

Becky:	Kenne mir uns am Café vor em Dans aadreffe? So baut siwwe Uhr.
Grace:	Yawell, dann kumm ich aa. Der Joe un ich dreffe eich datt aa.
Joe:	Sell is gut, bis schpaeder.

2. *Mach selle Sentences faddich.* Complete each sentence with the appropriate forms of the verbs. You will not need all the verbs listed.

wolle	schpiele	sei	geh
kumme	aadreffe	hawwe	waerre

1. Die Becky un die Maria _____ fer schur zum Dans.

2. Es letschde Mol hot die Baend net gut _____.

3. Der Joe _____ mit der Becky un der Maria zum Dans geh.

4. Die Baend _____ aus Oley.

5. All viere _____ nooch vorher dem Dans zu en Café geh.

Maria:	Na endlich! Die Becky un ich waarde schunn lang.
Grace:	Es dutt mir leed. Ich hab unsere Maschien gwesche. Fer sell hot mir mei Daadi zehe Daaler gewe.
Becky:	Die Kaart koscht sechs Daaler. Do kannscht du mit deinem Geld net viel duh.
Grace:	Du bischt recht. Ich hab awwer aa annere Geld vun meine Eldre.
Becky:	Meins hawwich schunn gschpent.

Joe:	Ich hab ya aa glee bissel Geld. Aerscht laad ich eich zu zwee Cappuccinos ei.
Maria:	Der Joe is allsfatt so en Scheenermann!

3. *Richdig odder Falsch?* Determine whether the following statements are correct or incorrect. If they are incorrect, provide a correct statement *in Deitsch*!

1. Die Grace hot en Maschien gewesche.

2. Der Joe hot schunn lang gwaard.

3. Die Becky hot noch Geld.

4. En Kaart zum Dans koscht zehe Daller.

5. Der Joe will fer die Cappuccinos bezaahle.

6. Die Grace hot vun ihre Eldre Geld grickt.

4. *Antwadde selle Frooget!*

1. Fer was glaabt die Becky as der Joe ken Aage hot?

2. Was will der Joe vun der Becky wisse?

3. Waerd die Grace mit dem Dylan zum Dans geh?

4. Fer was will die Grace net zum Dans geh?

5. Is die Baend aus West Chester?

6. Um wie viel Uhr kumme all zum Café?

7. Fer was hen die Maria un die Becky uff die Grace gwaard?

8. Was grickt die Grace vun ihrem Daadi un ihrer Mudder?

Schprooch

The Preterite form of SEI

The only verb in PD which has a preterite form is *sei*. Below is the conjugation of *sei* in the preterite:

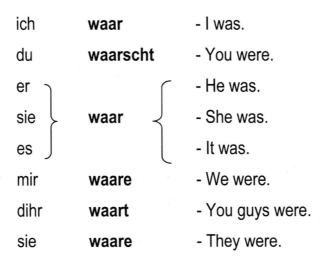

ich	**waar**	- I was.
du	**waarscht**	- You were.
er		- He was.
sie	**waar**	- She was.
es		- It was.
mir	**waare**	- We were.
dihr	**waart**	- You guys were.
sie	**waare**	- They were.

5. Fill in the proper form of the preterite form of *sei:*

1. Er _____ der beschde Schpieler.

2. _____ mir in Philadelfi im Tschulei?

3. Ich _____ hungrig var ich en Pizza gesse hab.

4. Der Hund _____ zu schnell.

5. _____ du an der Karich Picknick?

Eppes zu lese

En Schulrees

Die Schieler der Fraa Sieber vun re Hoch Schul in Lebnen hen ihre Schulrees schunn var en paar Woche ausgemacht. Ihre Schulmeeschderin un zwee Eldre gehne mit de fimf un zwansich Schieler. Sie blaane, vun Lebnen noch Ephrata un Landis Daal zu faahre.

Am Munndaag baut acht Uhr faahre sie mit em Bus un kumme noch vatzich Minudde in Ephrata aa. Sie gehne graad zu der Ephrata Cloister. Datt mache sie en Tour vun der Cloister. Sie lanne viel vun em Lewe am Cloister un aa vun dem Conrad Beissel, as der Cloister gegrindt hot. Darich die Tour hen die Schieler viel Gebeier gsehne. Wu der Tour faddich waar, hen paar Schieler Frooge gfroogt. Die Tourguide hot echde Cloister Gleeder gedraage.

Noch der Tour sin die Schtudente un die Uffgwaxner fer Middaagesse gange. Sie sin zu me gleene Essblatz gschwischich Ephrata un Landis Daal gange. Noch dem Middaagesse sin sie widder uff em Bus neigeschtiege. Noch fuffzeh Minudde sin sie an naegschde Blatz kumme: die Landis Daal Museum.

An der Landis Daal hen sie widder en Tour gemacht. Selle Mol hen sie viel vun die Pennsylfaanisch Deitsch gelannt. Sie hen viel vun em Lewe de achtzeht un neinzeht Yaahrhunnert gelannt. Die Landis Daal Tour dauert baut zwee Schtund.

Wu alles faddich waar, hen sich die Schieler der Tourguide bedankt. Die Schieler sin widder uff em Bus gange un zerick noch Lebnen gefaahre. Alli-epper hen en gude Erfaahring ghatt.

6. *Was is nett richdich?*

    1. En Uffgwaxener is mit de Schieler gange.

    2. Die Drupp faahrt en Schtund mit em Bus noch Ephrata.

    3. Die Cloister is in Laengeschder.

    4. Am Nummidaag hen sie yuscht Eisraahm gesse.

    5. Der Conrad Weiser hot die Cloister gegrindt.

    6. Die Landis Daal Museum legt die Gschicht vun den sechzeh Yaahrhunnert aus.

    7. Der Landis Daal Tourguide bedankt sich bei de Schieler.

7. *Mach en "Virtual" Bsuch!* Below are the websites for both the *Ephrata Cloister* and the *Landis Valley Museum*. Visit both websites and share something that you find interesting with the class.

    Ephrata Cloister: http://www.ephratacloister.org

    Landis Valley Museum: http://www.landisvalleymuseum.org

The following is PD comedic play. Perhaps your class would like to perform it?
Make a list of unknown words and reference a dictionary for assistance.

Geduld halde [*Keep your patience!*]
Peter V. Fritsch

Characters: Milton (Milt) Warremkessel
              Angelina (Ang) Warremkessel
              Host/Hostess
              Waiter/Waitress

Props: Small table, two chairs
              Menus, two place settings
              Two plates of food
              Coffeepot, two coffee cups

[Sketch opens with hostess at side stage checking names and reservations as in a restaurant. Milt, followed by Ang enter, Milt impatiently speaks to the hostess.]

Milt: [Almost pushing up against hostess.] Sin yusht zwee vun uns! Wu sette mer uns hocke?
Hostess: Ich bin sorry, mir sin all uffgfillt. [Looking at watch.] Ihr misse baut zwanzich Minutt waarde bis en Dish leer is.
Milt: [Loudly] Was?? Mir sin yusht zu zwett!!
Hostess: Sorry…Zwansich Minutt. [She turns and busies herself backstage.]
Ang: Nau Milt…Des nemmt net so long. Halt dei Geduld.
Milt: [Grumbling] Wann der Parre net so lang gebredicht hett!! Ich kumm eemol in die Karich un er mehnt er muss uffmache fer all die Zeite as ich net datt waar!!
Ang: Hosht nix aus'em Gebreddich grickt? Es waar vun dem Job sei Geduld.
Milt: [Sarcastically] Huh! Des hot dem JOB sei Geduld genumme fer so lang hocke un der Parre abharriche! Er hot drei mol "AMEN" gegrische un hot ennihau fattgemacht!! Seller lang-windicher… [Ang interrupts]
Ang: Nau, Nau Milt…Halt dei Maul. Guck!! Ich glaab as selli Leit ball reddi sin zu verlosse. [She points toward table on stage and imaginary people sitting there.]

236

Milt: Well sis baut Zeit!! Guck mol an ihre Dish!! Es guckt wie en Sei-Benn!! [Ang nudges him as if attempting to quiet him.]

Ang: Nau awwer ruhich! Un behaeff dich. [She straightens her hat as if to change the subject.] Dem Parre sei Breddich waar yusht paar Minutte iwwergange.

Milt: [Loudly] Paar Minutte!?! Des waar meh wie en Eewichkeit!! Un mei Maage hot aa so gemehnt!

Ang: Waar sell dei Maage as so an grummele waar?... Ken wunner hot der "Choir" die ganz Zeit uns aageguckt!!

Milt: [Looking at table.] Datt gehne sie!! Kumm aan, mir nemme selli Dish.

Ang: Milt, die Hostess hot unser Naame net geruffe!! [She is embarrassed.]

Hostess: [As though not seeing Milt and Ang, she calls in another direction.] Schneider! En Disch is reddi fer die Schneider Familye!!

Milt: [Pulling Ang to table.] Kumm aan! Hock dich hie gschwinnt!!

Ang: [Embarrassed] Mir sin aus "turn" gange! Der Dish waar fer die Schneider Leit. Hosht sie net gheert!? Sie hot uns net geruffe!

Milt: Ah-a-a, was macht's aus? Mir sin die Schneiders wennich vorgschprunge. Sie waare ennihau net reddi. Loss die Schneiders zwanzich Minutt waarde!!

Ang: Schemm dich!! Du settscht meh Geduld hawwe.

Milt: Loss die Schneiders Geduld hawwe!!

Waitress: Witt Koffee? [They nod, she pours.]

Ang: [Looking at coffee suspiciously.] Des guckt meh wie der Memm ihr Gravy!

Waitress: Witt Zucker odder Raahm?

Ang: [Still looking hard into cup.] Nee...yusht en Messer fer des Koffee riehre!

Milt: [Looking over menu.] So was witt hawwe Ang?

Ang: [Sarcastically] En nei-er Menu!!

Waitress: Sett ich zerick kumme?

Milt: Ya...die Frau muss meh Zeit hawwe. [She exits.] Dummel dich, mach dei "Mind" uff!

Ang: [Still looking at menu] Ei yei yei! Die Sei daheem esse besser as des. Ich kann mei "Mind" net uffmache zwischich GALLERREI SUPP udder HEXEBOHN-HINKELFIESS PLATTER!!!

Milt: [Impatiently grabbing menu] Oh, nemm der Roascht Beef graad wie ich!

Ang: Ferwas kummsht yusht do?

Milt: [Pulling out large coupon] Ei sie nemme Coupons!!

Ang: Ya...Du bisht der letscht vun die grosse "Schpenders"!! Du Geizbock!

237

Milt: Heh! Nau harrich mol… Ich hab en Zwansich-Daaler-Note im Offering Deller der marriye geduh!

Ang: [Quickly retorts] Ya!...Un du hosht aa Neinzeh Daaler wechsel raus genumme!!!

Milt: Well, was waar letz mit sell? [Waitress back on stage.]

Ang: Ei, alli-epper hott's gsehne un gelacht.

Waitress: Well nau, was wolle ihr hawwe?

Ang: [Sarcastically] Ei no-daut en Dokder wann mir fattich esse sin!

Milt: Oh ich nemm en Roascht Beef Sandwich.

Waitress: Un was witt die alt Gretz do? [Referring to Ang]

Ang: [Looking with murder in the eyes at the waitress] Well, ich mach's "easy" uff dir un der "Undertaker"…un nemm es same Ding, der Roascht Beef! [Waitress goes off stage long enough to grab two plates of food. She comes back and throws down the beef sandwiches and exits.]

Milt: [Proudly] Well…was denksht vun sell?? Sell hot net lang genumme! Sie misse des eirischde weit vannenaus.

Ang: [Looking at platter] Ya…weit vannenaus…wie letscht GRISCHDAAG!! [Milt begins eating very quickly.]

Ang: Muscht du esse wir en Sau!? Nemm dei Zeit!

Milt: Ich waar seilewwes net fer mei Zeit nemme, fer zerick schteh un waarde. Do kummt mer naryets im Lewwe wann zu viel Geduld hoscht! Do muss mer "grabbe" fer alles as mer kann! [A noisey commotion of celebration begins off stage.]

Milt: Geduldich Leit sin letscht im Roi un griege nix!!

Ang: Ich wunner was aageht datt drauss. [Off stage celebration gets louder. They both look back, wondering.]

Milt: [To waitress] Was geht aa datt draus? Was is die Commotion?

Waitress: Oh, epper hot en "Trip to Hawaii" gewunne, weil sie unser hunnerscht "Customer" waare!

Milt: Get out!!! Der hunnerscht Customer?? [He stands up.] Well was Nummer waare mir??

Waitress: [Looking at her order tablet.] Ihr waare neinunneinsichscht!

Milt: [Impatiently] Well, well…wie heesse die Leit as gewunne hen?

Waitress: Ei, SCHNEIDER!...sie hen en Disch grickt graad noch EICH!!

[Milt falls down in seat over table in despair, while Ang laughs.]

Schprooch

The Subjunctive Mood

The Subjunctive is used to express unreal conditions – things which might be true under other circumstances, but that are not true now.

Wann ich meh Geld hett, daet ich en nei-i Maschien kaafe.

> *If I had more money, I would buy a new car.*

Wann mir reich waere, daete mir efter reese.

> *If we were rich, we would travel more often.*

The Subjunctive of most verbs is formed by combining *daet* with an infinitive; this infinitive comes at the end of the clause. Example: Subjunctive of *mache*:

Ich daet mache	*I would make*
Du daetscht mache	*You would make*
Er, Sie, Es daet mache	*He, She, It would make*
Mir daete mache	*We would make*
Dihr daet mache	*You guys would make*
Sie daete mache	*They would make*

A few verbs, however, have a single-form subjunctive that has the following endings:

ich	**- t**	*mir*	**- te**
du	**- tscht**	*dihr*	**- t**
er		*sie*	**- te**
sie	**- t**		
es			

Example: *kumme* single-form subjunctive = *kaemt:*

Ich kaemt	*I would come*
Du kaemtscht	*You would come*
Er, Sie, Es kaemt	*He, She, It would come*
Mir kaemte	*We would come*
Dihr kaemt	*You guys would come*
Sie kaemte	*They would come*

Below is a list of verbs that have a single-form subjunctive:

Infinitive		Subjunctive
brauche	- *to need*	**breicht**
daerfe	- *to be allowed*	**daerft**
duh	- *to do*	**daet**
geh	- *to go*	**gengt**
gewwe	- *to give*	**geebt**
hawwe	- *to have*	**hett**
kenne	- *to be able*	**kennt**
meege	- *to like*	**meecht**
misse	- *to have to*	**misst**
solle	- *ought*	**sett**
wisse	- *to know*	**wisst**
wolle	- *to want to*	**wett**

The verb *SEI* has a unique single-form subjunctive:

ich	**waer**	*mir*	**waere**
du	**waerscht**	*dihr*	**waert**
er		*sie*	**waere**
sie	**waer**		
es			

8. Supply the correct subjunctive form:

1. Ich _____ en CD kaafe.

2. Er _____ (to go) heem.

3. Du _____ es Lied singe.

4. Der Belsnickel _____ (to come) wann du gut bischt.

5. _____ mir noch Kanadaa reese?

6. Wann er meh gscheit _____ (to be), _____ (to know)
   die Antwatt.

7. Wann die Katz schneller schpringe _____, _____
   er die Maus faange.

8. Dihr _____ (to give) die Gschenke.

9. Wann er es Buch lese _____, _____ du der
   Schulmeeschder alles auslege.

10. Wann er um siwwe Uhr _____ (to come),

    _____ (to be able to) eppes esse.

9. Translate the following sentences *in Deitsch*!

1. If he would want it, he would have it.

2. If she would be faster, she would be the winner (Winner).

3. If Dave would bring the game, we would have fun.

4. If Mom would bake the cake, we would wash the dishes.

5. If Dad would wash the car, we would be happy.

6. I would come home, if my sister would get a cat.

7. If the farmer would plant potatoes, then we would make Faasnachts.

8. If Emily would learn Spanish, then she would go to Mexico.

9. If Steve would drink coffee, he would not sleep as much.

10. If Jake would live with an Amish family, then he would speak good Deitsch.

Eppes zu wisse

Wie man en Brief odder EPoscht schreibt!

Diesember 8, 2008

Liewi Michelle un Liewer Dan:

Ich kann net waarde bis ich endlich eich bsuche kann. Ich denk as ich uff em 26 Diesember abfaahre will. Deswege kann ich Grischtdaag mit meinre Familye feiere. Es dauert baut drei Schtund noch eich zu faahre. Dihr wisst wie weit Philadelfi vun State College is. Un mit em Traffic, kann es lenger dauere. Was hett dihr geplannt? Ich will die Penn State University Campus sehne...abbadich die grosse Football Stadium. Ich hab gheert as es arig gross is! Es waer arig schee, wann ich der Nittany Lion aadreffe daet. Yawell, sell muss genung fer heit sei. Ich muss noch en glee bissel Grischtdaag eikaafe duh!

Macht's gut bis mir eich sehne!

Der Jeremy

Things to remember when writing a letter or an email in PD:

- If you are addressing a female, use *liewi*, if addressing a male, use *liewer*.

- It is common in PD to close your letter / email with the phrase *Macht's gut*! if writing to multiple people. Use the phrase *Mach's gut!* if writing to one person.

- Letters in PD follow the same format rules as letters in English.

Saag Eppes

Em Verschprechnis zu der Faahne

Ich verschpreche Gedrei zu sei zu der Faahne vun Amerikaa
un zu der Republik zu wem sie schteht,
ee Volk unnich Gott, Unverdeelich
mit Freiheit un Gerechtichkeit fer alli-epper.

[Reprinted from the Baerricks Kaunty
Versammling Programm vun 2004]

Die alt Mammi Schwank

Die alt Mammi Schwank,
Sie geht an der Schank
Un sucht ihrem Hundel en Gnoche;
Do waar nix zu finne
Wie Schtaab un Schpinne
Es Hundel hot g'schnuffelt, geroche.

Noh geht sie zum Becker
Un kaaft en Leeb Brot,
Un kummt sie zurick,
Datt leit er wie doot.

Dann geht sie zum Schneider
Un kaaft em en Rock,
Un kummt sie zurick,
Do reit er der Bock.

Zum Schuhmacher geht sie
Un kaaft em Paar Schuh,
Do hot er die Katz
Ins Bett geduh.

244

Sie geht in der Schtor
Un kaaft em en Hut,
Un kummt sie zurick,
Do schpielt er die Flute.

Noh geht sie ans Wattshaus
Fer'n Kessel voll Bier,
Un kummt sie, do batzelt
Er hinnich de Dier.

Mol is sie am backe,
Macht Kuchedeeg schteif,
Do hockt er am Offe
Un schmokt noch die Peif.

Sie geht in der Keller
Fer'n Pitcher voll Wei,
Do nemmt er der Kiwwel
Un fiedert die Sei.

Sie gebt em aa Schlecksach
So oft wie sie kann,
Do fresst er 're aa noch
Die Wascht aus de Pann.

Des Hundel is owets
Als wacker gebliwwe,
Hot Bicher gelese
Un alsemol g'schriwwe.

Die Mammi waar aarm,
Doch nir net in Not.
Wann's Hundel noch lebt,
Dann is es net doot.

[Reprinted with permission from: Sauer, Walter, ed. Mammi Gans: Mother Gooose's Nursery Rhymes, translated and adapted by John Birmelin. Neckarsteinack: Edition Tintenfass, 2003.]

Kuldur

> ### *Pennsylvania Dutch in the 21st Century*
> *Dr. Michael Werner, editor of* Hiwwe wie Driwwe
>
> The book is old. It was published in 1870. Maybe you saw it for the first time at your grandparent's house. The binding is plain – with a gold harp on the middle of the cover. The book has an odd title: *"Harbaugh's Harfe"*. Perhaps your grandparents would sometimes speak in a language that you didn't understand, just like the fact that you couldn't read the words in that book. In any event you have chosen to learn the language of your forefathers: Pennsylvania Dutch. Therefore you should page through that book by Henry Harbaugh (1817-1867), who is considered the most famous Pennsylvania Dutch author. His "Harfe" was found in thousands of homes in southeast Pennsylvania and beyond. Today, you do not have to go to archives in order to find Pennsylvania Dutch books and newspapers. Today, Pennsylvania Dutch titles are continually being published. In the last few years many new publications have been produced. Some of which are listed below:
>
> Horst, Isaac R.: *Bei sich selwer un ungwehnlich. Alt Mennischde Weg vun Lewe in Ontario. Separate and Peculiar. Old Order Mennonite Life in Ontario*. Waterloo, Ontario. 2001.
>
> Committee for Translation: *Es Nei Teshtament. Pennsylvania Deitsh un English. Mit Di Psaltah un Shpricha*. Bilingual Edition. Sugar Creek, Ohio. 2002.
>
> Birmelin, John: *Hans un Yarrick. En Buweg'schicht in siwwe Schtreech. A Story in Seven Tricks*. Neckarsteinach, Germany. 2002.
>
> Birmelin, John: *Mammi Gans. Mother Goose Nursery Rhymes*. Edited by Walter Sauer. Neckarsteinach, Germany. 2003.
>
> Martin, Gladys S.: *Kumm Laaf mit Mir. A Collection of Pennsylvania German Poetry*. Gordonville, Pennsylvania. 2005.
>
> Zimmerman, Thomas C.: *Die Nacht vor der Grischtdaag*. Edited by Walter Sauer. Neckarsteinach, Germany. 2005.

Saint-Exupery, Antoine de: *Der glee Prins. Mit der Schreiwer sei eegni Pickders.* Translated by Mark L. Louden. Neckarsteinach, Germany. 2006.

German-Pennsylvania Association (ed.): *Mit Pennsylvaanisch-Deitsch darich's Yaahr. A Pennylvania German Reader for Grandparents and Grandchildren.* Neckarsteinach, Germany. 2006.

Besides these books, which can easily be ordered over the Internet, there are the following newspapers and magazines that include Pennsylvania Dutch texts:

Journal of the Center for Pennsylvania German Studies. Ed. by C. Richard Beam. Published four times a year. Millersville University. Millersville, Pennsylvania.

Hiwwe wie Driwwe – Die Pennsylvaanisch-Deitsch Zeiding. Ed. by Michael Werner. Published two times a year. Ober-Olm, Germany.

Here is a short list of dictionaries and grammar books that have been recently republished:

Frey, J. William: *A Simple Grammar of Pennsylvania Dutch.* With preface by C. Richard Beam. Lancaster, Pennsylvania. 1985.

Beam, C. Richard et al. (Ed.): *The Comprehensive Pennsylvania German Dictionary.* 11 volumes. Millersville University. Millersville, Pennsylvania. 2004-2008.

Whoever thinks that the fountain of Pennsylvania Dutch materials has dried up would be very incorrect in their thinking. "Die Mudderschprooch" has recently gone "online". Much information printed in and about the dialect can be found on the following websites:

pdc.wikipedia.org (Pennsylvania Dutch Wikipedia Site)
www.pgs.org (The Pennsylvania German Society)
www.hiwwe-wie-driwwe.de (Website for the Hiwwe-wie-Driwwe publication)
www.amisch.de (Pennsylvania Dutch online Forum)
deitscheblog.wordpress.com (PA Dutch Blog)

The dialect can also be heard on the radio and on television:

Es Pennsylvaanisch-Deitsch Schtunn. Monthly TV program with the New Tulpehocken Choir on Berks County TV (Reading, Pennsylvania)

Die Alte Kumraade. Weekly Radio Program with C. Richard Beam on WLBR 1270 AM (Lebanon, Pennsylvania)

In 1861 when Henry Harbaugh was writing his poems for his "Harp," many people thought that the dialect would die out over the course of the next few generations. How wrong one can be! Since that time over 150 years have passed and Pennsylvania Dutch is still alive. Around 400,000 people today can still speak and understand the dialect. The children of the Old Order Mennonites and Old Order Amish have the ability to raise that number in the years to come.

As you can see, Pennsylvania Dutch is very much alive – and your decision to learn the dialect has helped keep our language alive into the 21st century. Hopefully one day your language abilities will be strong enough to enable you to read *Harbaugh's Harfe* from cover to cover. Set that as your goal, your time and energy will make the end product worth the work.

Rickguck

10. Put the following paragraph in the past tense. Use the praeterite form of *sei* when possible!

Ich bin en guder Schportler, awwer mei Bruder is besser. Unser Eldre sin arig schtolz mit uns. Mir sin schnell un kenne en Baseballe gut schmeisse. Sie sin froh wann mei Bruder am schpiele is. Sie saage: "Steve, du bischt der Bescht!" Ich bin aa froh wann mei Bruder en gudes Schpiel hot.

11. Fill in the blanks with the appropriate Subjunctive Verb forms!

1. Weil du net mitkummscht, muss ich mit meinre alte Maschien faahre. Wann du mit mir _____ (came), _____ mir mit deinre Maschien _____. (would drive)

2. Hariyesses, es regert! Wann es heit net _____ (weren't raining), _____ mir Tennis _____ (would play).

3. Kumm doch mit! Wann du daheem _____ (would stay), _____ du yuscht Guckbax _____ (would watch).

4. Er kann net genung fer mich duh. Wann ich ihn _____ (would ask), _____ er mir seinre Maschien (would give).

5. Meine Friend wuhnt arig weit vun do. Wann sie naeher _____ (lived), _____ ich sie efters _____. (would visit)

6. Der Movie schtoppt um Middernacht. Wann der Movie frieher _____ (ended), _____ mir noch dem Essblatz. (would go)

7. Laadet dihr denn der Matt net ei? Wann dihr ihn zur Party

_____ (invited), _____ er fer schur. (would

come)

8. Was willscht du denowed duh? Wann mir denowed in der Essblatz

_____ (would go), _____ ich mei scheener

Kleid _____. (would wear)

9. Nadierlich kenne mir ihn net. Wann mir ihn schunn _____

(knew), _____ mir net noch sei Naame _____.

(would ask).

12. *Schreib eppes!* Write a one-page letter to a class member. Be sure to write it following the proper format. Talk about an upcoming visit and what you would like to do or see while visiting.

13. Write a poem in Dutch. Present it to your class. Consider sending it to a local newspaper or one of the publications mentioned in the Kuldur section of this Kabiddel for publication.

Was weesscht du?

- *Ich will waericklich net datthiegeh!* Your friend is trying to convince you to come along to a dance. Give five reasons why you are not interested in going.

- *Was daetscht du mache?* Make a list of 7 things that you would do if you would win one million dollars. Make sure all of your sentences are in the Subjunctive!

  Wann ich en Millyoon Daaler hett, daet ich en BMW kaafe.

- *Was macht Schpass?* Imagine that you and your friends are planning a weekend away. Write a paragraph describing what you would do during the weekend for fun. Also, explain why the activities that you chose would be fun.

Waddelischt

aa/dreffe – to meet
ab/faahre – to depart
die Aerd – the earth, *f*
aus/lege – to explain
aus/mache – to plan
sich bedanke – to thank
blanne – to plan
der Dans (-e) – the dance, *m*
daeglich - daily
datthie/geh – to go there
dohie/geh – to go here
endlich - finally
die Erfaahring – the experience, *f*
es dutt mir leed – I am sorry
die Ewichkeit – the eternity, *f*
die Faahne – the flag, *f*
finne – to find
die Freiheit – the freedom, *f*
es Gebei (-er) – the building, *n*
es Gebet (er) – the prayer, *n*
die Gerechtichkeit – the justice, *f*
die Graft – the power, *f*
die Hallichkeit – the glory, *f*
Hariyesses! – Oh my goodness!

heilich – holy, blessed
der Himmel – the heaven, sky, *m*
die Iewele – the evil ones, *pl*
die Maus (Meis) – the mouse, *n*
die Middernacht – the midnight, *f*
es Mol - the time, *n*
es Reich – the kingdom, *n*
der Scheenermann – the gentleman, *m*
schpende – to spend
schpringe – to run
schtoppe – to end, to stop
schuldich - guilty
die Schulrees – school field trip, *f*
die Sind (-e) – the sin, *f*
der Uffgwaxner (Uffgwaxeni) – the adult, *m*
unverdeelich – indivisible
vergewe – to forgive
verspreche – to pledge, to promise
die Versuchung – the temptation, *f*
es Volk – the nation, *n*
vorher – before
die Wille – the will, *f*
die Yaahrhunnert – century, *f*
zamme - together

Guide to pronunciation

Though pronunciation may differ slightly from region to region, the spelling most closely resembles how the word is pronounced.

Vowels: Long vowels are doubled or followed by an h. In most cases, short vowels are followed by two consonants.

Consonants: Most of the consonants of PD are pronounced much like they are in American English, but there are some exceptions noted in the chart. Some sounds do not exist in American English: palatal ch, velar ch, intervocalic g. Some native speakers of PD employ an American r in certain positions. Others use a slightly trilled *r* in an initial and medial position. The final *r* is much like the Standard German *r*.

Aside from listening closely to your instructor, audio files can be found on the internet:

www.pgs.org
www.hiwwe-wie-driwwe.de

or on CD:

Fritsch, Peter V. Der Haahne Greht. Morgantown, PA: Masthof Press, 2005.

Letter	Example	English approximant
a (short)	Sache	a in what
aa (long)	Aag	aw in saw
ae (long)	Baer	ea in bear
ae (short)	Maetsch	a in match
a(r) (long)	darf	a in father
e (long)	geht	a in gate
ee (long)	weech	a in gate
e (short)	fett	e in get
i (long)	ihn	ee in see
ie (long)	Biewel	ee in see
i (short)	bin	i in pin
o (long)	rot	o in low
u (long)	Blut	oo in moon

u (short)	dumm	oo in cook
au	laut	ow in cow
ei	leicht	i in pine
oi	Roi	oy in boy
b	Bank	b in bank
	ab	p in bump
ch	ich	*
	mache	*
ck	packe	ck in picky
d	Daal	d in dog
	ald	t in tall
	Dodder	dd in buddy
f	finne	f in find
	hoffe	ff in huffy
g	Geld	g in gold
	Aage	y in yes
	Aag	k in kick
h	Hut	h in hat
	Uhr	*silent
k	Keenich	k in king
l	Leicht	l in light
	Millich	ll in silly
m	Mann	m in man
n	Not	n in not
	Menner	nn in banner
ng	Ring	ng in ring
nk	genunk	nk in sink
p	Paare	p in pastor
	Lumpe	b in number
	Kipp	p in help
	roppe	bb in robber
s	sadde	s in sort
	Boss	ss in boss
sch	Schul	sh in shop
t	Tee	t in tea
	datt	t in debt
v	verrickt	f in for
w	Wasser	w in water
x	Hex	x in axe

y	yung	y in yard
z	Zucker	ts in hats

[Reprinted with permission from: Beam, C.R. et al (eds). The Comprehensive Pennsylvania German Dictionary. Morgantown, PA: Masthof Press, 2004ff.]

Personal Pronouns

Singular	Nominative	Accusative	Dative
1st person	ich	mich	mer
2nd person	du	dich	der
3rd person	er	en	ihm
	sie	sie	re
	es	es	em
Plural			
1st person	mir	uns	uns
2nd person	dihr	eich	eich
3rd person	sie	sie	ihne

Definite Article

	Singular			Plural
	Masculine	Feminine	Neuter	
Nominative	der	die	es	die
Accusative	der	die	es	die
Dative	dem	der	em	de

Indefinite Article

	Singular			Plural
	Masculine	Feminine	Neuter	
Nominative	**en**	**en**	**en**	**kene**
Accusative	**en**	**en**	**en**	**kene**
Dative	**me**	**re**	**me**	**kene**

Regular Verb Forms – Present Tense

	gucke	saage	mache
ich	**guck**	**saag**	**mach**
du	**guckscht**	**saagscht**	**machscht**
er, sie, es	**guckt**	**saagt**	**macht**
mir	**gucke**	**saage**	**mache**
dihr	**guckt**	**saagt**	**macht**
sie	**gucke**	**saage**	**mache**

Irregular Verb Forms – Present Tense

	hawwe	sei	duh
ich	**hab**	**bin**	**duh**
du	**hoscht**	**bischt**	**duscht**
er, sie, es	**hot**	**is**	**dutt**
mir	**hen**	**sin**	**duhne**
dihr	**hett**	**sint**	**duhnet**
sie	**hen**	**sin**	**duhne**

Negation

- Verbs (net) – *Kummscht du net mit uns?*
- Nouns (ken) – *Ich hab ken Zeit.*

Modal Auxiliaries

	brauche	daerfe	kenne	meege	misse	solle	wolle
ich	**brauch**	**daerf**	**kann**	**maag**	**muss**	**soll**	**will**
du	**brauchscht**	**daerfscht**	**kannscht**	**maagscht**	**musscht**	**sollscht**	**witt**
er sie es	**braucht**	**daerf**	**kann**	**maag**	**muss**	**soll**	**will**
mir	**brauche**	**daerfe**	**kenne**	**meege**	**misse**	**solle**	**wolle**
dihr	**braucht**	**daerft**	**kennt**	**meegt**	**misst**	**sollt**	**wollt**
sie	**brauche**	**daerfe**	**kenne**	**meege**	**misse**	**solle**	**wolle**

Future Tense (*waerre* + infinitive)

ich	**waer**
du	**waerscht**
er, sie, es	**waerd**
mir	**waerre**
dihr	**waerret**
sie	**waerre**

257

Reflexive Pronouns

Singular	
1st person – *ich*	**mich**
2nd person – *du*	**dich**
3rd person – *er, sie es*	**sich**
Plural	
1st person – *mir*	**uns**
2nd person – *dihr*	**eich**
3rd person – *sie*	**sich**

Prepositions

Dative	Accusative	Two-Way
aus	**bis**	**an**
bei	**darrich**	**gschwischich**
in blatz vun	**fer**	**hinnich**
mit	**geeich**	**in**
mitaus	**gege**	**iwwer**
noch	**um**	**newe**
vun	**unne**	**newich**
weeich	**wedder**	**uff**
wege		**unnich**
zidder		**var**
zu		

Possessive Adjectives

	Singular			Plural
	Masculine	Feminine	Neuter	
Nominative	**mei**	**mei**	**mei**	**mei**
Accusative	**mei**	**mei**	**mei**	**mei**
Dative	**meim**	**meinre**	**meim**	**meine**

Irregular Verbs – Present Perfect Tense (Past Participle)

Infinitive	Past Participle	English
beisse	**gebisse**	*to bite*
bleiwe	**gebliwwe**	*to stay*
bringe	**gebrocht**	*to bring*
drinke	**gedrunke**	*to drink*
duh	**geduh**	*to do*
esse	**gesse**	*to eat*
fliege	**gflogge**	*to fly*
geh	**gange**	*to go*
gleiche	**gegliche**	*to like*
griege	**grickt**	*to get*
hawwe	**ghatt**	*to have*
heesse	**gheesse**	*to be called*
helfe	**gholfe**	*to help*
kumme	**kumme**	*to come*
laafe	**geloffe**	*to run*
lese	**gelese**	*to read*
nemme	**genumme**	*to take*
reide	**geridde**	*to ride*
rieche	**geroche**	*to smell*
schmeisse	**gschmisse**	*to throw*
schreiwe	**gschriwwe**	*to write*
schteh	**gschtanne**	*to stand*
schwimme	**gschwumme**	*to swim*
sehne	**gsehne**	*to see*

sei	**gewest**	*to be*
singe	**gsunge**	*to sing*
sitze	**gsotze**	*to sit*
verschteh	**verschtanne**	*to understand*

Adjective Endings

Weak Adjective Endings – following a Definite Article				
	Masculine	Feminine	Neuter	Plural
Nominative and Accusative	der **yung( )** Mann	die **yung( )** Fraa	es **yung( )** Kind	die **yunge** Menner
Dative	dem **yunge** Mann	der **yunge** Fraa	em **yunge** Kind	de **yunge** Menner

Mixed Adjective Endings – following an Indefinite Article				
	Masculine	Feminine	Neuter	Plural
Nominative and Accusative	en yung**er** Mann	en yung**i** Fraa	en yung**es** Kind	ken yung**e** Menner
Dative	me yung**e** Mann	re yung**e** Fraa	me yung**e** Kind	ken yung**e** Menner

Strong Adjective Endings – not following a DA or IA				
	Masculine	Feminine	Neuter	Plural
Nominative and Accusative	yung**er** Mann	yung**i** Fraa	yung**( )** Kind	yung**e** Menner
Dative	yung**em** Mann	yung**er** Fraa	yung**em** Kind	yung**e** Menner

Passive Voice

(*waerre* + the past participle)

- Die Maschien waerd gwesche. – *The car is being washed.*

- Die Bicher waerre glese. – *The books are being read.*

Subjunctive Mood

(*daet* + infinitive)

- Wann ich en Maschien kaafe daet, daet ich es faahre. –

    If I would buy a car, I would drive it.

Single-Form Subjunctive

Infinitive		Subjunctive
brauche	- *to need*	**breicht**
bringe	- *to bring*	**breecht**
daerfe	- *to be allowed*	**daerft**
duh	- *to do*	**daet**
geh	- *to go*	**gengt**
gewwe	- *to give*	**geebt**
griege	- *to get*	**greecht**
hawwe	- *to have*	**hett**
kenne	- *to be able*	**kennt**
kumme	- *to come*	**kaemt**
meege	- *to like*	**meecht**
misse	- *to have to*	**misst**
solle	- *ought*	**sett**
wisse	- *to know*	**wisst**
wolle	- *to want to*	**wett**

The verb *SEI* has a unique single-form subjunctive:

ich	*waer*	mir	*waere*
du	*waerscht*	dihr	*waeret*
er		sie	*waere*
sie	*waer*		
es			

Deitsch - English

The numbers following the meaning of individual words or phrases indicate the particular chapter in which they appear for the first time.

A

aa – also 2
aa/dreffe – to meet, 12
sich aa/duh – to get dressed 7
aa/fange – to start, to begin 7
es Aag (e) – the eye, *n* 7
aa/greische – to yell at 7
aa/gucke – to look at 7
aa/hawwe – to have on 7
aa/kumme – to arrive 7
der Aarem – the arm, *m* 7
aa/schreie – to scream at 7
aa/schtreiche – to paint 11
ab/faahre – to depart 12
ab/fliege – to take off 11
ab/nemme – to take pictures 9
der Abnemmer – the photographer, *m* 10
die Abrigos (-e) – the apricot, *f* 5
die Aeddick – the attic, *f* 5
die Aent – the aunt, *f* 3
die Aerbs (-e) – the pea, *f* 4
die Aerd – the earth, *f* 12
aerscht – first 2
aerschtmol – at first 7
allebeede – both 9
allerdings – above all, by all means 10
alli-epper – everyone 8
allsfatt – always 2
alt – old 1
der Amerikaaner – the American, *m* 3
die Amische – the Amish, *pl* 3
an – at, on 9
angle – to fish 11
anne/beschtelle – to announce 11
sich anne/hocke – to sit down 7
annere – others 5
die Antwatt (-e) – the answer, *f* 2
appeditlich – delicious 5
arig – very 2
die Arznei – the medicine, *f* 10

as – that 10
aus – from 1
aus/dauere – to last 11
aus/figgere – to figure out 4
aus/gewe – to spend 7
aus/lege – to explain 10
aus/lehne – to borrow 6
aus/mache – to matter 7
aus/seh – to look like 7
awwer – but 2
die Axel – the shoulder, *f* 7

B

sich baade – to bathe 7
die Baadschtubb (-schtuwwe) – the bathroom, *f* 6
der Baadzuwwer – the bathtub, *m* 6
der Baam (Beem) – the tree, *m* 5
die Baawoll – the cotton, *f* 6
es Babier – the paper, *n* 2
baddere – to worry about 10
die Baend – the band, *f* 2
die Baenk – the bank, *f* 10
der Balle – the ball, *m* 9
sich balwiere – to shave 7
bassiere – to occur, to happen 7
der Bauer (-e) – the farmer, *m* 3
es Bauerehaus (-heiser) – the farmhouse, *n* 4
die Bauerei – the farm, *f* 4
baut – about 8
der Becker – the baker, *m* 6
sich bedanke – to thank 12
begaabt – talented 5
begegne – to meet 10
beginne – to begin 2
es Beh – the leg, *n* 7
bei – at the house of, by 6
der Beidel – the purse, the handbag, *m* 11
bei/kumme – to come from 1

beisse – to bite 11
beschenke – to give a gift 8
es Bett (-er) – the bed, *n* 6
die Bettschtubb (-schtuwwe) – the bedroom, *f* 6
bewillkumme – to greet 11
bissel – a little 3
blanne – to plan 12
blanse – to plant 4
bleed – shy 3
der Bleipensil – the pencil, *m* 2
bletzlich – right away 10
bloss – only 8
der Blug (Blieg) – the plow, *m* 4
der Blutdruck – the blood pressure, *m* 10
der Blutsfreind – the relative, m 11
der Boi – the pie, *m* 3
es Boot (s) – the boat, *n* 8
die Bortsch – the porch, *f* 5
brauche – to need 2
brenne – to burn 5
der Bresident (-e) – the president, *m* 3
es Bretzel – the pretzel, *n* 5
der Brief (-e) – the letter, *m* 3
die Briefmark (-e) – the stamp, *f* 9
der Briefumschlag – the envelope, *m* 10
die Brieh – the gravy, *f* 5
bringe – to bring 3
es Briwwi – the toilet, *n* 6
es Brot – the bread, *n* 5
browiere – to try out 10
der Bruder (Brieder) – the brother, *m* 3
die Bruscht – the breast, *f* 7
der Bu (-we) – the boy, *m* 1
es Buch (Bicher) – the book, *n* 1
es Buchlaade – the bookshelf, *n* 6
die Buhn (-e) – the bean, *f* 4
die Bus – the bus, *f* 7
der Butscher – the butcher, *m* 6
butze – to clean 4

D

der Daadi – the father *m* 2
die Daafel – the chalkboard, *f* 2
der Daag (-e) – the day, *m* 1

es Dach (Decher) – the roof, *n* 6
daeglich – daily 10
daerfe – to be allowed 5
daheem – at home 2
dahie/geh – to go there 7
Dankfescht – Thanksgiving 8
es Dans (-e) – the dance, *n* 6
danse – to dance 8
darr – dry 4
datt driwwe – over there 1
datt/hiegeh – to go there 2
dauere – to last 9
der Deeg – the dough, *m* 3
dehinner – behind 1
deier – expensive 5
Deitsch – Pennsylvania German 2
denke – to think 3
dennot – then 2
der Deppich – the bedspread, *m* 6
dernoh – afterwards 4
deswege – therefore 8
dichter – closer 12
die Dier (-e) – the door, *f* 6
dihr – you (plural) 1
der Disch – the table, *m* 2
do – there 1
die Dochder (Dechder) – the daughter, *f* 3
der Dochdermann – the son-in-law, *m* 10
dohie/geh – to go here 12
draage – to carry, to wear 6
die Draen – the train, *f* 7
draus – outside 8
der Dreck – the dirt, *m* 4
drenke – to water (animals) 4
drieb – cloudy, overcast 4
die Driese – the glands, *pl* 10
drinke – to drink 5
driwwe/kumme – to come over 11
drum – about (a thing, fact) 8
du – you (singular) 1
duh – to do 4
dumm – dumb 1
sich dummle – to hurry oneself 2
dunkel – dark 5
dunnere – to thunder 4

E

eb – before, whether 10
es Eel – the oil, *n* 5
efders – often 5
der Eifluss – the control, *m* 10
der Eikaafer – the customer, *m* 6
es Eikaafsack – the shopping bag, *n* 11
ei/laade – to invite 7
die Eilaading – the invitation, *f* 8
die Eisbax – the refrigerator, *f* 6
eisich – icy 4
die Eldre – the parents, *pl* 3
endlich – finally 8
die Englisch – English, *f* 2
ennihau – anyhow 7
en Paar – a few 9
die Ent (-e) – the duck, *f* 4
eppes – something 1
er – he 1
die Erfaahring – the experience, *f* 12
es – it 1
es dutt mir leed – I am sorry 12
es gebt – there is, there are 2
esse – to eat 3
der Essblatz – the restaurant, *m* 5
es Ess-sach – the food, *n* 5
die Ewichkeit – the eternity, *f* 12

F

die Faahne – the flag, *f* 12
Faasnacht – Shrove Tuesday 8
der Familyebaam – the family tree, *m* 3
der Familyenaame – the last name, *m* 1
fange – to catch 8
die Fareb (Faerewe) – the color, *f* 5
fechde – to fight 10
die Fedder – the pen, *f* 2
feicht – damp 4
feiere – to celebrate 8
es Feld (-er) – the field, *n* 4
Feldi – Valentine's Day 8
die Fens (-e) – the fence, *f* 4
es Fenschder (-e) – the window, *n* 4
fer – for 3
die Ferien – the vacation, *f* 10
fer was – why 2

es Fescht (-er) – the festival, *n* 11
die Fieber – the fever, *f* 10
fiehle – to feel 10
finne – to find 12
der Finger – the finger, *m* 7
der Fisch (-e) – the fish, *m* 5
es Fleesch – the meat, *n* 5
fliege – to fly 4
die Floete – the flute, *f* 7
die Flugkaart (-e) – the airplane ticket, *f* 11
folye – to follow 2
die Fonnummer – the phone number, *f* 1
die Fraa – the woman, Mrs. *f* 1
der Frack (-e) – the dress, *m* 6
Franzeesisch – French 11
die Freiheit – the freedom, *f* 3
die Freindschaft – the relative, *f* 10
die Freizeit – the free time, *f* 9
fresse – to eat (animals) 4
frieh – early 2
frisch – fresh 4
der Fuuss (Fiess) – the foot, *m* 4
der Fuussballe – the football, *m* 9

G

gaar – absolutely 3
die Gaarde – the garden, *f* 4
es Gaardesach (-e) – the vegetable, *n* 3
die Galluun (-e) – the gallon, *f* 9
der Gans (Gens) – the goose, *m* 4
die Gas-schtation – the gas station, *f* 10
der Gaul (Geil) – the horse, *m* 4
es Gebei (-er) – the building, *n* 12
es Gebet – the prayer, *n* 12
der Gebottsdaag (-e) – the birthday, *m* 6
gebrode – fried 5
es Gedier (-e) – the animal, *n* 4
der Gees – the goat, *m* 4
die Gegend – the area, *f* 11
geh – to go 2
die Gehlrieb (-riewe) – the carrot, *f* 4
die Geig – the violin, *f* 5
geizich – frugal 6
es Geld – the money, *n* 3
die Gelegeheit – the possibility, *f* 9
Gell? – Right? 4

gemaeschde – mashed 5
die Gerechtichkeit – the justice, *f* 12
es Gschenk (-e) – the present, *n* 3
gewiss – indeed 8
gewwe – to give 3
gheere zu – to belong to 6
die Gitarre – the guitar, *f* 7
glaar – clear 10
es Glaffier – piano, *n* 3
die Glapperbax (-e) – the piano, *f* 3
glee – small 2
die Gleeder – the clothes, *pl* 5
es Gleederkemmerli – the closet, *n* 7
gleiche – to like 3
es Glick – the luck, *n* 11
die Gluck – the hen, *f* 4
es Gnie – the knee, *n* 7
graad – right away, now 2
graad um's Eck – right around the corner 1
es Graas – the grass, *n* 4
die Graft – the power, *f* 12
es Grankehaus – the hospital, *n* 10
die Gratsch – the garage, *f* 6
die Greess – the size, *f* 6
die Greid – the chalk, *f* 2
greische – to scream, cheer 9
greislich – terrible 10
griege – to get, receive 2
die Grienebuhne – the green beans, *pl* 5
Grischtdaag – Christmas 8
gross – big 1
der Grossdaadi – the grandfather, *m* 3
die Grosseldre – the grandparents, *pl* 3
die Grossmudder – the grandmother, *f* 3
die Grummbier (-e) – the potato, *f* 4
Grundsaudaag – Groundhog Day 8
gschehe – to happen, to occur 7
gscheit – smart 1
die Gschicht – the history, story, *f* 2
der Gschmack – the taste, *m* 3
gschpassich – fun 1
gschwinder – more quickly 10
g'schwischich – between 9
gschwolle – swollen 10
gsund – healthy 10
die Gsundheit – the health, *f* 2
die Guckbax – the television, *m* 4

gucke – to look, to see, to watch 4
die Gummer (e) – the pickle, *f* 8
gut – good 1
gutguckich – good looking 3

H

der Haahne – the rooster, *m* 4
die Haaptschtadt (-schtedt) – the capital, *f* 11
es Haar (e) – the hair, *n* 7
der Hals – the neck, *m* 7
die Hallichkeit – the glory, f 12
es Halsband – the necklace, *n* 8
es Halsduch (-dicher) – the scarf, *n* 6
es Halsweh – the sore throat, *f* 10
halwer – bottom of the hour, half 2
der Hand – the hand, *m* 7
Hariyesses! – Oh my goodness! 12
hatt – difficult 2
hawwe – to have 2
die Heemet – the home, *f* 11
die Heemschtubb – the homeroom, *f* 2
heere – to hear 3
hees – hot 4
heess – hot 8
heilich – holy, blessed 12
heit – today 2
der Held – the hero, *m* 9
helfe – to help 5
hell – light 5
es Hemm (-er) – the shirt, *n* 6
es Henkeglaas – the mug, *n* 5
die Hensching – the gloves, *pl* 6
her/kumme – to come from 7
hesslich – ugly 3
hie – hither 6
der Himmel – the heaven, sky, *m* 12
es Hinkel – the chicken, *n* 4
der Hinnerhof (-hef) – the back yard, *m* 8
hinnich – behind 9
hitze – to heat 5
hoch – high 8
Hochdeitsch – German 11
hocke – to sit 5
der Hockblatz (-bletz) – the seat, *n* 11
hoffentlich – hopefully 8

die Hosse – the pants, *pl* 6
der Hambariger – the hamburger, *m* 5
der Hund (-e) – the dog, *m* 3
der Hut (Hiet) – the hat, *m* 6
es Hutsch – the colt, *n* 4

I

ich – I 1
iewe – to practice 9
die Iewele – the evil ones, *pl* 12
die Iewing – the practice, *f* 9
ihr – her 1
in – in 1
in Blatz vun – in place of 6
inderessant – interesting 2
in guder Form – in good shape 9
iwwer – over, above, past, after, across 9
iwwerfalle – to surprise 10
die Iwwerhosse – the jeans, *pl* 6

K

kaafe – to buy 3
die Kaart (e) – the card, *f* 8
kaempe – to camp 5
der Kaffi – the coffee, *m* 5
kalt – cold 4
der Karebet – the carpet, the rug, *f* 1
die Kareer – the career, *f* 9
die Karich (-e) – the church, *f* 4
die Kasch (-e) – the cherry, *f* 3
der Kaschde – the box, the package, *m* 11
die Katz (-e) – the cat, *f* 3
die Katzhosse – the shorts, *pl* 6
ken – not, any, none 2
kenne – to know 2
kenne – to be able to, can 5
die Kerz (-e) / Inschlichlicht – the candle, *f* 11
die Kich – the kitchen, *f* 5
es Kichli (-n) – the cookie, *n* 3
kiehl – cool 4
die Kiehler – the refrigerator, *f* 6
es Kinn – the chin, *n* 7
die Kinner – the children, *pl* 1
es Kittel – the blouse, *n* 6
die Klaess – the class, *f* 2

die Klaessschtubb – the classroom, *f* 2
die Klarinet – the clarinet, *f* 7
koche – to cook 3
der Kopp (Kepp) – the head, *m* 2
die Kuh (Kieh) – the cow, *f* 4
kumme– to come 1
der Kumpanie – the company, *m* 10
die Kunscht – the art class, *f* 2

L

laafe – to walk 3
es Land (Lenner) – the land, country, *n* 4
die Landkaart (-e) – the map, *f* 2
langsam – slow, slowly 2
langweilich – boring 2
der Lattwarick – the apple butter, *m* 5
laut – loud 2
die Leckdrick – the electricity, *f* 3
leer – empty 2
die Lefts – the lips, *pl* 7
der Leftsschdift (-e) – the lip stick, *m* 6
lege – to lay 4
die Leibsklaess – the favorite class, *f* 2
leicht – easy 2
lese – to read 2
es Lied (-er) – the song, *n* 3
liewe – to love 2
die Licht (-e) – the light, lamp, *f* 6
los – loose 9
losse – to let 9

M

der Maage – the stomach, *m* 5
mache – to make, to do 2
Mach's gut – take care 1
maehe – to mow 4
der Mann – the man, husband, Mr. *m* 1
die Mannschaft (-e) – the team, *f* 9
die Marick (-e) – the grade, *f* 2
mariye – tomorrow 2
der Mariye – the morning, *m* 1
es Mariye-esse – the breakfast, *n* 5
die Maschien (-e) – the car, *f* 6
es Maul (Meiler) – the mouth, *n* 7
die Maus (Meis) – the mouse, *n* 12
es Meedel (Meed) – the girl, *n* 1

meege – would like to 5
meh – more 5
mehne – to be of the opinion 3
mer – one, as in a person 5
messe – to measure 10
es Middaagesse – the lunch, dinner, *n* 2
die Middernacht – the midnight, *f* 12
middes in der Schtadt – downtown 1
die Millich – the milk, *f* 4
die Minutt (-e) – the minute, *f* 2
mir – we 1
misse – to have to, must 5
mitaus – without 6
mit/bringe – to bring along 7
der Mithelfer – the colleague, *m* 10
mit/kumme – to come along 7
mit/nemme – to take along 5
es Mol – the time, *n* 12
die Mudder (Midder) – the mother, *f* 3
die Myusick – the music, *f* 2

N

der Naame (Naeme) – the name, *m* 1
die Naas (Nees) – the nose, *f* 7
die Nacht (-e, Nechde) – the night, *f* 1
nadierlich – naturally 6
naehe – to sew 4
nass – wet 7
nau – now 1
naus/geh – to go outside 7
die Nei-ichkeede – the news, *f* 10
neischteige – to board 11
Neiyaahrsdaag – New Years 8
net – not 2
net weit weck – not far away 1
es Netz (-e) – the net, *n* 9
newe – next to, near 9
newich – next to, near 9
newwlich – foggy 4
niwwer – over 2
nooch eppes – something else 5
der Noochber (-e) – the neighbor, *m* 10
die Nodel (-e) – the needle, *f* 6
es Noochesse – the dessert, *n* 5
es Nootbichli – the notebook, *f* 2
die Nummer (-e) – the number, *f* 1

der Nummidaag (-e) – the afternoon, *m* 1

O

odder – or 10
der Offe (Effe) – the stove, *m* 5
es Ohr (e) – the ear, *n* 7
der Ohrring (-e) – the earring, *m* 6
es Oi (-er) – the egg, *n* 4
der Onkel – the uncle, *m* 3
Oschder – Easter 8
der Owed (-e) – the evening, *m* 1
es Owedesse – the dinner, supper, *n* 4

P

der Pack (Peck) – the package, *m* 10
packe – to pack 11
parke – to park 9
der Parre – the pastor, *m* 6
der Peffer – the pepper, *m* 5
picke – to pick 4
der Pill (-e) – the pill, *m* 10
pinktlich – punctual 2
die Polies – the police, *f* 10
die Poscht – the mail, *f* 10
die Poschtaffis – the post office, *f* 10
die Poschtbax – the mail box, *n* 5
der Poschtmann – the mail man, *m* 10
der Preis – the price, *m* 6
der Puls – the pulse, *m* 10

R

die Raawerei – the robbery, *f* 10
die Rechelklaess – the math class, *f* 2
die Rechling – the bill, *f* 10
die Rees (-e) – the trip, *f* 11
reese – to travel 11
reeschde – roasted 5
reggere – to rain 4
der Reggeschaerm – the umbrella, *m* 8
es Reich – the kingdom, *n* 12
reide – to ride 4
die Reseet – the recipe, *f* 5
der Rewwer – the river, *m* 8
es Rickmeesel – the pork chop, *n* 5
es Ricksack – the back pack, *n* 11
der Riggelweg – the railroad, *m* 6

rischde – to set the table 8
der Rock (Reck) – the coat, *m* 6
die Rockmyusick – the rock music, *f* 3
roppe –to pick 4
die Rotrieb (-riewe) – the red beet, *f* 4
ruhich – quiet 2
rum/bringe – to spend time 7

S
saage – to say 2
es Sals – the salt, *n* 5
sammele – to collect 3
die Satt (-e) – the sort, type, *f* 6
die Sau (Sei) – the pig, *f* 4
saufe – to drink (animals) 4
es Schach – the chess, *n* 9
schaele – to peel 5
der Schaffmann (-menner) – the employee, *m* 11
der Schannschtee – the chimney, *m* 6
scharmand – elegant 6
schaue – to check, to look 5
der Schdor (-e) – the store, *m* 4
schee – pretty 1
der Scheenermann – the gentleman, *m* 12
die Scheier (-e) – the barn, *f* 4
die Scheierhof – the barnyard, *m* 4
scheine – to shine, to appear 4
der Schenk – the closet, *m* 6
es Schiff – the ship, *n* 11
es Schlaggding – the drum, *n* 7
schlagge – to hit 9
der Schlagger – the racquet, club, *m* 9
schlecht – bad 1
schloofe – to sleep 5
schlucke – to swallow 10
schmeise – to throw 9
der Schmierkaes – the cottage cheese, *m* 5
schmodich – humid 4
der Schmok – the smoke, *m* 10
der Schmuck – the jewelry, *m* 6
schnee-e – to snow 4
schneide – to cut 5
schnell – quickly 3
es Schof – the sheep, *n* 4
die Schokolaad – the chocolate, *f* 6

der Schopp – the shed, *m* 4
schpaeder – later 1
der Schpeck – the bacon, *m* 5
der Schpeicher – attic, *m*
schpende – to spend 12
die Schpielbank (-benk) – the sink, *f* 6
schpiele – to play 3
der Schpieler – the player, *m* 9
der Schpiggel (e) – the mirror, *m* 7
der Schport – the sport, *m* 9
schportlich – athletic 9
schpot – late 2
die Schprooch (-e) – the language, *f* 11
schpringe – to run 12
Schpuckdaag – Halloween 8
der Schreibdisch – the desk, *m* 6
schreiwe – to write 3
schtarewe – to die, 10
schtecke – to place 10
schtehe – to stand 4
schteif – stiff 9
die Schtelle – the place, the standing, *f* 9
es Schtick (-er) – the piece, *n* 6
die Schtiwwel – the boots, *pl* 6
der Schtock (Schteck) – the skirt, *m* 6
schtoppe – to stop 9
sich schtraele – to comb oneself 7
es Schtroh – the straw, *n* 4
der Schtrump (Schtrimp) – the stocking, *m* 6
die Schtund (-e) – the hour, *f* 7
der Schtul (Schtiel) – the chair, *m* 2
die Schuh – the shoes, *pl* 6
die Schul – the school, *f* 2
die Schularewet – the homework, *f* 2
schuldich – guilty 12
der Schulmeeschder – the male teacher, *m* 2
die Schulmeeschdern – the female teacher, *f* 2
die Schulrees – the field trip, *f* 12
die Schulsack (-e) – the school bag, *f* 2
es Schunkefleesch – the ham, *n* 5
schunn – already 4
der Schwans – the tail, *m* 4
die Schweschder (-e) – the sister, *f* 3
schwetze – to speak 2

der Schwetzkaschde – the radio, *m* 5
sehne – to see 1
sei – his 1
sei – to be 4
der Seide – the silk, *m* 6
seidich – silken 6
der Selaat – the salad, the lettuce, *m* 5
die Selaatbrieh – the salad dressing, *f* 5
sell – that 1
der Selleri – the celery, *m* 3
sie – she, they 1
die Sind (-e) – the sin, *f* 12
singe – to sing 3
so as – so that, in order that 10
es Sofe – the sofa, *n* 6
der Sohn (Seh) – the son, *m* 3
solle – to be supposed to 5
suche – to look for, to search 11
suchtich – addicted 6
der Sudd – the south, *m* 4
suddlich – drizzling 4
der Suit – the suit, *m* 6
die Sunn – the sun, *f* 4
der Supermarrick – the supermarket, *m* 5
die Supp – the soup, *f* 5
es Sweder – the sweater, *n* 6
es Swetschirt – the sweatshirt, *n* 6

T
der Tee – the tea, *m* 5
es Tennisblatz – the tennis court, *n* 9
der Tennisschlagger – the tennis racquet, *m* 8
der Tschimm – the gym class, *m* 2
es Tomaet (-s) – the tomato, *n* 4
der Traktor (-s) – the tractor, *m* 4
der Trompet – the trumpet, *m* 7

U
uff – on 4
uff/basse – to pay attention 7
der Uffgwaxner (Uffgwaxni) – the adult, *m* 12
uff/rischde – to prepare a meal 5
uff/schteh – to wake up 5
sich uff/wecke – to wake up 5

die Uhr (-e) – the clock, *f* 1
um – at 2
es Umgraut – the weed, *n* 4
unfreindlich – unfriendly 1
die Unnersuch – the research, *f* 11
unnich – under 9
unverdeelich – indivisible 12

V
es Vaddel – the advantage, *n* 9
Vaddel eb – quarter of 2
Vaddel nooch – quarter after 2
var – before, in front of, ago, of (telling time) 9
verbinne – to combine 2
verbrenne – to burn
vergewwe – to forgive 12
der Verkaafer – the salesman, *m* 6
sich verkelde – to catch a cold 7
verlewe – to spend time 11
verninfdich – reasonable 6
versammle – to collect 9
die Versammling (-e) – the meeting, *f* 9
verschpreche – to promise 6
die Versuchung – the temptation, *f* 12
viel – much 3
es Volk – the nation, *n* 12
vorbereide – to prepare 8
vorher – before 12
vun – of, from 3
vun wege as – because, because of the fact 10

W
der Waage (Wegge) – the wagon, *m* 4
die Waahl – the selection, *f* 6
es Waardeschtubb – the waiting room, *n* 10
es Waddebuch (-bich) – the dictionary, *n* 5
waericklich – really 2
waere – to wear 6
waerre – will 5
der Wammes – the jacket, *m* 6
wandere – to hike 11
wann – when, if 10
warm – warm 4
was – what 1

was fer – what kind of 2
die Waschbank – the sink, *f* 6
die Wascht – the sausage, *f* 5
der Wasserloch (-leecher) – the pond, *m* 8
die Weckeruhr – the alarm clock, *f* 6
es Wedder – the weather, *n* 1
weech – soft 5
weeich – on account of 6
wege – on account of 6
sich weh/duh – to hurt oneself 7
der Wei – the wine, *m* 5
weil – because 10
weller – which 2
der Weeze – the wheat, *m* 4
der Welschhaahne (-hinkel) – the turkey, *m* 4
es Welschkann – the corn, *n* 4
wesche – to wash 4
wessere – to water plants 4
wichdich – important 2
wie – how, what 1
wie viel – how much 2
Wie bischt du? – How are you? 1
der Wille – the will, *f* 12
der Winder – the winter, *m* 4
windich - windy 4
winsche – to wish 8
wisse – to know a fact 3
die Wisseschaft – the science, *f* 2
die Woch (-e) – the week, *f* 2

die Woll – the wool, *f* 4
wolle – to want to 5
wu – where 1
wuhne – to live 1
die Wuhnschtubb (-schtuwwe) – the living room, *f* 6
die Wund – the wound, *f* 10
die Wunner – the wonder, *f* 7
wunnerbaar – wonderful 3

Y
die Yaahrhunnert – the century, *f* 12
yammere – to make noise 4
yung – young 1

Z
der Zaah (Zaeh) – the tooth, *m* 7
zaart – tender 5
zamme – together 12
die Zeiding (-e) – the newspaper, *f* 1
zeige – to show 11
die Zeit – the time, *f* 2
der Zelt – the tent, *m* 10
zidder as – since 6
zimmlich – reasonably, rather 1
zu – at, too 2
der Zucker – the sugar, *m* 3
zwelft – twelfth 8
die Zwiwwel (-e) – the onion, *f* 5

English - Deitsch

A

to be able to, can – kenne
about - baut
about (a fact or thing) - drum
above – iwwer
above all, by all means - allerdings
absolutely - gaar
(on) account of – weeich, wege
across – iwwer
addicted – suchtich
adult – der Uffgwaxner
advantage – es Vaddel
after – iwwer, nooch
afternoon – der Nummidaag
afterwards - dernoh
airplane ticket – die Flugkaart
alarm clock – die Weckeruhr
to be allowed - daerfe
already - schunn
also - aa
always – allsfatt, allfatt
American – der Amerikaaner
Amish – die Amische
animal – es Gedier
to announce - annebeschtelle
answer – die Antwatt
any – ken
anyhow – ennihau
apple butter – der Lattwarick
apricot – die Abrigos
area – die Gegend
arm – der Aarem
to arrive – aa/kumme
art class – die Kunscht
at – um, zu , an
at first - aerschtmol
athletic – schportlich
to pay attention – uff/basse
attic – die Aeddick, der Schpeicher
aunt – die Aent

B

back pack – es Ricksack

back yard – der Hinnerhof
bacon – der Schpeck
bad – schlecht
baker – der Becker
ball – der Balle
band – die Baend
bank – die Baenk
barn – die Scheier
barnyard – die Scheierhof
to bathe – sich baade
bathroom – die Baadschtubb
bathtub – der Baadezuwwer
to be – sei
bean – die Buhn
because – weil
because of the fact – vun wege as
bed – es Bett
bedroom – die Bettschtubb
bedspread – der Deppich
before – eb, var, vorher
to begin – beginner, aafange
behind – dehinner, hinnich
to belong to – gheere zu
between – g'schwischich
big – gross
bill – die Rechling
birthday – der Gebottsdaag
to bite - beisse
blood pressure – der Blutdruck
blouse – es Kittel
to board – neischteige
boat – es Boot
book – es Buch
bookshelf – es Buchlaade
boots – die Schtiwwel
boring – langweilich
to borrow – aus/lehne
both – allebeed
bottom of the hour – halwer
box, package – der Kaschde
boy – der Bu
bread – es Brot
breakfast – es Mariye-esse
breast – die Bruscht

to bring - bringe
to bring along – mit/bringe
brother – der Bruder
building – es Gebei
to burn – brenne
bus – die Bus
but – awwer
butcher – der Butscher
to buy – kaafe
by, at the house of – bei

C

to camp - kaempe
candle – die Kerz, Inschlichlicht
capital – die Haaptschtadt
car – die Maschien
card – die Kaart
career – die Kareer
carpet, rug – der Karebet
carrot – die Gehlrieb
to carry - draage
cat – die Katz
to catch – fange
to celebrate – feiere
celery – der Selleri
century – die Yaahrhunnert
chair – der Schtul
chalk – die Greid
chalkboard – die Daafel
to check, to look – schaue
cherry – die Kasch
chess – es Schach
chicken – es Hinkel
children – die Kinner
chimney – der Schannschtee
chin – es Kinn
chocolate – die Schokolaad
Christmas – Grischtdaag
church – die Karich
clarinet – die Klarinet
class – die Klaess
classroom – die Klaessschtubb
to clean – butze
clear - glaar
clock – die Uhr
closer - dichter
closet – es Gleederkemmerli, der Schenk

clothes – die Gleeder
cloudy, overcast - drieb
coat – der Rock
coffee – der Kaffi
cold – kalt
to catch a cold – sich verkelde
colleague – der Mithelfer
to collect – sammele, versammle
colt – es Hutsch
color – die Fareb
to comb oneself – sich schtraele
to combine – verbinne
to come – kumme
to come along – mit/kumme
to come from – bei/kumme, her/kumme
to come over – driwwe/kumme
company – der Kumpanie
control –der Eifluss
to cook – koche
cookie – es Kichli
cool – kiehl
corn – es Welschkann
corner – die Eck
cottage cheese – der Schmierkaes
cotton – die Baawoll
cow – die Kuh
customer – der Eikaafe
to cut – schneide

D

daily - daeglich
damp – feicht
dance – der Dans
to dance - danse
dark – dunkel
daughter – die Dochder
day – der Daag
delicious - appeditlich
to depart – ab/faahre
desk – der Schreibdisch
dessert – es Noochesse
dictionary – es Waddebuch
to die – schtarewe
difficult – hatt
dirt – der Dreck
to do - duh
dog – der Hund

door – die Dier
dough – der Deeg
downtown – middes in der Schtadt
dress – der Frack
to get dressed – sich aa/duh
to drink – drinke
to drink (animals) – saufe
drizzling – suddlich
drum – es Schlaggding
dry – darr
duck – die Ent
dumb – dumm

E

ear – es Ohr
earring – der Ohrring
easy - leicht
earth – die Aerd
early - frieh
Easter – Oschder
to eat – esse
to eat (animals) – fresse
egg – es Oi
electricity – die Leckdrick
elegant – scharmand
employee – der Schaffmann
empty – leer
English – die Englisch
envelope – der Briefumschlag
eternity – die Ewichkeit
evening – der Owed
everyone – alli-epper
evil ones – die Iewele
expensive - deier
experience – die Erfaahring
to explain – aus/lege
eye – es Aag

F

family – die Familye
family tree – der Familyebaam
farm – die Bauerei
farmer – der Bauer
farmhouse – es Bauerehaus
father – der Daadi
favorite class – die Leibsklaess
to feel – fiehle

fence – die Fens
festival – es Fescht
fever – die Fieber
a few – en Paar
field – es Feld
field trip – die Schulrees
to fight - fechde
to figure out – aus/figgere
finally - endlich
to find – finne
finger – der Finger
first – aerscht
fish – der Fisch
to fish - angle
flag – die Faahne
flute – die Floete
to fly – fliege
foggy – newwlich
to follow - folye
food – es Ess-sach
foot – der Fuuss
football – der Fuussballe
for – fer
to forgive – vergewwe
freedom – die Freiheit
free time – die Freizeit
French – Franzeesisch
fresh – frisch
fried - gebrode
from – aus, vun
in front of – var
frugal – geizich
fun – gschpassich

G

gallon – die Galluun
garage – die Gratsch
garden – die Gaarde
gas station – die Gas-schtation
gentleman – der Scheenermann
German – Hochdeitsch
to get, to receive – griege
girl – es Meedel
to give a gift - bschenke
glands – die Driese
glory – die Hallichkeit
gloves – die Hensching

goat – der Gees
to go - geh
to go here – dohie/geh
to go outside – naus/geh
to go there – dahie/geh
to go there – datthie/geh
good – gut
good looking – gutguckich
goose – der Gans
grade – die Marick
grandfather – der Grossdaadi
grandmother – die Grossmudder
grandparents – die Grosseldre
grass – es Graas
gravy – die Brieh
green beans – die Grienbuhne
to greet – bewillkumme
Groundhog Day - Grundsaudaag
guilty - schuldich
guitar – die Gitarre
gym class – der Tschimm

H
hair – es Haar
half – halwer
Halloween – der Schpuckdaag
Ham – es Schunkefleesch
hamburger – der Hambariger
hand – der Hand
to happen - geschehe
hat – der Hut
to have – hawwe
to have to – misse
to have on – aa/hawwe
he – er
head – der Kopp
health – die Gsundheit
healthy - gsund
to hear – heere
to heat – hitze
heaven – der Himmel
to help – helfe
hen – die Gluck
her – ihr
hero – der Held
high – hoch
to hike – wandere

his – sei
history – die Gschicht
to hit – schlagge
hither – hie
holy – heilich
home – die Heemet
homeroom – die Heemschtubb
at home – daheem
homework – die Schularewet
hopefully – hoffetlich
horse – der Gaul
hospital – es Grankehaus
hot – heess
how – wie
how much – wie viel
how are you? – wie bischt du?
humid – schmodich
to hurry oneself – sich dummle
to hurt oneself – sich weh/duh

I
I – ich
icy - eisich
important – wichdich
in – in
indeed – gewiss
indivisible – unverdeelich
interesting – inderessant
invitation – die Eilaading
to invite – ei/laade
it - es

J
jacket – der Wammes
jeans – die Iwwerhosse
jewelry – der Schmuck
justice – die Gerechtichkeit

K
kingdom – es Reich
kitchen – die Kich
knee – es Gnie
to know – kenne
to know a fact – wisse

L

land, country – es Land
language – die Schprooch
to last – dauere
to last – dauere
last name – der Familyenaame
late – schpot
later – schpaeder
to lay – lege
leg – es Beh
to let – losse
letter – der Brief
light - hell
light, lamp – die Licht
to like - gleiche
lips – die Lefts
lip stick – der Leftsschdift
a little - bissel
to live – wuhne
living room – die Wuhnschtubb
to look, to see, to watch – gucke
to look at – aa/gucke
to look like – aus/seh
loose - los
loud – laut
to love – liewe
luck – es Glick
lunch, dinner – es Middaagesse

M

mail – die Poscht
mail box – die Poschtbax
mail man – der Poschtmann
to make, to do - mache
to make noise – yammere
man, husband – der Mann
map – die Landkaart
mashed - gemaeschde
math class – die Rechelklaess
to measure – messe
meat – es Fleesch
medicine – die Arznei
to meet – aadreffe, begegne
meeting – die Versammling
midnight – die Middernacht
milk – die Millich
minute – die Minutt

mirror – der Schpiggel
money – es Geld
more – meh
morning – der Mariye
mother – die Mudder
mouse – die Maus
mouth – der Maul
to mow – maehe
much – viel
mug – es Henkeglas
music – die Myusick
must – misse

N

name – der Naame
nation – es Volk
naturally - nadierlich
neck – der Hals
necklace – es Halsband
to need – brauche
needle – die Nodel
neighbor – der Nochber
net – es Netz
New Years – Neiyaahrsdaag
news – die Nei-ichkeede
newspaper – die Zeiding
next to, near – newe, newich
night – die Nacht
none – ken
nose – die Naas
not – ken, net
not far away – net weit weck
notebook – es Nootbichli
now – graad, nau
number – die Nummer

O

to occur, to happen – brassiere, gschehe
often – efders
Oh my goodness! – Hariyesses!
oil – es Eel
old - alt
on – uff
one, as in a person – mer
onion – die Zwiwwel
only - bloss
to be of the opinion – mehne

or – odder
others – annere
outside – draus
over – iwwer, niwwer
over there – da driwwe

P
to pack - packe
package – der Pack
to paint – aa/schtreiche
pants – die Hosse
paper – es Babier
parents – die Eldre
to park – parke
past – iwwer
pastor – der Parre
pea – die Aerbs
to peel – schaele
pencil – der Bleispensil
pen – die Fedder
Pennsylvania German – Deitsch
pepper – der Peffer
phone number – die Fonnummer
to photograph – ab/nemme
photographer – der Abnemmer
piano – die Glapperbax, es Glaffier
to pick – picke, roppe
pickle – die Gummer
pie – der Boi
piece – es Schtick
pig – die Sau
pill – der Pill
to place – schtecke
place, standing – die Schtelle
in place of – in Blatz vun
to plan – aus/mache
to plan – blanne
to plant - blanse
to play – schpiele
player – der Schpieler
plow – der Blug
police – die Polies
pond – es Wasserloch
porch – die Bortsch
pork chop – der Rickmeesel
possibility – die Gelegeheit
post office – die Poschtaffis

potato – die Grummbier
power – die Graft
practice – die Iewing
to practice – iewe
prayer – es Gebet
to prepare – vorbereide
to prepare a meal – uffrischde
present – es Geschenk
President – der Bresident
pretty – schee
pretzel – es Bretzel
price – der Preis
to promise – verschpreche
pulse – der Puls
punctual – pinktlich
purse – der Beidel

Q
quarter after – Vaddel noch
quarter of – Vaddel eb
quicker – gschwinder
quickly – schnell
quiet - ruhich

R
racquet, club – der Schlagger
radio – der Schwetzkaschde
railroad – der Riggelweg
to rain - reggere
to read - lese
really – waericklich
reasonable – verninfdich
reasonably, rather – zimmlich
recipe – die Reseet
red beet – die Rotrieb
refrigerator – die Eisbax, die Kiehler
relative – der Blutsfreind
relative – die Freindschaft
research – die Unnersuch
restaurant – der Essblatz
to ride – reide
right? – Gell?
right away – bletzlich, graad
river – der Rewwer
roasted – reeschde
robbery – die Raawerei
rock music – die Rockmyusick

roof – es Dach
rooster – der Haahne
to run – schpringe

S
salad – der Selaat
salad dressing – die Selaatbrieh
salesman – der Verkaafer
salt – es Sals
sausage – die Wascht
to say - saage
scarf – es Halsduch
school – die Schul
school bag – die Schulsack
science – die Wisseschaft
to scream - greische
to scream at – aa/schreie
to search – suche
seat – der Hockblatz
to see – sehne
selection – die Waahl
to set the table – rischde
to sew – naehe
in good shape – in guder Form
to shave – sich balwiere
she – sie
shed – der Schopp
sheep – es Schof
to shine, to appear – scheine
ship – es Schiff
shirt – es Hemm
shoes – die Schuh
shopping bag – es Eikaafsack
shorts – die Katzhosse
shoulder – die Axel
to show – zeige
Shrove Tuesday - Faasnacht
shy - bleed
silk – der Seide
silken – seidich
sin – die Sind
since – zidder as
to sing – singe
sink – die Schpielbank, die Waschbank
sister – die Schweschder
to sit – hocke
to sit down – sich anne/hocke

size – die Greess
skirt – der Schtock
sky – der Himmel
to sleep – schloofe
slow, slowly – langsam
small - glee
smart – gscheit
smoke – der Schmok
to snow – schnee
so that – so as
sofa – es Sofe
soft – weech
something – eppes
something else – noch eppes
son – der Sohn
son-in-law – der Dochdermann
song – es Lied
sore throat – es Halsweh
sorry (I am sorry) – es dutt mir leed
sort, type – die Satt
soup – die Supp
south – der Sudd
to speak – schwetze
to spend – aus/gewe, schpende
to spend time – rum/bringe, verlewe
sport – der Schport
stamp – die Briefmark
to stand – schtehe
to start – aa/fange
stiff – schteif
stocking – der Schtrump
stomach – der Maage
to stop – schtoppe
store – der Schdor
story – die Gschicht
stove – der Offe
straw – es Schtroh
sugar – der Zucker
suit – der Suit
sun – die Sunn
supermarket – der Supermarrick
supper, dinner – es Owedesse
to be supposed to – solle
to surprise – iwwerfalle
to swallow – schlucke
sweater – es Swedder
sweatshirt – es Swettschirt

swollen – gschwolle

T

table – der Disch
tail – der Schwans
to take along – mit/nemme
take care – mach's gut
to take off – ab/fliege
talented - begaabt
taste – der Gschmack
tea – der Tee
teacher (male) – der Schulmeeschder
teacher (female) – die Schulmeeschdern
team – die Mannschaft
television – die Guckbax
temptation – die Versuchung
tender – zaart
tennis court – es Tennisblatz
tennis racquet – der Tennisschlagger
tent – der Zelt
terrible – greislich
to thank – sich bedanke
Thanksgiving - Dankfescht
that – as, sell
then - dennot
there - do
there is, there are – es gebt
therefore - deswege
they – sie
to think - denke
to throw – schmeisse
to thunder – dunnere
time – es Mol
time – die Zeit
today – heit
together – zamme
toilet – es Briwwi
tomato – es Tomaet
tomorrow – mariye
too – zu
tooth – der Zaah
tractor – der Traktor
train – der Draen
to travel – reese
tree – der Baam
trip – die Rees
trumpet – der Trompet

to try out – browiere
turkey – der Welschhaahne
twelfth - zwelft

U

ugly – hesslich
umbrella – der Reggeschaerm
uncle – der Onkel
under – unnich
unfriendly – unfreindlich

V

vacation – die Ferien
Valentine's Day – Feldi
vegetable – es Gaardesach
very – arig
violin – die Geig

W

wagon – der Waage
waiting room – es Waardeschtubb
to wake up – auf/schtehe, sich uff/wecke
to walk – laafe
to want to – wolle
warm - warm
to wash – wesche
to water (animals) – drenke
to water plants – wessere
we – mir
to wear – waere
weather – es Wedder
weed – es Umgraut
week – die Woch
wet – nass
what – was
what kind of – was fer
wheat – der Weeze
when – wann
where - wu
whether - eb
which – weller
why – fer was
will – waerre
will – der Wille
window – es Fenschder
windy – windich

wine – der Wei
winter – der Winder
to wish – winsche
without – mitaus
woman – die Fraa
wonder – es Wunner
wonderful – wunnerbaar
wool – die Woll
to worry about – baddere
would like to – meege

wound – die Wund
to write – schreiwe

Y

to yell at – aa/greische
you (plural) – dihr
you (singular) – du
young – yung

About the Authors

Joshua R. Brown is currently a Ph.D. candidate at The Pennsylvania State University. He teaches courses in German language, culture & civilization, business German, and linguistics. He graduated from Millersville University with a Bachelor's degree in German, minoring in Slavic and Classical Languages. He also attended the Philipps-Universität in Marburg, Germany. He has worked as a research assistant on the Comprehensive Pennsylvania German Dictionary project at the Center for Pennsylvania German Studies and the Hessen-Nassau Dictionary project at the Research Institute for the German Language (Deutscher Sprachatlas) in Marburg.

Brown has co-edited and edited several books in Pennsylvania Dutch, as well as about the Anabaptists. His primary research interests are in sociolinguistics, the sociology of language & religion, linguistic anthropology, and language & gender.

Douglas J. Madenford, a native Pennsylvania Dutch speaker, is currently the German Instructor for the Keystone Central School District located in Mill Hall, PA. He is also an Instructor of German at The Pennsylvania State University—Altoona campus. He graduated from Lock Haven University of Pennsylvania with a B.A. in German and a B.A. in International Studies. He has attained a M.Ed. in German from Millersville University of Pennsylvania. Madenford completed his education and pedagogical studies at Susquehanna University and also has an Oberstufe Zertifikat in Sprach- und Literaturwissenschaften from the Universität-Gesamthochschule Paderborn, Paderborn Germany.

Madenford grew up in a PD speaking household in the northern part of Berks County, PA. He has authored articles and essays on PD language and education. He has also lectured on the culture and history of the Pennsylvania Dutch. He is the author of the Pennsylvania Dutch Blog: *Nau loss mich yuscht eppes saage* which can be found at http://deitscheblog.wordpress.com.